Essentials of Period Style

Essentials of Period Style: A Sourcebook for Stage and Production Designers covers the visual, social, and political dynamics of multiple epochs and cultures, and discusses how these trends affect the design of the architecture, costumes, and furnishings of the time. It then relates these characteristics and cultural movements to the design needs you'll encounter as you design a period production. Each chapter contains examples of period style in both theater and film from a variety of notable productions and a glossary of specialized terms and words used in the chapter. Technological and aesthetic developments that affect design, lighting, and music are also included.

* Contains 16 chapters on Western civilization from ancient Greece through the Postmodern world
* Five additional chapters include coverage of pre-Columbian, Egyptian, Indian, Chinese, and Japanese styles
* Contains over 400 full-color illustrations from both contemporary and period sources

Hal Tiné designed the sets for the Broadway productions of *Jerry's Girls, The Trip Back Down*, and other National Tours. He has worked extensively, designing over 300 productions for regional theaters, off and off-off Broadway, and regional opera and ballet, including over 20 for the New York Grand Opera. Mr. Tiné taught stage design and period style in the Design/Tech program at Purchase College for many years and recently retired from the Production Design program at the Savannah College of Art and Design where he continued to develop his period style curriculum. He is a full member of United Scenic Artists, local 829, and a member of USITT.

Trelliswork tunnel, Hampton Court, UK.

Matthew Tiné

Tea infuser, Marianne Brandt, 1924.

The Fine Art Society, London, UK/Bridgeman Images

Scottish bagpiper in full dress, Edinburgh.

Chris Tiné

Reflections—Big Ben in layers, London.

Matthew Tiné

ESSENTIALS OF PERIOD STYLE

A Sourcebook for Stage and Production Designers

Hal Tiné

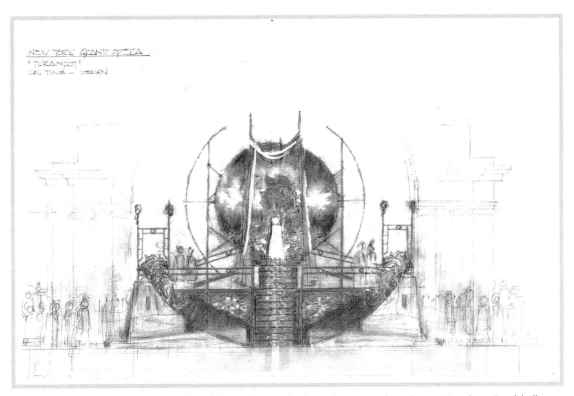

Sketch for *Turandot*, by Hal Tiné, NY Grand Opera, Vincent La Selva, founder and conductor, Naumburg Bandshell, Central Park, New York City.

Routledge
Taylor & Francis Group

LONDON AND NEW YORK

First published 2016 by Focal Press

Published 2018 by Routledge
2 Park Square, Milton Park, Abingdon, Oxon OX14 4RN
52 Vanderbilt Avenue, New York, NY 10017, USA

Routledge is an imprint of the Taylor & Francis Group, an informa business

Library of Congress Cataloging in Publication Data
Tiné, Hal.
Essentials of period style : a sourcebook for stage and production designers / Hal Tiné.
pages cm
Includes index.
1. Theaters--Stage-setting and scenery. I. Title.
PN2091.S8T575 2016
792.02'5--dc23
2015018082

ISBN: 978-1-138-93617-1 (hbk)
ISBN: 978-0-415-71005-3 (pbk)

Typeset in Helvetica Neue
by Servis Filmsetting Ltd, Stockport, Cheshire

Contents

Finials at moonrise.

Matthew Tiné

Foreword

Hal Tiné, my dear friend, and colleague of many years and many productions, on Broadway, at Lincoln Center, and events and programs around the world, in which we were a part of the telling of the tales of our history, has put together a vast information data base. It is a quick and easy visual reference for the director, designer, writer, animator, and Imagineer.

We do not just live in architecture (or caves) or just sit on chairs (or rocks) or just wear clothes (or, alas, animal skins). And as we get together around the campfire (or in the theatre) we tell the stories and sing the songs of our history and future. So—we need to know all about all our stuff and how it interfaces in one ever-evolving stream.

Hal, the brilliant theatre designer and teacher, has been pointing out these histories and attitudes of style for nearly half a century. He has now made it possible for the rest of us story tellers to see the stuff and hear the language of all the "periods" in a series of beautiful "quick takes."

He provides a guide for us, in every epoch, presenting the "Mad Men" in their white shirts and grey flannel suits sitting around a mahogany conference table with a pitcher of water, glasses and yellow pads, along with skyscrapers glistening outside the window. As these "guys" "run it up the flag pole" to see if anybody salutes—

We salute you Hal!

Peter Wexler—Co-artist and theater worker with Hal Tiné

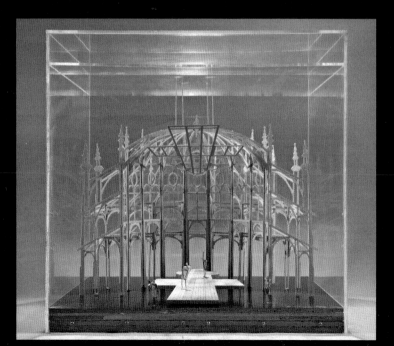

Le Prophète, by Giacomo Meyerbeer, The Metropolitan Opera Co., 1975; scenery and costumes designed by Peter Wexler. This model is the basic setting with cruciform floor, by Hal Tiné, Associate Designer. Collection of the McNay Art Museum, gift of The Tobin Theatre Arts Fund © Peter Wexler.

Photograph by Michael Jay Smith. For additional images for both Peter Wexler and Hal Tiné, see their websites and Peter Wexler Digital Museum at Furman University.

Preface

Working both as a professional NY Broadway and off-Broadway theater designer for sets, costumes, and lighting, as well as working in opera, TV, commercials, and museum exhibits, and teaching, I have often wished for a concise guide that combined architecture, décor, and costumes. There are many reference books and now the Internet that deal at length or in brief with treatments of these individual subjects, but none that treats them as interrelated within a single volume. Many years ago, I began developing classes in the history of period style with these three disciplines and as the classes evolved I added historical, intellectual, and artistic, and other background contextual information that was helpful in explaining why things had developed or changed within the periods, as they often had something important to say to each other. This book is not meant to be an exhaustive academic document nor encyclopedic, but a relatively concise overview. Its purpose is first to familiarize the emerging designer with the style images of past periods and to suggest an interconnectedness of period style motifs and influences in architecture, costume, and décor. And second, to suggest that those forms and treatments we find in period style carry with them meaning either understood by their inventors or given to them by us and that these meanings are the raw material of our designs.

I purposely wanted this to be primarily a visual reference that could be used by the designer or instructors of period style so I have slanted it that way. I have included over 400 illustrations and as often as possible period images as I think they are more accurate and genuine. Furthermore I have cited many additional references throughout the book and also included suggestions for films, TV, or other media that can enlarge our visual knowledge and vocabulary and design concepts. The Internet has become ubiquitous and is becoming, in many instances, more reliable, such as the ever improving and expanding Wikipedia. There are also many art, décor, and costume museums and other specialized ones around the world, historic houses and properties with images of architecture and décor, and libraries, and books that can also be accessed in traditional ways. It would also be useful to reference the artists and architects I mention to see examples of their work as they often have further beneficial visual information.

Background image: The ceiling inside the gateway, Taj Mahal, Agra, India.

Chris Tiné

Introduction

This is not a traditional art history book and I have formatted it in a different way. There are 16 chapters that concern Western civilization from Classical Greece through the Postmodern world. In addition there are five further chapters: pre-Columbian, Egypt, India, China, and Japan. In each chapter I give some background, reflecting historical, political, artistic, or other important influences. I also reference films, operas, and plays and frequently put an asterisk next to the ones I think best. This will be followed by sections on architecture and décor with illustrations, explanatory captions, and bullet point texts, and image citations. At the end of this section will be "keywords," which is a glossary with definitions of specific terms used by designers to refer to the elements of each period style. I have given a production design-specific definition for each of these terms but they can also be searched digitally or traditionally for a broader meaning, context, or visual image. This format will then be repeated for clothing and costumes.

In addition to the contemporary visual language that we all speak, production designers for film, theater, gaming, and themed events must bring to life stories from an imaginative world which might include both past and future influences from our own, or other, cultures. Our productions first take place in our imaginations and in our efforts to give them a specific design identity we make use of both past, future, and imagined style motifs. Whether to use period style, in what combination, and in what forms is the individual designer's choice, to give meaning to their work. I hope this book will serve as a guide and reference for some of the choices open to the production designer in imagining new visual worlds.

An inventive refracted image of the thirty-story gold mirror glass cones that frame the Presidential Palace, Astana, Kazakhstan.

Susana Ramalho

Acknowledgments

There are many people to thank for helping to make this book possible. As Meagan White, Senior Editorial Project Manager at Focal Press, reminded me—"it definitely takes a village to create a book." She was patient and supportive from the start; and I also thank Nicola Platt and Jaya Dalal. Thanks are due to Jody Potter, my illustrations editor, for her extraordinary resourcefulness; to my agent, Rita Rosenkrantz, for taking me one step further; and to my teachers, fellow designers, and colleagues who shared my love of history and the magic that period style can create. A special thank you to my two sons, Christopher and Matthew, who have contributed to the book in more ways than they or I could have imagined—they have been outstanding. And lastly I thank my wife, Louisa Rawle Tiné, for her support, knowledge, suggestions, and tireless energy.

Galeries Lafayette, a fashionable Art Nouveau Department Store, Paris, built 1912.

Chris Tiné

CHAPTER ONE

Greece: The Hellenic Period, 475–375 BCE

Figure 1.1 The Temple of Concord in the Valley of the Temples, Agrigento, Sicily, Italy. It is one of five temples built high on a series of hills overlooking the Mediterranean Sea. It was built by the Greeks in this colony c. 440–430 BCE and is considered an iconic image of a Greek temple, as it is a clear example of Doric architecture and because of its high degree of preservation. As it contains most of the important elements of Greek architecture, they will be described individually in this chapter.

Author photo

A Little Background

The forms and shapes of ancient Classical Greek and Roman architecture, costume, and decorative arts continue to resonate in our built environment today. Our sense of architecture and proportion, of how and where to use decoration, and what that decoration is and means, is still shaped by the examples from Greece and Rome that were periodically reinvented and updated over the intervening centuries. Classical builders invented much of the visual and tactile language of the decorative arts that characterize American, European, and Islamic forms today. These are the concepts and motifs that are familiar to us in the built world we live in and are what we use in our production design work, so it is important that we familiarize ourselves with them.

Western decorative arts, including furnishings and décor, as well as costume, share this Classical trajectory in American and European performing and visual arts. A look at this ancient culture and its preferences and how it relates to what we do today can help a designer better apply those design motifs to a built environment in today's performance world.

Who They Were

*   Ancient Greek history is divided into three periods; Archaic, the time of Greek mythology; Hellenic, the Classic age dominated by Pericles of Athens; and Hellenistic, the period of Roman penetration and Alexander the Great.

*   The Archaic period saw the rise and fall of the Minoan and Mycenaean cultures around 1600 BCE to 1200 BCE, on which many Classical Greek myths and dramas were based.

*   In the Hellenic period, sometimes referred to as "The Classical Period" and also "The Golden Age of Athens," Greek culture reached its height. It arose among a collection of competing and warlike city-states headed by Athens and Sparta on the Greek peninsula and islands that shared the same language and customs. It flourished for only 75–100 years (475–375 BCE) before the Persians defeated them.

*   Later Classic Greek culture was called the Hellenistic period (375–30 BCE). It saw contact with the Romans. During this time, Alexander the Great expanded the Greek Empire as far east as western India.

*   Classical Greeks were aware of and celebrated their Archaic founding myths of 1,000 years earlier and were proud of their art and culture, which they extended eastward.

*   Art was integral to politics and society and was used to idealize beauty, war, and conquest. It was used as an instrument of politics as well as culture.

*   Greek Classical culture strove for an ideal of personal moral purity combined with physical beauty. They believed in the unity of mind and body.

*   They stressed a philosophical and social emphasis on purity of thought, personal, and artistic beauty and also honesty in personal and political relationships.

*   The Greeks developed sciences and philosophy based on a rational, not spiritual worldview.

*   Theirs was a polytheistic, nature oriented religion based on mythological characters and images, which they used as metaphors for human activities and relationships.

*   In Athens the most powerful city of Classical Greece the primary god was a woman, Athena, who represented both war and justice. She gave her name to the city. See Figure 1.16.

*   Greek religious drama and myths were based on centuries-old Mycenaean legends of southwest Greece from 800 to 1200 BCE and were passed down as recited stories. These became religious

festivals honoring the gods, particularly Dionysus, and were meant to instruct and inspire religious awe in the audience.

* The Hellenic age was also the Golden Age of Greek Drama. The four Classical playwrights Aeschylus, Sophocles, and Euripides left 36 surviving tragedies and Aristophanes wrote comedies. These plays became the literary foundation of Western drama and literature. Drama was a religious not a secular activity engaged in by the whole population during week-long religious festivals. They used the spoken word, sung passages, dance, and music to advance their complex plots.

* Their theater was called a *theatron* and had three elements: the orchestra—a circular area where plays, dance, and festival took place; behind it was a rectangular building, the skene, which was the backstage, dressing rooms, and also for storage; and the audience, which were the raked seats built into a hill. See Figure 1.6.

* They also had *eccyclema* that were wheeled platforms to roll in furniture or bodies and *periaktois* that were three-sided painted panels that revolved to show different localities, and a machine and also theatrical plot device called a "Deus ex Machina" that allowed gods to suddenly appear via a crane from above or below through a trap door to alter the outcome of plots. This plot scheme has been used throughout literature when a character or event happens without warning or reason. J.R.R. Tolkien called it *eucatastrophe* and can be seen in his books and films—*The Hobbit* and *Lord of the Rings*.

* They used highly stylized, exaggerated masks and costumes to identify characters and emotions, so that audiences could see them from far away. None of these survive, but there are many images of them found on pottery. See Figure 1.17.

* The Greeks developed a highly sophisticated written literary tradition that included the sciences, medicine, law, philosophy, literature, and the arts.

* Greeks saw life as an organic whole governed by the gods and the laws of rational men. Gods were partly mortal and interacted with men on an equal footing.

* Women were idealized in art but confined to the house in society.

* There are many films and TV shows about ancient Greece, these are a few suggestions: *300* (2007), *Helen of Troy* (2003), *Jason and the Argonauts* (2000), *Troy* (2004), *Socrates* (1997), *Clash of the Titans* (2010), *Wrath of the Titans* (2012), *Hercules* (1997), and *Minotaur* (2006).

* A number of Classical Greek dramas have been adapted to film and are worth watching: *Oedipus Rex* (Dr. Guthrie (1957)*, Christopher Plummer (1968)*), *Iphigenia*, *Antigone*, *Electra*, *Phaedra*, *Medea*, *The Trojan Women*, and Peter Hall's *The Orestia Trilogy*.

* Many operas have been adapted from Greek tragedies and most have been forgotten, but these five have endured and are still performed around the world: Gluck's *Alceste* (1767) and Cherubini's *Médée* (1797) both after Euripides, *Les Troyens* (1863) by Berlioz based on Virgil's epic poem the *Aeneid*, Strauss's *Elektra* (1909), and Stravinsky's *Oedipus Rex* (1927) both after Sophocles.

Background image: Author photo

The Greek Material World

Figure 1.2 This is a conjectural National Geographic illustration showing a religious procession entering the sacred precinct of the Acropolis. The viewpoint is from the front of the Parthenon looking towards the entrance portals in the distance and shows several of the other buildings that make up the compound. One can also see various colors and styles of clothes. The large red-brown statue is Athena and the article to her far right is a brazier used for both light and heat.

H.M. HERGET/National Geographic Creative

Figure 1.3 This is a 19th-century print of the three Greek orders—Doric, Ionic, and Corinthian. Each had noticeable characteristics that were reflected in art, architecture, and fashion, which will be described in detail in keywords. Generally Doric was the earliest and simplest; next was Ionic, which had a delicate and elegant style; and last was Corinthian, which was the most ornate and featured acanthus leaves on the capital.

duncan1890/iStock

What They Made

Figure 1.4 The Porch of the Maidens, also known as the Caryatids, on the Ionic Temple of the Erechtheum, c. 421–406 BCE. This is part of one of the many temples in the Acropolis complex, and it is a rare but important example of figurative sculpture used as a structural architectural element, instead of columns that hold up the entablature. The maidens are wearing Ionic chitons.

Renee Vititoe/Shutterstock.com

Figure 1.5 The Parthenon. The Doric Temple of the Greek goddess Athena considered the protector of Athens; built between 447 and 432 BCE under the general supervision of the sculptor Phidias. This is the view that visitors would see as they ascended the Acropolis and approached the temple. The building is sited to emphasize its size and importance.

Mark Fiennes/Bridgeman Images

Figure 1.6 The Theater of Dionysus in Athens built in the 6th century BCE, and with later additions. This view shows the stepped seating built into the hillside, surrounding an open performing area called the Orchestra. The stage was originally circular but was reduced to a semi-circle by the Romans when they conquered Greece in the 3rd century.

Figure 1.7 This is a contemporary production of *The Bacchae* by Euripides in the 5th-century BCE Greek theater in Syracuse, Sicily. It was reconstructed in the 3rd century BCE by the Romans and is basically the same today. The round gold raked stage and silver truss work are for modern productions. The grey circular stage is the original space known as the orchestra. In today's production, like the original, it combined acting, singing, and dance with highly dramatic costumes that could be used in many different configurations.

* The purity of Greek religion and philosophy was reflected in an emphasis on purity of design, materials, and its execution. Classical Greeks preferred the unity of a single, unified design material for most important projects.

* They expressed a deep interest in realistic representation and a fascination with the observable, natural world expressed most dramatically in extremely sophisticated sculpture. See Figures 1.16 (Athena) and 1.18 (Demosthenes).

* Major durable buildings were religious. They were built of solid marble or granite and were brightly painted and embellished both inside and out with metal and precious stones.

* Public and religious buildings emphasized exterior design, three dimensionality, and decoration to be experienced as sculpture from all sides, which accentuated their communal public social functions.

* Most ceremonial and religious buildings were rectangular in plan and the majority of them were surrounded by a peristyle (row) of columns on all sides lending a unity and dignity to their designs. There were a few examples of small circular temples. See Figures 1.1, 1.2, 1.4, and 1.5 for peristyle.

* Informal town planning, roads, and construction followed natural contours of the land with buildings often placed for visual prominence rather than their utility.

* The major social, political, and commercial gathering place was the agora or marketplace near the center of the city. Here government affairs were conducted outside and in public with the participation of all citizens.

* Temples and adjacent theaters, which were also considered religious structures and part of the sacred area, were located in rural settings. They were often situated on an elevated position and close to nature that emphasized their religious function. See Figures 1.1, 1.2, 1.5, 1.6, and 1.7.

* Greek architects developed a highly sophisticated and organized system of decorative architectural orders and proportions that allowed repetition, codification, and extension of Classical styles. Each element of a building was codified and modified over the centuries and many are still used today. A Classical Greek or Roman person would recognize today's columns, molding shapes, and details.

How They Decorated

* The Classical Greeks developed a system of three decorative Orders or styles of decoration and proportion: Doric, Ionic, and Corinthian were applied to important religious structures to allow repetition in varying scales. The Orders were named for the regions of the country in which they developed and do not signify high or low rank. In fact the largest and most important temples were in the simplest Order, the Doric.

* Their principal buildings used the very simple post and lintel construction system consisting of a horizontal beam or lintel supported by vertical posts. The applied orders and a peristyle or surround of columns gave them unity and meaning. See Figures 1.3, 1.8, and 1.9.

* Only decorated pedimented tile roofs were considered sacred and were used only on temples, and followed the order of the rest of the building. Undecorated pedimented and gently peaked tile roofs were used on secular buildings. See Figures 1.1, 1.2, 1.8, 1.9, and 1.10.

* Arches were known but not used by Classical Greeks until the Roman influence in the late Hellenistic period, 3rd century BCE.

Figure 1.8 This is a conjectural illustration of a wealthy Greek home. A peristyle of Doric columns is organized around an atrium with an ornamental pool and open to the sky. Different living quarters surround this space, one of which shows an *oikos* with a banquet taking place. There are also good examples of the three zone wall decorations, painting, and their use of color. Also notice the Greek Key design on the entablature and the painted wooden ceiling.

Bibliothèque des Arts Decoratifs, Paris, France/Archives Charmet/Bridgeman

Figure 1.9 This is a reconstruction of the largest of three excavated houses from the late Classical period, 4th century BCE in Athens. The Greeks used an inward-looking plan in order to create a living compound. Houses were generally two stories high and were organized around a rectangular atrium that was open to the sky. The atrium and its surrounding promenade were the main public living spaces used by the family. It also shows the women's living quarters (*Gynaikeion*) upstairs. On the right are examples of interior wall treatments showing the horizontal three-layer decorative zones.

akg-images/Peter Connolly

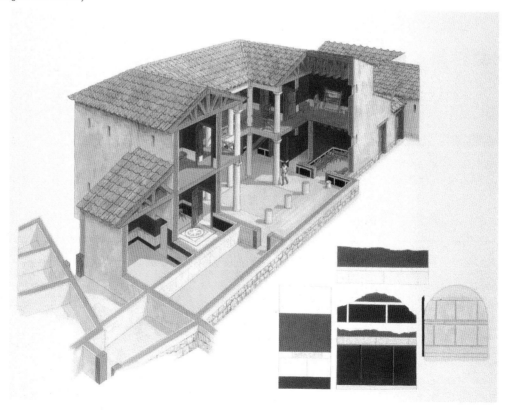

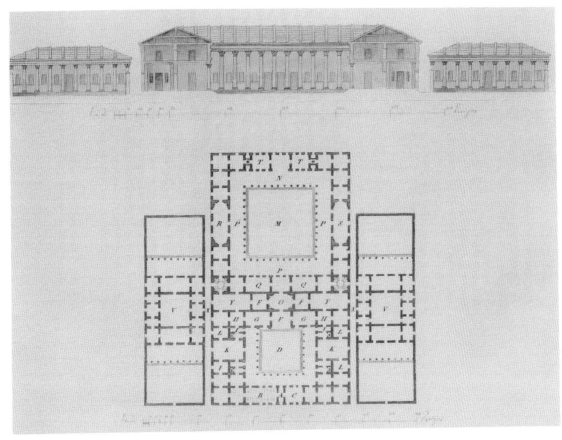

Figure 1.10 This is an 18th-century engraving showing a recreation of the elevation and plan of a hypothetical house for a wealthy Greek merchant. The main, center building consists of two zones, each defined by an atrium with a fountain in the center and surrounded by living spaces.

DEA/A. DAGLI ORTI/The Granger Collection

Figure 1.11 Terrace House Number 2, from the 3rd century BCE, Ephesus, Turkey. The rooms of this site clearly show the mosaic floors and the stuccoed walls with their three zones of decorations and figurative painting. These are similar to those of "The Golden Age" in the 5th century BCE.

Marshall Ikonography/Alamy

Figure 1.12 This is an early 6th-century BCE polychrome funerary stele depicting a potter holding two drinking vessels and sitting on a *diphros*—a typical simple stool. Steles were common in Greece and generally stone or wooden slabs that were erected as commemorative pieces—such as this for a funeral, or to explain other information. Steles are used by many different cultures around the world. They can be incised, painted, or in bas-relief as this one.

PRISMA ARCHIVO/Alamy

* Greeks took pride in extending and imitating Classical styles in their expanding empire during the Hellenistic period. Greek style spread throughout the Roman and Persian empires eastwards to India with the conquering armies of Alexander the Great. Later Roman style was almost wholly based on earlier Greek examples.

* Greek residences were one and two stories and made of brick and stucco (see Figure 1.11). They featured rooms organized around a central open atrium containing a pool of water often with a peristyle of columns and surrounded by domestic rooms. See Figures 1.8, 1.9, and 1.10.

* The open atrium at the center of each home was used as the main reception area for personal, business, and religious affairs conducted in the home. There were often multiple atria and these public rooms were lavishly decorated. This area was called the *oikos*, meaning a family room.

* Private family member rooms, servants' quarters, and food preparation areas were behind the atrium and less lavishly furnished. Men, women, servants, and slaves occupied different zones of the house. See Figure 1.9.

* Plain, windowless exteriors were used in urban settings and faced inwards to the atrium, which emphasized a private, interior life.

* Temples and wealthier homes featured marble and highly detailed mosaic floors. Residences also had plaster walls frescoed in three zoned color schemes using bold red, yellow, white, and black colors with intricate geometric borders framing realistic images. See Figures 1.8, 1.9, and 1.11.

* Wall painting often imitated costlier materials like finished wood and marble in modest homes.

* Ceilings were of carved and painted wood. Roof surfaces were gently angled inward to direct rainwater into a pool located in the center of the atrium. This pool was both decorative and the main source of water for the home. See Figures 1.8, 1.9, and 2.14.

* Simple furniture was made of carved or turned wood, sometimes upholstered in fabric or leather. In wealthier and sacred settings, furniture frames could be cast in metal. See *kline*/bed 1.8, 1.13, and 1.15, *klismos*/chair 1.15, *diphros*/stool 1.12.

Building and Décor Keywords

acropolis (a-CROP-o-lis) – This is a generic name, literally meaning "high city" and found in several Greek cities. The Acropolis was the name of the elevated promontory outside of Athens on which the Parthenon and its attendant buildings and theater were located and is the most famous. See Figures 1.2, 1.4, and 1.5. The image of the temple from Agrigento is also a part of an acropolis, Figure 1.1.

Order – This was the style of standardized details identifying the column and entablature system in Classical architecture. See Figure 1.3.

Doric Order – The Greek Order characterized by sturdy proportions and having a cushion capital, a frieze of alternating triglyphs (three vertical grooves in a panel) and metopes (low relief sculpted panels). This style originated in western Greece; it echoed earlier wood construction and was influenced by Egyptian and Etruscan art and used simple, strong, and powerful forms. See Figures 1.1, 1.2, 1.3, 1.5, and 1.8.

Ionic Order – The Greek Order characterized by elegant detailing, longer proportions, and with a capital consisting of a pair of large volutes or spirals, a continuous frieze, and a dentiled, tooth-like cornice. From eastern Greece and Asia Minor, it was more refined and sensuous than the Doric and incorporated sculpture into the architecture. See Figures 1.3 and 1.4. The Caryatids were on an Ionic Temple, but are not Ionic columns.

Corinthian Order – The slenderest and most ornate of the Greek Orders, it used bell-shaped capitals consisting of two rows of acanthus leaves surmounted by small spiral volutes and an elaborate cornice. It was from southern Greece where the style developed from motifs used in interior decoration and furniture that later spread to architecture. See Figures 1.3 and 2.1 and the capitals in The House of the Faun in Pompeii 2.14.

post and lintel – An ancient and universal construction system in which evenly spaced vertical posts set side by side on or in the ground are capped by a lintel or horizontal bar that then supported a roof. See Figures 1.8 and 1.9.

pediment – The low triangle at either end of a Greek temple roof above the cornice, often filled with sculpture that indicated its sacred nature. These also appeared on other buildings and temples, but with no decoration. See Figures 1.1, 1.2, 1.8, 1.9, and 1.10.

entablature (en-TAB-la-chure) – In Classical architecture, the elaborated horizontal beam (lintel) carried by columns (posts) and divided horizontally into three descending zones: cornice, frieze, and architrave. See Figures 1.1, 1.2, 1.3, 1.4, 1.5, and 1.8.

peristyle – A row of identical columns supporting an entablature and surrounding a temple or an atrium. See Figures 1.1, 1.2, 1.4, 1.5, 1.8, and 1.10.

cornice – The upper horizontal band of the entablature capped by a projecting cornice or crown molding. See Figures 1.1, 1.4, and 1.5. It was also the upper decorative zone of an interior wall. Both were characterized by a cyma-recta or s-curved molding.

frieze (freez) – The middle, horizontal band of the entablature; sometimes it contained pictorial or running decorative motifs, such as the Greek Key in Figure 1.8.

architrave – The lower, molded horizontal portion of the entablature. In Figure 1.1 it was blank.

capital – The decorative cushion at the top of a column that supported the architrave. See Figures 1.1, 1.2, 1.3, 1.5, and 1.8.

shaft – The vertical support or post of a column system that displayed a swelling called entasis and was often decorated with fluting. See Figures 1.1, 1.2, 1.3, 1.5, and 1.8.

entasis (ENTA-sis) – The narrowing, curved tapering of the top two-thirds of a Classical column. See Figures 1.1, 1.2, and 1.4.

fluting – Decorative vertical grooves carved into the surface of a column shaft. See Figures 1.1, 1.3, 1.5, and 1.8.

dentils – A band-like decoration that consisted of block-like forms resembling teeth spaced at even intervals. They were usually found as part of a cornice in the Ionic and Corinthian orders. See Caryatids Figure 1.4.

triglyphs (TRI-glifs) – Literally "three strokes," one of two kinds of horizontal repeating and alternating decorative panels on Doric entablatures, which resembled three sculpted vertical v-shaped channels. See Figures 1.1, 1.3, and 1.5.

Figure 1.13 This is an example of a c. 6th-century BCE red-figure Greek drinking vessel, a *kylix* for drinking wine at "symposiums," which were men's drinking and debating parties. It shows a man reclining on a woven cushioned *kline* with a pillow behind his back and next to it a low table. In his right hand he is holding the same type of cup and in the other appears to be a plate. He is dressed in a himation and beside him is a typical walking stick/crutch. Also notice the circular design around the image that is a common graphic feature, known as a Greek Key, and is found on everything from pottery, clothing, to the interior and exteriors of buildings.

metopes (MET-o-pez) – This was the other kind of decorative panel on Doric entablatures that contained relief scenes of mythological figures. In simpler structures they were painted rather than sculpted. See Figure 1.3.

stylobate – The stepped platform that supported Greek Doric temples. See Figures 1.1 and 1.5.

base – This was a molded cushion at the bottom of an Ionic or Corinthian column shaft. Note that the Doric column has no base. See Figure 1.3.

crown – This was the upper decorative zone of an interior wall. See Figures 1.8, 1.9, and 1.11.

field – This was the wide, middle decorative zone of an interior wall. See Figures 1.8, 1.9, and 1.11.

dado (DAY-doh) – This was the lower decorative zone of an interior wall. See Figures 1.8, 1.9, and 1.11.

thronos (THRONE-os) – The large, solid seat with a back meant for a king or god in a Greek theater. It was often carved of stone and it is where our word "throne" comes from.

agora (a-GOR-a) – This was the open meeting and marketplace at the center of each Greek town or city that was the site of commerce, government, educational, and cultural activities.

atrium (A-tree-um) – In a Greek home it was the ceremonial center of the house. It often contained a pool of water and was surrounded by a peristyle of columns. See Figures 1.8, 1.9, and 1.10.

oikos (OY-kos) – The Greek word for the family unit that was headed by a male. It was also the name of the room in a house where the patriarch greeted and entertained guests, and was usually located just off an atrium. See Figure 1.8.

klismos (KLIZ-mos) – It was a light, armless chair with outward curved front and rear legs and an inward curved backrest for the comfort of the back and shoulders. The style of this chair has been adapted in several periods, particularly Neoclassical and Modern. See Figure 1.15.

diphros (DIF-ros) – It was a three- or four-legged stool with turned or carved legs often in the shape of animal legs. See Figure 1.12.

trapezai (trap-EEZ-eye) – These were small, three-legged portable tables used for dining. Some examples are also found with animal-style legs. See Figure 2.15.

kline – This was a decorated and upholstered or cushioned couch for sleeping, sitting, and dining, usually made of wood and often with decorated side, head and footboards. It was the primary article of furniture in a prosperous Greek house and came in many sizes and decorative treatments. The basic shape will be adapted countless times through Western decorative arts to the present time. See Figures 1.8, 1.13, and 1.15.

caryatids (car-ya-TIDs) – These are sculptures of women used instead of a column to support the entablature. The most famous example is shown in Figure 1.4. Like many other examples this Greek form would be used by the Romans, notably in the Pantheon and the Forum and then would later appear in the Renaissance and would continue to be in use both on exteriors and also in interiors, particularly in fireplaces. Also see pre-Columbian similar use in Toltec Warriors in Chapter 17.

deus ex machina (machine of the gods) – This was a crane-like machine that allowed gods to suddenly appear from above or below. It was also a literary device used to alter plots to create happy or dramatic endings and often used by Shakespeare, 19th-century operas, comic books, soap operas and J.R.R. Tolkien.

The Greek Clothing and Costume World

How They Dressed

* Classical Greek clothing was draped loosely and conveyed dignity, elegance, stability, and permanence; and it took on the form of the wearer. Fluid, lively garments were of simple, elementary forms and were usually of linen or wool. Clothing fabric was rectangular and in a single woven piece. It was folded or draped in various ways, but never in curves or shapes.

* Men and women took great pride in elegantly draped and detailed garments and considered refined drapery essential to sophistication.

* Men's and women's costumes were both made of a single draped and pinned piece of rectangular fabric that came in various sizes according to use. Dress and formal garments were of finer fabric and were longer than utilitarian garments, which were shorter and of rougher material.

* Greeks seemed distrustful of complex, intricate pattern, which might have reminded them of or suggested the decorations of their enemies, the Persians. They kept their fabrics simple, emphasizing elegance. Fabric edges were sometimes elaborated with stencil and embroidered borders but otherwise left plain. They never used fringed edges. For many years it was thought that they were always white, because of the statues, but it is now known they were also dyed. See Figure 1.2.

* Only very young boys were clean-shaven. The beard was an important symbol of virility to the ancient Greeks. After Alexander the Great men began to shave.

Figure 1.14 This is a detail from a red-figure pottery deep-bowled drinking vessel, a *skyphos*, showing a woman wearing a decorated peplos in a sheer material, notice the folded over fabric from her waist—this is the distinguishing feature of a peplos. She is holding a mirror and a jewel or make-up box.

Erich Lessing/Art Resource, NY

Figure 1.15 The young woman on the left is seated on a *klismos* and wearing a himation, also notice her hairstyle. She is holding a distaff in her right hand. The other woman is holding a loom. Women traditionally did spinning and weaving, which were usually done in the home. To the far left can be seen the end of a room with a *kline* and pillow. This is a red-figure pottery vessel from Athens c. 430 BCE called a *pyxis*, which were small round lidded boxes for storing jewelry and cosmetics.

© RMN-Grant Palais/Art Resource, NY

* Women wore their hair long and sometimes caught up in the back with bands and ribbons but with little other decoration. See Figures 1.14, 1.15, and 1.16.

* The clothing of common people and slaves often reflected Persian tunics and trousers, especially in the Hellenistic period and were of rough fabrics.

* Both sexes wore sandals. Women's versions were sometimes highly laced. Soldier's sandals could be quite complicated and the ties could extend up to the knees. Actors also wore sandals known as buskins.

* There was no uniformity in Greek military costume as each soldier was responsible for his own garments and armament. Soldiers wore both the chlamys and himation in shorter versions for mounted riding. These could be worn with a rigid or semi-rigid breast and back plate, and a helmet with a semispherical crown, a nose guard, cheek guards, and a horsehair crest. See Figure 1.2, statue of Athena.

* Theatrical costume was highly codified and actors were always masked according to the character represented. Tragic kings and queens wore floor-length sleeved tunics over padding and cothurnus or raised boots to increase their stature. Gods wore insignia as identification and lesser characters dressed in rougher fabrics.

Clothing and Costume Keywords

peplos (PEP-los) – This was the most distinctive basic Greek garment. It consisted of a large rectangle of cloth with the top folded down around the torso and pinned on each shoulder with a fibulae and was open on one side. They were often ankle-length and worn by both sexes; and shorter versions were worn by young men and soldiers. The peplos in various ways will be used in fashion again and again and is still in use today. See Figures 1.14 and 1.16.

chiton (KEY-tawn) – This was also a basic Greek garment worn by men and women. It could be worn alone, as an undergarment with the peplos, and also with the two capes, described below. This was a loose garment resembling a tunic, closed up to the arms and pinned at the shoulders with broaches (fibulae) and belted around the waist or under the breasts.

Doric chiton – This early version was usually simple and made of wool. It varied in length—for young men it was shorter to the knees, for older men and higher rank it was worn to the ankle and usually only fastened at one shoulder, and for women it was floor-length.

Ionic chiton – By the 5th century BCE it had evolved into a more graceful gown-like garment made out of a more lightweight fabric such as linen and later silk, which allowed it to be intricately draped with folds and pleats. It was now made out of a much wider piece of fabric and pinned or buttoned along the shoulders in as many as 10 places to create sleeves. This style of dress for women would reappear throughout the centuries till our present time. See Figure 1.4, the Caryatids and Athena, 1.16. The Inca in Chapter 17 would use a simpler version.

himation (hi-MAT-e-on) – A long cloak also worn by both sexes, it was made from a large rectangle of cloth that could be draped in various ways. It was commonly used as a cloak covering the head and also as a sleeping garment. See Figures 1.2, 1.13, 1.15, 1.17, and 1.18.

chlamys (CLAM-iss) – This was a short, light, rectangular over-garment cloak, pinned at the right shoulder or in the middle below the throat that was worn by younger Greek men, soldiers, and women. See Figure 18.16. Also see Figures 3.12 and 3.13, which show a longer Byzantine version.

fibula – A large pin or brooch used by Greeks and Romans to fasten male and female garments.

Figure 1.16 This is a statue of Athena wearing a peplos over an Ionic chiton and sandals. It shows the naturalism and elegance of Greek sculpture and also of her clothes. It pictures her with her symbolic military details—the ornate *gorget* around her neck, a symbolic shield with the head of a Gorgon, a crested helmet, and carrying a spear; all to portray her as the Goddess of War.

Ken Welsh/Bridgeman Images

Figure 1.17 This is an excellent example of a black-figure vessel called a *hydria*—for carrying water, c. 520 BCE. The scene is "The Judgment of Paris" and shows figures from Homer's epic poem *The Iliad*—Hera, Athena, and Aphrodite, led by Zeus with the Goddesses competing for Paris. This is part of the Greek myth about Paris and Helen and The Trojan Wars. It was also the subject of many Greek and later plays and paintings well into the 19th century. It also shows both men and women wearing different variations of the himation.

akg-images

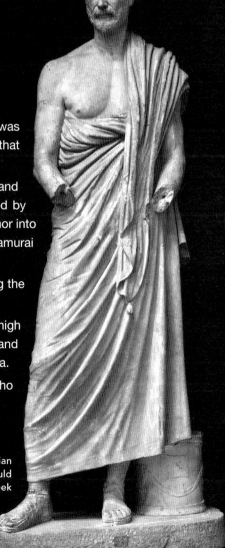

hoplite (HOP-lite) – An individual Greek foot soldier. He was responsible for his own clothing, weapons, and equipment that could vary greatly in style and materials.

Greek cuirass (kwi-RAS) – This was a military breastplate and back plate either woven or formed of metal and connected by leather or fabric straps. A version of this will continue as armor into the 20th century in Europe. See Figure 1.2 Athena and the samurai Figure 21.16.

greaves – These were shaped metal or leather panels covering the shin and ankle as armor and were often highly decorated.

Spartan helmet – A nearly fully enclosed battle helmet with a high standing center crest of horsehair or feathers, and rigid nose and ear guards. It was favored by the army from the city of Sparta.

cothurnus – The large, raised boots worn by Greek actors, who represented royalty or gods.

Figure 1.18 Demosthenes was a 4th-century BCE prominent Athenian statesman and considered one of its greatest orators; whose writings would have lasting impact. This is an example of the realism attained by Greek sculptors of this period and is the model for many sculptures in the Western canon. Typical of the time, notice his beard and short hair, his sandals, and the elegant drape of his himation.

Alinari/Art Resource, NY

CHAPTER TWO

Roman: 3rd Century BCE–476 CE

Figure 2.1 Maison Carrée, Nîmes, France. This typical Roman temple is raised on a podium, as opposed to a Greek *stylobate*, with a broad staircase accessible from the front. Though similar to the Greek temple form, the Roman temple is closed on three sides and has a massive central entrance, and continues to use the Greek pedimented roof, entablatures, and Corinthian columns.

Edler von Rabenstein/Shutterstock.com

A Little Background

Roman culture developed from the Etruscan culture on the central Italian peninsula. Beginning around 300 BCE they came in contact with the Greeks and adopted and continued the design features of Greek life, infrastructure, and culture but modified and extended them for their own commercial and imperial use. In many ways the two cultures blended during the 2nd and 1st centuries BCE and it is often difficult to separate one from the other. Eventually the Romans dominated the Greeks, overpowered and incorporated Greek influences and grafted them onto a new, far-flung and dynamic commercial and military empire. Roman culture extended eastward to India, as did the Greek Empire, but it also extended west to present-day Spain and England, north into today's Germany, and south to Egypt and North Africa, picking up local influences along the way. The Romans codified the Greek orders of architecture and added two of their own: the simple Tuscan Order and the most complex of all, the Composite Order.

As in architecture, Roman patrician clothing and decorative arts continued to be dominated by Greek design and mythology. Variety in clothing was achieved by adding the tunic, both long and short, for men and women of all classes as a foundation garment and the toga for the wealthy.

Who They Were

*   Roman culture and founding mythology developed before 400 BCE from the indigenous early Etruscan tribes of central Italy.

*   Early Romans came in contact with the Greeks in the 4th century BCE. They admired and copied Classical Greek art, building, and clothing adapting it to their uses.

*   They conquered Greece in the 2nd century BCE during the Hellenistic period and brought Greek culture and art to Rome and later assimilated and redirected it for political purposes.

*   At its height, in the 1st century CE, the Roman Empire administered a broad, well-organized, tolerant, multicultural, and multiracial empire of local cults, diverse nationalities, and Eastern religions. It was a secular empire devoted to conquest, trade, and administration, spreading and administering Roman culture. Romans did not require conquered peoples to give up their culture and identities as long as they acknowledged Roman authority. Those who did not acknowledge Roman authority like the Christians and the Jews were persecuted.

*   The Roman civilization was originally a Republic that was governed by elite elected representatives to the Senate, which was a limited representative government. It divided citizens into wealthy Patricians, lower middle class Plebeians, and poor Slaves. Only the Patricians could vote, make laws, or hold office in the elected Senate.

*   In 60 BCE Julius Caesar instigated a coup and reduced the power of the Senate and started the First triumvirate. He was assassinated in 44 BCE and in his will named his relative Augustus Caesar as his heir.

*   In 27 BCE Augustus Caesar ended the Republic and took supreme power for himself and became the first Roman Emperor of an Imperial state—now Imperial Rome—and ruled until 14 CE.

*   Architecture tended to be fairly consistent throughout the Empire because of its function as the official cultural and political propaganda presence. Rome also had uniform legal and administrative systems, which were used among all her colonies. Costume and the decorative arts, though, achieved great variety and liveliness reflecting the local influences of the diverse commercial empire and the richness and individuality of the conquered cultures.

*   Imperial Rome became highly expansionist, and this period saw the greatest growth and development of the commercial and military reach of the Empire.

*   Romans connected cities of the Empire by complex travel and communication systems. They built and maintained 50,000 miles of paved roads, sea-lanes, and hundreds of cities, many of which are still inhabited today.

*   Romans increased and stratified its social divisions. They practiced slavery of conquered peoples to a much greater extent than the Greeks.

*   Romans led a complex, cosmopolitan social life, continuing the humanism of Greece but coupling it with a secular commercialism.

*   Romans believed in the superiority of the mind over the body, but the body was the province of each individual.

* Roman social activity was focused on creating a decent secular life mediated by the state and laws. Romans systematized life by applying rationalist organization, recordkeeping, and administration.

* They did not copy the Greek alphabet but developed the Roman Capital script and numerals that are still in use.

* Most major buildings were secular, not religious, and were organized along streets in planned cities often based on grids and behind defensive walls.

* Art and architecture were in the service of the state and politics. Buildings served as propaganda and symbols of power.

* Public spectacle in amphitheaters, racetracks, bathhouses, and theaters was used as a political tool to control unrest as well as to provide entertainment.

* Emperor Constantine designated Christianity as an approved religion in 313 CE and Christianity became the official religion of the Empire a century later.

* Women achieved higher status, education, and culture than in Greece. Imperial mothers, wives, and daughters were often influential behind the scenes in Imperial politics.

* Theater was an important part of Roman life and a good website is: http://www.crystalinks.com/rometheatre.html

* There are a number of operas that have been set in ancient Rome and several of these are: *Giulio Cesare*, Handel (1724); *La Clemenza di Tito* ("The Clemency of Titus"), Mozart (1791); *L'ultimo Giorno di Pompei* ("The Last Day of Pompeii"), Pacini (1825); *Antony and Cleopatra*, Barber (1975).

* Some suggestions of TV shows and movies that could be useful research are: *Rome* (TV series) (2005–2007)*, *I, Claudius* (TV series) (1979)*, *Gladiator* (2000)*, *Spartacus* (2004), *Spartacus: War of the Damned* (2013), *Julius Caesar* (1970), *Empire* (2005), *Rome* (2005), *Imperium: Augustus* (2003), *Ben-Hur* (1959, remake forthcoming), *Barabbas* (2012), *Cleopatra* (1963)*, and *The Robe* (1953)* and *A Funny Thing Happened on the Way to the Forum* (1996). In addition, there are a number of excellent movies, TV programs, and documentaries about Pompeii.

The Roman Material World

What They Made

* The Romans organized cities around rationally planned public forums and marketplaces derived from the Greek agoras, and the cities were connected with paved roads.

* Unlike those of the Greeks, Roman monumental buildings had only one central entrance. See Figure 2.4.

* Also unlike the Greeks, the Romans eliminated natural obstacles when they were building. They built where they wanted, not just where nature allowed.

* The Romans adopted Greek architectural style and then added codified arched construction, including arcades, vaults, and domes which allowed freer and larger interior spaces and larger, more complex building forms. See Figures 2.2, 2.4, 2.5, 2.6, 2.8, 2.9, and 2.10.

* The Romans ranked the Greek architectural Orders into a hierarchy from the simple Doric to the more complex Ionic to the most elaborate Corinthian. This was done to signal the relative importance of each building type. The Romans added the Tuscan Order below the Doric for rough

Figure 2.2 This contemporary photograph is of the interior of the Pantheon, Rome, built 118–125 CE. This temple is proportioned to enclose a perfect sphere—in other words, its diameter horizontally is exactly equal to its height. Much of the marble is original; however, the floor has been replaced. The coffered ceiling would originally have been covered with gold, and the oculus—the round opening in the roof—is open to the sky.

Vanni Archive/Art Resource, NY

stables and farm buildings, and the Composite Order above the Corinthian for use on the most important temples and government buildings. In addition, the Romans redesigned the Doric Order to more closely align with the look of the other orders. See Figure 2.3.

* Public art was in service to state propaganda. The frequent succession of power in the Imperial period required an industry producing political art on a commercial scale as emperors rapidly followed one another and their official images changed.

* The Romans borrowed and modified the Greek temple form by closing off the sides and back, adding the podium, front entrance, and staircase, and by locating them in cities rather than in the open countryside. They also moved their theaters from the country into their urban centers. See Figure 2.1.

* The Romans perfected multi-story residential buildings. They developed the first five to six-story apartment houses. These became the most common residential building type and outnumbered single houses 20 to 1.

* The Romans made many innovations in building including concrete construction, plumbing, central heating, public water supply, fountains, sewerage systems, and aqueducts. Additionally, they made many engineering advances in the organization of complex civic structures and systems.

Figure 2.3 This is a graphic depiction of the five Roman Orders of architecture. The Romans kept the three Greek Orders, but modified them and added two new ones. Starting on the left is the first new Roman Order, which is the simple Tuscan Order; 2nd is The Doric—modified with fluting on the column and a cushioned capital and molded base; 3rd is the Ionic; 4th is the Corinthian; 5th is the new Roman Composite Order, which combined Corinthian and Ionic elements. This drawing also shows important proportional elements.

Private Collection/Bridgeman Images

Figure 2.4 The Pantheon, exterior, built 118–125 CE, era of Hadrian, Rome. This is the best-preserved structure from ancient Rome and has been in continuous use ever since. Its design has influenced many architects, artists, and numerous buildings since the Renaissance throughout the world.

Gianni Dagli Orti/The Art Archive at Art Resource, NY

Figure 2.5 This is a contemporary model of ancient Rome during the Imperial Age, which shows the density of the city. By the 1st century CE it had 1 million people and it would be almost 1,800 years until London would have that number. Romans built multi-story domestic apartment buildings and the precursor to our shopping malls and clustered them closely with civic structures. The model shows this; other prominent features are the semi-circular theater in the foreground, the large buildings with the pitched roofs in the center, which are the Baths of Nero (public baths or *thermae*, with their gardens, a long arcade, and the *palaestra* for sports, games, and competitions), and the Pantheon, which is the round-domed building in the upper right.

Mondadori Portfolio/Electa/Andrea Jemolo/Bridgeman Images

Figure 2.6 This model is a reconstruction of the Theater of Marcellus in Rome. The theater was completed in 13 BCE. It was the largest and most spectacular ancient Roman theater, seating 12,000 people, but with a capacity of much more. It would serve as the model for many Roman theaters throughout the Empire and also the Roman Coliseum (Colosseum). This theater has the most typical features of a Roman theater and shows many of the differences from a Greek one. First it is a freestanding, semi-circular, concrete structure using Roman arches. The arches not only provided support for the raked seats, but also provided entrances, which were tunnel-like structures called vomitories. Unlike the Greek theater, which was primarily religious, Roman theater was an entertainment venue not only for drama and song, but also for political propaganda and was usually situated in cities.

Scala/Art Resource, NY

Figure 2.7 The 2nd-century CE Roman theater, in Bosra, Syria. Roman "Bostra" was the thriving provincial capital of the province of Arabia Petraea. This picture shows the other major innovations: the addition of the three-story stage house called the *scena frons* with its permanent scenic openings, the raised rectangular stage below it, and in front of it another adaptable, semi-circular space called the orchestra, which was surrounded by the steeply raked seats. Notice the three levels of seating, the wedges that allowed for stairs, and the vomitories between sections; importantly, this is the origin of our modern stadium seating.

jasminam/iStock

Figure 2.8 The Coliseum in Rome, built 70–80 CE was the largest amphitheater in the Roman Empire with an estimated capacity of over 50,000 people. It was used for a variety of entertainments such as gladiators, public spectacles, and battle re-enactments. Notice that the column Orders—Doric, Ionic, and Corinthian—ascend with each tier of the building, which is true of most theaters and arenas. The row of brackets, just above the small windows, once held a retractable canopy, called a valerium. The Coliseum features prominently in the video game: *Assassin's Creed: Brotherhood.*

abadesign/Shutterstock.com

BATHS OF CARACALLA.

Figure 2.9 This artist's rendering of an interior in The Baths of Caracalla, Rome, shows what it might have looked like. They were built from 212 to 216 CE and were one of the most monumental and impressive complexes of buildings with baths, sports, shops, libraries, and gardens. For propaganda purposes the unpopular Emperor Caracalla built this extensive facility that was open to all classes. Bathing was an important social activity for wealthy Romans, but the *thermae*, or bathhouse, was not only for bathing, but was also the site of important social and civic activities. By the 4th century CE there were at least 900 baths in Rome. Today the Baths of Caracalla are an important ruin in Rome and in the summer the home of the Teatro dell' Opera.

North Wind Picture Archives/Alamy

Figure 2.10 Basilica of Constantine in Trier, Germany, 310 CE. A late example of the Roman law court that was later used as the prototype of Western Christian churches. The semi-circular apse was originally where the Roman Judge sat, but when the building was converted into a Christian church it became the site of the altar and behind it was usually a mosaic of Christ.

lexan/Shutterstock.com

* The important introduction and use of concrete allowed the Romans to build much faster and larger than the Greeks. They perfected its use for underwater construction, bridges, aqueducts, buildings, and roads.

* The Roman architect Vitruvius wrote the first surviving treatise on Roman architecture around 25 BCE. This book was later an influence on Renaissance architects.

How They Decorated

* Classic Roman architectural decoration is based on the five Roman orders, which dictate how to design structural members such as columns and lintels. See Figure 2.3.

* Romans developed decorative elements of the orders such as pilasters, entablatures, and broken pediments as both exterior and interior motifs. In interiors they were often executed in relief and in partial perspective. See Figures 2.3, 2.5, 2.9, and 2.14.

* The patrician Roman house continued the Greek domestic practice of inward-looking rooms built around one or more atriums open to the sky, highly decorated rooms with painted stucco or relief walls, mosaic or marble floors, and rich furnishings. See Figures 2.2, 2.9, 2.11, 2.14, 2.15, and 2.16.

* As in Greece, the home was the center of personal, social, business, and religious practice. The rooms were laid out with an inward-facing orientation with plain exteriors and richly decorated interiors. See Figures 2.13 and 2.14.

* The homes also had elaborate and costly furnishings. They used finely detailed and crafted couches, chairs, stools, and tables. They also invented the candle. Google "Imperial Roman Furniture" and it will lead to several sites.

Figure 2.11 This fresco from a wall painting in Pompeii c. 79 CE shows the beginning of the use of the three kinds of perspective—a mastery of linear, positional, and atmospheric perspective. The Romans were the first to incorporate all three types of perspective into their painting, giving their landscape, figurative, and still life works a highly realistic effect. Also notice the subtle and realistic use of color.

Scala/Art Resource, NY

* The Romans continued and elaborated the Greek style of wall painting and experimented with early forms of linear and atmospheric perspective. See Figures 2.11, 2.15, and 2.16 and look at "Villa of The Mysteries, Pompeii" for more exceptional and interesting mosaics.

* The Romans continued the Greek mastery of freestanding realistic sculpture and invented the freestanding equestrian statue. See Figures 2.17, 2.18, and 2.19.

Building and Décor Keywords

Tuscan Order – A simplified version of the Doric Order was added by the Romans, with a plain frieze, and no fluting on the column. See Figure 2.3.

Composite Order – An elaboration of the Corinthian Order was also added by the Romans, combining the capitals of the Corinthian and Ionic Orders, and characterized by elaborate details that were only used on buildings of a high stature. See Figure 2.3.

Roman Doric Order – Replaced the Greek Doric Order with a slimmer column with smaller fluting, a small cushion capital, and a molded base. See Figure 2.3.

podium – This was the raised base of Roman temples that replaced the Greek stylobate (platform). See Figure 2.1.

Roman arch – A half-circular curved support member instead of a lintel that spans an opening between columns. It was developed from a single radius point located in the middle of the spring line. This allowed columns to be spaced farther apart and buildings to be larger and stronger. The arch is the most important feature of Roman architecture. See Figures 2.5, 2.6, 2.8, 2.9, and 2.10.

Figure 2.12 This is an artist's reconstruction of a typical street scene in the Via dell' Abbondanza, Pompeii, Italy, showing residential and commercial buildings along a wide cobblestone and concrete street with a market and pedestrians. Urban streets had two common features, large raised curbs, and elevated stones for people to cross the street. The graffiti on the walls refers to a local election. Also notice the square stone public water fountain.

akg-images/Peter Connolly

pier (PEER) – This is a massive, rectangular support, similar to a column, to carry an arch or dome, it can also be seen on bridges and aqueducts and is pictured in the plan of Hagia Sophia. See Figure 3.10.

pilaster – This is a square column that can stand alone or be engaged in a wall. See Figure 2.14.

forum – The Roman version of the Greek agora marketplace but expanded to include political and governmental as well as commercial buildings. Unlike the agora, it often included temples. See Figure 2.5.

amphitheater – A circular or oval arena for public celebrations and staged combat surrounded by seats and open to the sky. The Coliseum is an example; see Figure 2.8.

basilica – A public building or Roman law court that was a large, oblong building with a semi-circular apse usually at one end for a judge. This was the precursor of the Western church form. See Figure 2.10, the Basilica of Constantine.

circus – A long oval raceway surrounded by seats that was used for chariot races.

thermae (THER-my) – A Roman public bathhouse composed of three zones: a cold water bath, a warm water bath, and a hot water bath. In larger examples it could also contain shops, libraries, restaurants, and gaming facilities, as was the case of The Baths of Caracalla and The Baths of Nero. See Figures 2.5 and 2.9.

aqueduct – The Roman system of water channels that were on raised arcades and were used to supply water to cities from faraway sources.

insula (IN-sula) – A rectangular Roman apartment house often four or five stories high with rooms facing inward to an open courtyard containing a communal well.

scena frons (SKEN-a FRONS) – The highly decorated rear stage wall of a Roman theater containing ordered columns, statuary, and surmounted by a wooden roof. It contained five entry arches, three from the rear and one from each side of the stage. See Figures 2.6 and 2.7.

vomitory – This was the tunnel that the audience used to get to their seats in a Roman theater or amphitheater. See Figures 2.6, 2.7, and 2.21.

arcade – This was a connected series of arches joined side by side and supported by columns or piers. See Figures 2.5, 2.6, and 2.8.

vault – A series of masonry arches placed face to face and extended in depth like a tunnel. See Figures 2.5 and 2.6.

groin vault – The intersection of two barrel vaults meeting at 90-degree angles. Sometimes also called a cross vault.

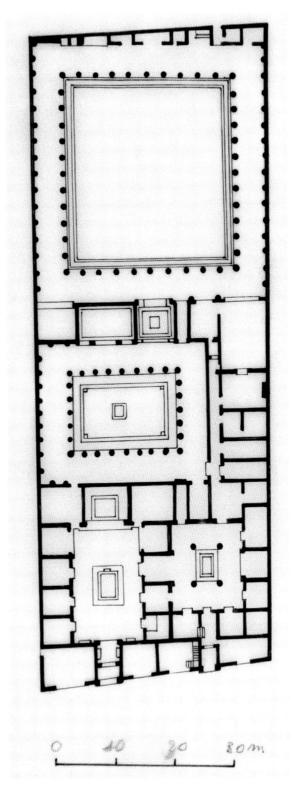

Figure 2.13 This is a reconstruction of a plan of the House of the Faun in Pompeii, 1st century CE. The houses were constructed with solid outer windowless walls designed to provide privacy and reduce noise. There are four distinct atriums, the two smaller and more private ones also contain fountains in the center, and the central atrium would have been used for entertainment and to conduct business. The fourth large atrium at the back would probably be a clipped and green garden in most homes. The entrance to the compound is through the atrium on the lower left, which opened onto the street.

Figure 2.14 This is a reconstruction illustration of House of the Faun in Pompeii. It shows three atriums open to the sky and a pool in the center with a decorative statue/fountain. The water collected in these pools was the primary source of water for the household and notice how the roof slants down to enable this and the three round waterspouts. Notice also the decorative marble floor and the walls, which could also be marble, painted to look like marble, or with other decorative or figurative paintings as in Figure 2.11. You can also see the smaller rooms adjoining this space. There are fluted pilasters on either side of the main passageway and the two side walls that also have Corinthian capitals. The partial ceiling and the full ceilings were made of wood and often decoratively painted.

De Agostini Picture Library/Bridgeman Images

dome – A rounded, curved roof structure spanning an enclosed space, often hemispherical, usually on a circular plan, based on the principle of a rotated arch. See The Pantheon, Figures 2.2 and 2.4.

spring line – The point on a vertical support at which an arch begins to curve.

radius point – The point from which the radius of an arch is measured.

valerium (Val-ER-ium) – A retractable fabric canopy used for shade over an amphitheater and other theater structures. See Figure 2.21.

The Roman Clothing and Costume World

How They Dressed

*   In the Republic from c. 300–100 BCE the Romans adapted and modified Greek clothing.
*   Romans introduced the toga, which was an enlargement of the Greek himation. Initially it was worn by men and women, but by the 2nd century BCE primarily by men. See Figure 2.18.

Figure 2.15 This is a fresco of women dressing and is a rare example showing fabric and female hairstyles. Note the *tunicas* and *stolas* and the ladies on the left with *pallas*; and the elegant fashion sense and subtle use of color in the fabrics. The large candle in the lower left, which was a Roman invention, the three-legged table—called a *trapeza*—and the delicate rendering of a glass pitcher lend realism to the scene.

Figure 2.16 This mosaic from Pompeii, 62–79 CE, shows a rehearsal for a satyr play which was the third type of Roman drama after tragedy and comedy. Note the detailed props, masks, and costumes being used by the actors. Masks were a particularly important part of Roman drama and were colorful and expressive, which could easily convey a character or emotion and also allowed the characters to be seen from far away. They also permitted an actor to play multiple parts. The man in the center is playing an *aulos*, a Greek and Roman wind instrument.

Museo Archeologico Nazionale, Naples, Italy/Bridgeman Images

* Late Republican and early Imperial fashion from 100 BCE to 200 CE for both men and women was dominated by the elaborately draped toga and *palla*. The toga was a large fold of cloth cut in a semi-circular pattern that was worn over a tunic for formal and ceremonial occasions and worn with sandals. See Figure 2.15 and 2.18.

* Later Imperial patrician fashion after 200 CE became complex and highly competitive and concerned with rank and wealth for both sexes. As the Empire spread there was the introduction of styles and materials from across the Empire; particularly furs from the north and exotic colors and materials from the east.

* Older women also wore the *stola*, a long, thin tunic, and the *palla*, a scarf that could function as a hood, separately or together. See Figure 2.15.

* Tunics and undergarments were often shaped and sewn from two pieces of cloth and dyed bright colors.

* Military clothing continued Greek forms, which became more standardized, and added the shaped metal cuirass or breastplate and boots instead of sandals. These were adaptable for varying climates of the Empire. See Figure 2.19, 3.18, and 5.17.

* The military used rough togas but often wrapped them around their waists. Short and long cloaks could be used for a hood.

* Bronze or iron helmets had a smooth crown, a neckpiece, a visor, and cheek guards. See Figures 2.20 and 2.21.

* Lower classes shortened the toga into a cape worn over a wide variety of tunics, breeches, and leather boots.

* Men of all ages were clean-shaven with short, cropped hair; scholars and slaves were often bearded.

* Women were fashion conscious and competitive. They wore their hair up and highly decorated with ribbons, jewels, and exotic ornaments.

* Religious costume was much the same as civilian costume, based on the toga, often with the addition of special insignia and a veil to denote religious function.

* Men and women wore sandals. See Figures 2.16 and 2.19.

Clothing and Costume Keywords

tunica – A Roman name for a tunic. It was worn by men and women. It was a linen garment similar to and adapted from the Greek chiton, but sewn from two pieces of flat cloth with sleeves, slipped over the head, and tied at the waist with a belt or sash. There were many variations in length and type of decoration. Generally for the wealthy, it was made of a good fabric, frequently with decoration and worn under a toga. Rougher forms and materials were characteristic for common people and slaves. See Figures 2.12, 2.15, 2.16, and 2.17.

toga – The main Roman formal garment for upper class men and women during the Republic and early Imperial periods. It was a single semi-circular piece of cloth, often 8–9 feet in diameter, draped elaborately around the body and held in place by the left hand. Its folds were often used as pockets or for concealing valuables or weapons. In rougher versions it could be used as a blanket at night. See Figures 2.9, 2.11, and 2.12.

Figure 2.17 This is a marble relief from the 2nd century CE. It portrays a woman and a child, a little dog, and a bird. A maidservant is bringing a dish laden with food. They are relaxing on an upholstered and pillowed couch called a *lectus*. The decorations on the wall behind them are a garland with three putti and above that shells and ribbons. Notice the women's hairstyles and clothes—*tunicas* and *stolas*.

De Agostini Picture Library/A. Dagli Orti/Bridgeman Images

Figure 2.18 This is a statue of Emperor Tiberius showing the Imperial toga and tunic. Only wealthy and politically prominent men would have worn a toga of this size and complexity. Also notice that he is clean-shaven and with the typical short, combed-forward Roman hairstyle. Roman and Greek sculptures were usually painted.

De Agostini Picture Library/A. Dagli Orti/Bridgeman Images

Figure 2.19 This is a statue of Emperor Trajan (53–117 CE) showing his short skirt, long cloak, armor, breastplate, high laced sandals, and sword. This was the basis of all military garments, which were provided to soldiers by the state. This military uniform would continue basically unchanged for the next 800 to 1,000 years. See the Tetrarchs, Figure 3.18, and the soldiers in *Charles the Bald*, Figure 5.17.

Claudio Divizia/Shutterstock.com

toga praetexta (TOGA pri-TEXT-a) – An Imperial toga with additional fabric in its circumference and with a purple band along its outer curved edge denoting high status. It was only worn on formal occasions. See Figure 2.18.

licinium (li-SIN-e-um) – A linen loincloth, knotted at the waist, that originally was the only Roman undergarment. By the time of the Empire it was only worn by workmen and athletes. See Figure 2.21.

femoralia (fem-o-RAY-lia) – These were half-length trousers worn under a toga and also with military clothing.

greaves – This was a piece of armor to protect the shins and used by gladiators. See Figure 2.21.

stola – This was the typical and basic outer garment of a Roman woman and worn over the tunica. It had sleeves and was worn long and loose often with two belts, one under the breasts and one on the hips. It was made of wool, linen, or cotton, and for the very wealthy, silk. Unlike men's clothes they came in a variety of bright colors. See Figures 2.15 and 2.17.

palla – This was the Roman adaptation of the Greek himation, and was the female version of the male toga. It was wrapped and draped over the *stola* and could be used as a head covering or a veil. See Figure 2.15.

Roman cuirass (kwi-RAS) – The military torso protector made of two rigid metal or leather panels shaped to the upper body, connected by straps under the arms and worn on the chest as armor. Often highly decorated and worn with a leather fringed skirt. See Figure 2.19.

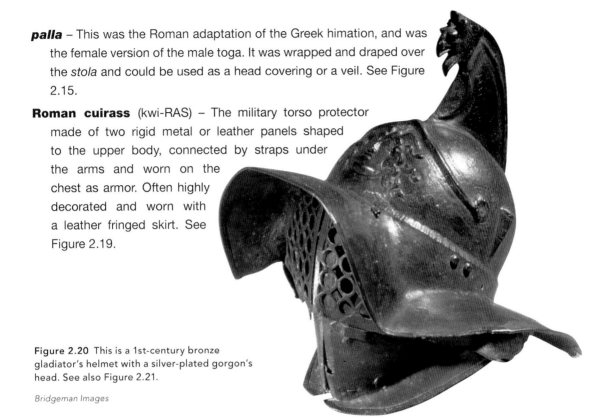

Figure 2.20 This is a 1st-century bronze gladiator's helmet with a silver-plated gorgon's head. See also Figure 2.21.

Bridgeman Images

Figure 2.21 This is a carefully researched reimagining of gladiatorial combat in the Coliseum, painted by Jean Léon Gérôme in 1872 entitled *Pollice Verso* (Thumbs Down)—a rejection. On the gladiators notice the different helmet details, the loincloth (*licinium*), the greaves on his shins, the articulated armor on his arm, daggers and shield. In the middle is the emperor's box with the red columns and banner and Imperial Roman eagles and to the left is a vomitory entrance. The dark shadow would have been cast by the valerium, above, which is not shown.

Phoenix Art Museum, Arizona, USA/Museum purchase/Bridgeman Images

CHAPTER THREE

Early Christian: 313–800 CE, Byzantine: 313–1453 CE

Figure 3.1 The Basilica of Sant' Apollinaire in Classe, Italy, was consecrated in 549 CE. This shows the wide nave with arched columns and two smaller side aisles in the long basilica style; this characteristic rectangular plan would influence Western church construction for the next 1,500 years. The massive polygonal apse features a mosaic of the Saint as "shepherd" surrounded by his "flock" in a flat graphic style very typical of medieval painting that has moved away from the realism of Classical styles. Also at the top is an image of Christ and the four Evangelists and the 12 sheep represent the Apostles.

A Little Background

Constantine was a Roman military commander who became a Christian in 313 CE and conquered the city of Rome and then became emperor. Shortly after this, he divided the Roman Empire into two parts to make governing and administration easier. He founded the city of Constantinople, on the site of an ancient Greek port, Byzantium, now present-day Istanbul in Turkey, as the city's location was at an important intersection of trade routes and at the most eastern edge of the Empire. He named the city for himself and made it the capital of the eastern half of the Empire or now the Byzantine Empire. The western half remained in Rome after Constantine's division. Christianity was accepted in both halves and it would later become the official state religion. In the form of the Byzantine Empire the eastern half continued for another thousand years under a series of emperors, until it fell to the Ottoman Turks in 1453. The Western European portion of the Empire gradually declined and mixed its Roman identity with the individual tribal identities of the pre-Roman peoples. In 476 CE northern German and Celtic tribes overran Rome and this is frequently called "the fall of the Roman Empire" in the West.

The introduction of Christianity, then one of a number of Eastern mystical religions, and later Islam, transformed the visual and stylistic tastes of the next thousand years by shifting the visual emphasis in pictorial design from the secular realism of Classical design themes to the subjective spiritualism of the faith-driven Christian and Muslim religions in both halves of the Empire.

Who They Were

* The Western Empire declined drastically in wealth and cohesion after the sack of Rome in 476 CE; however, functioning remnants of the old empire survived for another 500 years and mixed with the tribal cultures and influences from northern Europe. They coexisted with elements of the new Christian faith in planting the seeds of a new European culture.

* The Western Empire (Early Christian) based first in Rome and Milan and then Ravenna eventually produced the Roman Catholic Church of Western Europe. The Eastern Empire (Byzantine) based in Constantinople produced the Greek, Baltic, and Russian Orthodox Churches.

* Early Christianity remained the sole transnational force in Europe and occupied the vacuum left by the political decline of the Western Empire and the physical abandonment of Rome. The Church had the only remaining literate and administrative institutions.

* In the West no permanent civic or secular structures or institutions survived the barbarian invasions. Although often referred to as the Dark Ages, there was significant intellectual and religious activity in the monastic system that developed as a result of the spread of Christianity.

* Militarization of the aristocracy in the West isolated the peasantry and created serfdom, in which the poor, who were 90 percent of the population, supported the wealthy and were little more than slaves. This was the beginning of feudalism. See costume illustrations, Figures 3.15 and 3.16 for peasants and laborers.

* Altered and much reduced Classical forms became the foundation of the architecture of medieval Western Europe. In the Byzantine Empire it combined with Arabic architecture and it produced the architecture of Asia Minor.

* This period saw the increased influences of Northern and Eastern cultures; and trade brought furs, rich fabrics, gems, and spices especially to the Eastern Byzantine Empire.

* Some films, including adaptations of two Shakespeare plays include: *King Lear* (1971 and 1999)*, *Hamlet* (1990)*, *Beowulf* (2007)*, *Beowulf & Grendel* (2005), *The Lord of the Rings Trilogy* (2001, 2002, 2003), and two films about the legendary Pope Joan that would be good costume resources, *Pope Joan* (1972 and 2009)*.

The Early Christian/Byzantine Material World

Figure 3.2 This is the ancient Basilica of St. Peter's in Rome. This a 14th-century fresco of the 4th-century CE building, as it appeared when it was constructed at the time of Constantine. This cut-away shows the typical shape of a basilica looking toward the apse with the long nave and the five aisles each of which contained a row of columns. This was on the site of St. Peter's grave and now the present St. Peter's in The Vatican.

Scala/Art Resource, NY

What They Made

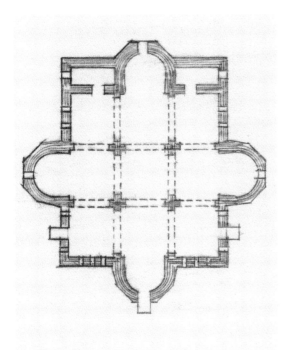

Figure 3.3 This is a floor plan of a Central or Greek Cross Church and was the plan characteristic of Eastern Church architecture. See Figures 3.6, San Vitale, and 3.9 and 3.10, Hagia Sophia.

Author drawing

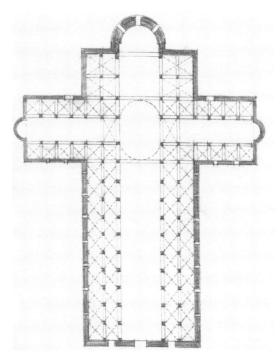

Figure 3.4 This is a floor plan of a Latin Cross Church that became characteristic of Western Church architecture in the Romanesque period. See the words section for a more comprehensive description.

Author drawing

Figure 3.5 Sant' Apollinaire in Classe, Italy, is in the long basilica style built from 532 to 549 CE and is an important example of Early Christian architecture. This was a further evolution of the basilica—see Figure 2.10, the Basilica of Constantine in Chapter 2. In this view we see the short front end of the nave rising above a horizontal narthex or porch with the main entrance. This and the building to the left were added at a later date. The round bell tower with mullioned windows is from the 9th century.

Scala/Art Resource, NY

Figure 3.6 This is an exterior view of the Basilica of San Vitale, 526–548 CE, in Ravenna, Italy. It is a central plan—Byzantine design, based on an octagon. The diagonal buttresses to the left and right were added later to help stabilize the building. Buttresses will be discussed more fully in Chapter 6, Gothic. The church was a gift from the Eastern Roman Emperor Justinian to his counterpart in the West, whose mosaic portrait and that of his wife, Theodora, figure prominently on the apse walls. See Figures 3.12 and 3.13.

Gerard Degeorge/Bridgeman Images

Figure 3.7 The Interior of San Vitale is a blaze of rich color with mosaics, which some consider the best in the Western world. The beautiful decorative marble columns feature a new innovation for a column style known as a basket capital with a tapered impost block on top of it holding up the arch. See websites: www.khanacademy.org and www.sacred-destinations.com/italy/ravenna-san-vitale

De Agostini Picture Library/A. de Gregorio/Bridgeman Images

Figure 3.8 The Basilica of San Vitale is most famous for its magnificent mosaic walls reaching to the ceiling vaults. All of the decoration shown here is original and reflects its debt to Classical Roman painting and the Byzantine style of the figures. See Figures 3.12 and 3.13 for the images of Justinian and Theodora and their retinues.

Alfredo Dagli Orti/Art Resource, NY

* Religious buildings were often the only form of permanent architecture. Almost all large secular and commercial buildings were abandoned as the Western Empire lost interest in the secular world and Roman civic organization deteriorated and reverted back to local traditions.

* Early church forms of the Western Empire, called Early Christian, were longitudinal, based on the Roman basilica or law court. It had a single apse, a large central nave or corridor, with two small side aisles, and a wooden roof. It was much reduced in scale from Classical Roman buildings. See Figure 3.2, St. Peter's Basilica.

* Early church forms of the Eastern Byzantine Empire were centralized, based on circle, square, cross, or octagon plans and often maintained or exceeded the size and grandeur of Classical Roman buildings, such as Hagia Sophia in Constantinople (now Istanbul, Turkey) built by Justinian from 532–537 CE. Also see a smaller version San Vitale, Ravenna, Figure 3.6, and Greek Cross plan, Figure 3.3.

* As the Christian church gained control and dominance in both parts of the Empire, secular building, cosmopolitan life, and public entertainment were abandoned and seen as sinful and transitory.

* Secular buildings were reduced in scale with plain exteriors and emphasis was placed on the highly decorated interiors.

* In the West only religious and some defensive buildings were built permanently; and in the Eastern Empire only major cathedrals, palaces, and defensive structures were built on a large scale.

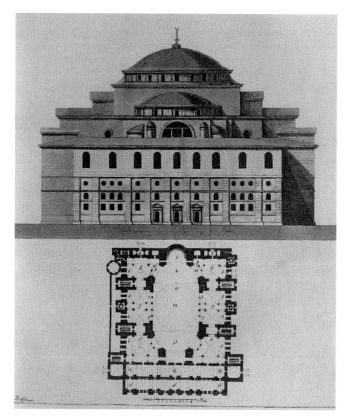

Figure 3.9 This image is a floor plan and drawing of Hagia Sophia in Istanbul, Turkey, showing its massive size and its central plan style. It was an extraordinary example of engineering and building, as it was the largest building and dome in the world for 1,000 years. The dome is supported by four triangular pendentives, two of them are noticeable in the photo below on either side of the apse. Five Pantheons could fit inside of it and it was built at the same time as the much smaller Ravenna churches. The four enormous freestanding rectangular supports in the center of the plan are piers.

De Agostini Picture Library/Bridgeman Images

Figure 3.10 This is a contemporary photograph of the interior of Hagia Sophia. Originally it was built by Justinian as a Christian church, but with the conquest of the Ottomans in 1453 it was converted into a mosque, which is why the large green medallions with Arabic calligraphy are noticeably displayed. Many of the early Christian images and symbols were also covered over with Islamic ones. Its form served as a model for many other mosques. Now it is a museum; the round golden chandeliers were added later.

INTERFOTO/Alamy

How They Decorated

Figure 3.11 This mosaic is from the mausoleum of Galla Placidia, Ravenna, Italy, c. 440 CE. This is a lunette under a vaulted ceiling, and it is believed to be Saint Lawrence of Rome standing next to the gridiron with flames on which he was martyred and burned. Next to that is a cupboard, which has four books with the names of the Apostles. The entire ceiling of the mausoleum is covered with stars, part of which can be seen here. The rectangle in the center is an alabaster window. Above the stars is a Greek Key design that can use many different configurations and in this instance it is made to look three-dimensional.

Mountainpix/Shutterstock.com

* In artistic visualization there was increased influence of the spiritual, symbolic, and the abstract to convey emotion and mystery that resulted in the elimination of realistic representation and rejection of the realism of the Classical and secular world.

* This period saw the abandonment of freestanding sculpture with individualized features. They were replaced by art that was flat, two dimensional, and low relief, which used frescoed or mosaic figurative images of a stylized identity.

* The systematic use of the Classical Orders was also abandoned as many building parts were scavenged from ruined Classical buildings and then recombined and reused in new structures. An example of this is San Vitale, which used bricks and stones from Roman buildings and also the new column style. See Figure 3.7.

* The invention of the impost block in interior decoration characterized almost all Early Christian and Byzantine construction. This was a tapered block placed between the top of a column capital and the base of the arch to lengthen its vertical proportion. See Figure 3.7, San Vitale.

* The rise in the use of mosaics was seen on walls and ceilings of churches in place of frescos because of their dramatic color and emotionalism when seen against the dark interiors of religious buildings. See Figures 3.1, 3.7, 3.8, 3.10, 3.11, 3.12, and 3.13.

* The development of the illuminated manuscript occurred during this period.

Building and Décor Keywords

Latin Cross (Cruciform) plan – The plan of a church in which two main aisles of unequal length crossed at right angles with the shorter aisle crossing the larger at a point east of its center, resulting in a cross plan with approximately three equal arms and one longer arm. This was characteristic of Western Church architecture. See Figure 3.4.

central plan or Greek Cross – The plan of a church based on a circle, square, hexagon, or octagon in which all sides were of equal length and produced a large center sanctuary. This was the plan characteristic of Eastern Church architecture. See Figures 3.3, 3.6, 3.9, and 3.10.

impost block – This was a unique feature of Early Christian and Byzantine architecture, in which a tapered block was placed between the top of a capital and the spring line of an arch. See Figure 3.7.

basket capital – A basket-shaped capital was often square or rectangular in plan, and had relief carved and interlaced bands resembling woven strips or reeds. Sometimes it was also used in conjunction with altered Classical capitals. See Figure 3.7.

Byzantine Arch – An adaptation of the semi-circular Roman arch that used a smaller radius in relation to the height of the column and raised the spring line by the addition of an impost block between the capital top and the spring line of the arch. See Figure 3.7.

pendentives – These are triangular segments of a sphere that are used as supports that allow the placing of a circular dome over a square space. Pendentives were commonly used in Orthodox, Renaissance, and Baroque churches. See Figure 3.10.

lunette – This is a crescent-shaped painting sometimes in a niche. It can also be a semi-circular window in a domed ceiling. This form of painting was a favorite of Italian Renaissance artists, but also the form is used in many other cultures. See Figure 3.11 as a type of lunette.

Greek key – This was a repeating border or pattern that could come in different variations, but always used a continuous line. It was a prominent decorative feature in Western architecture and décor from Classical times onward and was also frequently used in Asian designs as well. See Figure 3.11.

The Early Christian/Byzantine Clothing and Costume World

How They Dressed

* Introduction of trousers from Persia for aristocratic dress, combined with Hellenistic Greek costume, produced the typical look of the Byzantine style that consisted of a tunic and trousers with a cloak clasped at the right shoulder. An enlarged form of the Greek chlamys or cloak replaced the toga, with a decoration of a rectangular *tablion*, as the garment of royalty and the upper classes especially in the Byzantine territories. Western and Eastern ecclesiastical garb developed from the Greek chlamys and Roman toga forms into the dalmatic. See Figures 3.12 and 3.15.

* The lower classes continued the use of long tunics for women and short tunics over leggings for men. See Figures 3.15 and 3.16.

Figure 3.12 This image of Justinian at the Basilica of San Vitale shows a rare example of secular mosaic portraits. The Emperor Justinian is in the center wearing an Imperial purple robe over a long tunica with an enlarged version of the chlamys, now called a *paludamentum*, with a large fibula and holding a paten, which is a bowl to hold the bread for a Eucharist mass. His courtiers to the left also have purple *tablions* and there are soldiers in military costumes to the far left. On his other side is his head general, then the Bishop of Ravenna, wearing a chasuble and stola and, holding a jeweled cross. The other members of the clergy are holding a Bible and incense burner, and all of them are wearing dalmatics with black banding. Not shown, but the portrait of Christ in the apse dome is also wearing a purple robe—also signifying him as royal. The borders in this and the companion piece are typical Byzantine decorative designs and colors.

De Agostini Picture Library/A. Dagli Orti/Bridgeman Images

Figure 3.13 This other mosaic pictures Justinian's wife, the Empress Theodora with her court. She and her courtiers are also shown in purple and she is holding the jeweled chalice for the mass. Also notice Theodora's lavish jeweled *maniakis*—collar, and crown—stemma. The woman next to her is Antonina, the wife of the general. The other women attendants are wearing exquisite dalmatics made of richly colored and decorated fabrics, probably of silk, and jewels—earrings, rings, bracelets, and necklaces. Also notice the colored and patterned drapery.

Tarker/Bridgeman Images

Figure 3.14 This is a French manuscript *The Breviary of Alaric*, 506 CE with a text in Latin. It shows on the upper left the King of the Alamans, Lodhanri, with a crown, next to him a bishop—notice his halo—and below a duke and a count. These were codexes of law that continued Roman practices in the south and east of present-day France, now no longer part of the Roman Empire but controlled by the Visigoths. Although the drawing is crude it is still possible to see that the clothing has hardly evolved since the 1st and 2nd centuries CE and includes the belted short and long tunics and cloaks. Compare this illustration to the much more realistic and sophisticated art from Classical times in Chapters 1 and 2.

Bibliothèque Nationale, Paris, France/Flammarion/Bridgeman Images

Figure 3.15 *The Chronicle of the Months*, this is a page from an early Carolingian manuscript. The illustration shows the labors of each month and displays a wide variety of tasks, implements, and seasonal garments; and if you look carefully you can make out the names of the months. Notice the similarity to Roman garments, particularly the way the cloaks are fastened and draped, worn over their tunics, leggings and pants.

Erich Lessing/Art Resource, NY

Figure 3.16 This is an 11th-century CE Byzantine illuminated manuscript page from a *Book of Hunting* showing a variety of clothing types of laboring men and women. The men are wearing variations of tunics and decorated leggings, particularly the man on the lower left. The two women on the upper left are wearing simple belted dalmatics with wide flared sleeves. First on the left they are gathering olives, then smoking out bees and collecting honey, and then an unidentified scene, and finally a man slaughtering a ram.

Scala/Art Resource, NY

Figure 3.17 This is a Byzantine buckle with an embossed head in profile from c. 400 to 600 CE. It is gold, lapis lazuli, and glass and is a sample of the exquisite craftsmanship of the time and what was available to the wealthy.

Cleveland Museum of Art, OH, USA/Grace Rainey Rogers Fund/Bridgeman Images

Figure 3.18 This is a stone statue of the Four Tetrarchs from St. Mark's Cathedral, Venice. These four men were co-emperors about 305 CE. Recently it has been discovered that the statue was originally from Constantinople and brought to Venice during the 4th Crusade. When it was installed at St. Marks it was broken in half to fit the corner. Important to us is their military clothing and the weapons, which hardly changed since Classical times. Notice the eagles on the hilts of the swords. This is a rare purple rock, porphyry, from Egypt and its use was reserved for royalty and emperors.

Renata Sedmakova/Shutterstock.com

* The Eastern Empire saw the introduction of Persian and Arabic motifs, jewels, and metallic fabrics. See Figures 3.13 and 3.17.

* They used luxurious fabrics, with the extensive use of silks and metallic threads. By the 6th century CE they were making silk in the Byzantine Empire. The quality of the cloth and the richer levels of ornament and decoration indicated social status. See Figures 3.13 and 3.17.

* Jewelry and embroidery were used extensively, particularly on Imperial costumes for both men and women. All Byzantines liked bright, rich colors and as in Imperial Rome the color purple was reserved for the emperor. See the clothing and jewelry of Justinian and Theodora, Figures 3.12 and 3.13.

* In the Eastern Empire men were often clean-shaven and women wore their hair up and decorated in the Classical fashion. See Figures 3.12 and 3.13.

* The Western Empire saw the introduction of Celtic motifs, leathers, and furs. Men were clean-shaven and often had long hair. Women also wore long hair and in braids. See Figures 3.14, 3.15, and 3.18.

* There was an increase in caste and rigid social systems in both the East and the West that was exemplified by extravagant clothes to define class lines.

* Unlike in Rome that had sumptuary laws and therefore people were told what they could wear, in the Byzantine Empire they could wear whatever they could afford.

Clothing and Costume Keywords

Early Christian, Byzantine Costume styles – They descended from Classical examples retaining the tunic and cloak or a full wrapped over garment often over trousers for men and a simplified form of the *palla* for women. See Figures 3.12, 3.13, and 3.15.

cote, surcote (surcoat) – The long fitted tunic worn by both sexes that gradually replaced the Classic tunic and became the basis for both men and women's clothing. See Chapter 5 for examples.

dalmatic (dal-MATIC) – A long, wide or tight sleeved tunic falling to the feet with a rounded neck. For the wealthy, they were decorated with vertical bands. Originally Roman, it was also worn by the Byzantines and then it was adopted for Early Christian liturgical dress. It is still worn by clergy in the Eastern Orthodox Churches. See the clergy in Figures 3.12 and 3.13.

tablion (TAB-lee-on) – This was an oblong or square panel on a chlamys worn by Byzantine emperors and their attendants as a mark of rank. There is a patterned one on Justinian and purple ones on the courtiers in Figures 3.12 and 3.13.

maniakis (mani-AK-is) – The flat, wide, highly decorated collar worn by Byzantine Empresses. See Theodora in Figure 3.13. Notice how similar this was to the *usekh*, Figures 18.10, 18.11, and 18.12, and also the collar on the *chacmool*, Figure 17.16, and the Inca necklace, Figure 17.27.

stemma – The crowns set with gems and decorated with hanging ornaments worn by Byzantine Empresses and in a variation by emperors. See Figures 3.12 and 3.13.

CHAPTER FOUR

Islamic: 622–1100

Figure 4.1 The *mihrab* (prayer niche) in the Mezquita Mosque-Cathedral in Córdoba, Spain created in 961 CE. The *mihrab* is one of the three elements found in most mosques. This exquisite example is embellished with gold, calligraphic, geometric, and plant forms. This is also an example of a Moorish arch that re-curves on itself. Unlike most *mihrabs* that generally face east to Mecca this one faces south. There will be a fuller explanation in the body of the text and in "Keywords" at the end of the section.

Matt Trommer/Shutterstock.com

A Little Background

A new religion, Islam, arose in Arabia and centered on the person and teachings of the prophet Mohammed; it quickly swept across the Arabian Peninsula and into North Africa. It shared many tenets of Old Testament practices and beliefs with Christians and Jews, but developed its own religious and political structure, culturally related to Arabic tribal practice. For the first time, Mohammed unified Arabia into a single polity.

Who They Were

* Islam began in Arabia in 7th century CE with the teachings of Mohammed and later writings in the Qur'an.

* Arabia was originally in the Arabian Peninsula centered between the Red Sea and the Persian Gulf and its northern borders were present-day Jordan and Iraq. It was the homeland of the Arab people and the prophet, Mohammed, who was born in the city of Mecca in 570 CE. Later in the 7th century CE Mecca (now in Saudi Arabia) was considered the holiest city and was the center of this new religion.

* Through rapid military conquest Islam spread extensively across the Arabian Peninsula to North Africa to the Iberian Peninsula (Spain, Portugal, and southern France), and later to Sicily, Persia (now Iran), Turkey, most of the Middle East, and then further east.

* Islamic society was organized as a theocracy in which the Caliph was the religious, secular, and military leader.

* Because of its Arabic origins early Islamic culture was nomadic and primarily in the desert with no fixed architecture; and it adapted to the architecture of these conquered people.

* In newly conquered areas Muslim rulers often preserved and adapted local cultural traditions including local styles of architecture and dress. The Arab conquerors remained separate from the conquered people and lived and governed from separate enclaves.

* The Moors, who were descended from Arabs and Berbers (North African people), invaded the Iberian Peninsula from Morocco and conquered it in 711 CE and called it Al-Andalus.

* The Islamic "Golden Age" ran roughly concurrent with the Middle Ages in Europe from the end of the 8th century through to the 13th century. Muslim scholars preserved Classical learning by saving Greek and Roman texts, translating them into Arabic and other languages and adding to them. They also created a learned literary and scientific culture of their own. Many of their texts and much Classical learning came to Europe from them during the Renaissance and their "Golden Age" would start to fade. See Figure 4.11.

* Islamic scholarship and culture made great advances particularly in the fields of medicine, mathematics, and astronomy. They invented the much more flexible Arabic numeral system, the basis of our Western numbering system.

* Córdoba, Spain, was the capital of the Caliphate; it was the intellectual, cultural, and artistic center of medieval Europe and the city had the largest population including Muslims, Christian, and Jews. There were reported to have been 700 Mosques, 60,000 palaces, and 70 libraries. It was said they had some of the finest book illuminators and that some were women. Muslim rule ended when the city of Granada, their last holdout, fell and the Catholic, Spanish King Ferdinand and Queen Isabella came to power and expelled the Muslims and Jews in 1492.

* There are a number of 19th-century American, English, and other artists that painted very accurate and detailed paintings of the Islamic world and especially Egypt and India that would be very useful references; many of their images are on the Internet. The style of painting is known as "Orientalism." Several to look for are: John Frederick Lewis, R.K.K. Zommer, Giulio Rosati, William Holman Hunt, Edwin Lord Weeks, Rudolf Ernst, Lawrence Alma-Tadema, and Frederick Bridgeman.

* *The Message* (1977)* is a film about the birth of Islam. *El Cid* (1961)* was a spectacular film about 11th-century Spain and won an Academy Award for Best Art Direction. Two movies set in the 20th century, *Lawrence of Arabia* (1962)* and *A Dangerous Man: Lawrence After Arabia* (1990), might be useful to designers. An early Middle Eastern fantasy video and 2010 film *Prince of Persia: The Sands of Time* is worth seeing. Two romantic silent films starring Rudolph Valentino, *The Sheik* (1921) and its sequel *The Son of the Sheik* (1926), are entertaining.

The Islamic Material World

Figure 4.2 The Great Prayer Hall in the Mosque-Cathedral of Córdoba. Originally a church built by The Goths in c. 600 CE, from 710 it was a shared mosque and cathedral, and then a mosque from 784–1236 CE, and then after the expulsion of the Muslims/Moors only a Catholic cathedral. There are 856 red and white arches that were made from recycled Roman ruins. The double-height columns supporting the Moorish arches were a new architectural feature.

Ken Walsh/Bridgeman Images

What They Made

Figure 4.3 This is an aerial view showing part of the exterior of the huge Mosque-Cathedral of Córdoba complex with the courtyard garden and entrance.
In the center of the picture is the Christian Cathedral that was added to the center of the Mosque in the 8th century CE.

akg-images/Jean-Louis Nou

Figure 4.4 This is a contemporary photograph showing the exterior of Hagia Sophia in Istanbul, Turkey, that began as an Eastern Christian church in 537 CE, but was converted to a mosque when the Eastern Empire fell in 1453. It shows the four minarets, which are one of the important features of mosque architecture.

ruzgar344/Shutterstock.com

Figure 4.5 A contemporary photograph of the Sheikh Lotfollah Mosque, Isfahan, Iran, showing the dome and the main entrance gateway. The top of the gateway is covered with honeycomb work in the Persian style, which was popular and used throughout the Islamic world in the 12th century. The building is completely covered in intricate decorative tiles in the 17th-century innovative new process called the "7 colors technique," mostly variations of blues with gold. It was built for the Shah Abbas in his new Persian capital from 1602 to 1619 as a private royal mosque for him and his harem. It was not open to the public so the minarets are noticeably missing as there was no need to call worshipers to prayer.

Andrea Jemolo/Scala/Art Resource, NY

Figure 4.6 The Courtyard of the Myrtles is a residence in the Alhambra complex, Granada, Spain. Built by Yusuf I between 1333 and 1354, this particular house was patterned on Mohammed's home in Mecca, Arabia. It also shows a typical long Islamic reflecting pool fed by fountains at either end that bisects the courtyard and is surrounded with a marble walkway and myrtle bushes. Above the columns is a fretwork screen and the larger central large arch also has *mocarabes* (honeycomb) decoration as also seen in Figure 4.5. Also rising behind the building is a crenellated wall with two 19th-century towers that also indicate that the Alhambra was also a fortress.

Adam Lubroth/Art Resource, NY

Figure 4.7 This is a 19th-century engraving of ogival or ogee arches at Paisley Abbey, Scotland. This is an Islamic arch that became very popular with Western architects at the beginning of the Victorian period. It is constructed of four radii, two in the normal lower position and two in the opposite direction above it.

DavidBukach/iStock

Figure 4.8 This is the Al-Madina Suk in Aleppo, Syria. This is a contemporary photo showing people walking down one of the many corridors inside this historic *suq*, or market, that dates from the 16th century and is the largest permanent covered market in the world. Usually *suqs* were temporary and often seasonal and open-air structures in the Middle East and North Africa. Notice that they were lit by holes in the ceilings. The lack of windows was also so the buildings stayed cool in this hot climate.

jcarillet/iStock

Figure 4.9 This is an extremely simple Bedouin tent in Tunisia. Notice the woven fabric and straw sleeping pallets and that everything could be rolled up and carried on a camel or horse. They have essentially remained unchanged for centuries. Bedouins (Bedou means desert dweller) were nomadic tribes throughout the Middle East and North Africa and still exist.

LUke1138/iStock

* Early Islamic culture reflected its Arabian cultural roots of nomadic tribes of animal herders with no fixed residences. For shelter they used tents that they carried with them. These could be as simple as a piece of fabric held up with sticks to extremely large lavish affairs with colorful rugs and decorations with many ornamental as well as utilitarian objects. There are numerous images of styles and varieties on the Internet—"Bedouin Tent," click on images.

* Another type of market was the bazaar, which also used tent-like coverings instead of a roof as these were frequently temporary markets. Edwin Lord Weeks' painting of a 19th-century *Moorish Bazaar,* the Persian equivalent term for a market, is a good image (http://en.wikipedia.org/wiki/Edwin_Lord_Weeks or http://www.the-athenaeum.org/art/list.php?m=a&s=tu&aid=330). Notice the red and white striped arch that is similar to the Prayer Hall, Mosque in Figure 4.2. There are also good costume and color references in this painting. E.L. Weeks was a 19th-century American Orientalist painter and traveled widely in the Middle East and India. He did many paintings of these countries and they are an excellent research source.

* Islamic architecture was not standardized but reflected and adapted local building styles. The four major building forms remained the same throughout the diaspora and fell into four categories: mosque, palace, tomb, and fort.

* Because of religious strictures against portraying living beings, decorative expression was primarily calligraphic and geometric in religious art, texts, and buildings. These restrictions did not apply to secular, scholarly, and literary works. See Hagia Sophia Figure 3.10—the huge green calligraphic medallions that were made in the 19th century by the famous calligrapher K.M.I. Effendi and name Allah, Mohammed, and other notables. Also see Figure 4.5.

* All mosques had at least three features in common: the *mihrab*, the *minbar*, and *maqsura*. See Figure 4.1 for the *mihrab*, Córdoba. See Figure 4.12 for the *minbar*.

* Minarets although not original to mosques became a significant part of mosque architecture and were associated with the *muezzin* singing worshipers to prayer. See Figure 4.4.

* Mosque architecture, like in many religious spaces, was inward looking, and concentrated on the spiritual not secular world. It was egalitarian in the sense that men of all ranks prayed together; however, the women were separated. See Figure 4.12.

* The *madrasa* was and still is a school for the teaching of secular and religious values. Like a mosque it had no prescribed shape or composition. See Figure 4.12.

* *Caravansari* were fortified enclosures for the shelter and replenishing of caravans along their journey that often took on the function of military forts. There are many images on the Internet of old and new ones; search "Silk Road" for further information.

* There were few examples of royal palaces as they were often destroyed when their rulers changed. They were usually seen as the ostentatious dwelling of a single person rather than a multigenerational family home. The prime exception to this, although built at a later date (1248–1354), was the Moorish palace—the Alhambra in Granada, Spain: the last holdout of the Muslim rulers in Europe. See Figure 4.6 Alhambra (means red castle in Persian).

How They Decorated

* John Frederick Lewis (1805–1875) was another prolific English Orientalist painter, who lived in Cairo in the 1840s, and was known for his highly detailed paintings and sketches, all of which could be useful research for the designer and are easily accessed. His 1873 painting *Reception* is

Figure 4.10 This is a typical Islamic prayer rug called a *sejadah*. For centuries it has followed the same basic principles and varies in color, designs, and materials from village to village, region by region. It is woven in a rectangular shape using traditional symbolic images, in this case a tree and abstracted floral designs. Characteristically there is a niche at one end that points the worshiper in the direction of Mecca and to the *mihrab* in the mosque.

tunart/iStock

an oil painting of Western women visiting an Egyptian harem and is a useful example of an interior (http://commons.wikimedia.org/wiki/Category:John_Frederick_Lewis). Notice the overall architecture of the room with wooden beams and high ceiling, and the details of the carved screens, which allowed for air circulation, and the stained glass all with repeating geometric patterns. Also notice the pool surrounded and edged with tiles, the ornate fountain, and the raised banquette with cushions and rug. The different figures are wearing typical Western and Egyptian period clothing; of note is the young girl in her baggy pants—an adaption of the earlier *sirwal* that came to be known as "harem pants" (baggy pants that were caught at the ankle or above).

* Interiors and exteriors of buildings, both religious, and secular, used decoration that was characterized by brightly colored, lavish, and profuse use of tiles, gold leaf, mosaics, and stained glass. See Figures 4.1, 4.2, 4.5, and the paintings *Moorish Bazaar* and *Reception*, and Chapter 19, "India."

* Because of the extreme geographic range, interior decoration varied widely from country to country; however, in the Middle East interiors also used tiles and mosaics and the use of multiple rugs—even in tents and modest homes. See the painting *Reception*.

* Religious prohibition of representations of living things in religious texts and structures resulted in a decorative style based on geometric patterns, such as arabesques, abstracted floral forms, and calligraphy. See Figures 4.1 and 4.5 and also the interior of the Hagia Sophia 3.10. These were also used in India particularly in the Mughal Empire—see Figures 19.7, 19.8, and 19.11.

Building and Décor Keywords

mosque – The principal religious dwelling of devotion in Islam. Its plan is often based on an open courtyard derived from the courtyard of Mohammed's home in Arabia, but there were no formal rules as to its configuration. The mosque often took the form of the local architecture, which varied from region to region from a simple mud structure in Mali to huge, complex tiled edifices in Turkey or Iran. See Figures 4.1, 4.3, 4.4, and 4.5, as well as 3.9 and 3.10.

minaret – A tall tower or usually four towers in or next to a mosque with stairs leading up to one or more balconies from which the faithful were called to prayer by a *muezzin*. See Figure 4.4.

mihrab (ME-hrab) – This is the most important decorative element in a mosque. It could vary in size and colors and have modified elements; but basically it was a semi-circular, arched niche in a mosque wall that indicated the direction of Mecca and therefore the congregation always faced it. It was usually carefully and exquisitely decorated with geometric and calligraphic designs, using tiles or mosaics. It was often decorated to look like a doorway thus a symbolic entrance to Mecca. See Figure 4.1.

minbar – Originally this was a three-step platform from which the Imam led prayers and spoke to the congregation. Later it was usually a small tower with stairs and a roof, it was akin to a Christian pulpit or lectern. See Figure 4.12.

maqsura – A prayer chamber or separate room in a mosque often with an openwork screen originally meant for the Sultan or Imam. There are a number of references and pictures on the Internet, but *use caution* as many images are not correct.

Moorish (horseshoe) arch – A round arch whose curve was a little more than a semi-circle so that the opening at the bottom was narrower than its diameter. See Figures 4.1 and 4.2.

ogival (O-gival) **or ogee arch** – A pointed arch based on an ogee or reverse curve shape, in which the curves of the arch take an S-shaped form. See Figure 4.7.

Persian arch – A pointed arch formed by two small-diameter arcs at the spring line supports that extended in a straight line towards each other to form an apex. See Figure 4.5, the large arch and the four smaller ones. Also see Figures 19.7 and 19.8.

suq (SOOK), **suk**, **souk**, and **sukh** – This was a large, often covered market with shops grouped according to the commodity being sold. See Figure 4.8, which is an important historical *suq* in Aleppo, Syria.

bazaar – This was the Persian word for a market and can also be in the open air or enclosed. They are found in all Islamic and other countries as well. See E.L. Weeks' painting *Moorish Bazaar*.

arabesque – This was one of the primary Islamic styles of decoration and can be found on all types of their architecture, household items, and illustrations. These are intricate designs based on repeating geometric, curvilinear, and abstracted plant forms. They represent an infinite pattern and therefore symbolized the infinite – the one God, Allah. See the Mosque dome, Figure 4.5.

mocarabes – The honeycombs that are frequently found embellishing Islamic architecture. See Figures 4.5 and 4.6.

sejadah – These were and are Islamic prayer rugs. See Figure 4.10.

The Islamic Clothing and Costume World

Figure 4.11 This illustration is from a 13th-century Arabic version of Dioscorides' book *De Materia Medica*, a 1st-century Roman doctor whose seminal work in Greek is about herbs and their remedies. These scholars are wearing *thaubs* and turbans on their heads. Also notice their fabrics and the use of gold leaf for the background.

Werner Forman Archive/Bridgeman Images

How They Dressed

Figure 4.12 *Left:* In this illustration (1237) Abu Zayd is teaching to men and veiled women in a *Madrasa* in Raiy. In the 8th century it was an important ancient city near Tehran, Iran, which is now destroyed. Notice the blue tiled steps that he is preaching from, which form a *minbar*; the women are segregated and seated on a balcony. Shown are a variety of colorful and patterned clothes and headdresses of both the men and women and the flat two-dimensional style of painting typical of Persian miniatures.

bpk, Berlin/Bibliothèque Nationale, Paris, France/ Art Resource, NY

Figure 4.13 *Below:* These are three contemporary Islamic women showing different styles of head coverings, the general term is *hijab*. In all of their manifestations the important thing is to cover the head, hair, and shoulders. The woman in the middle is wearing a version called a *niqaab* where she also veils her face.

Juanmonino/iStock

Figure 4.14 *Left:* This photograph shows a different variation of the turban on a Muslim man in Tozeur, Tunisia, Africa. It is believed that Mohammed wore a white turban as it is the holiest color.

Bill Bachmann/Alamy

Figure 4.15 *Below:* This is a contemporary photo of four men in the United Arab Emirates. They are wearing traditional *thaubs*, *kufi*, and *taqiyah*. Notice the necklines, embroidery on the third man's clothing, and also the variety of facial hair.

Jeff Greenberg 5 of 6/Alamy

* The Qur'an recommended that all Islamic clothing for men and women should emphasize modesty and piety. Traditional Muslim garments for both men and women were loose fitting so as not to call attention to the physical body. Mohammed did not specify the degree of covering; those traditions have evolved over many centuries and were also dependent on whether the person was in public or in their homes and also with members of the opposite sex. Traditions also suggested that clothing should not be opulent nor should it be in rags.

* Because Mohammed was from Mecca, in present-day Saudi Arabia, Islamic clothing was adapted from simple interpretations of the loose, flowing traditional Arabic dress developed for desert life and mounted travel. Later it incorporated Persian and Turkish influences, which resulted in a wide variety of styles of both loose and fitted garments, sometimes very plain and others that were colorful, highly decorated with embroidery, woven or printed, and of rich fabrics. Usually particularly for women ornate or colorful clothing would only be worn in the home or under a large over garment. See Figure 4.12.

* The origin of turbans (derived from a Persian word) is unclear, but they were found in many Muslim regions and in many styles. In the desert their use varied and they had many adaptations such as to protect from heat, sand, sun, and cold, as a pillow or covering. See Figures 4.11, 4.12, and 4.14. Also in Chapter 19, India, Figures 19.20, 19.21, 19.22, and 19.27.

* Many of the styles of clothing for men and women started in ancient times, and even some before Mohammed, and in some regions have changed very little. The biggest differences in clothing were regional styles mainly due to geography and climate, the available fabrics and dyes, and less due to different Islamic sects, ethnic, and national costumes, and until recently variations due to position, status, and wealth and now contemporary Sharia laws.

* Men and women had to have head coverings in public (also true in the US and Europe until very recently) and they both wore sandals, and boots for men and the military. As in Figures 4.8 and 4.15 contemporary people have adopted Western style footwear such as sneakers, and blue jeans have become ubiquitous in many Islamic countries.

* Only men were allowed to conduct religious services and they are usually referred to as clerics or mullahs. Their ecclesiastical garments were very similar to secular ones, but there is much variety again because of geography, climate, local styles, and also religious laws. However, they have always included a long robe and a head covering such as the turban. Today for convenience' sake they often wear trousers or some form of *sirwal* underneath. See the teacher in Figure 4.12 and notice the difference in his sleeves as opposed to the men in Figure 4.15.

* Military uniforms for the most part from the 7th century to the 12th century were often supplied by the individual or were a continuation of the Classical garments shown in Chapters 2, 3, and 5, when the older cuirass was replaced by a chain mail tunic worn over breeches and a shaped metal helmet with a mail neckpiece.

* Women's clothing has also adapted from the same traditions. In many parts of the Islamic world in the 21st century it has come under strict control. Through the centuries these Sharia laws have come and gone.

* *Hijab* is the general term for headscarf, but there are many different styles, colors, and materials, also driven by geography and sect and politics. In some countries *hijab* is also the religious code that governs clothing. To many, both men and women, it is a symbol of modesty as dictated by the Qur'an.

* Headscarves and veiling were not just an Islamic custom and have been worn since very early times. They were a common practice in Rome and the Byzantine Empire where they were considered a

sign of wealth and high status. Jews and Christians also wore them—the premier example would be all the iconography of Mary, who was always pictured with a large over garment.

Clothing and Costume Keywords

kufi – A small round cap worn by men that is similar to the Jewish *yarmulka*. See Figure 4.15.

taqiyah – This is also a small round flat-topped hat. It can be worn alone as in this picture, Figure 4.15, or under the *ghutra*.

ghutra – Another type of headdress for men also with regional variations in style and color, but basically it is a square scarf folded into a triangle with the fold in the front. It is held in place with an *igal* (egal). In the old style this was a thick double gold color band as seen on the Bedouin Prince Faisal in *Lawrence of Arabia*, Lawrence of Arabia, or the modern King Faisal of Saudi Arabia, and in the new style it is usually a double black band made of goat hair, famously worn with a red and white check *ghutra* by Yasser Arafat and now many contemporary Palestinians.

turbans – These are an additional variation of a hat for men and are basically a long cloth wrapped around the head. They come in numerous modifications, particularly in the way they are wrapped to make different shapes, the length of the cloth, and their color. Turbans are worn by Muslims all over the world and by Sikhs. See Figures 4.11, 4.12, and 4.14, and again in Chapter 19 on India, Figures 19.20, 19.21, 19.22, and 19.27.

thaub, **thobe**, **also called a dishdasha** – For many centuries this has been the most typical and basic Muslim costume. It is a long, loose robe with long sleeves and often a tailored top, like a shirt with buttons, which can also be embroidered. It can have a simple round neck or a small stand-up collar. Primarily worn by men, a modification is also worn by women. It is frequently worn with several layers such as loose trousers, a headscarf, an overcoat, or a shawl. In summer or hot climates it is usually white, but in colder areas or winter it is black or in dark colors. Frequently this was the only garment for children. See Figure 4.15.

bisht/aba – This is a robe worn over the *thaub*. Depending on the season, climate, wealth, and rank it can be quite simple or very elegant and made from cotton, camel, or sheep wool. For Imams, prominent men, and the wealthy they are usually embroidered with gold threads. See Figure 4.15.

sirwal, sarwal (SIR-wall) – In the olden days this was the basic undergarment of men and women that consisted of a single piece of fabric wrapped around the waist and between the legs. Today they are the loose pants often worn with a tunic, *thaub*, or even a T-shirt. See Figure 4.15.

shamla (SHAM-la) – A mantle or scarf worn over the head by men and women.

hijab – A headscarf or cowl that in all of its different manifestations always covers the hair and shoulders, but not the face. See Figure 4.13.

niqaab – This is a veil that covers the head and face with a slit for the eyes, but can vary so that it ties at the bridge of the nose. Another variety comes in three pieces and covers the chest as well with a veil that can be lifted to reveal the face.

kaftan – This was another typical and basic type of Islamic garment originally derived from Persian clothing and worn by men as a long tunic often with a wide sash. The type of fabric and decoration indicated wealth and rank. Again due to the region, the styles and fabrics could vary, but they were and still are made of camel or sheep wool, cashmere, silk, or cotton. It was adapted for women and later became popular in Europe and the US. Unlike many of the other clothes for women the contemporary kaftans are brightly colored, patterned, and decorated and made of expensive materials, clearly indicating that in most Islamic countries they would only be worn in the home.

abaya – This is also a basic women's garment and can come in a number of different styles and fabrics by region, status, and wealth. Mostly it is a long dress with either wide or narrow long sleeves often with embroidery at the neck and down the front and at the wrists. It usually opens with buttons from the neck to below the breasts and is embroidered.

There are a number of different variations of the outer female garments. Almost every region has a variation and different names. It would be wise for the production and costume designer to research the locale and the precise period, as there is much confusion in descriptions. This is a short list to show the variety and to get started on research.

burqua (BURK-a) – Originally this was the veil worn by all Islamic women when they appeared in public, and later it is the entire floor-length garment with a fitted cap and screen-like veil attached that originated in Pakistan and now is mostly worn in black, blue, or white versions in Afghanistan. See Figure 4.12 for the early version.

chador – It had its origins in ancient times and is mostly worn in Iran today. It is a full body and head covering cloak made in a large semi-circle and held together in front with the hands. It is usually black.

haik – This was and is a traditional Algerian woman's full body and head covering robe, usually in white and a lightweight fabric similar to the traditional flowing men's Arabian clothes. It is having a renaissance in their country.

kebaya – This is a variation of the word *abaya* and is a type of traditional full robe worn in Indonesia and warmer climates also of lightweight fabric and frequently colorful.

CHAPTER FIVE

Romanesque: 800–1100

Figure 5.1 Abbey Sainte Foy, Conques, France, 11th century. This cathedral is in the new Romanesque style. This is the West Front showing the bell towers; projecting pedimented entrance of the Romanesque doorway with an arched canopy and a sculpted narrative tympanum were also added features of Romanesque style. Windows were small and arched and widely spaced. Originally it was in the basilica plan of the early Christian churches, but in the 11th century these alterations and the use of masonry vaulting made this and the new church form both dramatic and useful and the West Front became functional, elaborated, and instructive.

Paul Maeyaert/Bridgeman Images

A Little Background

Named for its resemblance to previous Roman examples, the Romanesque style with the use of Roman masonry arches and columns spread across Europe in both the church and military buildings.

In the vacuum created by the dissolution of the Roman Empire in Europe, this period saw the continued slow development of local languages, cultures, and political and military units that would eventually define the Western European nation states. Several social systems arose at this time: a new international religious organization called monasticism, a new secular organization called feudalism, as well as a reorganization of the military structure with power diffused among local barons and their courts with no transnational authorities.

In what is now northern France and Germany, Charlemagne ruled as a civilized leader on the Roman model in the 9th century. He briefly reunited elements of the Roman Empire, preserved Classical texts, and developed the first secular law system since Rome. Charlemagne saw himself as a successor to the Roman emperors but his reign and influence were short.

Who They Were

* The Carolingians or scholars of Charlemagne's court developed an architectural style based on Roman and Early Christian examples with a conscious attempt to revive the scale and grandeur of Classical building and learning. See Figure 5.2.

* Carolingian scholars and scribes invented lower case letters of the Roman alphabet in order to make writing faster and easier. This style of calligraphy was known as Carolingian minuscule. Due to its clarity and legibility it spread quickly through Western Europe and is still used today.

* Norman, sometimes called Viking, culture spread south from present-day Norway and Sweden to Scotland, England, Ireland, France, Spain, Italy, and into the Holy Land.

* Monasticism from the Eastern Empire developed as a way of organizing far-flung monasteries and was characterized by self-governing and self-sufficient, celibate religious communities that were connected by an international network of traveling monks. Originally monasteries were exclusively male, but shortly women were organized into nunneries also known as convents. See Figures 5.5, 5.6, and 5.7.

* This culture expressed a strongly anti-humanist religious sentiment and stressed mystical and judgmental themes.

* This period saw the development of the Romance languages including French, Italian, Spanish, and Romanian from Latin. The Catholic Church continued to use Latin in its services and most written manuscripts also used it.

* Scholars and teacher monks were educated in monasteries and were the guardians of order and learning and preserved and studied Classical texts. See Figures 5.5, 5.6, and 5.7.

* With the monastic system the Catholic Church became more unified and the period also saw the rise of Papal authority in Rome.

Background image: Monreale Cathedral, Palermo, Italy, is a superior example of 12th-century Norman architecture. Author photo.

* Feudalism developed as a military and judicial system of local barons with their own military, political, and economic systems. They were perpetually contending with each other for riches and prestige.

* The constant warfare among these competing barons resulted in massive defensive castle-building projects throughout Europe.

* Diminished commercial trade during this period resulted in an impoverished peasantry who were dependent on their local barons for their livelihood. There was a reduction of the use of currency, which had been prevalent in Classical times, in favor of barter.

* The first Crusades were mounted and attempted to take Jerusalem from the Muslims.

* These are some suggestions for films of the period: *Becket* (1964)*, *The Lion in Winter* (1968)*, *Murder in the Cathedral* (1951)*, *The Vikings* (1958), *The Vikings* TV mini-series (2013, 2014, and 2015), *Erik the Conqueror* (1961), and *Alfred The Great* (1969).

The Romanesque Material World

Figure 5.2 Charlemagne's Palatine Chapel consecrated 805 CE, Aachen, Germany. Charlemagne saw himself as a continuation of the Roman Empire and made many important innovations, but he wanted to revive the glory of Imperial Rome and so he copied their architecture and the decoration of San Vitale in constructing his magnificent chapel, rather than the new Romanesque style.

Danita Delimont/Alamy

What They Made

Figure 5.3 Abbey Sainte Foy, Conques, France, 11th century. This is the nave looking toward the east emphasizing small windows and round arches. The new Romanesque style abandoned the flat wooden roof in favor of an arched masonry roof and with the double arches allowed for a much higher nave. This new cathedral form also created the Latin Cross plan by the addition of a perpendicular aisle and a transept or crossing of the nave. The apse was now also roofed by a masonry rather than wooden dome.

Scala/Art Resource, NY

Figure 5.4 Abbey Sainte Foy. Column capitals in this period became lively storytelling devices with both sculpture and painted images. This one shows a man blowing a horn and masons erecting a wall.

Hervé Champollion/akg-images

Figure 5.5 Fontenay Abbey, Burgundy, France is a 12th-century Cistercian monastery complex. This shows the façades of some of the buildings, including the dormitory, left, chapter house and scriptorium, center, and the church, right, and medicinal garden in the foreground. It was founded in 1119 by St. Bernard of Clairvaux and like many monasteries was isolated and the monks dedicated to prayer, poverty, and self-sufficiency. In addition to the above buildings it had an excellent dovecote, iron works, bakery, and refectory as well as vineyards and agricultural fields.

Gianni Dagli Orti/The Art Archive at Art Resource, NY

Figure 5.6 This is the view from the other side showing the Romanesque cloister and its small steeple. It is characterized by simple, unadorned decoration and the squat Roman arches. The cloister is a four-sided enclosed space surrounding a covered arcade, and this is an early use that evolved from the Classical atrium, but now associated with a monastery, nunnery, and their churches, usually with a water feature in the center. The pathways here lead to the larger arches that are entrances, and the double arch enclosed in a larger arch is also a typical Romanesque feature.

Manuel Cohen/The Art Archive at Art Resource, NY

Figure 5.7 This is the monks' dormitory, which is just one large space with a vaulted wooden ceiling, in which they all slept together on the floor. They wanted all of these buildings, including the church, to be stark like this so as not to distract or disturb them from prayer. Monasteries could be either male or female and were organized communally with the members sharing religious devotions, sleeping, eating, and work facilities.

Gianni Dagli Orti/The Art Archive at Art Resource, NY

Figure 5.8 The Church of the Holy Sepulchre, which locally is called The Round Church. This contemporary photograph shows a round Romanesque church in Cambridge, UK. The church shows several Romanesque features such as the general heavy stone appearance, the lack of windows on the first floor, the multiple stepped back columned doorway with its relatively small wooden door with large decorative hinges. The windows also have stepped back Romanesque arches with thin colonettes and dentil-like projections above them.

Chris Tiné

Figure 5.9 Pembroke Castle, Wales, UK. Illustration by Harry Green (b.1920). This is a 12th-century Norman castle and like in monasteries secular life centered on self-sufficient communities. Unlike monasteries these were fortified and were the center of a feudal lord's domain. The castle was the home of the local lord, his family, his court, and soldiers and was protected by one or more walls of defensive battlements. The walls and towers were characteristically built with crenellations so that soldiers could hide behind them and they protected them from projectiles. Castles were often located on a hill and also behind a moat or a river bend as shown here. For more images of UK castles go to www.webbaviation.co.uk/castles/castles.htm and then aerial photographs of castles.

Look and Learn/Bridgeman Images

Figure 5.10 Pembroke Castle: this is the imposing view invaders would have had when attacking from the river. It shows the massive size of the castle, the defensive walls, towers, and large circular keep. The building to the right with contemporary scaffolding is the gatehouse; although not in this case, it would frequently be entered over a drawbridge, which could be raised and lowered over a moat.

garyforsyth/iStock

Figure 5.11 The Great Keep at Pembroke Castle. A keep or don-jon is the largest round tower in a castle compound and the last refuge in time of war. Around the inside of this circular one are holes for timbers which once supported the floors. It would have had a circular stone staircase and this one also has a stone roof, so that flaming arrows wouldn't light it on fire.

Flynt/Dreamstime.com

Figure 5.12 Stokesay Castle in Shropshire, England, with the adjacent Parish Church graveyard in the foreground. The rectangular part in the front and the wall to the left are the original 11th-century castle and were built as a fortified manor house. Castles were often topped with half-timbered living quarters. The large brackets under the upper story allowed this space to be enlarged and are typical of this period and would continue into the 17th century. The small vertical windows in the lower stone part were for defensive purposes and could be closed in time of attack, as could the small upper windows, which would have been small leaded panes and would have interior shutters. The two small, triangular, hipped roofs were common on houses and farm buildings and were vented to allow for better air circulation. The additions to the rear with the four gabled roofs and Gothic windows were from the 13th century.

BackyardProduction/iStock

Figure 5.13 Interior "Great Hall" in Stokesay Castle. This was the main central living area where the soldiers, servants, workers (yeoman), and farm animals slept on the floor, which was covered with straw. It was also used for other gatherings, meetings, and eating. In the center was a fire pit and directly above it a vent in the roof. The fire was used for both heating and cooking and was active day and night. There would have been heavy crude furniture such as trestle tables that could be broken down, benches, chairs, and chests. The lord of the manor and family lived in the rooms at the top of the stairs and they slept on piles of straw covered with furs. The complex timber roof with its massive arched, horizontal, and vertical beams would be the pattern for future Gothic pitched roofs in England and Northern Europe.

age fotostock/SuperStock

Figure 5.14 The small white house on the left is a medieval Norman residence in Cluny, France. The small arched windows use the typical Romanesque arch. It was also fairly common to use a pair of rectangular windows. The house to the right with the half-timbering and the square windows, whose windowpanes have been modernized, are markers for a Gothic house. They have been joined and now have a shared tiled roof, which would also have been a medieval feature. The bottom story with the large arches that have been altered were most likely shops or entrances to inner courtyards.

akg-images/Yvan Travert

* The majority of permanent structures were for religious and military architecture and were characterized by heavy defensive stone construction, small windows, and bare, dark interiors. See Figures 5.1, 5.2, 5.3, 5.4, 5.5, 5.6, 5.7, 5.8, 5.9, 5.10, and 5.11.

* Towns and cities were organized as defensive structures behind fortified walls with the local church or cathedral as the central focus. The idea of the Classical forum was reinvented as the town squares where the church and local government offices were located and where processions and festivals were held. These squares were the sites of religious celebrations, public executions, royal weddings and funerals.

* The Early Christian basilica church form was enlarged and combined with stone vaulting systems to gain dramatic height. The West Front of the church was further elaborated and elevated to the principal entrance. This produced the first true Western cathedral form. See Figures 5.1 and 5.3.

* The Cruciform or Latin Cross church plan was formalized and standardized throughout Western Europe. It was characterized by an emphasis on large, heavy stone construction, small windows, and verticality on a cruciform plan. See Figure 3.4.

* The development of monastic community architecture made possible the spread of these self-sufficient religious communities throughout Europe. See Figures 5.5, 5.6, and 5.7.

* The main entrance to religious buildings was characterized by a single large arched opening, decorated by multiple, stepped back concentric Roman arches, often with a roofed porch and decorative relief tympanum. See Figures 5.1 and 5.8.

* The Normans revived the Classical arch and column forms for castle architecture, but thickened, exaggerated, and simplified them.

* Norman castles developed at this time and extended throughout Europe, Asia, and North Africa. These complexes supported the large mobile populations of civilians and soldiers as well as The Knights Templar during the multiple Crusades. http://www.britannica.com/EBchecked/topic/586765/Templar

* The typical castle complex came in a variety of configurations, but most often included a moat, a gatehouse usually with a portcullis, the iron grate that could go up and down, a barbican and drawbridge, a ring of curtain walls, defensive towers, a courtyard, a keep (known at that time as a don-jon), and often utilitarian dependencies for people and animals. They were effective defenses until gunpowder was introduced in the late 17th century. See Figures 5.9, 5.10, 5.11, and 5.12.

* The renewed use of Classical scale and proportion at the end of this period encouraged the development of sophisticated mathematics that was needed to build the increasingly large, complex structures of church and castle architecture. *The Pillars of the Earth* was a 2010 TV mini-series based on the Ken Follett book about 12th-century England and building a cathedral.

* The Bayeux tapestries were made from c. 1070s to 1077 CE, shortly after the Norman Conquest by William The Conqueror over the English Anglo-Saxons at the Battle of Hasting in 1066 CE. Not really a tapestry they are an embroidered cloth about 230 feet long and 20 inches high and tell the story of the lead-up to and the battle in 50 illustrations with Latin text. This battle that changed English history took place on October 14, 1066 CE and caused the death of King Harold and his brothers and saw the ascendency of William as the first Norman King of England. It is really the first sequential art. Although their origin is uncertain, they are now in a museum in Bayeux, France, therefore their name. They are an iconic source for costumes of all different kinds of people—men, women, kings, clerics, and soldiers. They also show rudimentary architecture, agriculture, and military costumes, horses, weapons, battle scenes, and ships. http://www.bayeuxtapestry.org.uk/Bayeux14.htm

How They Decorated

Figure 5.15 *Left:* This is a Romanesque chair from Gotland, Scandinavia. Most furniture of the period is freestanding and heavy but portable based on simple shapes like squares and rectangles; the frames of this chair and the next chest are made of turned wooden spindles and have braces at the feet for strength. Other decoration is often a miniaturization of architectural forms as seen in the profile of the skirt of the chair and its incised patterns that use a simplified Celtic design.

National Historical Museum Stockholm

Figure 5.16 *Below:* This is a Romanesque chest from Gotland, Scandinavia. This chest is a companion to the chair and was part of a larger set. It uses the same turned spindled framework and the interesting simple linear decorative wooden panels. The fretwork arches and columns are similar to what would be seen on a church. The tilted lid could also be used for holding, reading, and writing manuscripts.

National Historical Museum Stockholm

* The increased emphasis on the spiritual and judgmental in art and decoration resulted in less realistic, more abstract forms in hierarchical compositions in both interior and exterior decoration.

* Classical decoration was partially revived but simplified and often mixed with Celtic and northern motifs.

* The spring line of the Romanesque arch dropped to create a vertical, elongated arched window form and for decoration and also widened to create deep, horizontal architectural entrances. See Figures 5.1, 5.2, 5.3, 5.5, 5.6, 5.7, 5.8, 5.11, and 5.14.

* The impost block was eliminated and was replaced by larger, highly narrative column capitals. They often depicted figurative representations of Biblical and other stories. See Figure 5.4.

* The perfection of the pointed arch as a structural and decorative motif, probably borrowed from Persia, later in the period spurred the building of larger, more open and more complex church structures.

* The blind or filled-in arch and arcade were used as a repeating decorative device on upper building façades and underneath the crenellations of military structures.

* Mosaic decoration was replaced by frescos in church interiors.

* Manuscript illustration was perfected in the scriptoriums or copy rooms of the monasteries.

* Furniture and furnishings remained heavy, simple, utilitarian, and portable. See Figures 5.15 and 5.16.

* Tapestries were developed to help insulate stone buildings in northern climates as well as to provide visual decoration for interiors.

* Toward the end of this period, the development of eating utensils, especially the fork, signaled the beginning of an increased sophistication in social manners.

Building and Décor Keywords

Carolingian (karo-LIN-jan) – Refers to the Empire established by Charlemagne and his successors in Germany, France, and Italy during the 9th century that briefly reunited elements of the former Roman Empire. Carolingian architecture was based on late Roman and Early Christian styles. See Figure 5.2.

Norman style – The heavy, defensive castle architecture developed by the French and English military that spread throughout Europe at the time of the Crusades. See Figures 5.9, 5.10, 5.11, and 5.12.

Celtic (KEL-tic) **style** – The highly stylized and elaborate organically inspired decoration brought by Celtic tribes from Scandinavia, Ireland, and Scotland to central and southern Europe during the Early Christian and Romanesque periods. http://www.britishmuseum.org/research/research_projects/complete_projects/technologies_of_enchantment/the_celtic_art_database.aspx

Romanesque arch – A semi-circular Roman arch made up of multiple concentric arch forms superimposed upon one another whose radius was large in relation to the height of the supporting columns, which resulted in a heavy, squat profile. This description is for architecture; there was also a more decorative Romanesque arch that was longer and narrower and often paired or in groups. See Figures 5.1, 5.2, 5.3, 5.5, 5.6, 5.7, 5.8, 5.14, 5.17, and 5.18.

tympanum – The semi-circular space under the central large entry way arch on a Romanesque church. It usually was decorated with moralistic religious relief sculptures. See Figure 5.1.

nave – The middle and largest aisle of a Latin Cross church or cathedral, intended primarily for the congregation. See Figure 5.3.

transept – The shorter transverse aisle of a Latin Cross church that crossed the nave at a right angle just to the east of the nave's center, producing a cruciform plan.

groin vault – A compound vault that resulted from the intersection of two barrel vaults at right angles. Adapted from Roman examples, it allowed higher and wider bays between the columns. See Figure 6.4.

rib vault – A groin vault in which the ribs rather than the surface of the arch supported the weight of the vault.

castle – The typical Norman defensive complex came in a variety of configurations and after William the Conqueror was constructed out of stone, which then was the primary building material used throughout Europe, Asia, and North Africa. See Figures 5.9, 5.10, 5.11, and 5.12.

barbican – The fortified gatehouse or the towers over the gatehouse that could be part of castle compounds or the entrances to cities and towns with their walls.

keep or don-jon – The large, central structure inside the walls of a castle that contained the living quarters and food storage. It was the last line of defense in time of attack. See Figures 5.9 and 5.11.

moat – A large dry or water-filled defensive trench that surrounded a castle or military structure. See Figures 5.9, 5.10, and 5.11.

crenellation (cren-ih-LA-shun) – The alternating high and low masonry blocks along the top of a castle wall, tower, or keep that afforded protection to the archers positioned behind them. See Figures 5.9 and 5.10.

curtain wall – The fortified wall that wrapped around a castle or city. See Figures 5.9 and 5.10.

blind arcade – An extended row of small, blind arches used as a decorative device at the top of a Romanesque wall or building.

The Romanesque Clothing and Costume World

How They Dressed

* The main feature of medieval garments in Europe was the adaptation of Roman clothing to the clothes of the native people. The Celts, Britons, Gauls, and Franks wore short-belted, tight-sleeved tunics over pants with leggings and hose, and cloaks and mantles. See Figures 3.14, 3.15, and 3.16.

* Until the 14th century and the Renaissance most clothing in Europe remained simple for men and women and was mostly of wool and linen and made at home. It used simple banding at the neck, wrists, sometimes hems, and embroidery. See Figures 5.18, 5.19, and 5.20.

* Generally men and women had two or three tunics and/or gowns of different lengths, which could be worn individually or over each other, but usually over a simple washable undergarment—the chemise. Confusion of terms for costumes begins, as at different times and in different localities there was a wide assortment of names and different words for similar garments.

* By the 11th century clothing was becoming more differentiated for men and women and more decorated and elaborate.

Figure 5.17 King Charles II, "The Bald" (823–877), reigned (840–877 CE) receiving a Bible (the large red and black object, center left) from Count Vivian and the Monks of Saint-Martin de Tours. The image is from the first Bible of Charles the Bald, 843–851 CE. It shows the French monarch on his throne decorated with "fleurs de lis," a symbol of French royalty, and his red robe and gold cloak with a gold crown and holding a staff. Next to him are two courtiers dressed in kirtles and long cloaks, boots, and hose and on either side of them are soldiers, on the left holding a long spear and on the right a bundle of spears, the fasces—a Roman symbol of "strength through unity." Their military garments are also closely related to Roman examples. See Figures 2.19 and 3.18. In a semi-circle below and in front are the count and clergymen in assorted vestments and most seem to have tonsure hair treatments. Like the Romans this illustration is using an architectural feature—the draped arch and columns—to act as a frame. The hand in the center at the top is the hand of God and is a very typical feature of illuminated pictures.

Bibliothèque Nationale, Paris, France / Bridgeman Images

Figure 5.18 This scene from the Bayeux tapestries shows Harold as the new King of England sitting on his throne in the throne room, wearing a large dark cloak over his golden long tunic and wearing a crown. It is January 6, 1066 and King Edward had died that morning. To the far upper left is Halley's comet that to the medieval world was a sign of great change and was called the "terror of kings." The courtier, approaching him to tell him about the comet, is wearing the typical kirtle; notice the round slitted neckline, long sleeves, and banded and belted kirtle, hose, and pointed poulaines shoes. Although the architecture is crude all the details are characteristically Romanesque, such as the arches, small windows, towers, and thick walls. Underneath in the lower border to foretell the bad omen are symbolic, pale grey Norman ships. http://www.bayeuxtapestry.org.uk/BayeuxContents.htm

jorisvo/Shutterstock.com

Figure 5.19 *Left:* This is a miniature illumination from *The Hunterian Psalter*, c. 1170. This medieval psalter or prayer book has over 200 exquisite illuminations and calligraphy using tempera and gold on vellum. The texts are of the psalms, Old and New Testament stories, and other useful information for its medieval reader, such as astrological positions and meanings. The two laborers are wearing basic clothes—the man on the left has the typical kirtle with banded neck, sleeves, and hem and on the right, also typical, are the loose pants, sometimes referred to as breeches or braies. Notice the interesting and artistic rendering of their draped fabrics and their long hair. This would be an excellent source for costumes, activities, and props. Parts of this manuscript can be seen on the University of Glasgow, virtual exhibition website: http://www.gla.ac.uk/services/specialcollections/virtualexhibitions/hunterianpsalter

Glasgow University Library, Scotland/Bridgeman Images

Figure 5.20 *Below:* This is a detail of Saint Giles from a fresco in a 12th-century crypt in the church of Saint Aignan-sur-Cher, France. He wears a floor-length cote and offers his surcote to a beggar; notice his scraggly beard and long hair. The saint in the center wears a cloak over his surcote and his servant wears a simpler shorter cote. Both saints have halos to make it clear to the viewers of their holy position.

akg-images/De Agostini Picture Library/G. Dagli Orti

Figure 5.21 This illustration is from the *History of Costume*, by Auguste Racinet, published 1867–1888. It covered world costume from ancient times through the 19th century and although flawed is still a valued textbook. This plate is for Romanesque costumes and shows a wide variety of clothes. On the left are soldiers with typical weapons and different types of helmets and tunics over chain mail, then a falconer, a court jester, with ladies in waiting and then queen and king, also wearing typical gowns and robes. The closure on his cloak is a distinctive feature. The lower panel shows a Knight of the Templar in the very distinctive outfit that was always white with a red cross. Next to him is a cavalry soldier in full chain mail, notice the coverings for his knees, hands, and head and also his spurs and the typical kite-shaped shield. A noble woman is next wearing an elegant gown with an over garment and wimple around her neck and head. The bishop on the right is wearing a full set of ecclesiastical vestments—alb, stole, dalmatic, and blue-lined chasuble with a miter and large ornate cross.

akg-images

* Male dress was characterized by the kirtle, cote, surcotes, robes, and cloaks. These could vary in length mainly because of their use and the age of the wearer. They wore hoods and a phrygian cap, which was a symbol that they were not Greek or Roman and was associated with freedom.

* Women wore different kinds of gowns, but they were always long to the ankle or floor, usually had wide sleeves, and sometimes were belted with "a girdle." Frequently they were augmented with cloaks and a hooded *palla*, veil, or mantle.

* Celtic and northern clothing styles and materials included wool and linen, but more importantly introduced furs and animal skins, which continued to influence clothing. Furs were worn as surcotes and also used as linings.

* They did have intricate jewelry and other metal artifacts as seen from the archeological site and museum at Sutton Hoo, UK.

* The majority of Norman men wore their hair short and cropped at the back of the neck and were clean-shaven and the English wore theirs long and often with beards. See Figures 5.18, 5.19, and 5.20. Also see Bayeux tapestries.

* Women's hair was worn long and down the back and was often braided.

* Another illuminated manuscript is the *Hortus Deliciarium*, *The Garden of Delights*, a 12th-century manuscript (1167–1185) that was an early encyclopedia written and illustrated by Herrad of Landsberg, the abbess at the Hohenberg in Alsace, for her nuns' edification with the text in Latin and German. The most famous illumination is *Philosophy and the Seven Liberal Arts* and shows seven women in a transitional style of dress from the Romanesque to the Gothic in a variation of the

bliaut with a tight fitting bodice, a flared skirt, and long bell-shaped sleeves over a simple chemise under garment. There are 336 illustrations in the manuscript mostly symbolic and interesting images of Biblical and philosophical ideas, but many could be useful references for the designer and the book is easily referenced on the Internet.

* Ecclesiastical garb continued its development and differentiation, which would continue into the next period as well, but most of it derived from the dalmatic of the late Roman and Byzantine era, usually with wide sleeves and a slit skirt. In the Bayeux tapestries there are a number of images such as in scene # 30 the Arch Bishop Stigant is wearing a long clerical robe, the alb, and a cope, which is a liturgical cloak fastened with a morse at his throat and he holds a stole in his hand. Also see Figure 5.17.

* Military outfits based on Roman and Early Christian styles remained and also reintroduced metal armor and with chain mail. See Bayeux tapestries and Figures 5.17 and 5.21.

Clothing and Costume Keywords

kirtle – This was one of the basic garments of the Middle Ages from the 10th to 16th century for men and women. For men it varied slightly but mostly it was knee length and consisted of a tunic with long sleeves and a circular neck opening with a vertical slit at the breastbone and banded decoration at the neck, wrists, and hem. The women's version had flaring sleeves and was floor length. See Figures 5.18 and 5.19.

cote masculine, cotte feminine – Another basic garment that was likely a variation of the Byzantine tunic, the dalmatic. It was a long outer garment with sleeves usually of cloth worn by men and women, which was pulled over the head fitted at the waist and a close fitting round neck. Men's sleeves were narrow and women's usually long and flared, both could be worn with belts. Peasants and soldiers wore shorter versions. See Figure 5.20.

surcote, surcoat – This was worn over the cote and also the kirtle, and therefore usually slightly larger. It could be sleeved or sleeveless and also for men, with a hood. See Figure 5.20.

bliaut – A man and woman's over garment that appears in the Bayeaux tapestries and continued into the Gothic period. It was characterized by long loose pleated skirts and usually fitted on the top and for women had distinctly long flared sleeves. See the *Hortus Deliciarium*.

robe – This was a long, loose outer garment worn by men and women and distinguished from a cloak as it had sleeves and went to the ankles or feet. See Figure 5.17.

poulaines, crakow – These were the pointed shoes worn during medieval and Gothic times, usually made of leather. The points could be as long as two feet for royalty and they had to be tied up for walking or running. The Hunterian Psalter referenced above has an image of "Gemini"—the twins wearing identical short kirtles, red hose, and these fashionable shoes. They are also sharing a gold, jeweled studded long, kite-shaped shield that is typical of this period, and two long spears. See Figure 6.16.

chemise, shift – This was an undergarment worn by men and women from the Middle Ages until the 18th century. It was usually made of linen and often the only piece of clothing that was washed.

wimple – A white cloth worn around a lady's head and over the neck and shoulders signifying the modesty and propriety of a married or widowed woman. See Figure 5.21.

phrygian cap (FRIG-ian) – This was a tight, fitted pointed cap with the point bent forward worn by Anglo-Saxons and Gauls to show that they were not Greeks or Romans. This cap has been worn since antiquity to symbolize freedom and was a prominent symbol during the French Revolution and has been seen throughout Western civilization. Today it is seen in video games, such as *Assassin's Creed* and *The Legend of Zelda*, Disney features, many seals in the US and coats of arms of many South American countries, and even the smurfs.

cope – This was the large liturgical cape worn by Catholic priests, fastened at the neck with a decorated object known as a morse. It was worn over a simple long robe known as an alb, which derived from the long Roman tunic and Byzantine dalmatic.

tonsure – The clipped, circular haircut of a monk symbolizing humility before God. See Figure 5.17.

chain mail – This was the primary covering for European mounted and foot soldiers and was used until the 13th century and probably of Persian origin. It was lengths of small metal chain that were tied or woven together and could be used on any part of the body and usually worn over a padded under garment.

hauberk – This was the armor transitioning to plate armor and used primarily for cavalry soldiers. These chain mail tunics were usually long-sleeved, knee-length and had a slit at the back and center that made them easier for riding a horse.

CHAPTER SIX

Gothic: 1100–1450

Figure 6.1 Cathedral of Notre Dame, Reims, France. The building was completed by the end of the 13th century at the height of the Gothic period and the West Front was added in the 14th century based on the 13th-century designs. The highly elaborate façade shows the Late Gothic style and it completes the transition from the austere Romanesque to the lively Renaissance. The building both inside and out is covered with hundreds of figurative statues giving a sculptural effect to the whole massive façade that is decorated on all four sides. The three highly decorated entrances have numerous sculptures in their Gothic arches. The main portal also has many figures rather than a tympanum and also two stained glass rose windows. The two smaller flanking entrances have quatrefoils below trefoils. The two large bell towers were never completed to their intended height, but notice they are partly transparent.

Pecold/Shutterstock.com

A Little Background

This period saw the development of the large European commercial and religious centers and the growing importance of international trade, finance, commerce, and manufacturing. In architecture the major design features of this period were the final development of the sophisticated cathedral form in Europe. There was also a revolution in fashion brought about by the development of spinning, tailoring, and the differentiation of men and women's clothing.

Religious images changed dramatically from Old Testament anger and retribution by an adult Figure of Christ to images of the Holy Family groupings with Christ portrayed as an innocent child. Abbot Suger in France abandoned Romanesque darkness and ordered his new church, the Basilica of St. Denis, filled with light. Religious buildings became much larger and for the first time since antiquity secular and civic buildings were built for permanence.

Who They Were

* This period saw the crystallization of the European nation states and their newly developing languages from their earlier Latin and Celtic roots.

* Universities were founded in major cities for religious, philosophical, medical, and legal training, which reflected a growing need for a literate segment of the population.

* The building of cathedrals became a religious and civic duty for the clergy and wealthy donors. Competitive cathedral building between cities became a defining feature of Gothic architecture and spurred technological innovations. The large building projects created a need for a higher degree of social organization to complete them.

* The rise of a new merchant class and increased trade in Europe and with the Eastern Empire encouraged the growth of trade guilds, the reintroduction of currency, and the use of credit.

* Continued Crusader activity brought Eastern influences to Europe. Eastern fabrics such as silk made their way westward.

* Musical notation was developed in Italy, allowing music to be written down for the first time and therefore saved.

* The cult of chivalry among noble men, knights, and women emphasized loyalty, courage, purity, and respect for women. Songs were composed about art and love, not war. Love poetry became fashionable among the wealthy and this was also the age of the troubadours and wandering minstrels, who spread songs and poetry from town to town.

* This period saw the development of religious plays—the Passion, Mystery, Miracle, and Morality plays. They were first acted in churches, then in front of them, and then later out in front in public squares. The Passion plays developed first as part of the liturgical Easter story into huge elaborate presentations in the 15th century and are still performed all over the world; as well as the more secular Morality play *Everyman*, also still performed today. See Figure 6.11.

* Paris became the commercial, intellectual, and artistic center of Europe.

* England developed the Perpendicular Gothic style of architecture that lasted into the 17th century. See Figures 6.6, 6.7, and 6.8.

* Sumptuary laws restricted or forbade costly and ostentatious goods as a reaction to the increase in wealth, trade, and desire for fashion.

* At this time there was keen interest in the stories of King Arthur and the Round Table and members of his court. The stories were told in poems and songs and illustrated in many medieval illuminations. No one knows for sure if this late 5th-century, early 6th-century English court was fact or legend but their popularity has never waned and there are countless versions in paintings, books, films, and operas. Some of the most famous contemporary ones are Disney's *The Sword and the Stone* (1963), the musical *Camelot* (1960)*, adapted into a film (1967), *Merlin and the War of the Dragons* (2008), *Excalibur* (1981), *Monty Python and the Holy Grail* (1975), *A Knight's Tale* (2001), *Arthur—The Once and Future King*—a documentary is on YouTube, and also newer updates and spoofs. The Arthurian legends also include the stories of Guinevere, Tristan and Isolde, Parsifal, and others.

* Although written in 1820 Sir Walter Scott's seminal book *Ivanhoe* took place in 12th-century England and dealt with many aspects and people of this period including knights and their ladies, kings, Crusaders, clerics, and also introduced Robin Hood and his merry men. There have been many adaptations of both in many media from the historical to the romantic to the absurd, such as Mel Brooks' film *Robin Hood: Men in Tights* (1993) and also including several operas. Scott was also credited for introducing the craze for Neo-Gothic and medievalism in the 19th century.

* Some films of the period: *Braveheart* (1995), *The Canterbury Tales* (1971), *The Hollow Crown* was a PBS TV mini-series of Shakespeare's plays—*Richard II*, *Henry IV*, and *Henry V*—and *Henry V* (1944) is a classic, *The Seventh Seal* (1957)*, *Brother Sun, Sister Moon* (1972)*, *Alexander Nevsky* (1938)*, and *The Name of the Rose* (1986)*.

The Gothic Material World

Figure 6.2 The stained glass windows of the Basilica of St. Denis are considered some of the finest and best preserved in Europe. Seen here are the two top levels: the clerestory windows are the large stained glass ones and below them the triforium gallery and its windows, which were a new addition to Gothic cathedrals and therefore a new innovation.

stockcam/iStock

What They Made

Figure 6.3 The Basilica of Saint Denis, Paris, is considered the first Gothic church. It was conceived, produced, and supervised by Abbot Suger from 1135 to 1140 as an abbey church for his Benedictine Monastery. It introduced a number of important Gothic elements that would influence all Gothic cathedral building. This early Gothic West Front and its elaboration on all four sides reintroduced decoration that had been abandoned since the Classical period. The increased décor such as the large verticals separating the three entry doors, the horizontal courses under the windows, and the use of figurative sculptures on the exterior, the large rose window, the other larger windows, and steeply pointed nave windows, and the use of stained glass also introduced recognizable features of the Gothic style to distinguish it from the Romanesque. Usually French churches had two bell towers on the West Fronts as seen in Figures 6.1 and 6.5, as did this one, but only the south tower survives.

funkyfood London—Paul Williams/Alamy

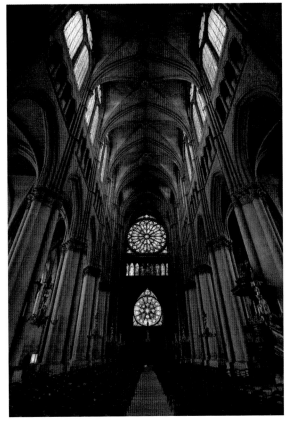

Figure 6.4 Interior of Cathedral Notre Dame, Reims, France. It is an important example of the mature Gothic style, for instance, in this view it shows the vertical emphasis of the nave columns that go from floor to ceiling that is characteristic of the French style, and the massive nave arches; the English style will be explained and shown in Figure 6.7. Other examples are the very large upper clerestory windows, the huge nave windows that are not shown here, and the double rose windows of the West Front. In this picture you can see the triforium gallery with its smaller windows that don't open to the outside. This is a passageway that goes from the back of the church to the front and is accessible from stairways so that the congregation and the service below are not disturbed. At the center, the ceiling shows a good example of groin vaulting.

PHB.cz/Shutterstock.com

Figure 6.5 This is the exterior of Notre Dame Cathedral, Paris, photographed from across the Seine. Flying buttresses were an external brace placed outside the nave to help reinforce the walls that were load bearing and supported the massive ceilings and roofs. They also allowed the walls to be higher and therefore created a lighter appearance. Also note that the décor surrounds the entire building and that even the transepts have double rose windows. The ornate spires are also typically Gothic.

oalexand/iStock

Figure 6.6 This is Salisbury Cathedral, Salisbury, England, exterior, showing the characteristic English Cathedral style with its horizontal emphasis and the single bell tower at the central crossing. It was built from local stone and very quickly from 1220 to 1258 so that it has great unity. The exterior is less lavishly decorated than the French cathedrals and they also placed less emphasis on the West Front. This is the tallest spire in England and was added from 1310 to 1333, but in the same style as the rest of the cathedral and the same stone so it is fully integrated.

Mark Eaton/Dreamstime.com

Figure 6.7 This is the interior of Salisbury Cathedral also showing the English style that uses horizontal emphasis as opposed to the French that was more vertical. This was done through its use of different alternating bands of light and dark marble and with the horizontal moldings. The three elements of all mature Gothic-style cathedral interior architecture are clearly seen in this example and illustrate the three-layer organization. At the bottom is the large arcade with Gothic arches, next the enlarged triforium gallery, and then the clerestory windows at the top.

Andreas Juergenmeier/Shutterstock.com

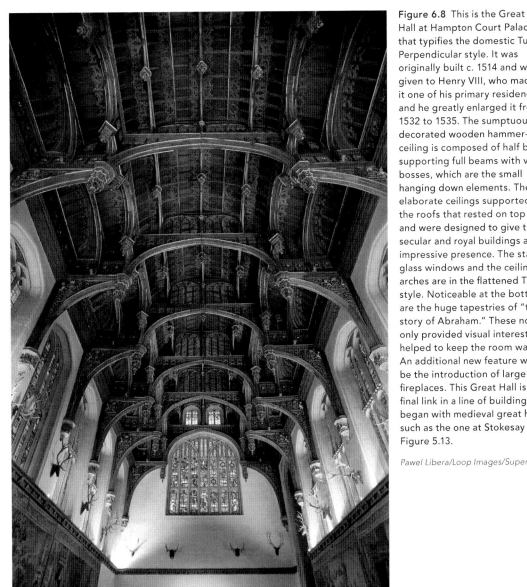

Figure 6.8 This is the Great Hall at Hampton Court Palace that typifies the domestic Tudor Perpendicular style. It was originally built c. 1514 and was given to Henry VIII, who made it one of his primary residences and he greatly enlarged it from 1532 to 1535. The sumptuously decorated wooden hammer-beam ceiling is composed of half beams supporting full beams with vertical bosses, which are the small hanging down elements. These elaborate ceilings supported the roofs that rested on top and were designed to give the secular and royal buildings an impressive presence. The stained glass windows and the ceiling arches are in the flattened Tudor style. Noticeable at the bottom are the huge tapestries of "the story of Abraham." These not only provided visual interest but helped to keep the room warm. An additional new feature would be the introduction of large fireplaces. This Great Hall is the final link in a line of buildings that began with medieval great halls, such as the one at Stokesay Castle Figure 5.13.

Pawel Libera/Loop Images/SuperStock

Figure 6.9 "Shakespeare's Birthplace" in Stratford-Upon-Avon, England. This is an example of a 16th-century wooden half-timbered house with wattle and daub construction. The exposed half-timbering shown is the frame of the house and in between the beams the walls are composed of wattle and daub. This technique is similar to interior lath and plaster and used woven lattice, which is the wattle, and filled in between or attached is the daub, which is a mixed assortment of materials such as clay, soil, sand, and straw. When they were dry it was white washed. An oriel window is shown on the second floor center and all the windows use the small diagonal panes of glass.

warasit phothisuk/Shutterstock.com

Figure 6.10 This is the main market square in Mittenberg, Germany, a historic town in Bavaria, in Southern Germany, founded in 155 CE by the Romans. These red half-timbered houses with steeply pitched roofs are very typical of German half-timbering. The large house in the center with additional smaller beams with this particular shape is also a typical Southern German style and these are purely decorative. Also notice the house is five stories high, which is unusual for the Gothic period in other countries but was used in Germany and combined with the decorative beams, indicating a wealthy owner. The large central fountain is original to this period and would have been the source of water for the surrounding homes.

PRILL/Shutterstock.com

* There was a pronounced movement away from the symbolic and abstract representation of the Romanesque era toward a new realism and desire for exterior decoration in architecture and painting. See Figures 6.16 and 6.18.

* The Gothic marked the end of Romanesque massiveness and frontality in building. Exterior church decoration emphasized taller and lighter compositions and expertly carved details. There was a renewed interest in the exterior decoration of buildings. Churches were designed with approaches from three sides and were profusely decorated on all sides.

* Abbot Suger of St. Denis defined the new Gothic architecture as a search for "Holy Light." Light was symbolically associated with divinity, truth, and the Creation of the Universe. This became the motivating factor in the development of the new Gothic style. "Lightness" was expressed in construction as well as in transparency, verticality of structures, and illumination of interiors. There is a scholarly book about St. Denis and is available at http://www.metmuseum.org/research/metpublications/Abbot_Suger_and_Saint_Denis

* This era saw the origination of sophisticated engineering concepts and skills applied to buildings. Complex vaulting systems were invented and were in different shapes and styles because of the distribution of downward force from the ceilings; before they were only circular or rectangular. Flying buttresses kept the force in check and both of these techniques increased the height and transparency of the Gothic cathedrals. See Figure 6.4 for groin vault and Figure 6.5 for flying buttress.

How They Decorated

Figure 6.11 This is a 19th-century drawing of a Mystery play being performed in the 16th century at Coventry, England. Scenes from the Bible were enacted on decorated wagons. The design of the cart is conjectural, but taken from original sources. There would be one cart for each scene of the story and they would circle the town square repeating the scene over and over. The Miracle plays also used religious stories, and saints' lives, and were often about the Virgin Mary. In both the Miracle and the more secular Morality plays like *Everyman*, the stage was stationary at different locations and the spectators rotated around the square.

Gianni Dagli Orti/The Art Archive at Art Resource, NY

Figure 6.12 *Top:* This is a grand Gothic house of a wealthy French merchant, Jacques Coeur, in the city of Bourges, France. The steeply pitched roofs are introduced in this period and are typical throughout Northern Europe. The horizontal decorative trim under the roof will become Renaissance balustrading. Most residential decoration such as the tall Gothic dormer windows and the tower with a spire that are seen here are copying liturgical style. The multiple chimneys indicate the introduction of enclosed fireplaces in many rooms. The house itself is based on the Roman model, which has a series of rectangular rooms surrounding a courtyard. This façade is facing the street, but a Roman house would not have windows like this but a plain façade.

Photononstop/SuperStock

Figure 6.13 *Left:* These are two smiling angel statutes on the Cathedral of Notre Dame, Reims, France. This Cathedral has hundreds of classically inspired sculptures both on the exterior and interior. This period marks the return of full round three-dimensional sculptures showing sensitive portraits of individuals and realistically rendered clothing of men and women; shown here are a version of the kirtle, surcote, cloak, and mantle. There are many pictures of the Cathedral and sculptures and stained glass available.

hartcreations/iStock

* A new visual vocabulary of décor based on exaggerated Classical forms and freely interpreted natural and vegetative forms was used both inside and outside buildings. This new style was used both graphically in paintings and manuscripts and dimensionally in carved interior and exterior decoration. This can be seen on the columns in the image in Figure 6.13. Wealthy residences, as seen in Figure 6.12, also used the same decorative vocabulary as religious buildings.

* The development of stained glass technology in this period allowed construction of huge, colorful, backlit narrative windows that replaced frescos as storytelling devices. See Figures 6.1, 6.2, 6.3, 6.4, and 6.8.

* Now highly elaborate carved exteriors were on churches, which also brought narrative to the outside of these buildings. See Figures 6.1, 6.5, and 6.6.

* Religious symbolic emphasis shifted from Old Testament judgment to New Testament redemption. The cult of Mary, St. Francis of Assisi, and the Christ child as savior replaced the image of an adult Christ as an angry Judge. The Holy Family became the focus of worship and the metaphor for a moral life.

* This period saw the reintroduction of freestanding figurative sculpture. For the first time since the Classical age religious sculptures were expressed in human terms and sculpted in full round. Classical draped garments and more natural body postures were adopted. See Figure 6.13.

* Book illumination became highly refined and elaborate musical, religious, and secular texts were transcribed and painted by hand in monastery scriptoriums and secular workshops. See the film *The Name of the Rose* for a real scriptorium and its use.

* This was the height of illuminated manuscripts in "the International style." There are many examples of original manuscripts, books, and videos about them that would make excellent references. Two of the most famous are *The Très Riches Heures du Duc de Berry*, a scanned copy of which can be seen at Wiki commons, and the *Belles Heures du Duc de Berry*, which is at the Met, New York; for more information about it see http://blog.metmuseum.org/artofillumination

* Furniture and furnishings became lighter and more elaborated but were still collapsible and portable. Carved decoration became prominent and furniture was still built primarily of wood with cloth or leather upholstery.

* There is an interesting BBC video about medieval English Cathedral stained glass and also how it was made: *Britain's Most Fragile Treasure: Stained Glass in Medieval England*; look on YouTube.

Building and Décor Keywords

Gothic arch – An arch form developed by the intersection of two semi-circular arches that overlapped one another creating a pointed arch; this was probably of Persian origin. Its main advantage was structural as it allowed thinner and stronger arch supports. See Figures 6.1, 6.2, 6.4, 6.5, 6.6, 6.7, and 6.11.

Ogee (OH-gee) **arch** – An arch using two opposed S-curves above the spring line that formed a point at the top. It was similar to the Byzantine arch. See Figure 4.7 on a Scottish building.

Perpendicular or **Horizontal Gothic style** – The architectural style of the Gothic period in England that balanced the vertical thrust of buildings with a horizontal emphasis in composition. See Figures 6.6, 6.7, and 6.8.

Tudor – The English secular architectural, decorative, and furniture style during the reign of Henry VIII and Elizabeth I that retained Gothic forms but combined them with Classical influences. This architectural style was characterized by large, bold sculptural elements, half-timbering, and heavy wooden paneled interiors and strapwork plaster ceilings and decorations. See Temple Newsam House, Leeds, UK, and Anne Boleyn's childhood home http://www.hevercastle.co.uk/visit/hever-castle/rooms-exhibitions for this and many other Tudor and Jacobean features.

strapwork – A type of surface ornamentation of the Tudor and Jacobean styles that consisted of a flat fillet or band that was crossed, folded, or interlaced. Often it resembled a belt or a ribbon and was used in decorative plaster ceilings as well as in wall ornamentation. See Temple Newsam House, Leeds, UK, for this and many other Tudor and Jacobean features.

Tudor arch – A flattened Gothic arch developed from four radial arcs. It was similar to a Persian arch and characteristic of English Perpendicular Gothic architecture. See Figure 6.8.

West Front – The western front of a church or cathedral enlarged and decorated to signify its symbolic importance as the main and royal entrance. Its orientation ensured that the laity always faced east to Jerusalem during services. See Figures 6.1, 6.3, and 6.6.

triforium (truh-FORIUM) **gallery** – A shallow passageway above the arches of the nave and below the clerestory. It allowed passage for churchmen from the front to the rear of the building without disturbing the services being conducted below. See Figures 6.2, 6.4, and 6.7.

clerestory (clur-REST-ory) – The upper part of the nave that contained a series of windows, which let in light. See Figures 6.2, 6.4, 6.6, and 6.7.

buttress – A masonry brace that was built perpendicular to an exterior wall in order to stabilize it. See exterior San Vitale, Figure 3.6.

flying buttress – A freestanding buttress connected to the building with one or more arches. See Figure 6.5.

fan vault – A concave conical vault usually found in English architecture whose ribs radiated from the spring line like the ribs of a fan. It was typically decorative rather than structural. Two early examples were at King's College chapel, Cambridge University, UK, and the cloister at Gloucester Cathedral, UK, and in the Neo-Gothic Strawberry Hill House interior, Figure 11.4.

hammer beam roof and ceiling – A wooden roof supported by frames made of two or more short horizontal members attached to the foot of a principal rafter by means of a Tudor arch. See Figure 6.8.

great hall – A high, large single room in English buildings that served as the primary living and eating space. In the early examples such as Stokesay Castle Figure 5.13 it had a pitched wooden roof and a smoke hole as there was a fire pit in the middle of the room. In more rustic examples it also provided shelter for livestock. This room was the origin of the living room in English architecture. The Tudor great hall at Hampton Court was much improved and enlarged and now included a large fireplace but it was still the center of banqueting, parties, and theatricals. See Figure 6.8.

half-timbering – The style of domestic architecture of the Gothic period in England, France, and Germany characterized by walls constructed of visible heavy wood beams with spaces filled in with wattle and daub. See Figures 6.9 and 6.10; Stokesay Castle 5.12, Cluny 5.14, Speke Hall 7.6, Old Globe 7.8, Dürer 7.9.

lancet window – A tall, narrow Gothic arched window that often contained stained glass. See Figures 6.1, 6.6, and 6.11.

bay window – A floor-length window that projected beyond the outside wall of a building and rose one or more stories from the ground. See Figures 6.10 and 6.11.

oriel (or-YELL) **window** – A small waist-high window that projected beyond the outside wall of a building on an upper floor. See Figure 6.9 and in Chapter 19, Figure 19.10.

diamond pane windows – The first large practical glass windows with panes made of small diamond-shaped hand blown glass that was held in place with a network of lead frames. See Figures 6.9.

thatched roof – A roof covering of woven straw laid on rough wooden rafters and used on modest stone and plaster homes and farm buildings in England, Ireland, and Northern Europe.

trefoil (TREH-foil) – An arch, window, or panel whose inner edge had three lobes. Other variations included quatrefoil with four lobes; cinquefoil with five lobes, etc. See Figure 6.1.

crocket – This was a projecting ornament, often vegetal in form, regularly spaced along sloping or vertical edges of spires, pinnacles, or gables. See Figure 6.1.

gable – The high, vertical triangular portion of the end of a building having an A-shaped sloped roof. It was steeper than a pediment, but was less than 90 degrees. See Figures 6.5, 6.6, 6.9, 6.10, and 6.11.

bargeboard – In Gothic domestic buildings, a decorative, carved board that hung from the projecting end of a gable roof, often it was elaborately carved and ornamented. See Figure 6.11.

gargoyle – A waterspout projecting from the roof gutter of a building, often carved grotesquely. Many images and lots of information are available.

colonette (colo-NETT) – This was a decorative column that was often narrow or elongated and was also an element in compound piers. See Figure 5.8.

wainscot – A decorative facing such as wood paneling that was applied to the dado or lower portion of an interior wall. See Temple Newsam House and Hever Castle.

dado (DAY-dough) – This was the bottom third of an interior wall often decorated with paneling and of a darker color. See Temple Newsam House and Hever Castle.

linenfold – A carved paneling or decorative motif often on a wainscot or door or furniture that represented a symmetrical fold of linen cloth. There are a number of websites that have wonderful pictures; also look on Pinterest, there are several companies in England still making furniture; also look in museums such as the V&A, and on Flickr, Jacobean interiors, and YouTube.

The Gothic Clothing and Costume World

How They Dressed

* During the Gothic period, clothing design and manufacture were revolutionized with technological innovations. The invention of the spinning wheel, the carding of wool, and improvement in looms increased variety, quality, and availability of fabrics.

* The development of complex cloth-making techniques, of harvesting, weaving, dyeing, and cutting spurred the development of textiles and fabrics. They were the first truly international business commodities.

* The new craft of tailoring, sophisticated and intricate pattern making, sewing skills, and a high degree of decoration and rich materials characterized these new garments.

* Increased wealth and the rise of a highly developed sense of stylish fashion in the courts and among the wealthy sparked great competition that was consistent throughout Europe.

Figure 6.14 Sir Geoffrey Luttrell on horseback with his wife and daughter-in-law from the *Luttrell Psalter*, c. 1325–1335. This was an example of heraldry applied to a knight, his lady, his horse, and armor in preparation for a joust during the High Middle Ages. Although heavily decorated this is an accurate depiction of the horse and knight's costumes for a jousting tournament, which at this period had become a sporting event for nobility. Note their armor, chain mail, headgear, jousting stick or lance, and large saddle. Notice the elegant ladies are holding a shield and a flag also with the knight's emblems and their long flowing gowns now have low necklines.

Figure 6.15 This is a miniature painting of Saint Ursula and her companions from a 14th-century Book of Hours, Lombardy, Italy. She is shown to the right with a crown and halo and holding a banner. She is pictured here with 10 other virgins as their legend says that she and 11,000 maidens were beheaded in Cologne, Germany, by the Huns; so they represent one for each thousand. Most of the ladies' dresses have a low, curved neckline, no elaboration at the waist, and trailing hemlines. Also notice the variety of small headpieces, colors, and the patterns on the fabrics that were made possible by the new technology of carding and weaving.

Figure 6.16 This is another miniature painting from an illuminated manuscript, the *Chronique des Empereurs*, c. 1460, titled *How Bernard de Ray, a hermit, claimed to be Baudouin V, Count of Flanders and Hainaut, 1150–95*; he is shown begging for mercy and a man behind him is about to be hanged from a gallows. In addition to the return of figurative painting and perspective, we see a variety of examples of male and female costumes. Both ladies' and men's favor larger and more elaborate hats and thicker fabrics. The women's dresses have a pronounced belted waist and now v-neck bodices are also seen, but most distinctive of this period are the variety of *hennin* hats, all of which could vary by region and nationality. Many of the men's fashions have been seen before, but now noticeable are the men's *pourpoint* or doublet, chausses, and elegant pointed shoes, known as *poulaines* or *crakows*. The two monks are also wearing typical medieval monastic clothing of a belted tunic with a scapula and cowl or hood.

Kharbine-Tapabor/The Art Archive at Art Resource, NY

* Clothing abandoned all Classical influences and also became differentiated by sex and both had more variety of styles to choose from.

* Women wore elaborately tailored gowns with clearly defined parts and headdresses. See Figures 6.16 and 6.18.

* In the north women's fashion favored a profile with a defined waist, in England a square neckline on the bodice and in France and Holland they preferred a V-shape bodice also with a belted waist. Their hair continued to be worn long and down the back, but was also braided and sometimes coiled around the ears. See Figures 6.16 and 6.18.

* Southern women favored a horizontal or gently curved, low neckline without a defined waist. Their hairstyles were smaller and shorter and they favored blonde hair, which they bleached if it wasn't natural. They had many different hair and head decorations and always covered their heads. See Figure 6.15.

Figure 6.17 This is an illumination *Le Charivari* from the *Story of Fauvel* by Gervais du Bois in a 14th-century French manuscript. Charivari was a loud mock serenade with people singing raucously, banging on pots and pans, and parading around in silly costumes. It was often performed at the homes of newlyweds. For a different reason it was also used to show displeasure over other disapproved social behaviors. It occurred in many parts of Europe and England. In this illumination notice the adaptations of medieval clothing and particularly the cowl. The spires on the towers are very Gothic and similar in feel to those on cathedrals such as Notre Dame, Paris, and represent churches and have the disapproving clergy looking on. The custom and practice of Charivari continued into the 18th century.

Bibliothèque Nationale, Paris, France/Flammarion/ Bridgeman Images

Figure 6.18 This is a 15th-century painting *Garden of Love at the court of Philippe III the Good,* Duke of Burgundy (1396–1467) in the gardens at Hesdin Castle in 1432. It shows the wedding party for Chancellor Andre de Toulongeon and Jacqueline de Tremoille and shows a wide variety of elegant men and women all dressed and themed in white and gold. The only exception is the man lower right in red who appears to be a priest or cardinal. Also notice the herald, upper left, with long trumpet with the coat of arms and the wedding banquet feast. The painting is noticeably showing the use of foreground, middle ground, as well as the return of atmospheric and linear perspective.

Bridgeman Images

* There was much variety in styles of headwear from simple veils and caps to complex and increasingly taller headdresses. The turban developed into a padded halo and then double horns with a veil called an escoffin. See Figures 6.13, 6.15, 6.16, 6.17, and 6.18.

* Men favored fitted, tailored garments, characterized by short tunics, leggings, and headwear. See Figures 6.16 and 6.18.

* Men's over garments became shorter and exposed the legs. Decorated hose or chausses became fashionable for men and continued as the basis of men's fashion for the next 400 years. See Figures 6.16, 6.17, and 6.18.

* Shoes and hats became elongated and highly elaborate and decorative and functioned as a statement of wealth and fashion. See Figures 6.16, 6.17, and 6.18.

* Men's hair was worn shoulder length and cropped into a square shape with bangs, and faces were clean-shaven. Later in the period they also featured bobbed hair with curls and trimmed beards. See Figures 6.14, 6.16, 6.17, and 6.18.

* The development of the *houppelande* defined fashion for both sexes. These heavy, front buttoned, fitted tailored over garments had large, flaring sleeves, and stiff, pleated lower panels that came to typify Gothic fashion for both men and women. Men's versions were short for young men exposing the legs and longer and more robe-like for older men. The woman's *houppelande* had a fitted bodice and a flaring skirt that reached the ground. See Figures 6.16 and 6.18.

* This period saw the introduction and perfection of articulated plate armor for military and ceremonial use.

Clothing and Costume Keywords

sumptuary (SUM-tree) **laws** – These were royal or ecclesiastical edicts intended to limit and control excessive decoration and consumption of luxury or ostentatious goods. They were often used to enforce social conformity by specifying the clothing types, furs, and fabrics permitted for each class of society.

heraldry – The system of pictorial symbols and colors that identified persons and families that was used on their clothing, armaments, including their horses and flags, and documents. See Figures 6.14 and 6.18.

surcote – This was a long outer garment worn by men and women over another garment. It was open at the front and either sleeveless or with varying sleeve lengths. It was also worn by knights over their armor to protect from rain so their chain mail did not rust. After the Crusades it was often white to help deflect the sun. Like Figure 6.14 it also showed the knight's symbols, which is where we get the term "coat of arms." See St. Giles 5.20, 6.14, and 6.16 (man in green and right in blue).

cotehardie (coat-har-DEE) – A long, A-line, fitted, buttoned gown with short sleeves, often with trailing tippets and later with wide dagged sleeves, worn by both men and women. See Figure 6.14.

dagging – These were the decorative rounded or pointed edges of sleeves or hems fashionable in the 14th and 15th centuries. See Figure 6.18.

houppelande (HOOP-a-land) – A full tailored Gothic overdress worn by both sexes with full, flaring sleeves, a tight waist, and a funnel-shaped, high collar, which opened at the front. Often it was worn with a pleated front and lined in a contrasting fabric or fur. It was worn below the knees for men and long and floor length for women. See Figures 6.16 and 6.18.

doublet or ***pourpoint*** (POUR-point) – Originally this was a tailored, quilted military undergarment, later it became a man's quilted, decorated, and padded outer garment with tight sleeves and a short, tight waist and peplum. The sleeves and front were closed with numerous buttons and it had a high collar and a linen shirt was worn under it. Later in the period the sleeves were enlarged and the peplum shortened. See Figures 6.16 and 6.18.

peplum – The flaring of fabric at the waist of a fitted garment, which was seen on both men's and women's garments. It derived from the Greek peplos and continues to be used today. See Figures 6.16 and 6.18.

jacque or **jack** – This was the short, close-fitting *pourpoint*. It had larger sleeves than a doublet and an elongated hood. This is the origin of our word jacket. See Figure 6.18.

liripipe (LYR-a-pipe) – Originally this was the elongated hood of a *jacque* and long tails of other hooded garments, which could be coiled around the head and shoulders in a decorative manner.

habit – The traditional dress of nuns that consisted of a loose floor-length tunic of simple black fabric, tied with a cotton belt at the waist. A white cotton wimple was worn over the head, and a black fabric veil worn pinned over the wimple. The shape and cut of the wimple could be quite complex and signified the nun's order.

monk's clothing – This consisted of a belted tunic with a scapula worn over the shoulders with a hole for the head, usually with a cowl or hood attached and secured in the front with a rectangular piece of fabric. The different orders had different colors. See Figure 6.16.

chausses – This was the medieval term for hose or leggings. See Figures 6.16, 6.17, and 6.18.

tabard – A men's short outer garment similar to a tunic and open at the sides, but without sleeves. It was sometimes worn over armor and often decorated with heraldic devices. See Figure 6.16, the two guards in red and blue.

armor – At this time armor could be chain mail, metal, or plate and was hammered into the outer shape of body parts and joined with leather straps or metal hinges. In ceremonial versions the fabric-covered form was richly decorated with heraldic designs and in the plate armor it often used intricate etchings. It was also worn by horses and varied greatly in style by region and period. See Figure 6.14.

CHAPTER SEVEN

Renaissance: 1450–1600

Figure 7.1 Villa Capra, "La Rotonda," Vicenza, Italy, built 1565–1592. Designed by Andrea Palladio, it is often called the "perfect house" because of its beautifully proportioned four identical classical façades. It has since influenced hundreds of buildings and architects in the US and abroad. In turn Palladio used the Pantheon as his inspiration for this building.

Fedecandoniphoto/Dreamstime.com

A Little Background

The rediscovery and excavation of Classical Roman ruins in Rome and central Italy reawakened European interest in the Classical past. Artists and builders began to study Classical authors and imitate Classical examples of building and decorative arts, much of which still survived, and applied them to their contemporary design. In Italy and especially in Rome and Florence this resulted in a new artistic vision and an architectural style based on Classical examples. In the 19th century this period was termed the Renaissance, a literal translation from French to English meaning rebirth or reawakening. Starting in Italy it spread to major cities throughout Europe.

The prevailing Gothic style remained in northern Europe. England continued its development of the Gothic, but it was inflected by the new Renaissance classicism. The Renaissance in the northern countries was primarily a scientific and literary movement. This rise in humanist activity in the arts and literature weakened the dominance of the Catholic Church and helped produce the Protestant Reformation.

Who They Were

* Rediscovered Classical humanism became the driving force for artistic achievement. Man became the measure of all things. The importance, dignity, and the value of the individual person were recognized, as was the pursuit of personal pleasure. The economic and cultural flowering of European cities and the rediscovery of their Classical heritage encouraged cosmopolitan thinking among artists and intellectuals.

* The Southern Renaissance was in Italy, Spain, and Portugal, where there was a maturing of the Classical artistic principles. This maturity was characterized by humanism, individualism, intellectualism, naturalism, and a renewal of realism and perspective in art. Artists and intellectuals made conscious comparisons and imitations of Classical Athens and Rome in their work.

* The Northern Renaissance in England, France, Holland, and Germany primarily developed scientific observation, religious reforms leading to different Protestant sects, and the beginning of the rise of nationalism.

* Individualism became the model for personal achievement. Artists signed their names to their work. Doubt and skepticism were given intellectual value.

* Reduced warfare and the end of The Hundred Years' War combined with expanded Gothic economic power increased the secularization of society and its institutions.

* The invention in 1450 of the printing press and movable type by Johannes Gutenberg led to the rapid and wide circulation of books and therefore knowledge, which was a significant component in the weakening of the intellectual and religious monopoly of the Catholic Church.

* It was also important for the spread of art, literature, music, architecture, and fashion. Both images and information were disseminated across Europe and copied from country to country.

* The development of modern international banking and financial institutions brought the cultures and economies of Europe closer together.

* This era marked the beginning of the development of the modern theater building, moving it into its own designated indoor building and the establishment of the proscenium stage with illusionistic, moving scenery. See Figures 7.10, 7.11, and 7.12.

* Guilds organized and codified craft professions including painters, builders, and architects who also provided scenery and costumes for public processions and both public and private performances and festivals. See Figures 7.11 and 7.12.

* This period saw the development of architecture as a profession. For the first time buildings were planned, modeled, and drawn in advance. Previously buildings were built by teams of masons, led by a master mason, who often remained anonymous and often spent a lifetime finishing his task. See Figures 7.1, 7.2, 7.4, 7.5, and 7.7.

* Also as a result of decreased warfare between cities and states and an increase in wealth, this period saw the beginning of the era when large country houses and gardens were built. See Figures 7.1, 7.6, and 7.7.

* The end of the 15th century and 16th century was known as "The Age of Discovery" as most European countries were exploring all around the world; and they embarked on the colonization and exploitation of the New World. They brought back gold and silver, but also many plants and spices, particularly from the New World, which would completely change the diets of Europeans and also their domestic animals.

* Playwrights: Shakespeare, Marlowe in England, Lope de Vega in Spain.

* Novelists: Cervantes in Spain, Petrarch and Boccaccio in Italy, in England Chaucer's *Canterbury Tales* were first published in 1478.

* Poets: Shakespeare, Milton, and Donne in England.

* Artists: Brunelleschi, Raphael, Michelangelo, Masaccio, Da Vinci and Palladio in Italy, Dürer in Germany, El Greco in Spain, Holbein, the younger in England.

* There are many movies about the individual people and this period and these are some suggestions: *Elizabeth* (1998)*, the sequel—*Elizabeth—The Golden Age* (2007)*, *Shakespeare in Love* (1998)*, *Anne of a Thousand Days* (1969)*, *The Private Life of Henry VIII* (1933)*, *A Man For All Seasons* (1966)*, *Life of Leonardo DaVinci* (TV series 1972), *The Agony and the Ecstasy* (1965)*, *Romeo and Juliet* (1968; dir. Zeffirelli)*, *The Return of Martin Guerre* (1982; César and Academy Awards)*, *Andrei Rublev* (1966)* and any adaptations of Shakespeare and these other writers.

* Two excellent TV mini-series for sets and costumes were *The Tudors* (2007–2010) and *The Borgias* (2011–2013).

The Renaissance Material World

What They Made

* Artists and architects favored simple, geometric shapes arranged symmetrically in calm, balanced compositions. Their work was based on the rediscovery of Roman and Greek forms and ornaments. Gothic mystery and emotionalism were now often rejected in favor of a restrained Classical rationality. See Figures 7.1, 7.2, 7.3, 7.5, and 7.7.

* Andrea Palladio developed an architectural style for palazzo and villa designs using Classical forms which had a lasting effect on English and American architecture. He wrote a treatise on architecture and design. He provided designs and plans for many country and city houses in the Veneto as well as the Venetian churches of Il Redentore and San Giorgio Maggiore. See Figure 7.1.

* Palladio also designed the Teatro Olympico in Vicenza, northern Italy (built 1580–1585). It was the first indoor theater in Europe and he based it on Roman examples. See Figures 7.10 and 7.11.

* Great advances were made in stage building and machinery, much of it based on winch and pulley engineering borrowed from naval technology.

* Building design and technology were improved so that a building could be designed and built in a few years instead of a lifetime. This combined with the prevailing humanism of the time made individual architects and designers more prominent and encouraged them to take and receive credit for their work. See Figures 7.1, 7.2, 7.3, 7.5, 7.7, and 7.10.

Figure 7.2 Palazzo Farnese, view of the courtyard inside the building. The square interior courtyard or cortile echoes both Gothic cloisters and earlier Roman atriums. This courtyard was designed by Michelangelo. The three distinct levels use the ascending orders referencing it to its Roman heritage, each level being more sophisticated.

Scala/Art Resource, NY

Figure 7.3 Ospedale degli Innocenti in Florence, Italy. Designed by Filippo Brunelleschi, who received the commission in 1419, it was originally a children's orphanage. This is the first building to abandon the Gothic style and to return to Classical forms of architecture, based on surviving Classical buildings, which was the beginning of the new Renaissance style.

pio3/Shutterstock.com

Figure 7.4 *Left:* Ospedale degli Innocenti. This is a detail of a Classical Composite column capital in the new Renaissance style, showing its resemblance to Classical models; however, it is simplified and more abstracted and now has a small impost block.

Scala/Art Resource, NY

Figure 7.5 *Below:* Farnese Palace, Rome, started 1514. This east façade is a supreme example of the mature Palazzo style and like the interior (Figure 7.2) uses the three levels of ascending orders. High Renaissance elements are the decorative quoins at the corners, the complex projecting cornice by Michelangelo, the massive central doorway, the second floor (piano nobile) ceremonial window with a balcony and large coat of arms, the alternating pediments of the windows, and blind balustrades on all three levels. The plan was rectangular with an open atrium in the center. In Puccini's *Tosca* it is the site for the scene with police chief Scarpia.

Claudio Zaccherini/Shutterstock.com

Figure 7.6 Speke Hall, a Tudor Manor House built in 1530, Liverpool, England, showing the garden front. Northern European design still followed Gothic forms throughout the Renaissance. Northern countries like England where wood was plentiful preferred to use it, even for large projects like this wealthy residence. England continued to favor the Gothic style in architecture, construction, and decoration.

Kps 1664/Dreamstsime.com

Figure 7.7 Longleat House, Wiltshire, England. Completed in 1580 this is the Palazzo style applied to English Tudor forms and is considered a prime example. As at Longleat, later and even more costly buildings were influenced by Renaissance examples that paired Renaissance organization using the rectangular plan, the three level façade, and the use of a balustrade on the edge of the roof with Gothic details, such as the crenellations on the roof and the dome-like towers.

hallam creations/Shutterstock.com

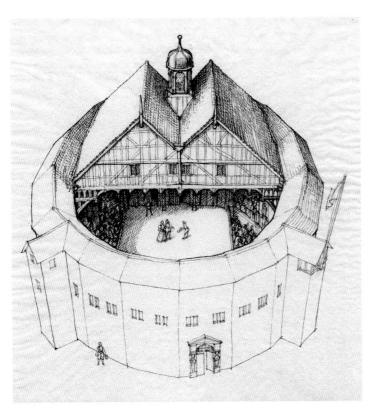

Figure 7.8 This is a bird's eye view of an artist's interpretation (1973 by C. Walter Hodges for The Folger Library) of the second Globe Theater and stage house, London, England. It was built in 1614 shortly after the first one's thatch roof caused a fire. It was modified with a safer tile roof and eliminated the columns on the stage. It would be one of the last outdoor theaters before European-style indoor proscenium theaters supplanted them after the restoration of the monarchy in 1660. From 1992 to 1997 a reconstruction of the original 1599 Globe Theater was built with modern amenities.

Folger Shakespeare Library

Figure 7.9 Albrecht Dürer (1471–1528) was the most famous Northern Renaissance artist. This is a view from his house in Nuremberg, Germany. The casement windows are made up of small, round pieces of glass called roundels. It would be another 100 years before glass panes could be made much larger than 10"x10". The house was built circa 1420 and he lived and worked here from 1509 until his death in 1528. Its upper three stories feature painted red half-timbering like the house outside the window. This type of Gothic design in architecture continued throughout the Renaissance in the northern countries.

Erich Lessing/Art Resource, NY

How They Decorated

Figure 7.10 *Top:* Teatro Olimpico, Vicenza, Veneto, Italy. Palladio's classic design was the first indoor, secular theater. It is based on a Roman theater plan but now indoors and on a more intimate scale and the seating continues to use steeply raked seats. The audience would enter through the loggia, the columned space above them, which also has freestanding Classical statues on top of it.

Austrophoto/SuperStock

Figure 7.11 *Left:* Built after 1580, Teatro Olympico contained some of the first three-dimensional perspective scenery. The stage has three perspective vistas, an arched one in the center, flanked by two rectangular openings. Each is built in forced perspective and meant to be seen only from the front to maintain the perspective illusion.

Erich Lessing/Art Resource, NY

Figure 7.12 This set design sketch, pen and ink on paper by Inigo Jones (1573–1652) is a one-point perspective scene design for the new proscenium-style theater. Painted scenery was themed not by the time and play but by its subject matter. The three types of scenery followed the example of the Roman theater: comedy, tragedy, and satyr plays. Shown here is the scenery for a tragic scene, meaning the type of play. These designs were generic images that could be used for many plays. The decorative element is the top of the proscenium frame.

* In painting realism of form, lighting, and perspective replaced the inward-looking subjectivity and emotionalism of the Gothic style. Theatrical space characterized painting and sculpture by reviving the Classical foreground, mid-ground, and background used by the Romans and Greeks. See Figures 7.11, 7.12, and 7.13.

* Linear and atmospheric perspective were refined and codified by Brunelleschi in Florence and rapidly employed by his fellow artists and architects. See Figure 7.11.

* Portraiture flourished as a way to realistically record images of people and their surroundings and the use of props showed their accomplishments. Oil painting techniques were perfected allowing paintings to become portable and personal, a commodity that could be bought and sold. Painting became separated from architecture. See Figures 7.16 and 7.14.

* At the same time fully developed fresco painting techniques were also perfected for large projects.

* Theatrical scenery was painted by artists and was confined to imitations of fanciful Classical images and scenes. See Figures 7.11 and 7.12.

* Furniture and furnishings continued the Gothic preference for large, heavy, and ornate forms but with added Classical details. Pieces were still portable and could be broken down for travel.

Building and Décor Keywords

piazza (pee-AT-za) – An open plaza in an Italian city, usually with a church or cathedral on one side. They were often the site of markets, festivals, celebrations, executions, and other public gatherings. It was a descendant of the Classical Forum and similar to the town squares of northern towns and cities.

palazzo (pal-AT-zo) – A wealthy urban Italian residence. It gave its name to the Palazzo style of architecture developed during this period. See Figures 7.1, 7.2, and 7.5.

Figure 7.13 Vittore Carpaccio was a Venetian painter (1455–1525), *Dream of St. Ursula*, 1495. His exquisitely detailed paintings are always set in *his* present time and are a rich source of costume, prop, and décor material for Renaissance decoration. Here the angel Gabriel summons Ursula from her bed. Notice the roundels again in the windows.

Cameraphoto Arte Venezia/Bridgeman Images

Palazzo style – Literally, palace. This style of wealthy Italian domestic city architecture was defined by a classically designed horizontal façade of two or three stories, each treated with an ascending Classical order and built around a courtyard in the Classical manner. Often the windows displayed Classical pediments and a new feature, the balustrade at the roof level. It featured a large central ceremonial entrance and a second floor window above it bearing a carving of the coat of arms of the family. See Figures 7.2, 7.5, and 7.7.

villa – A wealthy Italian residence and its dependencies in the country. Highly influenced by Andrea Palladio who helped bring the Classical style to residential architecture. See Figure 7.1.

hotel (o-TEL) – A wealthy French residence in the city, the equivalent of the palazzo, that was also influenced by Classical design.

château (sha-TOE) – A wealthy French residence and its dependencies in the country, often in a variation of the Palazzo style and similar to the Italian villa.

Palladian Arch or window – An arched composition perfected by Andrea Palladio in which a Roman arch is flanked by an additional column or pilaster on either side, with the columns creating two rectangular openings. Often there were decorative circular openings above these rectangular openings beside the main arch. See Figures 8.11 Teatro Farnese, and 10.3.

Tudor – This was the style of secular English architecture and clothing during the Renaissance reigns of Henry VIII and Elizabeth I. In architecture it was characterized by heavy Gothic forms, flattened arches and half-timbering and in costume, wide, heavy profiles. The English Tudor and Jacobean styles were only minimally influenced by the revival of Classical design. English architecture kept its Gothic flavor until the Baroque period. See Figures 6.8, 6.9 and 7.6 and 7.8.

Jacobean – The English Renaissance architecture, decorative, and furniture style from the death of Elizabeth I in 1603 to the Cromwell Revolution in the 1640s. It reflected Classical influences applied to Tudor Gothic forms. The style was characterized by flatter, low relief sculptural elements. The name referred to James I, the successor to Elizabeth I.

balustrade (BAL-is-trad) – An entire railing system that included a molded handrail, balusters (turned spindles), and a bottom rail. They could be found either inside or outside a building. This was a Renaissance invention applied to Classical architecture but not used by the Romans or Greeks. They frequently were seen on staircases and on roof edges. If they were not open with railings they were called blind. See Figures 7.2, 7.5, and 7.7, and Figure 9.3.

blind door or **window** – A decorative or false dimensional door or window frame with no practical opening. They were routinely used to balance an asymmetrical composition. See Figure 8.11 Teatro Farnese.

quoins (KWOINS) – Large decorative stones used to reinforce or elaborate the external corner of a building or palazzo. See Figure 7.5, Farnese Palace.

rustication (rusti-CAY-shun) – The intentional use of large, rough or partially carved stones on the lower level of a palazzo that indicated its lower order and utilitarian function as the basement of the house and later as a decorative element. See Figures 7.5, 10.2, and Figure 13.14.

grotto – A natural or artificial cave in a garden or landscape commonly decorated with shells and stones often incorporating a water feature.

marquetry (MAR-ketry) – Wood or stone inlay of representational subject matter used in floors and furniture.

parquetry (PAR-ketry) – Also wood or stone inlays, but of abstract or geometric subject matter that was used in furniture. See Figure 13.9.

parquet (par-KAY) – Geometric wood or stone inlay used for patterned floors.

trestle table – A collapsible wooden table supported by two piers that are large, flat legs connected by a horizontal brace. Often they were elaborately carved and made to be portable.

X chair or **Savonarola chair** – A large, low-backed armchair with a flexible sling back supported by a folding "X" frame rather than legs. Commonly it was upholstered and highly decorated. Developed during the Gothic period, it became very popular in the Renaissance.

credenza (cre-DEN-za) – A tall, wooden storage cupboard for clothing or linens.

cartouche (car-TOOSH) – A decorative frame attached to a wall resembling a shield, often with a coat of arms and inscription. Could be used on either architecture or furniture. See Figure 7.5, and Figure 7.12, Proscenium frame, Figures 8.1, 8.11, 8.12, 8.14, and Figure 9.3.

theatrical space – The Classically based Renaissance painting technique used in perspective views that divided the pictorial space into foreground, mid-ground, and background with the major narrative action occurring in the mid-ground. Oftentimes the figures in the foreground are looking away from the viewer, "upstage" into the picture space. See Figures 7.12 and 7.13, and 8.12, 8.13, and 8.14.

linear perspective – A drawing system developed in the Renaissance to portray the realistic depth of space. It employs a horizon line and vanishing points from a single viewpoint to enable an artist to represent the visible world in a convincing illusionistic way. Objects of a similar size in the foreground become progressively smaller as they are seen in the mid-ground and background. See Figures 7.11, 7.12 and 8.12, 8.13, and 8.14.

false perspective – Is similar in concept to linear perspective, using one-point perspective, but is only applied to built scenery or architecture. See Figures 7.11, 8.1, 8.2, and 8.14.

atmospheric perspective – A painting technique that creates the illusion of depth by the progressively blurring and softening of faraway forms and colors in distant objects in comparison to foreground objects. See Figures 2.11, 7.12, 9.12, and 12.13.

positional perspective – A perspective painting technique in which objects of the same size in reality are shown larger, darker, and in more detail in the foreground than in the mid-ground or background. These three types of perspective are often combined in the same painting and are what distinguish Renaissance painting from earlier styles. See Figures 7.11, 7.12, and 8.12, 8.13, and 8.14.

The Renaissance Clothing and Costume World

Figure 7.14 *Henry VIII* portrait by Hans Holbein the Younger, 1537. Henry's power and pride are evident, as are his fashionable slash and puff garments, rich fabrics, and his hose. Note the square-toed shoes (sometimes referred to as duckbill shoes) and padded shoulders, characteristic of the English style. Hans Holbein became his court painter in 1555 and painted many notable portraits, festival designs, and designed other objects including jewelry. He is known for his highly refined precise technique and his many portraits and objects would be a good source for designers.

Walker Art Gallery, National Museums Liverpool/ Bridgeman Images

How They Dressed

Figure 7.15 Vittore Carpaccio, *Two Venetian Ladies*. These Italian courtesans wear the latest gowns with tied-on sleeves. The woman on the right is wearing a tie-on bodice and puffed sleeves. Both are wearing lifts, a type of shoe, under their skirts, and wear their hair up and gathered into a bun on top of their heads. Note the child playing in the upper left, and the wealth of detail. Also notice the low necklines and simple cut of the Southern-style garments and lack of rigid structure.

Bridgeman Images

Figure 7.16 *Elizabeth I when a Princess*, 1546, at age 13, by Flemish artist Guillaume Scrots. She is showing the English flat downward curved neckline, a stiff bodice with a stomacher, and the skirt that was supported by the bell-shaped farthingale. This costume is stiffer and less revealing than the Italian, Southern style. Also notice her jewelry and jeweled headpiece. Scrots painted many highly refined and detailed portraits, which would make good resource material.

Royal Collection Trust/Her Majesty Queen Elizabeth II, 2014/ Bridgeman Images

Figure 7.17 *A Ball at the Court of King Henri III*, 1581–1582. This view of a wedding fête shows the latest Northern style of fashions with their more structured clothes with clearly defined waists, the newly fashionable starched ruff collars, and tall hats for both sexes; and the farthingale and huge stuffed sleeves for the ladies.

Louvre, Paris, France/Bridgeman Images

Figure 7.18 This is a late 16th-century drawing: *A Game of Real Tennis*, to distinguish it from "lawn tennis," being played on an indoor tennis court. Notice the puff-style breeches, the doublets with wings, and the various shapes of the tall hats that were formal garments worn even for sporting activities. In the 1530s Henry VIII had an indoor tennis court built at Hampton Court.

Private Collection/Bridgeman Images

Quando pila et Sphæræ flectuntur corporis artus,   So oft ich thue den Ballen schlagn,
Corpus erit levius, pectus erit levius.   Erfrisch ich mir hertz tragen vnd magn

Figure 7.19 Pieter Brueghel, the Younger (c. 1564–1638), Dutch. *The Peasant Wedding Dance*, 1623, which shows a wealth of detail on Northern peasants and the variety and colors of their clothing. Peasants' garments were similar in cut to wealthy examples but of cheaper and more serviceable materials and with little decoration. Also notice the tied-on parts of clothes with laces and eyelets.

Art Gallery of Ontario, Toronto, Canada/Gift of Mr. and Mrs. W. Redelmeier, 1940/Bridgeman Images

* Both Henry VIII and his daughter Elizabeth I were very fashion conscious and liked clothes and fancy and sumptuous decorations. They set the standard for fashionable costume throughout the courts of Europe. See Figures 7.14 and 7.16.

* Clothing continued to elaborate the tailored Gothic forms for royal and noble men and women during the Renaissance and added decorative variety and expensive materials. See Figures 7.14, 7.16, 7.17, and 7.18.

* There were many introductions of fabric and metallic threads from the East, but also rich fabrics such as silk, satins, velvets, damasks, and lace were now being manufactured in Europe. See Figures 7.14, 7.15, 17.16, 7.17, and 7.18.

* Cloth and well-made garments were so expensive that they were bequeathed to descendants in wills or recycled into other or smaller clothes, pillows, or upholstery.

* This period was noted for these exquisite fabrics but also for its luscious colors, textures, designs, and the addition of jewels. See Figures 7.14, 7.15, 7.16, 7.17, and 7.18.

* Gothic tailoring techniques were perfected and in many cases applied to heraldic designs that identified family members.

* Fitting and tailoring of garments became highly sophisticated and encouraged stylish and competitive fashion with much variation from country to country. See Figures 7.14, 7.15, 7.16, 7.17, and 7.18.

* This period saw the introduction of the "slash and puff" decorative fashion for men and women in which an outer garment was pierced with a decorative pattern of slits like large buttonholes that was worn over a loose undergarment that was then pulled through the slashes and puffed out. See Figures 7.14, 7.15, and 7.16.

* Notable in women's clothing was the development of a separate bodice with tied-on sleeves and a separate skirt. See Figure 7.15, the woman in red.

* The introduction of the farthingale structure for women's skirts occurred during this period. It was the first structured garment with rigid framing elements and it allowed skirts to have a larger, more dramatic shape. See Figures 7.16 and 7.17.

* National styles developed and became differentiated. In women's garments Southern styles preferred an open, off the shoulder boat neckline, while Northern bodices continued with the square neckline, covered shoulders, and had a pronounced waist. See Figure 7.15, Southern, and Figures 7.16 and 7.17, Northern.

* In the mid to late 15th century *hennin* hats began to appear predominantly on the Continent. This was the ubiquitous "fairy tale princess hat" that was a tall conical hat with a veil, a *cointoise*, that could fall to the shoulders or to the floor or cover the face. See Figure 6.16. See http://en.wikipedia.org/wiki/Hennin

* Different styles of hoods for women became common, particularly the pedimented, gable, diamond and French, which covered the back and sides of the head. These were worn on the back of the head to reveal a prominent forehead accentuated by a raised plucked, parted hairline and thin eyebrows. See Figures 7.16, 7.17, and 7.19 for head coverings for peasants.

* Fans and fancy lace handkerchiefs became fashionable accessories in European courts, particularly after the introduction of large feathers from South America for fans.

* Male costume featured leggings, sleeves, and codpieces, all of which could be laced and buttoned separately to the body of men's base garments and worn over trunk hose or tights. The lacing and holes are especially noticeable in Figure 7.19. See Figures 7.14, 7.17, 7.18, and 7.19.

* Men's hats varied greatly, also by region, from small caps and bonnets to tall and large decorated headwear, often with feathers. See Figures 7.14, 7.17, 7.18, and 7.19.

* The Tudor styles shared the same features as Continental fashions but were wider, fuller, and more solid in profile for men and women's garments. Shoe fronts were enlarged and squared off to complete the bulky silhouette. See Figures 7.14 and 7.16.

* Theatrical costume was a heightened and exaggerated version of contemporary court dress and was often provided by the actor.

Clothing and Costume Keywords

slash and puff – A style of Renaissance clothing in which an outer garment had many slits that allowed an undergarment to be pulled through in a series of puffs. See Figures 7.14, 7.15, and 7.16.

parti-colored or motley – Men's and women's garments that had parts of different, brightly colored fabrics and asymmetrical compositions. A style often adopted by young men and women, court fools, and jesters. See Figures 5.21 and 7.15.

ruff – This was a stiffened lace decorative collar worn at the neck and around the sleeves on men, women's, and children's clothing. Later it became fan-shaped and was worn behind the head and was termed a whisk collar. See Figures 7.17 and 8.16.

leg-o-mutton – The puffed shape of a sleeve that was large and rounded at the top tapering to a narrowing at the cuff. Figure 7.17 shows an elongated version that was very popular in England, France, and Germany. Later these will recur with just a larger puff at the upper arm and narrowing from the elbow to wrist starting in the 1820s and then later in the 1890s. See Figures 7.17, 11.7, and 14.6.

ropa – The Spanish women's full-length decorated over garment with long sleeves, which was worn as a robe.

farthingale – This Renaissance women's skirt structure started in Spain in the 1400s and moved to England and the Continent. It was a bell-shaped cage that was stiffened on a wire or wood frame and was worn under the skirt and connected at the waist by fabric or leather straps. It imparted a large, stiff, formal profile to the garment. In the 1500s it became wider on the sides and the back and lasted in England and the Continent until the 1590s. In theatrical costume it is now known as the "bum roll." See Figures 7.16 and 7.17.

stomacher – The front of a lady's bodice was a stiffened triangular piece that went from the neckline to below her abdomen. See Figures 7.16 and 7.17 and Figures 8.16, 8.17, and 8.20.

doublet – This was a men's short over garment with a tight stiff collar that buttoned up the front and ended at the waist. See Figures 7.17, 7.18, 8.16, 8.20, and 8.21.

jerkin – This was also a jacket worn over the doublet, usually belted, hip-length, and sleeveless, but sometimes with wings, and often made of leather.

trunk hose – This was the men's hose that started at the waist and was sometimes short and onion shaped and sometimes more elongated to halfway down the thigh. They could also be padded and were worn in the 16th and 17th centuries. See Figures 7.17, 7.18, and Figures 8.20 and 8.21.

codpiece – In men's clothing the separate piece of cloth or pouch that attached at the top of the hose or breeches at the crotch. See Figures 7.14, 7.17, and 7.19.

wings – These were the rolled fabric worn around the shoulders by both men and women. See Figure 7.18.

chain of office – This was a heavy metal chain worn over the shoulders and draped equally front and back, which has been used since ancient times to denote authority. Attached in the front was a badge, insignia, portrait or other image that represented rank, an office or organization. It is still in use today by royals, political offices, and university members. See Figure 7.14.

CHAPTER EIGHT

Baroque: 1600–1720

Figure 8.1 Gian Lorenzo Bernini (1598–1680) has been credited for creating the Baroque style of sculpture, but he was also one of its great architects as well as a painter and set designer. This is Scala Regia, the spectacular entrance to the Vatican Palace in which Bernini employs false perspective in the staircase and also the dramatic use of natural light; it would become a central and important feature of Baroque secular and religious art and architecture. One of his other innovations was the incorporation of realistic sculpture and narrative decoration with the architecture. These three elements—fusing architecture, lighting, and decoration—are significant developments of Baroque architecture and would characterize it in all of continental Europe, and primarily the Spanish New World. See the plan and elevation in Figure 8.3.

Bridgeman Images

A Little Background

The revived classicism of the Renaissance and the new spiritual demands of the Protestant reformation presented a challenge to the Catholic Church. It answered this difficult situation by mounting a determined building and artistic campaign to win back straying adherents to the Church by emphasizing the spiritual, theatrical, and emotional in religious practice. This movement was sponsored by the Church, and encompassed all of the arts. This period of turmoil and transition in politics and religion also influenced clothing.

Growing prosperity throughout Europe and the beginning of the commercial development of the New World and the Far East colonies brought Europeans into contact with new cultures, which fostered a cross-pollination of styles. Science continued to challenge religious doctrine in this period and established the foundations of scientific observation and methods.

Who They Were

* Most of Europe was ruled by Absolute Monarchs—the quintessence being Louis XIV, the Sun King in France. However, England had a civil war from 1642 to 1651, which deposed King Charles I, established the Commonwealth under the Puritans, and later in 1660 saw the Restoration of Charles II as a limited monarch with a Parliament.

* The flowering of scientific discovery and development occurred during this period of the 17th century known as "The Age of Science," from the invention of the telescope that enlarged the world, to the microscope that allowed the discovery of microorganisms. Francis Bacon, René Descartes, and Isaac Newton (*Principia*, 1686 and *Optiks*, 1704—the study of light and color) were responsible for new mathematic and scientific methods and controlled standards. Scientific observation became the key to unlocking the mysteries of the physical world and in conjunction with the growing rationalist philosophy challenged the old foundations of religious belief.

* The Counter Reformation was instituted by the Catholic Church to attract lapsed Catholics back to the Church with drama, passion, mystery, emotion, and a challenge to rationalist thought. This new style, Baroque, was characterized by a re-emphasis on passion and drama in religion, and was promoted and paid for by the Church. See Figures 8.1, 8.2, 8.3, 8.6, 8.7, 8.8, and 8.9.

* Art and architecture were put in the service of celebrating the Catholic Church and the Monarchy. Many European kings allied themselves with the Catholic Church to reverse the intellectual effects of the new sciences, the Protestant Reformation and innovations of the Renaissance, which weakened the power of civil and religious authority.

* For the first time since Classical times, "architecture" combined building, painting, and sculpture in a unified, dramatic whole. See Figures 8.5 and 8.6.

* Since the Renaissance music had been considered one of the "four liberal arts" with arithmetic, geometry, and astronomy as they all used number ratios and were seen as proof of the existence of God. Architecture was also closely allied to these as it also used mathematical calculations.

* The development of opera in Florence, Venice, and Rome unified poetry, music, dance, painting, and sculpture, and reimagined Classic Greek drama in contemporary settings and costumes. Its popularity first in the royal courts and then as public entertainment spurred the development of theater buildings and technology. See Figure 8.13.

* Music was a major component of court life in most of Europe. Both Louis XIV and the Stuart kings in England loved court spectacles and masques, which they and their courtiers took part in. These performances also combined poetry, singing, and dancing with lavish costumes and scenery. See Figures 8.10, 8.12, 8.13, and 8.14.

* Jean-Baptiste Lully (1632–1687) and Molière (1622–1673) initially were friends and favorites of Louis XIV and the two of them invented comedy-ballet with music, which they performed together. *Le Roi Danse* was a 2000 film about their collaboration. See Figure 8.13.

* This period saw the development of organized orchestras to accompany court celebrations, public spectacles, and the newly invented form of opera, ballet, and theater. The position of a conductor was invented. See Figure 8.12.

* The Puritan civil war of Oliver Cromwell outlawed theater and opera and marked the end of the Elizabethan theater stage and acting style.

* The English Restoration in 1660 re-established theater on the European proscenium model and permitted women on the stage. This period was known for heroic dramas and satirical and somewhat bawdy Restoration comedies, all heavily influenced by the French. See Figures 8.11, 8.12, and 8.14.

* For the first time this new theater and the new opera art form allowed women to become independent and wealthy because of their artistic talent.

* Playwrights: Molière, Corneille, Racine in France, Restoration and Ben Jonson plays in England. There are two bio films about Molière—1978 and a more loosely based one in 2007.

* Composers: Monteverdi, Telemann, Purcell, Vivaldi, Handel, J.S. Bach, Lully, Rameau, Charpentier, Marin Marais, Alessandro and Domenico Scarlatti, Corelli, Albinoni, Couperin, and Pachelbel. There is a 1994 documentary film about William Christie and his *Les Arts Florissants* and music of the Baroque. *Farinelli* (1994) is about a young 17th-century opera singer.

* Artists: Bernini, Caravaggio, Orazio and Artemesia Gentileschi, Rubens, Rembrandt, Velasquez, Anthony Van Dyck, and 17th-century Dutch flower and genre painters (especially useful to designers).

* Authors: Samuel Pepys—*Diaries*.

* Architects—Inigo Jones in England.

* There are several films that would be helpful: *Rembrandt* (1936 and 1999)* both sets and costumes, *Artemisia* (1997), *Caravaggio* (2007 TV), *The Girl With a Pearl Earing* (2003)*—Vermeer. Lavish sets and costumes abound in both dark and joyful films such as: *Witchfinder General* (1968), *A Field in England* (2013), *The Devils* (1971), *Day of Wrath* (1943). Also many adaptations of these two classics—*Cyrano de Bergerac* (1990)*, and *The Three Musketeers* (1973)*—*Tous Les Matins du Monde* (1991)*, *Marquise* (1997), *The Draughtsman's Contract* (1982), and *The New World* (2005).

The Baroque Material World

What They Made

* The Baroque style began with Bernini in Rome and spread to all of Italy, Spain, Portugal, and Germany and to a lesser extent France and England. See Figures 8.1, 8.2, 8.3, 8.6, 8.7, 8.8, and 8.9.

Figure 8.2 This is an aerial view of St. Peter's Piazza, Vatican City, Rome, with Bernini's exuberant addition to the piazza with its two massive semi-circular arcades, which symbolically evoke the welcoming arms of the Church inviting lapsed Christians to return to the church. Planned and constructed from 1655 to 1667 this enormous space holds huge crowds, who come to see and hear the Pope speak from the loggia of the Basilica or the balcony of the Palace. A 1st-century CE obelisk is in the center of what was formerly Caligula's Roman circus and the colonnade is topped with freestanding sculptures. In 1506 the old 4th-century CE Basilica of St. Peter's was replaced and for the next 150 years it was enlarged and reconfigured by most of the prominent architects of their time, including Michelangelo, who among other things designed the large dome that was completed shortly after his death in 1590. The dome has served as a model for numerous buildings, both religious and secular throughout the Western world, including the US Capitol in Washington, DC.

Figure 8.3 Plan and elevation of the Scala Regia by Bernini shows that it is built in theatrical false perspective. The staircase is shown in Figure 8.1. Bernini also took advantage of the existing angles of the adjacent buildings, which were not parallel.

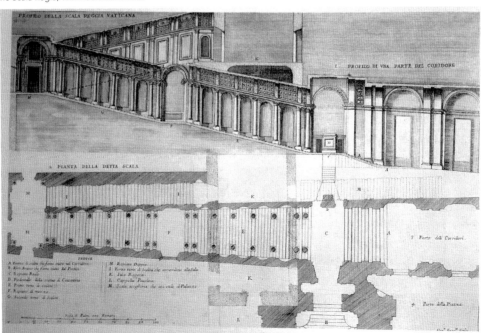

Figure 8.4 This is the exterior of the Château de Vaux-le-Vicomte, a prime and influential example of 17th-century French Baroque residential architecture. The house and garden were built 1658–1661, for Nicholas Fouquet, superintendent of finances for Louis XIV. Fouquet hired an architect, Louis Le Vau, a painter-decorator, Charles Le Brun, to do the interiors, and André Le Nôtre, a landscape designer, to work on this large project under his direction. It would be the first time these three disciplines would be used together and they created "The Louis XIV style." At the inauguration of the house in 1661 he had his friend and playwright Molière perform a fête to honor and impress the King. Unfortunately things did not go well and Louis was so jealous about the beauty of the château and its extraordinary gardens that he had Fouquet arrested and imprisoned for the rest of his life. He then took much of the things including the orange trees and the three designers and they transformed his palace of Versailles. Royalty and the very wealthy, to dramatically emphasize and reinforce the idea of their power and extended reach, used the symmetrical and extensive gardens disappearing into the distance. Also notice that the house is set in a moat, reminiscent of medieval castles. The James Bond film *Moonraker* was filmed here, as it was the home of the villain Hugo Drax.

CHICUREL Arnaud/Hemis.fr/SuperStock

Figure 8.5 *Left:* The "chambre du roi," the King's Bedroom, at the Chateau Vaux-le-Vicomte, designed by Charles Le Brun. The most fashionable in Baroque décor surrounds this bed that was designed as a miniature stage with a proscenium. In this palace and at Versailles Louis XIV configured his bedroom to accommodate his performances of rising in the morning and retiring in the evening. To be invited to these staged productions was considered an honor by his courtiers.

Erich Lessing/Art Resource, NY

Figure 8.6 *Below:* This is the church St. Andrea al Quirinal, Rome, 1658–1670, that Bernini designed for the Jesuits. Bernini's small but exquisite church is covered with animated sculptures and focus on a sun-lit altar behind a proscenium-like pedimented frame. Its dramatic lighting, oval plan, and integration of sculpture are his hallmark and major contribution to the Baroque style. Notice the subtle use of color and complex treatment of textures.

Photoservice Electa/Universal Images Group/SuperStock

Figure 8.7 *Left:* The exterior street façade of St. Andrea al Quirinal, Rome. The semi-circular walls on each side of the façade recall the curved arcades that surround the piazza of St. Peter's Basilica. The broken pediment with sculpture, the curved steps, the Baroque buttresses, and the large pilasters with the most complex capital—the Composite Order—are pure Baroque features.

Bridgeman Images

Figure 8.8 *Below:* The front façade of Syracuse's Duomo, Sicily, Italy, is typical of the European Baroque churches with its large complex columns, the strong vertical thrust, huge central doorway, and the use of freestanding sculpture. With regional variations this style extended across Europe and to the Spanish and Portuguese colonies in Central and South America.

ToolX/iStock

Figure 8.9 This is the south façade of Syracuse's Duomo, showing the integration of the massive Doric columns, with the Norman and Baroque features. Both the exterior and interior retain elements from all the many different periods in the life of this church.

Author photo

* Syracuse's Duomo has a unique place in religious architecture. It was started as a pre-Greek Ionic Temple by the native Sicilians and then later the Greeks transformed it into a Doric Temple to Athena in the 5th century BCE. With the advent of Christianity it became the first Christian Church in the West after Antioch. Then came the Byzantine conquerors, who converted it into a mosque and added their own architectural elements; next came the Normans, who added a stark Norman façade that was destroyed in the earthquake of 1693, but not the huge Doric columns. Then came the Spanish, who incorporated all of these elements and enveloped it in all this lavish Baroque architecture built from 1728 to 1753; and miraculously unlike many other churches in Sicily, it was not destroyed by the Americans during WWII. There are churches that have undergone similar reincarnations, but very few have such a rich history and varied architectural heritage that still survive. For a more complete history and photos see the wiki website: "Cathedrals of Syracusa," translate to English.

* The Baroque style was characterized by the use of Renaissance forms that were enlarged, multiplied, and articulated in a forceful manner. Diagonals and asymmetry were used to upset linearity of Classical forms.

* Baroque artistic subjects were formal, religious, Classical, monarchic, and dramatic as a result of Church and royal patronage. Michelangelo's frescos in the Sistine Chapel in the Pope's Palace are a pre-eminent example of the Baroque painting techniques of chiaroscuro and contrapunto. See Figures 8.1, 8.6, and 8.7.

* Český Krumlov Castle in the Czech Republic has a Baroque theater (1680–82) with its original stage machinery and many period sets, props, and costumes.

* Enormous, sprawling geometrically laid out gardens associated with massive palaces proclaimed the omnipotence of kings and symbolized their dominance of the physical world. These gardens, like architecture, décor, costume, and music, were raised to an exaggerated theatrical level. This and the Baroque ideal of controlling and manipulating Nature were epitomized by Louis XIV and Versailles. See Figure 8.4 as an example.

* The English, French, and Northern European Baroque was more linear, Classical, rational, and ordered than the Italian and German Baroque, which was more exuberant and passionate. Both emphasized massive size and scale.

How They Decorated

* Royal and Church architecture was characterized by heavy oval, twisted forms seen in highly dramatized lighting. It featured a profusion of carved and gilded, twisted, Classical cornices and ornament. Paintings and sculpture were also applied to ceilings that were divided into figuratively painted panels. See Figures 8.1, 8.2, 8.5, 8.6, 8.7, 8.8, 8.10, 8.11, 8.12, 8.14, and 8.15.

Figure 8.10 This is a Baroque Pageant Cart, which is the forerunner of our parade floats. This shows a festival celebration for Fernando VI, King of Spain in 1747. The Royal court members are standing on the arcaded balcony, and clergy and commoners are on the roof. The display is of allegorical figures and the portraits of the King and Queen are in the red throne- like structure, decorated with puttis. Notice the elegant period costumes, the men on horseback are wearing justacorps and tricorn hats. The 2011 movie *Pirates of the Caribbean: On Stranger Tide* has a fictionalized Fernando VI.

Album/Art Resource, NY

Figure 8.11 The interior of the Farnese Theater, Parma, Italy. This is believed to be the first theater to use a permanent proscenium arch and served as a model for other European theaters. It was started in 1618 and opened in 1628. It is a rectangular wooden structure with an elongated oval performing area surrounded by very steeply raked seats like the Roman stadiums. Above the benches were two rows of Palladian arches topped by a small gallery with statues, which is very similar to Teatro Olympico (7.10). The stage area was designed for perspective scenery using the wing and drop system. The square wooden proscenium was decorated with statues set into niches.

Robert Harding Picture Library/Superstock

Figure 8.12 This copper engraving is of Molière's comedy *Le Malade Imaginaire* (The Imaginary Invalid), from 1676, and he is seated at the center of the stage. Notice the lighting is by candled chandeliers that were lit and raised at the beginning of each performance. Like the Farnese the proscenium is classically styled with a pediment and Classical statues, but with a wider opening. The stage is raised to accommodate stage machinery and a full orchestra is in front of it to provide incidental music. This illustration treats the setting as a stage set in itself with the curtain raised and the audience seated in the foreground. The comedy premiered in 1673 with Molière playing the title role and he died after the fourth performance.

akg-images

Figure 8.13 This is the actual set design rendering for *Atys* by Jean-Baptiste Lully (1632–1687), oil painting on canvas. *Atys* was a tragic opera based on Ovid's *Fasti* and was one of Louis XIV's favorites. This view shows a perspective wing and drop set, in which each layer of scenery would have been painted on a separate piece of fabric. Sophisticated flying mechanics carried scenic elements and also allowed singers to be flown in at the climax, all contributing to a sense of magical realism.

Giraudon/Bridgeman Images

* Color and light were dramatically contrasted and surfaces were richly textured. The colors used were rich, dark, and saturated blues, maroons, browns, and golds; they were rendered in the chiaroscuro style, which emphasized extreme contrasts of light and shade. See Figures 8.13 and 8.14.

* Furniture of this period was characterized by large dark shapes. Casework furniture was heavy and square and used turned legs and frequently diagonal bracing. Chairs and tables used it as well as the simpler square braces. It used contrasting veneers for marquetry with different materials; especially popular were tortoise shell, metals, and different colored woods like ebony, oak, and walnut. See Figures 8.19 and 8.20.

* Furniture and décor in addition to the above later used curved and heavily carved and decorated gilded pieces and some things even in solid silver.

* Louis considered his clothes, furnishings, and palaces an expression of his wealth and also a symbol of his Divine power. He frequently had an "L," fleurs-de-lis, and sunburst on his furniture and other décor. See Figure 8.5 where a sunburst is woven into the rug.

* He started several furniture factories around Paris that produced furniture for him and his court and he extended the practice of competition of décor and furniture as he did for their dress.

Figure 8.14 The Interior of an Italian theater, c. 1700–1750. This view shows a perspective stage setting that during this period was painted on canvas and by the end of the century on rigid board. The stage is also high to allow for the scene changing crew and machinery located under the floor. Notice that now that this theater is in Italy the Italian Baroque style of the proscenium is more massive and elaborated.

National Gallery, London/Art Resource, NY

Figure 8.15 This is a façade at the Oberschleissheim, New Palace in Munich, built 1701–1719, showing French windows. They are casement windows that open outward from the window jambs. They frequently had a radiating pattern of panes above them in a semi-circular transom. They were invented earlier in this period, but they became extremely popular after their use at Versailles.

xyno/iStock

* A new type of furniture was the commode introduced in France about 1700 as a low chest with drawers and often veneered. It was immediately popular and the word was applied to different pieces of furniture like desks, lowboys, and tables as well as chests and its shapes also changed with the prevailing styles. After the Neoclassical period, in the US it frequently meant a toilet.

* This period saw the continued refinement of perspective techniques and the development of perspective tricks and false perspective techniques in painting. Their use expanded to include architecture and theater sets as well as easel painting. See Figures 8.1, 8.2, 8.12, 8.13, and 8.14.

* Theater forms and machinery were standardized and codified. The dominance of the proscenium configuration was established throughout Europe. The new "wing and drop" scenery shifted by winches was located under tracked stages and flying machinery was adapted from rope and winch naval technology all of which became universal. See Figures 8.11, 8.12, 8.13, and 8.14.

* Particularly in the Low Countries art was no longer just for the Church and monarchs, but was everywhere, in public buildings and private homes. The subject matter was also far broader not just religious, but included portraiture, still lives, history, genre, and mythological painting, as well as all of the natural sciences.

Building and Décor Keywords

chiaroscuro (key-ara-SCURA) – The treatment of contrasted light and shade in painting and drawing. Literally from the Italian and Latin light and dark. See Figure 8.13.

contrapunto – This refers to the dramatic, twisted shapes of much Baroque painting, sculpture, and architecture. Its sister word is counterpoint and is a major component of Baroque music.

axial planning – The rectilinear and symmetrical layout of a building or group of buildings and gardens along a single axis that implied a processional pathway. This type of plan became typical of the great palaces and churches of the Baroque style. See Figure 8.4.

baldachin (BAL-da-kin) – This was an ornamental canopy over an altar; usually held up on columns.

fête galante – An elegant outdoor entertainment often in a garden setting that was accompanied by dancing, music, song, and costumed guests and performers. See Figure 9.12.

french window or door – A pair of glass window or door casements hinged at the jambs that could open inwards or outwards. Often they were surmounted by an arched window. See Figure 8.15.

boiserie (BWOIZ-a-ree) – Usually carved interior wood paneling that went from floor to ceiling. In the Baroque period it was stained dark and painted in pastel colors during the Rococo. See Figures 8.5, 8.14, 9.5, and 19.11. See YouTube video: *Hôtel Violette—The Making of a French Salon in the Rococo Style with Boiserie*.

tall case clock – This was a full-length standing clock with pendulum and weights, which was oftentimes called a "grandfather" clock. This was a new 17th-century innovation and Louis XIV had one specially built at Versailles in about 1670, that showed hours, minutes, and seconds.

broken pediment – A pediment split apart at its apex and/or at the center of its base. Frequently it was decorated with an urn, sculpture, or cartouche in the break and often a feature of furniture decoration. See Figures 8.6, 8.7, 8.8, 10.5, and 10.16.

The Baroque Clothing and Costume World

How They Dressed

Figure 8.16 Peter Paul Rubens' self-portrait with his first wife Isabella Brandt in the honeysuckle bower, c. 1609. She is shown wearing the Northern European fashion with a conical hat, lace ruff and cuffs, and exquisitely embroidered rigid stomacher. Because it is early in this period, he is wearing a more Renaissance doublet, a flat lace collar, and orange hose with fashionable open-sided shoes, and also a conical hat. Reubens was one of the most famous and accomplished of the Northern Baroque painters. He is particularly noted for his voluptuous women.

Alte Pinakothek, Munich, Germany/Giraudon/Bridgeman Images

* Baroque costume abandoned Renaissance lightness and symmetry and became highly structured, heavy, and dark. It adopted saturated colors and abundant Classical details. "Slash and puff" and separate tie-on garment parts were abandoned. See Figure 8.16 and many of the "Dark" films sited.

* The French nobility developed an obsession with fashion and ornament under Louis XIV. Men vied with women to invent new fashions. One of the ways Louis controlled the aristocracy was by encouraging fashion competition among the nobles.

* Long-flowing wigs worn down over the shoulders for both men and women in natural colors became fashionable after Louis XIII lost his hair and adopted a wig. Court fashion always followed the king and queen. See Figure 8.19 and the film *The Draughtsman's Contract* (1982).

* Late Baroque costume became highly ornamented with jewels, ribbons, bows, lace, feathers, and heavy make-up for both sexes. Men and women wore decorated high-heeled shoes and adopted canes, fans, parasols, purses, and other artificial accessories. See the films: *Tous Les Matins du Monde* (1991) and *Cyrano* (1990).

Figures 8.17 and 8.18 Peasant woman and peasant man, France, 17th century. Prints by Jean de Saint-Jean in Georges Duplessis's book *Historical Costumes of the 16th, 17th, and 18th Centuries*, 1867. These clothes would have been simpler variations of more fashionable clothing and during this period peasants were clearly defined by regional variations. She is wearing an apron over her dress, which also has a stomacher and a large lace collar around her shoulders and soft cap. He is also wearing a less formal justacorps and tongued shoes, cravat and wide-brimmed hat, and notice his long hair without a wig.

Album/Florilegius/SuperStock

Figure 8.19 Louis XIV and his courtiers playing billiards at Versailles c. 1694. This is an early European version of billiards, which was played more like table croquet using a curved stick and small hoops. They are all wearing a form of the justacorps with wide cuffs, and the newly introduced style of neckware, the cravat, which could be tied in various ways, long hair, and high-tongued leather-heeled shoes. Louis is also wearing a large fashionable sash and a baldrick across his chest usually for holding a sword and also the new tricorn hat. Although the table is delicate it is representative for its rectangular shape and the "stringers"—the railings at its base.

Grafissimo/iStock

Figure 8.20 *Lady at her Toilette*, 1660, oil on canvas by Gerard ter Borch (1617–1681). This is a candid view of a lady and her maid and young boy, dressing in front of a mirror. She is wearing a low-cut stomacher over a white satin skirt with elaborate gold trim. She has a narrow mantilla around her shoulders that ties around her waist and the maid would be fastening it behind her with loop; it usually had long tails. The young boy is dressed as a page with fancy trunk hose with rosettes at his knees, and heeled leather "duckbilled" shoes with satin bows. He is wearing a very short doublet over a white shirt; black and white striped fabric was very fashionable at the time. Also notice the typical period hairstyles for men and women of long ringlets. Notice the architectural and furniture décor, which uses some significant Baroque features, such as the diagonal bracing of the turned legs on the substantial table and heavy square straight lines of the chair, both in dark wood that they preferred. Oriental carpets were also popular and used to cover tables like this. In the background is a canopied bed.

Detroit Institute of Arts/Bridgeman Images

Figure 8.21 *Cavaliers in a City Square*, pen and brown ink drawing by Jean de Saint-Igny (c. 1600–1647), a 17th-century French painter, designer, and engraver. In the center is a soldier wearing a doublet with a pointed hem, long pants, and bucket-topped boots. The man next to him on the left is wearing patterned onion-shaped trunk hose with a doublet and short cape and with stockings tied at the knees. The others are wearing asymmetrical style clothing that is characteristic of the Baroque "Cavalier style," which included their knee-length breeches over hose, fancy shoes, and large plumed hats and swords.

The Metropolitan Museum of Art. Image source: Art Resource, NY

* Collars were popular for both sexes and were used as a conspicuous display of wealth. Intricate ones for ladies were made of delicate wired and stiffened lace and were raised behind the neck. Other versions for men and women were large flat, lace or linen collars that could be plain, pointed, scalloped, embroidered or edged with lace. See Figure 8.16.

* By the 1670s the *mantua* was gaining popularity and became the principal female dress. This one-piece full long gown with ruffled elbow-length sleeves was worn over a chemise, a bodice-like corset, and a petticoat and was often swept up behind. It would be adapted in numerous ways and continued until the end of the 18th century. See Figure 9.8.

* Women's costume developed a separate boned bodice that was pointed at the waist, called a stomacher. This tailored bodice overlapped a skirt and was worn over multiple underskirts and a structured farthingale. See Figures 8.16, 8.17, and 8.20.

* Men's doublets become shorter, featured a waist, and were worn over a vest and shirt with a cravat and knee-length pants, which were worn over hose. See Figures 8.16, 8.20, and 8.21.

* Later in the period, the doublet developed into the justacorps when the lower panels were lengthened and the waist was eliminated. They started long and then got shorter toward the end of the Baroque period. See Figures 8.18 and 8.19.

* The "Cavalier style" of dress was worn by the supporters of Charles I during the period of the English Civil War and consisted of a military sword and high bucket-topped leather boots with spurs worn over different styles and colors of trunk hose. An asymmetrical cape and long hair became popular for young men, whether in the military or not; the outfit was often completed with a large soft floppy hat with feathers. Initially it was worn by the Cavaliers but became fashionable with nobles and the wealthy throughout Europe for most of the century. See Figure 8.21.

* Northern Protestants, Puritans, and the American colonists abandoned Baroque costume frills and decoration for a more restrained look, but the line was still bulky and sober with dark colors for men and women. This included replacing the ornamental lace collars with a plain white, broad, flat split collar at the neck. Men also wore high boots or simple shoes with a buckle and a tall, wide-brimmed hat. See Figure 8.18 and see the film *The New World* (2005).

* Rubens defined Baroque femininity and Rembrandt defined Baroque masculinity.

Clothing and Costume Keywords

Baroque (bar-OAK) – European clothing of the 17th and early 18th century that abandoned Gothic and Renaissance tailoring in favor of highly structured separate boned bodice and a structured skirt for women and the development of the justacorps, wigs, and high-heeled shoes for men.

doublet – This developed in the Middle Ages from a padded "double" garment worn under armor to a short, sometimes padded, men's coat worn from the 14th century to 1680s. See Figures 8.16, 8.20, and 8.21, and Figures 7.17 and 7.18.

justacorps (JUST-a-core) – A men's long coat that was flared below the waist, with long sleeves. It also had exaggerated buttons, pockets, and pocket flaps. It was worn buttoned closed and knee-length during the Baroque period, and three-quarter length and open during the following Rococo period. See Figures 8.10, 8.18, and 8.19.

pantaloons – These were a loose, ankle-length form of trousers popular in England in the 1660s and would evolve into long tight breeches in the 19th century. See Figure 10.18. Pantalone was a buffoon character in Commedia dell'arte and later pantomime shows.

trunk hose – These came in a number of different configurations, but the common ones were a short puffed, onion, or pear shape worn over regular hose. See Figures 8.16, 8.20, and 8.21, and Figures 7.17 and 7.18.

breeches – Men's half-length pants worn gathered under the knee and on top of the hose. See Figure 8.21.

cavalier boots, bucket-topped boots – These were a soft folded-over leather boot popular with the Cavaliers, and also in Dumas's novel, *The Three Musketeers* and Perrault's 1697 fairy tale, *Puss in Boots*. They were popular in Europe between about 1500 and 1700. See Figure 8.21.

boned bodice – A stiff, tight-fitting women's upper garment supported by thin bone strips to create a cone-shaped waist and flat-chested bodice. See Figure 8.16 and 8.20.

stomacher – A stiff, decorative triangular panel that was pinned to the front of a woman's bodice in the Baroque period. It hid the structure of the boned bodice underneath. See Figures 8.16, 8.17, and 8.20 and Figures 7.16 and 7.17.

virago sleeves – This was a style of women's sleeves that had a double puff tied with ribbons above the elbows.

mule – An open-backed, high-heeled slip-on shoe worn by men and women.

falling band – The linen or lace collar that replaced the ruff that went around the neck and lay on the shoulders, which could be very plain or highly elaborated. See Figure 8.16.

periwig – This was a long, curly stylized wig worn by men and women in an assortment of natural colors. See Figure 8.19.

gorget (GORE-jet) – This was a small, decorative armor plate worn around the neck. It was worn in formal and social situations with dress clothing to indicate military rank.

muff – This was a winter accessory popular with men and women to keep the hands warm; and usually it was made of fur. See Figure 11.8, *Morning, Noon and Night*.

tricorn – A round crowned, wide-brimmed men's hat with the brim lifted and pinned to the crown at three equal points producing three "corns" (corners) or points. It was developed during the late Baroque and worn into the Rococo and Neoclassical periods. See Figures 8.10, 8.19, and Figure 9.11, *The Beggar's Opera*.

CHAPTER NINE

Rococo: 1720–1760

Figure 9.1 *Declaration of Love*, 1731, Jean-François de Troy (1679–1752). A romantic drama in up-to-date fashions in a fanciful landscape. The latest fashion included the Watteau pleat, which can be seen prominently displayed. This painting typifies the new relaxed, secular spirit of the Rococo period, which lightens the palette and abandons religious and noble subject matter to concentrate on nature and romantic love.

Bridgeman Images

A Little Background

This style movement was relatively limited in its reach as compared with past style trends but its impact on the visual, artistic, and intellectual landscape was significant because it was popular with the intellectuals who were promoting Enlightenment ideas. Primarily a leisure style of the aristocracy, it was intimate and personal in scale. The Rococo visual style became associated with the new, liberal, and secular political ideas popular with the European and American rationalists and the political revolutions they fostered. The visual style was often seen as a frivolous one, as it focused on the informal, the natural, and the transient. It was not primarily an architectural style, but delighted in outrageous displays of clothing and interior décor. And yet it suggested a freedom from past dogma that was directly connected to the development of modern theatrical and dramatic writing styles and to the liberating influences of rationalism on the arts.

The name Rococo derived from the word rock, which it used as well as shells and other natural shapes in both flat and raised designs in their interiors. The subject matter of their designs was secular, pastoral, exotic, and intimate. Rococo and Neoclassicism overlapped one another toward mid-century.

Who They Were

* The rise of secularism during the period of Enlightenment ended Baroque seriousness and religiosity and initiated Rococo frivolity. The Rococo was an upper class artistic movement, but elements of the style were reflected in the manners and dress of some middle class citizens. It did not affect lower social orders. It was popular in France, Germany, the Austro-Hungarian Empire, and Italy and was embraced by the nobility of those countries. England and America rejected the Rococo's superficiality and excesses of style; and Americans associated it with the corruption of European royal courts.

* The period was also characterized by the rise of mass communication, like the introduction of newspapers, magazines, and handbills that created a market for news, gossip, and fashion.

* The rise of the middle class and commercialism reduced the powers of the Catholic and Protestant churches and royal courts later in the period.

* Scientific and art academies and societies, museums, and libraries were founded and spread throughout Europe and the eastern colonial American cities, which increased secular knowledge and ideas.

* The Rococo initiated the great age of classical music, opera, and the perfection of the modern orchestra.

* Theatrical stage techniques and machinery also developed with new innovations like scrims, transparencies, and translucencies. Stage lighting also had new special effects—such as lightning, smoke and fog, colored lights and the ability to raise and dim lighting, but all still used candles.

* Theatrical costumes were often heightened versions of contemporary fashion. For classical plays most sets and costumes were of contemporary design using grand imaginary locations favoring Classical scenes and subjects. Playwrights like Gay, Congreve, and Sheridan who were dealing with satire, humor or contemporary subject matter used less imposing scenery and frequently used one or two prescribed locales like the prison, tavern, or bedroom from stock scenery that could be used for more than one play.

* These films about this period have good images for sets and costumes: *Amadeus* (1984,* this film won Academy Awards for Art Direction and costumes and was adapted from Shaffer's 1974 play), *Marie Antoinette* (1938 and 2006)*, *Farewell My Queen* (2013), *Dangerous Liaisons* (1988)*, and *Belle* (2013)*.

Background image: akg-images/Erik Bohr

* The rising prominence and independence of women artists continued in this period. They were noteworthy in all the arts but especially in singing and painting.

* Rococo playwrights: Congreve, Wycherley, Sheridan, Racine, and Corneille.

* Rococo composers: Gluck, Haydn, Mozart, and Salieri.

* Novelists: Fielding, *Tom Jones*—also a 1963 movie;* Swift, *Gulliver's Travels*—also a 1977 movie;* and Voltaire, *Candide*—several adaptations including Leonard Bernstein's 1956 operetta, directed by Tyrone Guthrie with sets Oliver Smith and costumes Irene Sharaff; and 1973 revival, which won Tonys for Eugene and Fanne Lee's sets and costumes.

* Painters: Watteau, Boucher, Fragonard in France; Angelica Kaufman, Gainsborough, and Hogarth in England; Gian Battista Tiepolo—Italian, but also worked in Spain and Germany.

* Architects: Johan Balthazar Neumann, Germain Boffrand, and Francoise Cuvilliers.

The Rococo Material World

Figure 9.2 Main staircase in the Würzburg Residenz, Würzburg, Germany. The massive quadratura ceiling of the main hall is decorated by a single giant fresco by Giovanni Batista Tiepolo and his son, Dominico, and was painted in 1752–1753. These single-ceiling compositions were an important stylistic feature of this period. The Quadratura ceiling used forced perspective, foreshortening, and illusionistic painting techniques. This shows the ceiling painting with its foreshortened figures, representing the four continents, and painted architecture looking up to the painted open sky and then joining the real three-dimensional architecture underneath. In the Baroque and Rococo period, the staircase gained importance as part of a formal reception room. The staircase of the Würzburg residence spans its unsupported trough vault without pillars and is an outstanding piece of construction as well as painting.

Igor Plotnikov/Shutterstock.com

What They Made

Figure 9.3 Würzburg Residenz, Würzburg, Germany. The chief architect on this enormous palace project was J.B. Neumann, who oversaw an international array of other architects, designers, painters, and specialized craftsmen. The building was started in 1720 and the exterior was completed in 1744. The highly fanciful entablature and window treatments typify Rococo exteriors. The interior was not completed until 1780 and so incorporated Neoclassical elements as well.

akg-images/Bildarchiv Monheim Gmbh

* Although primarily an interior style there were architectural examples of Rococo exteriors as seen in the Würzburg Palace. Exteriors, particularly in larger and more formal buildings, retained Classical features, but what set the style apart was the new combination of it and the use of lighter, more graceful, and organically derived animal and vegetative forms for embellishment. See Figure 9.2.

* The Rococo interior style was characterized by secular wit and humor, and a rejection of Baroque seriousness and religiosity and the use of brighter and pastel colors as seen in these ceiling paintings. See Figures 9.2 and 9.4.

* Asymmetry continued to be a major feature of surface design and sculptural décor and decorative arts. See Figures 9.2, 9.4, and 9.7.

* Increasingly popular painted and gilded stucco wall decorations emphasized free-form compositions with few Classical references. See Figure 9.7.

* Ceilings in this period were notable for a large, single unified composition. Prior to this innovation, from the Renaissance through the Baroque, the ceiling decorations were always made up of a number of compartmentalized spaces, which used smaller, multiple images. In the Rococo the scenes were allegorical and used ornate plasterwork combined with painting. The artists went to great lengths to blur the line between the ceiling and the wall. The epitome of this technique was achieved by Tiepolo and his son. See Figures 9.2 and 9.4.

* In addition to these large palaces with their extensive formal gardens, they also incorporated smaller buildings like the hunting lodge and the Hameau de la Reine and the Petit Trianon at Versailles, and smaller gardens designed as settings for artistic and amorous activity with an emphasis on idealized nature. See Figure 9.5.and http://www.pbs.org/marieantoinette/life/hameau.html

How They Decorated

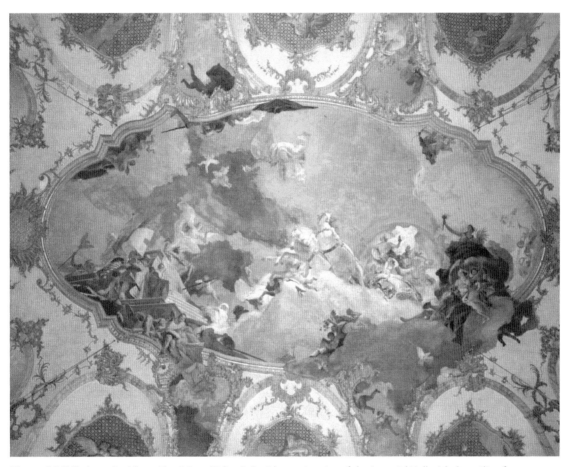

Figure 9.4 Würzburg Residenz, The Prince Bishop's Residence. Interior of the Imperial Hall with the ceiling fresco *Apollo Leads Barbarossa's Bride to his Altar* also by Tiepolo. In ceiling paintings like this all Classical rigor and accuracy of the imagery is abandoned to a free-flowing lyricism. The gold and white dimensional moldings dissolve into the painted ones and the painted perspective invites the eye upwards to the painted open sky. Notice that the infill in the golden ovals uses the decorative trellis-work.

akg-images/Erik Bohr

* Colors become lighter and they used pastels and sunlit shades. Baroque darkness and saturated colors were abandoned. See Figures 9.1, 9.2, 9.4, 9.5, 9.6, 9.7, and 9.12.

* Interior designs often reflected influences of Chinese, Japanese, and Turkish styles because of their increased contact with them. This created a "Turkish" fad for anything Eastern or exotic.

* This would be the first wave of "Orientalism" in architecture, décor, and the decorative arts, particularly the importing of "china." This was true in the British American colonies as well as Europe; after the American Revolution they would start their own "China Trade" (1783–1844). See Figure 9.7.

Figure 9.5 The Hall of Mirrors in the Amaliaburg hunting lodge at the Nymphenburg Palace, Munich, Germany. This is near the palace of the Holy Roman Emperor Charles VII and his wife Maria Amalia of Austria. This small building is one of the most complete examples of Rococo interiors. All Classical references are abandoned in favor of floral, garden, and hunting motifs. See more pictures on the Internet and videos on YouTube.

dieKleinert/SuperStock

Figure 9.6 Louis XV–style (c. 1750) gilt wood chair with an Aubusson tapestry upholstery. The Rococo transforms furniture from Baroque massiveness to a delicate elegance. All the elements flow together organically and gilt is used profusely. For the first time upholstery was using complete scenic images, and frequently they were pastoral themes using needlepoint, tapestries or printed fabrics like chintz. An example is toile that was originally produced in Ireland in the mid-18th century and became popular with the aristocracy in Britain and France and also colonial North America.

De Agostini Picture Library/C. Postel/Bridgeman Images

Figure 9.7 This gilded heavily ornamented carved wood and marble console table is very representative of Rococo style with its lightweight curvilinear construction and also subtle use of the insertion of the trellis motifs and abandonment of Classical references in linear forms and decoration. It is pictured with a Chinese-style vase that shows the new popular use of Chinese objects from "The China trade." The darker blue in the vase augments the pastel blue of the wall, which also features a typical example of their use of gold and white relief decoration using asymmetrical curves and playful suggestions of vegetative forms.

* Furniture and decorative objects, including mirrors, bric-a-brac, porcelain vases, and figurines became new status symbols. See Figure 9.7.

* European porcelain and china factories were also started and prospered at this time making fine quality utilitarian dinnerware and decorative objects, several notable companies were Royal Copenhagen (Flora Danica) in Denmark, Sèvres and Limoge in France, Meissen and Dresden in Germany, and Wedgewood, Spode, Coalport, and Minton in England. The light colors and subject matter of the Rococo style lent itself to their designs. Many of them are still in business today and have both their old and new current designs available.

* There was a rejection of Classical imagery in favor of natural, organic forms, often in themed and free-form compositions. Rococo style stressed more intimate interior spaces, secular, and romantic activities. In addition it glorified the joys and beauty of the natural world in pastoral and everyday scenes. See Figures 9.1 and 9.12.

* The "English style" of garden design was introduced later in this period and replaced the older axial designs with more naturalistic, free-flowing compositions. This garden style became the rage and quickly spread throughout Europe and the American colonies before and after the Revolution.

* Trellis-work and garden and plant references like vines and flowers were introduced into decoration, decorative objects, and clothing. For trellis-work see Figure 9.4, the orange infill in the gold arches in the ceiling, and also in the table, Figure 9.7, and for floral fabrics see Figures 9.8 and 9.10.

* The new refinement of watercolor pigments led to the improvement of watercolor painting and plein-air painting techniques, which continued the personalization of art by allowing even amateur artists to paint spontaneously and directly from nature.

* The Grand Tour of Europe was required and was considered part of the education of wealthy young men and women. They were encouraged to draw, paint, and write about their impressions of foreign lands and cultures and also to rediscover their Classical heritage. Prior to cameras they painted and wrote about these places so that they could share them with family and friends when

they returned. These tours could last for several months or several years and were similar to our "gap years." See http://www.getty.edu/art/exhibitions/grand_tour/index.html

* The Grand Tour also opened up a huge market for artists, print dealers, and buyers to purchase prints and other objects especially of the Classical sites—like souvenirs for them to take home. This also helped set the stage for the next style trend, Neoclassicism.

* Baroque theater forms and technology were refined and perfected. The introduction of sophisticated flying machinery, and scenic and lighting effects created great public demand for ever more spectacular theatrical effects. Rococo designs were still created by painters in the Classical style but featured freer interpretations in stage effects and lighting. Sophisticated lighting and projection effects were pioneered using candles, mirrors, and colored filters. See Figure 9.11.

Building and Décor Keywords

residenz – These were the enormous formal palaces of royalty, nobility, and Prince Bishops in Austria and Germany. See Figures 9.2, 9.3, and 9.4.

trelliage (TREL-ee -ahge) – Originally these were garden structures made of open, crisscrossed or gridded latticework slats meant for training climbing plants, but also for screening, arbors, and small garden buildings like summerhouses, and follies. This pattern was used as a decorative motif on walls, furniture, china, fabrics, and clothes. See Figure 9.4, in the ceiling the orange infill in the gold arches uses this, and the table in Figure 9.7, and the real trellis in Figures 7.13 and 14.9.

folly – An ornamental architectural structure usually in a garden or park, often a fake ruin or other historical anomaly, which was particularly popular in the 18th century. Wikipedia has some good pictures of them, under this keyword.

boiserie (BWOIZ-a-ree) – Usually carved interior wood paneling that went from floor to ceiling. In the Baroque period it was stained dark and painted in pastel colors during the Rococo. See Figures 8.5, 8.14, and 9.5 and 19.11. See YouTube video: *Hôtel Violette—The Making of a French Salon in the Rococo Style with Boiserie*. See https://www.youtube.com/watch?v=mPxUULiahhM

Chippendale – The English and American furniture style of the mid-to-late 18th century named after the English cabinetmaker, Thomas Chippendale. It incorporated Chinese motifs and mixed them with Rococo elements. Chairs featured an open ribbon work splat, a recurved crest rail, and cabriole legs with ball and claw feet derived from popular Chinese designs. Casework furniture also featured cabriole legs and ball and claw feet, as well as broken pediments. This Asian-influenced style was sometimes called Chinese Chippendale. The V&A museum has good examples of English pieces.

chinoiserie (shin-WA-so-ree) – This was the decorative style characterized by motifs and figures borrowed from Chinese and Japanese sources. It was also popular in fabric and plaster wall ornamentation and design. See Figure 11.5, Chinoiserie bed.

tester – The fabric covered canopy over a bed. It could either be supported by bedposts or hung from the ceiling or wall. See Figures 7.13 and 8.5.

chaise lounge (SHAZE- long) – A chair with an upholstered back, arms, and an elongated, upholstered seat resembling a couch with a back only at one end, similar to a Greek *kline* in Chapter 1.

bombé (bom-BAY) – The bulging shape in the front of a piece of casework furniture of the late Baroque and Rococo periods.

console table – A narrow tabletop that projected from a wall and was supported by brackets or legs. See Figure 9.7.

tall case clock – This was a full-length standing clock with pendulum and weights, which was oftentimes called a "grandfather" clock.

fête galante – An elegant outdoor entertainment often in a garden setting that was accompanied by dancing, music, song, and costumed guests and performers. See the pageant cart in Figure 8.10 and the reference in Figure 9.12.

quadratura (kuadra-TURA) – Quadra = four, so four sides of a ceiling. This was a ceiling decoration technique that used perspective, foreshortening, and trompe l'oeil effects to create the illusion of three dimensions. See Figure 9.2.

toile – This was a type of wood block printed fabric that was popular in France, England, and American colonies with the aristocracy. It used hand printed wooden blocks to depict small scenes often of pastoral, mythological, and later Chinese people and settings in a single color—initially red, blue or black on white cotton chintz. Originally it was for upholstery, later other fabrics, wallpapers, and decorative objects.

The Rococo Clothing and Costume World

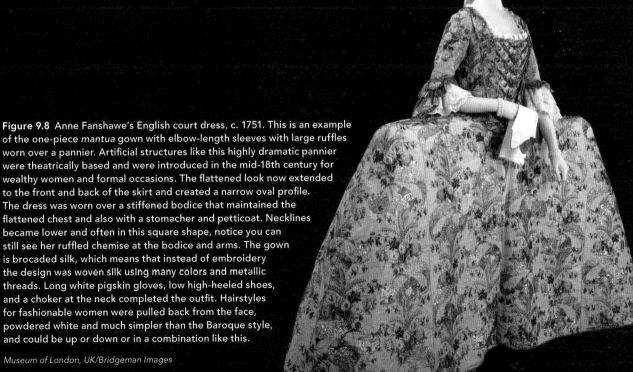

Figure 9.8 Anne Fanshawe's English court dress, c. 1751. This is an example of the one-piece *mantua* gown with elbow-length sleeves with large ruffles worn over a pannier. Artificial structures like this highly dramatic pannier were theatrically based and were introduced in the mid-18th century for wealthy women and formal occasions. The flattened look now extended to the front and back of the skirt and created a narrow oval profile. The dress was worn over a stiffened bodice that maintained the flattened chest and also with a stomacher and petticoat. Necklines became lower and often in this square shape, notice you can still see her ruffled chemise at the bodice and arms. The gown is brocaded silk, which means that instead of embroidery the design was woven silk using many colors and metallic threads. Long white pigskin gloves, low high-heeled shoes, and a choker at the neck completed the outfit. Hairstyles for fashionable women were pulled back from the face, powdered white and much simpler than the Baroque style, and could be up or down or in a combination like this.

Museum of London, UK/Bridgeman Images

How They Dressed

Figure 9.9 *Left: Young Woman Taking a Morning Walk*, from *Gallerie des Modes et Costumes Français*, hand-colored engraving by Nicolas Dupin, published by Esnauts et Rapilly, Paris, 1778. This is a magazine caricature lampooning Rococo ladies fashion. She wears a "milkmaid"-style skirt, showing a poof in the back, which is not a bustle but simply fabric gathered up behind. Hemlines now rose revealing ankles and low high-heeled shoes. Although exaggerated, her elaborate, decorated, and powdered oversized wig and props like her walking stick, pinned flowers, and fan were typical.

Museum of Fine Arts, Boston, Massachusetts, USA/The Elizabeth Day McCormick Collection/Bridgeman Images

Figure 9.10 *Below:* This is a page from a 1782–1805 French cloth sample book. Originally printing on fabric was done by hand using wood blocks, but in 1785 a roller printing machine was invented to print fabrics from metal plates, which allowed faster, more complex colors and patterns to be available; and also they no longer had to rely on the very slow process of decorative embroidery.

DHM/Bridgeman Images

Figure 9.11 William Hogarth, *The Beggar's Opera,* 1731. The scene is in the prison and the painted scenery would still be in the "wing and drop" style for the stonewalls, high barred windows, and metal restraints. The shield at the center top was a decorative element and part of the proscenium, and lower right the two metal handles are for raising a trap door. The play was a ballad opera by John Gay 1728, which used simple melodies and was a spoof of Italian opera and also a satire of English life. Theatrical costume was a heightening of fashionable clothing and hairstyles. Macheath, the hero, is in the red coat and his wife Polly and the other would-be wife, Lucy, are shown pleading with their fathers for his life. They are both wearing stylish *mantua* dresses with softer fabrics, low-cut necklines, elbow-length sleeves with white ruffles, and simple head coverings. Macheath is fashionably dressed wearing breeches, shorter hose, a justacorps over a vest with a stock at the neck, stylish high-tongued shoes with red linings, and a tricorn hat. Lucy's father, the jailer, is not well dressed, but in the old-fashioned Baroque style and poorer clothing. Also notice the variety of men's hairstyles. Honored guests, like the King and his court, sat onstage with the actors.

* Rococo costumes continued the forms of the Baroque but lightened and softened the shapes and colors, while they retained and increased the structure. See Figures 9.1, 9.8, 9.9, 9.11, and 9.12.

* French fashion spread throughout Europe and dominated it for the next 200 years. See Figures 9.1, 9.9, and 9.12.

* This was the beginning of the craze for the "Turkish" style, a word they used to refer to any exotic Eastern locale or Oriental fashions. This style would continue to resurface in later periods.

* Ornamentation and fabric patterns abandoned Classical motifs in favor of the floral and organic. These could be embroidered, printed or woven, like silk brocade. See Figures 9.1, 9.8, and 9.10.

* Fashion was highly influenced by the development of printed fabrics, dyes, and the popularization of cotton that allowed subtle and varied colorations. See Figures 9.9 and 9.10.

* There was an increased emphasis on the importance of comfort, convenience, and relaxation in daily costume, see Figures 9.1, 9.9, and 9.12; but formal wear was still highly structured and standardized, see Figure 9.8.

* Women had a variety of head coverings but with the "milkmaid" look and the romanticizing of the rustic, straw hats and bonnets became fashionable and in the 1760s with the "Turkish craze," a soft turban. See Figure 9.9.

* Men's fashions were also evolving, such as the justacorps into an open coat with a matching or contrasting vest and breeches with stockings. See Figure 9.1 and 9.11.

* Wigs were still worn by women as well as men, but were now powdered white. Wealthy women wore highly ornate and artificial hairstyles in wigs that were popular for social occasions. For court appearances they could be outrageously high and spectacularly decorated even with scenes and ships. See Figures 9.1, 9.8, and 9.9.

* Men's wigs become shorter, also powdered white, and pulled back and gathered at the back with a ribbon, bag or bow or with curls on the sides. The ribbons were usually black and sometimes the long tails were tied in the back and then again in a large bow at the throat. Old-fashioned Baroque hairstyles lingered with older men and stayed long to the shoulder. See Figures 9.1 and 9.11.

* Men and women continued to wear high-heeled shoes and often they were elaborately decorated with rosettes in the 1630s and with stiff bows in the 1670s and later with a variety of buckles. See Figures 9.1, 9.9, and 9.11.

* Men and women also used canes, fans, and other accessories and make-up to compete for attention among the fashionable. See Figures 9.1, 9.8, and 9.9.

Clothing and Costume Keywords

pannier (pan-YEA) – The wide sides and flat front and back of a boned or wired and hooped under skirt. They started out as a padded structure (the word derived from the French "bread," i.e. two loaves of bread), and they became underskirt structures worn by women at the height of the Rococo style. They developed from theatrical costume and were covered with a highly decorated fine fabric. See Figure 9.8.

bum-pad or false rumps – This was extra fabric or a pad worn under a skirt to enlarge the fanny in the back, but it is not a bustle. See Figure 9.9.

sack (or Watteau) gown – This wide, loosely draped women's over garment was open at the front and gathered at the back of the shoulders and flared to the ground in a single large pleat, and was emblematic of the Rococo style. Also derived from theatrical costume, it was of rich material and also worn over panniers. See Figure 9.1.

négligée (neg-li-ZJA) (in French means neglected) – This was a loose, light feminine garment of the Rococo style, which emphasized comfort and allure.

caftan – A full-length decorated Turkish garment that was open at the front and gathered at the back and fashionably worn as part of the "Turkish craze" by men and women.

striped fabric – Introduced to Europe and America from Muslim countries, it was also prominent as part of the "Turkish craze." See Figure 8.20 and 9.10.

fichu (FEE-shu) – A fine linen or cotton women's scarf folded into a triangle and worn around the shoulders that covered the open bodice. Older women wore it for modesty on low-cut dresses. It came in a variety of styles and could be pinned or tucked into the bodice or apron. Peasant women's fichu would have been made of a coarser fabric like muslin. It was a feature for most women during the 18th and 19th centuries. See Figure 9.11.

cravat (cra-VAT) – It started in the 1670s and was worn throughout the 18th century in assorted styles. It was a men's neckwear of narrow white fabric usually of linen and sometimes edged in lace that was wrapped and knotted at the neck in different ways, which is why it appeared differently. The length of the fabric also changed, which was another reason why it looked wider and bulkier. It was sometimes worn over an upturned collar and a thinner version of it was called a stock. It was the forerunner of the necktie. See Figures 9.1 and 9.11, 8.18, 8.19 and Beau Brummell, Figures 10.18 and 10.19.

waistcoat (vest) – These sleeveless garments were introduced in the 17th century and were worn over a shirt and under an overcoat, such as the justacorps and later coats, and still later frock coats. They varied in length and materials and decoration by period. See Figures 9.1 and 9.11 and later chapters for many others as they will be a staple of the men's three-piece suit—coat, vest, pants—that was now evolving.

pompadour – A men's and women's hairstyle where the hair was swept up from the face and worn high on the head. This style will be seen again in several periods, but especially noted by the Gibson Girls in the early 20th century and by Elvis Presley in the 1950s. It was named for the very influential Madame Pompadour, the official royal mistress to Louis XV, famous for her beauty, wit, and her "salons." See Figure 9.9.

Figure 9.12 Jean Antoine Watteau, *Embarkation for Cythera*, 1717, oil on canvas. Watteau is one of the iconic painters of the Rococo, with his lush palette and bucolic scenes often depicting allegories or mythological stories—a never-never land of nymphs and lovers. This scene shows stylish men and women preparing to sail off to the Greek island of Cythera, supposedly the birthplace of Venus, the goddess of sexual love. Her statue can be seen to the far right with the amorous couple next to it. Also notice the cherubs flying off to heaven. After this painting was accepted by the Academy a separate sub-genre was named for it as it depicted a "Fête Galantes" rather than a "history painting."

CHAPTER TEN

Neoclassical: 1750–1820

Figure 10.1 *Portrait of Madame Récamier* in the embodiment of the classic Empire gown is a painting by Baron François Pascal Gérard (1770–1837). She is sitting in a French Empire chair; the generous soft cushions are characteristic of the period as is the sleigh back that is also reminiscent of Roman styles. Gérard was an important and prolific painter during this period and painted history paintings and many portraits of Napoleon's court, the Bourbon monarchy and the aristocracy, as well as important people throughout Europe, all good sources for the designer. He was also well known for his salons. Clothing design made a clean break from the structured and ornate designs of the last period to harken back to Greek elegance and simplicity. Napoleon's admiration of Classical designs was reflected not only in clothing as shown here, but also in architecture, furniture design, and decorative objects.

Bridgeman Images

A Little Background

Almost simultaneous with the frivolous Rococo, the more sober and rational Neoclassical style once again looked back to Classical forms for inspiration. This was the style of art, architecture, and clothing popular throughout Europe and America in the late 18th and early 19th centuries. At this time the style was driven primarily by the excavations at Pompeii, which for the first time revealed evidence of Roman Patrician private life and once again inspired designers and artists to reinterpret their Classical heritage in contemporary terms.

It was characterized by a return to Classical proportion and style but in lower relief and shallower form and retained the lighter color palette of the Rococo.

Who They Were

* Neoclassicism reflected the prominence of new Enlightenment ideas, which regarded man as master of a perfectible world that emphasized doubt, questioning, reason, scientific inquiry, and progress.

* This trend continued the weakening of the Church and royal influence and encouraged the embrace of secularism.

* The American Revolution took place from 1765 to 1783. Unlike many wars, it did not affect architecture, décor or clothing, but did have a profound impact on political and governmental systems and established the first democratically elected representative government.

* During the Rococo period in France there was a growing resentment of the common people to the royalty and the aristocracy, who now controlled most of the wealth, government, and even the Catholic Church. This would eventually lead to the French Revolution from 1789 to 1799 and the end of "The Absolute Monarchy."

* Eventually Napoleon Bonaparte would take control and he established the Napoleonic Empire, which lasted from 1804 to 1815. It would have profound consequences for all aspects of Western civilization that are still with us today. For the designer it is the Neoclassical and Empire period in art, architecture, décor, and costume.

* The growth of liberal, democratic thought after the American and French Revolutions was spurred by the rationalist philosophies of Locke, Rousseau, and Diderot.

* The beginning of Historicism was bolstered by the discovery of Pompeii, and other Roman, Etruscan, Egyptian, and Greek ruins. These discoveries resulted in the expansion of the Grand Tour as a necessary component of higher education for men and women, as a sophisticated person was expected to know the Classics and have an understanding of the Classical foundations of their European world.

* Napoleon adopted design motifs associated with Imperial Rome for his court that influenced art and fashion in the first 20 years of the 19th century. He led or sponsored military and scientific campaigns to appropriate and document Classical art treasures from conquered Italy, Greece, and Egypt.

* Napoleon supported and encouraged the rigorous programs of The École des Beaux-Arts in Paris that taught classically based architecture, painting, sculpture, and the decorative arts. It had produced some of the world's great artists and continued to flourish during the Napoleonic Era.

It was also the founding school of the architecture movement, known as "The Beaux-Arts," that would become prominent in the late 19th century and will be addressed in Chapter 13.

* In the 1780s oil lamps replaced candles as a way of theater lighting. Now they would be used in chandeliers both on stage and in the audience, for foot lights, and on ladders between the wings.

* Artists: Gérard, Isabey, Houdon, Canova, Jacques-Louis David, Greuze, Chardin, Joshua Reynolds, Gainsborough, Zoffany, Angelica Kaufmann, Piranesi, and Ingres.

* Colonial American Painters: Benjamin West, C.W. Peale and his family, Inman, Sully, Stuart, Feke, and Copley.

* Writers: Samuel Johnson, aka Dr. Johnson—*Dictionary*, 1755; BBC 4 did a documentary *Samuel Johnson: The Dictionary Man*, with useful period images; Defoe—*Robinson Crusoe*; and the poet Robert Burns.

* Playwrights: von Goethe, Schiller, Richard Brinsley Sheridan, Sophie Lee, Goldsmith, and Beaumarchais.

* Composers: Mozart, C.P.E. Bach, Beethoven, and Haydn.

* Any of the Jane Austen adaptations would be good research for this period as well as movies about Napoleon and his court.

* These films were about the English colonies at this time: *Last of the Mohicans* (1992), *The Patriot* (2000), *John Adams* (2008); and these are in Europe: *The Madness of King George* (1994), *Jefferson in Paris* (1995), *Casanova* (2005), and *Goya's Ghost* (2006).

The Neoclassical Material World

Figure 10.2 Cheswick House, London, England. This is the English Neoclassic interpretation of Palladio's Villa Capra. Architecture returned to the stable, symmetrical forms based on Greek architecture and design.

Anthony Shaw Photography/Shutterstock.com

What They Made

Figure 10.3 *Left:* View of the Red Velvet Room in Cheswick House. Featured is the Palladian window, a Neoclassical invention; this interpretation and the miniaturization of the Palladian arch became a popular window design and continues until today.

English Heritage Photo Library/Bridgeman Images

Figure 10.4 *Below:* Monticello near Charlottesville, VA, was the plantation of Thomas Jefferson. In his Neoclassical house Jefferson used the principles Palladio described in his *Four Books*, which were about Classical forms that he adapted for his Renaissance architectural designs. Jefferson started construction in 1768, but after serving in France where he saw many Neoclassical buildings, from 1801 to 1809 he remodeled much of the house, which was now more like an Italian villa. The most significant and iconic feature was the addition of the central octagonal dome.

chrispecoraro/iStock

Figure 10.5 Hunter House in Newport, Rhode Island, was built between 1748 and 1754 and is a good example of a colonial Georgian house. The 18th century was Newport's "golden age" as it was an important cosmopolitan shipping and trading city and was also a center of fine craftsmanship for furniture and other decorative arts that rivaled Philadelphia. The north half of Hunter House was constructed in 1756, a second chimney was added and now it was a more formal central hall mansion. This is the front façade; notice there is a broken pediment over the door and the railing on the gambrel roof surrounds a flat platform. This structure is called "a widow's walk" and in coastal houses was used for looking for sailing ships. The sash windows were developed in England in the 17th century and were used in the colonies as they were more resistant to harsher weather than casement windows. They are also large using 12 panes over 12 panes, indicating great wealth, as normally they would be 6 over 6 or even smaller. Notice that there are contemporary storm windows covering the original ones, and also the skylight is new. In the mid-18th century Americans copied the silhouette of English houses but especially in the Northern colonies, were built with wooden clapboards, as wood was cheap, plentiful, and easy to construct in the cold climate rather than brick or stone.

AugustSnow/Alamy

Figure 10.6 The Royal Crescent, Bath, Somerset, England. Built 1767–1775. This is an early example of Georgian architecture and is a series of 30 terraced town houses in which every three columns marked a separate house. This semi-circular curved façade uses the Ionic order topped by a balustrade. House No. 1 now has a museum of Georgian life with period interiors. Jane Austen's *Persuasion* takes place here and it was used in the 2007 TV version and also in the 2008 film *The Duchess*.

ChrisAt/iStock

* Neoclassical art and architecture were based on a revival of Classical and Renaissance models of unity, rationality, clarity, and simplicity but with details presented in much lower relief.

* It emphasized the calm rationality and the appreciation of the ideal form of the Classical period.

* The Georgian Palladian style was a Neoclassical architectural and interior design style in England, America, and Germany that revived the work of Andrea Palladio and often featured a pedimented portico and one or more Palladian windows. See Figures 10.2, 10.3, and 10.4.

* This period brought the settlement, development, and exploitation of the North American colonies. As well as in the New England style wood clapboard house that is shown, in other parts of the colonies other European styles were also used and simplified and interpreted in stone and brick. Brick was more common in the mid-Atlantic and Southern colonies and was often used on wealthier dwellings in cities and large estates, and places like Williamsburg, the University of Virginia, and Tryon Palace, New Bern, NC. See Figures 10.4 and 10.5.

* There is an interesting video on YouTube from a British TV show *Restoration Home—Stoke Hall, Episode Three*.

How They Decorated

* Neoclassical interior design was influenced by the discovery of Roman interiors at Pompeii and Etruscan tombs in northern Italy; it featured low relief plaster moldings and highly painted interior decoration. See Figures 10.7, 10.11, and 10.17.

Figure 10.7 Osterly Park, Middlesex, England. The Neoclassic entry hall by Robert Adam (1728–1792) showed the strict symmetry and restrained color palate that he used and which made it a favorite of Neoclassical designs. Newly discovered examples in Pompeii influenced interior design preference for comparatively flat, classically inspired surface design. Also notice other elements of "the Adam style," such as the ornate plaster ceiling and wall decorations, the pilasters, the niched half-domed fireplace, and the marble floor, which is a reflection of the ceiling pattern. He is also using Classical-style urns and statues and typically long, low upholstered benches.

National Trust Photographic Library/Dennis Gilbert/Bridgeman Images

Figure 10.8 The bedroom of Empress Josephine (1763–1814), Rueil-Malmaison, France. Napoleon's Empress's fanciful and lavish bedroom was based on Roman-style campaign tents, beds, and furniture. Empire furniture and decoration and all of the other Neoclassical architecture and décor elements used Roman features that were based on geometric square, circular, or oval shapes. Also notice the large eagle carving above the bed that Napoleon adopted for his symbol.

Giraudon/Bridgeman Images

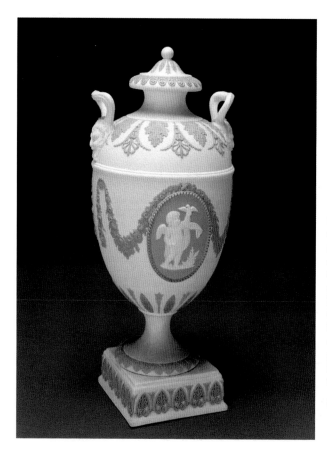

Figure 10.9 This is a three-colored Jasperware urn with putti, designed by the sculptor John Flaxman c. 1780. The use of color and raised decoration are very similar to "the Adam style." The shape is reminiscent of Greek vases and urns and the putti and garlands were Classical Roman images. See Greek (Figure 1.17) and Roman marble relief (Figure 2.17). Josiah Wedgewood, one of the leading china manufacturers in England in the 18th century, produced Jasperware and other china patterns, and they frequently used classically inspired motifs. The company is still in business today.

Private Collection/Photo © Mark Fiennes/Bridgeman Images

Figure 10.10 This is the parlor in the Hunter House (exterior 10.5) and shows good examples of 18th-century American architecture and furnishings in an elegant and refined manner. The painted wood paneling uses simple unadorned geometric shapes, as do the two symmetrically built-in glassed china cupboards with Roman arches. The fireplace surround with Delft tiles and the dark faux-painted marble pilasters is a stylish Georgian touch that adds grandeur to the room. The furniture is all Queen Anne and very representative. On the left there is a side chair with vase-shaped back splat and a small table that could be used for playing cards or serving tea, both with cabriole legs and slipper feet. The imported tea set has very typical Neoclassical shapes. A camelback sofa is behind it and to its right is a wing-backed chair with ball and claw feet that was popular and meant to be comfortable as well as protect from drafts. Next to it is a small tripod piecrust table also with cabriole legs. The portraits are good examples of Colonial American paintings. The fine damask fabrics and the Oriental carpet are other indications of the sophistication and wealth of the owner.

Gavin Ashworth. Photo courtesy of The Preservation Society of Newport County

Figure 10.11 This is the drawing room from the Lansdowne House, London, by Robert Adam (1728–1792) and shows the restrained color palette and low relief plaster decoration that characterized Neoclassical architecture and furniture. The decorations on the flat pilasters and the ceiling derive from Pompeian examples. When the house was remodeled this room and the dining room were removed and are at the Philadelphia Art Museum and Metropolitan Art Museum, New York City. The two large gilt upholstered armchairs in the style of Louis XVI and two fire screens are representative of the period.

Bridgeman Images

Figure 10.12 Writing desk with a lift-top and drawers, c. 1795–1810, from a design by Thomas Sheraton (1751–1806). On the top of the desk is an unusual oval mirror. The inlays are in geometric shapes that are based on examples found in Pompeii. The slender straight legs are an indicator of the Neoclassical style.

De Agostini Picture Library/Bridgeman Images

Figure 10.13 Hepplewhite style shield back side chair, 1794–1799, attributed to Samuel McIntire (1757–1811), Salem, Massachusetts. It is made of mahogany, ebony, ash, birch, and white pine. The straight legs and delicate line identify it as a Neoclassical style chair. The shield back was a common motif on many cabinetmakers' versions of the original Hepplewhite design. The gold design on the front is also typical and is made with brass "buttons."

Image copyright © The Metropolitan Museum of Art. Image source: Art Resource, NY

Figure 10.14 This is a scroll back side chair from the Duncan Phyfe work-shop, c. 1810–1820. The profiles of Phyfe's furniture such as the outward curve of the legs are based on Greek furniture designs. The crisscross back is based on a Roman design.

Bridgeman Images

Figure 10.15 These are a pair of Duncan Phyfe side chairs that use elements of the Greek *klismos* chair design, such as the inward curved back and outward curved legs. They also use the Greek lyre that was commonly found on Duncan Phyfe chairs and became his signature decoration.

Collection of the New-York Historical Society, USA/Bridgeman Images

Figure 10.16 American Queen Anne tiger maple highboy, sometimes also called a chest on chest, as the two major components can separate for travel and the legs and crest rail can also come apart. These standing chests were very popular in the 18th century and are an example of casework furniture because of their box-like construction. Notice the crest rail is in a broken pediment design; the two carved shell designs and the cabriole legs are also typical of the Queen Anne style.

Peter Harholdt/SuperStock

Figure 10.17 This is a Neoclassical portable writing desk with an integrated chair by Giovanni Socchi, Florence, Italy, 1807. Fold out furniture was a very popular novelty item and only wealthy people could afford it. The tilted writing surface folds down and then slides into an opening and then the two side pieces come together to make a flat oval table and the chair could slide under as well. The ormolu designs on the chair and the brass animal head feet are also characteristic of the period. Thomas Jefferson had a desk similar to this one. Notice the white on white low relief work on the wall behind.

akg-images/Rabatti–Domingie

* Both English (Regency) and French (Empire) embraced Neoclassicism and were also influenced by the recent archeological discoveries from Egyptian tombs with their relics, which were now being brought to Europe for collectors and the new museums. See Figures 10.2 and 10.6 (Regency) and 10.8 (Empire).

* This period was known as the Great Age of Interiors. The role of carefully designed interiors was applied to settings for both grand salons and in private homes for entertainment. See Figures 10.7, 10.8, 10.10, and 10.11.

* The Neoclassical interior styles like Robert Adam and the furniture styles of Sheraton, Phyfe, and Hepplewhite were picked up by the middle class in England and Colonial America. See Figures 10.7, 10.11, and 10.17 interiors; 10.12, 10.13, 10.14, 10.15, and 10.17 furniture.

* The style retained the pastel and light color schemes of the Rococo but reintroduced Classical imagery and decoration. It firmly abandoned the frivolity and asymmetry of Rococo for the slimmer, cleaner more Classical look of the Neoclassical design. See Figures 10.7, 10.9, 10.11, and 10.17.

* Interior design was characterized by elegantly scaled symmetrical motifs based on Greek and Roman formality and was often carried out in shades of white or off-white integrated with pastel shades. See Figures 10.7, 10.9, 10.11, and 10.17.

* In this period, rooms took on specialized functions of salons, living rooms, libraries, galleries, and bedrooms. See Figures 10.7, 10.8, 10.10, and 10.11.

* The new profession of interior design emerged to facilitate this specialization of interior spaces. For the first time designers gave their names to furniture and décor styles. See Figures 10.7 and 10.11 for Robert Adam interiors and for the individual furniture designers Figures 10.12, 10.13, 10.14, and 10.15.

* web addresses: for Neoclassical and Biedermier furniture and props see 1stdibs.com. French accents.com—17th-century, 18th-century and 19th-century French antiques, has good pictures and library. Google—"Louis XVI Furniture" at Wikipedia.

Building and Décor Keywords

Neoclassical – This was the style of art, architecture, and clothing popular throughout Continental Europe and America in the late 18th and early 19th centuries. It was characterized by a return to Classical proportion and design, but used shallower relief for surface design and retained the lighter color palette of the Rococo. See Figures 10.4, 10.7, 10.9, and 10.11.

Adam – The architectural and interior design style based on the work of Robert Adam and his brothers in England and copied in Colonial America in the late 18th century. It was influenced by Greek and Roman wall surfaces and other interior design elements. It was characterized by clarity of form, the use of subtle, often pastel colors, fine low relief detailing, and unified interior design schemes. See Figures 10.7, 10.9, and 10.11.

Regency – The English Neoclassical furniture, décor, and clothing styles that took place during the Regency period when George III's son, stood in for him (1810–1821), which was roughly equivalent to the Empire style in France. In England the term continued during his reign as George IV and his brother William IV until 1837. See Figures 10.1, 10.3, 10.6, 10.7, 10.9, 10.11, 10.12, 10.13, 10.14, 10.15, 10.17, and 10.18.

Georgian – An English and American architectural and furniture design style analogous to the Neoclassical style in Europe. In England it is often called Regency and later in America Federal or Palladian. It included the work of the American cabinetmaker Duncan Phyfe, and the English

Robert Sheraton and William Hepplewhite. See Figures 10.4, 10.5, 10.10, 10.16, and the individual designers, Figures 10.12, 10.13, 10.14, and 10.15.

Queen Anne – The English and American furniture style of the early to mid-18th century named after the English monarch of that name, who ruled much earlier (1665–1714). It featured chairs with cabriole legs and slipper feet, an elliptical crest rail, and a vase-shaped back splat. Casework furniture, furniture that had frames and drawers, also featured cabriole legs and slipper feet, and flat cornices. See Figures 10.10 and 10.16.

Biedermier – A German interior design and furniture style from the first half of the 19th century whose features are based on the Empire style, but with simpler lines, heavier forms, and contrasts in their toned wooden inlays. There are many websites and images available.

Sheraton – The Neoclassical English and American chair styles based on the designs of the English cabinetmaker, Robert Sheraton, featuring open splat backs in a square or rectangular shape, and sometimes featured urns and used slim, tapered Neoclassical legs. See Figure 10.12.

Hepplewhite – The Neoclassical English and American chair style based on the designs of the English cabinetmaker, William Hepplewhite; featuring open splat backs in a shield or heart shape and slim, straight tapered Neoclassical legs. Splat designs featured ribbon work decoration. See Figure 10.13.

Duncan Phyfe – A Neoclassical American furniture style named after this American cabinetmaker and characterized by legs with graceful outward curves on chairs, tables, and sofas. Seating pieces often had lyre backs, rolled or scroll top rails, and arms echoing Greek furniture lines. See Figures 10.14 and 10.15.

Palladian window – A Neoclassical window in which there are three openings: one larger arched central window that is flanked on both sides with smaller rectangular openings and using pilasters or columns as supports. This is also known as a Palladian Arch and can be a window or doorway. When it is used as a window or door the central one often opens as a French window/door, but the semi-circle light remains fixed. See Figures 10.3 and 8.11.

sash window – It was developed in England in the 17th century and used in the Neoclassic period and continues to be used on contemporary buildings. This new style was characteristic of English and American architecture, but not used in continental Europe. The window opening was fitted with vertically sliding panels (sashes) each containing glass panes. It replaced the older style hinged casement window. In a double-hung sash both parts slide and in a single-hung sash only the bottom half goes up. See Figures 10.4 and 10.5.

valance – This was a decorative fabric cover above a window that hid the drapery attachment.

crest rail – The top, horizontal frame member of a chair back or cabinet, whose shape or size defined its style. See Figures 10.3, 10.13, 10.14, 10.15, 10.16, and 10.17.

splat – This was the decorative vertical wood panel of an open back chair. Its shape and decoration often expressed the style of the chair. See Figures 10.10, 10.13, 10.14, and 10.15.

cabriole leg – This was an S-shaped furniture leg often with the features of an animal leg and based on Classical examples. See Figures 10.3, 10.10, and 10.16.

slipper foot – This was a carved chair or table leg with a foot on a cabriole leg that ended in a flat, pad-like foot. See Figures 10.10, 10.15, and 10.16.

sabre leg – These were the rear legs of an Empire chair that curved out and backwards from the seat, like a Greek chair. See Figures 10.13, 10.14, 10.15, 10.17, and 10.19.

ball and claw foot – Another variation, this was of a carved chair or table leg with a foot on both front cabriole legs that resembled a ball held in the claw of a bird or lion. See Figure 10.10.

Wedgewood – Their most famous china pattern of this Neoclassical period was in "the Adam style" and called Jasperware; it featured a surface decorated with low-relief Classical figures in white bisque on a colored bisque background. It was named for its inventor and manufactured by Josiah Wedgewood in his English factory in 1759. See Figure 10.9.

bisque – The matte chinaware finish made popular by the Wedgewood Chinaware Company of England. See Figure 10.9.

clapboard (CLAB-ord) – Horizontal, overlapping wooden siding typically used on colonial American homes. In England this term was weatherboard. See Figure 10.5.

Meet the Louis

Louis XIII Style (reigned 1610–1643) – **The Early Baroque Style.** This was more elaborate than the Renaissance and introduced more comfortable rectangular upholstered armchairs and the use of complex turnings on chairs, benches, and cabinets.

Louis XIV Style (reigned 1643–1715) – **The Baroque Style.** This featured Baroque curves and classically inspired decoration and ornamentation. It featured heavy, massive furniture in dark or gilded woods and dark upholstery. It introduced the commode, bureau, and more rounded open armchair. See Figures 8.5 and 8.19.

Louis XV Style (reigned 1723–1774) – **The Rococo Style.** This was light, elegant furniture that featured flowers, bright colors, elongated oval and curvilinear forms and metallic trim. It rejected the Classical shapes and favored nature-oriented decoration and light-colored upholstery. See Figures 9.6 and 9.7 and Figure 11.4.

Louis XVI Style (reigned 1774–1792) – **The Neoclassical Style.** This style roughly corresponded with his reign. It also used light, refined furniture, but this time rejected floral shapes, and featured geometric shapes for the chair seats and backs and straight tapered Neoclassical legs and light-colored upholstery. See Figure 10.11.

There are many websites available through antique dealers and museums for reliable information and images, such as French accents.com.

The Neoclassic Clothing and Costume World

How They Dressed

*   The three artists below were the leading painters in 18th-century England and would be a good resource for designers especially for costumes, colors, and fabrics.

*   Sir Joshua Reynolds (1723–1792) was probably the most accomplished and famous portrait painter of Georgian England and was known for his idealized style. He was also one of the founding members of the Royal Academy of Arts in 1768 and its first president.

    *   http://www.nationalgallery.org.uk/artists/sir-joshua-reynolds

Figure 10.18 *Left:* Portrait of George "Beau" Brummell, watercolor by Robert Dighton, c. 1805. Brummell was the men's fashion arbiter during the Neoclassical period in England, who popularized and set the high fashion standard for stylish men and who made long trousers acceptable for them. He was known for his immaculate cleanliness and this shows his quintessential outfit—a crisp white shirt, a short white vest, and an unusually large white cravat with a dark double-breasted cut-away tailcoat with brass buttons, and tight breeches or pantaloons, and tall boots.

Private Collection/Bridgeman Images

Figure 10.19 *Below:* A Parisian society ball, 1819. This shows a variety of fashionable men's and women's clothes and hairstyles as well as the room setting. Notice that some of the men are wearing the more current style of long pants and some still the knee-length with ribbons and both men and women are wearing soft dancing slippers. One of the distinguishing features of the dresses is the trim at the hems. Some typical Neoclassical details are the chair in the lower left and its similarity to a Greek *klismos*, the chandelier and light sconces, the parquet floor where the carpet has been removed for dancing, the very high ceiling, and the complex drapery patterns.

Giraudon/Bridgeman Images

* * http://www.bbc.co.uk/arts/yourpaintings/artists/joshua-reynolds
  * * http://en.wikipedia.org/wiki/Joshua_Reynolds
* * Thomas Gainsborough (1727–1788) was a rival of Reynolds and another esteemed painter of portraits and landscapes and also a member of The Royal Academy.
  * * http://www.nationalgallery.org.uk/artists/thomas-gainsborough
  * * http://www.bbc.co.uk/arts/yourpaintings/artists/thomas-gainsborough-658
  * * http://en.wikipedia.org/wiki/Thomas_Gainsborough
* * Johann Zoffany (1727–1810) was also known for his portraits and especially of the leading actors and actresses of his day and often painted them in their costumes. These theatrical portraits became a distinctive genre and part of the "conversation piece" style, whose paintings of groups of people later made into mezzotint prints were popular with the middle class; both would make excellent resources. The lead painting in Chapter 9 by Jean Francois de Troy (1679–1752) of the Watteau gown is an example of the "conversation piece style."
  * * http://www.tate.org.uk/art/artists/johan-zoffany-620
  * * http://www.bbc.co.uk/arts/yourpaintings/artists/johann-zoffany
* * After the French Revolution costume made a clean break with the structure and frivolity of the Rococo period and Neoclassical clothing looked back to Greek and Roman elegance and simplicity for women and simplified, clean lines for men. See Figures 10.1, 10.18, and 10.19.
* * Before the emergence of the Empire dress fashionable dresses were still of silks and satins and had full and substantial skirts and low necklines.
* * In addition particularly in France after the French Revolution, to show the rejection of the monarchy, wigs, high-heeled shoes, and all of the elaborate decorations were abandoned.
* * The period of Empire style was notable for refined fashions for men and women. It is thought that the tape measure was introduced in England early in the 19th century and allowed for much more precise tailoring and garment making.
* * In the Empire style women abandoned the corseted look for a simple, sheath dress with a high waist, square neck, short puffed sleeves, large bonnets, and soft slippers. Their clothes featured lighter, thinner, often white or later pastel fabrics. They continued to wear a more flexible and discreet corset under their dresses. See Figures 10.1 and 10.19.
* * Also another influence of the Greek and Roman clothing, large shawls were popular in this period and were adapted from the himations and *pallas*. They were also useful to provide warmth over their delicate dresses. See Chapters 1 and 2, and Figure 11.7.
* * Women wore their hair long, but piled up with short curls around the face in imitation of the Classical Greeks and the styles shown in the Pompeian wall paintings. They decorated their hair with ribbons or small tiaras for formal occasions. See Figures 10.1 and 10.19.
* * The late 18th century saw the emergence of the milliner as a separate profession, who designed and made trims for hats and dresses. Hairdressers for men and women also started as an occupation and the first hairdressing school opened in Paris.
* * The Neoclassical men's look saw the introduction of full-length, snug trousers with high waists for day and eveningwear. Their outfits included coats that were both single and double breasted with high standing collars and tails, vests, and larger, bulkier cravats. See Figures 10.18 and 10.19.
* * These clothes were worn with high riding boots that curved at the knee and top boots with a broad tan band. See Figure 10.18.

* The frock coat was a men's woolen winter overcoat that evolved during the mid-19th century from an earlier simpler version, into a long coat with a full skirt and waist with turned over lapels, which could be single or double-breasted. It continues to be used today as our overcoat.

* Men were clean-shaven with short hair brushed forward in the Classical Roman style. They wore flat top and bicorn hats. See Figure 10.18.

* Any of the Jane Austen adaptations would be good research material.

Clothing and Costume Keywords

Beau Brummell – He was a good friend of the regent, the future King George IV, and had enormous influence on him and his large circle of friends. He set the model for Regency fashion and popularized the outfit shown in Figure 10.18 with cut-away tails, tight breeches, spotless white accessories, high boots, top hat, gloves, and the cane that completed the picture.

Directoire (direc-TWAR) – This was the costume style during the era of the French Directorate (1795–1799). It was a transitional style after the French Revolution but before the full more restrained Empire style in which elements of simplified Classicism began to replace the more formal period of Louis XVI and the older Rococo style.

Empire (om-PEER) – A clothing style characteristic of the Napoleonic Empire (1804–1815) that attempted to evoke the elegance and simplicity of Classical garments for women. See Figures 10.1 and 10.19.

Empire waist – The high gathering of fabric just below the bosom seen in a Directoire or Empire dress. See Figures 10.1 and 10.19.

sans culottes (SANZ coo-LOT) – Long, loose trousers worn by gentlemen in imitation of and in sympathy with French peasants who had been engaged in the Revolution. The phrase alluded to the common worker's trousers and they were worn in opposition to the aristocrat's silk knee breeches.

redingote for men (reddin-Goat) – This was an English overcoat that evolved into a double-breasted coat with wide lapels and a long full skirt and was later adapted in France.

redingote for women – This was an adaptation of the female riding habit and was a simple undecorated coatdress with long sleeves, usually of wool. Toward the end of the century it had evolved into a lightweight dress with wide lapels, and often worn with a fichu and/or apron. It would continue to evolve through the 19th century.

bicorn – A large round man's hat of the Revolutionary, Directoire, and Empire styles with two sides pulled up and pinned with a cockade. This was the signature hat worn by Napoleon.

cockade – A round, gathered, red, white, and blue ribbon worn on a hat or bonnet in sympathy with the Revolution.

phrygian cap – This cap was commonly worn by the revolutionaries during the French Revolution as a symbol of their freedom. It was mentioned in Chapter 5, Romanesque.

indispensable – This was the English word for a small handbag carried by women in the Empire period that dangled from the wrist.

CHAPTER ELEVEN

Romantic: 1750–1840

Figure 11.1 Royal Pavilion in Brighton, England, 1783. It was built as an exotic summer seaside retreat for entertaining and recreation by the Prince Regent, who would become George IV. Among the first of this type of building, it was very influential in catering to the taste for the exotic and Mughal that marked this era and later would spark the Victorian taste for the romantic past and their craze for the extravagant. The pavilion uses a pastiche of diverse Asian features such as ogee arches, minarets, pointed cupolas, and onion domes, all of which contribute to this flamboyant building.

Dmitry Naumov/Shutterstock.com

A Little Background

The Romantic revolution in design and clothing was partly a result of the looting of antiquities from Greece and Egypt by Napoleon and Lord Elgin of England, as well as by the earlier Roman archeological discoveries at Pompeii. As artists and designers gradually became conscious of the historic style trends that preceded their own era they included them in their work. This required scholarly study of past historical styles and the creation of the research process still used today.

The Romantic style arose as historical subjects in both art and performance were interpreted in the dress and locales in which they were supposed to take place rather than in a contemporary style. Suddenly Shakespeare's Julius Caesar was dressed in a toga instead of a justacorps and acted out his tragedy among Roman columns instead of Rococo palaces. In design, Romanticism was the reimagining of historical events in an idealized past, and its ally Historicism, the setting of stories and/or artwork in the period in which they actually occurred. Architectural and interior styles also responded to Historicism by producing a series of revival styles that looked back at past eras for inspiration and treated buildings and rooms in a fanciful way.

Who They Were

* The picturesque and pastoral influences of the Rococo continued and combined with the new Historicism to produce early Romanticism.

* Romanticism was primarily a reimagining of historic periods in costume, literature, music, architecture, and the decorative arts.

* Many, particularly in polite society, sought to escape from the harsh realities of industrialization into a romantic world of historical imagination, exoticism, and political idealism.

* Romanticism was identified with the rise of middle class values in style and fashion and an overall rise in prosperity brought on by the Industrial Revolution and by colonialism.

* Romanticism also introduced magic, xenophobia, and parochialism as serious artistic subjects.

* The writing and art of William Blake on the spiritual and sublime nature of man was very influential in defining Romanticism for the public.

* The 18th century and early 19th century saw the development of the modern novel in all of its forms from the romantic, historical, to the satirical. There were a number of notable women writers like the Brontë sisters and the epitome was Jane Austen; most of their novels have been made into films and some several times—*Sense and Sensibility* (1995)* is an especially beautiful one and there is a 2007 movie *Becoming Jane*.

* The "Gothic" or horror story was also popularized by the author Mary Shelley, the wife of the poet, Percy Shelley, with her book, *Frankenstein* (1818). There have been many, many adaptations in numerous languages; among the films from 1910 to 2015 Boris Karloff's 1931 movie is still iconic. Shelley was widely imitated and one of these imitators was Jane Loudon, who in 1827 anonymously published *The Mummy!: Or a Tale of the Twenty-Second Century*, a pre-cursor to fantasy, science fiction. Although later Bram Stoker's 1897 novel is in this genre and has had many adaptations, particularly worthwhile is Francis Ford Coppola's 1992 *Dracula* with fantastic costumes by Eiko Ishioka.

* This was probably the most important period of English poetry and saw the great Romantic poets: Byron, Keats, Coleridge, Wordsworth, Shelley, and Arnold.

* Partly as a reaction to the rationalists, the Romantics viewed sentiments and emotions as valuable assets to a complete personality and they thought that life without them was meaningless.

* The Romantic period in Germany was also one of their and Europe's most important literary and musical periods. It was known as "Sturm und Drang" and was exemplified by von Goethe, who wrote about many subjects in several different forms, and Friedrich "Fritz" Schiller, both of whom wrote plays and together established the Weimar Theater.

* Victor Hugo (1802–1885) is perhaps the best known of the French Romantics for his works *Les Miserables*, *The Hunchback of Notre Dame*, and *Hernani*, all three of which have been adapted to opera, plays, musicals, or films. *Les Miserables*, is also an Andrew Lloyd Webber 1983 musical and 2012 film.

* Theater, opera, and orchestral music were enormously popular as both entertainment and also through attendance and appearances at performances became signs of social status.

* Melodrama also appeared in theater and was popular especially among the growing middle class. Melodrama, literally melody and drama, was an acting style that emphasized emotionalism and sentimentality onstage. Performances were always accompanied by musical underscoring similar to the use in early silent films and today's film scoring.

* The new "Bel Canto" or "Beautiful Song" style of opera used a highly ornamented style of singing. It emphasized historic subjects often in exotic locales with period settings. It popularized opera for the middle classes. It was best represented by Rossini, Bellini, and Donizetti and many of their operas are available on video.

* This period saw the emergence and flourishing of celebrity performers, writers, and composers that began at the end of the Rococo period.

* Composers: Schubert, Liszt, Carl Maria von Weber, Berlioz, Bruckner, and Beethoven. There are several biopics including *Copying Beethoven* (2006) and *Immortal Beloved* (1994).

* Artists: J.M.W. Turner, Constable, Blake, Goya, Fuseli, Girodet, Delacroix, and Thomas Cole. The 2014 movie *Mr. Turner* is an excellent example of sets, costumes, and lighting in the Romantic period. In addition there is valuable visual information and also about the craft of painting.

* Architect: John Nash.

* Many movies were set in this period, as well as those already mentioned, the following would also be useful resources: *The Count of Monte Christo* (2002), *Vanity Fair* (2004), *Beau Brummell: The Charming Man* (2006 TV), *Amazing Grace* (2006), and in the US, *The Alamo* (1960 and 2004).

The Romantic Material World

Figure 11.2 The Music Room, Royal Pavilion, Brighton, England. The Prince Regent, later King George IV, was fond of music and often entertained in this room. This view shows the newly invented pianoforte, the forerunner of our grand piano. The gilded domed ceiling is made up of hundreds of plaster shells and the room is lit by nine lotus chandeliers. The red and gold walls are in the chinoiserie style and they are complemented by the complex blue window drapery. Dragon motifs are used throughout the room. The exquisite handmade oval carpet is an Axminster carpet. See Brighton Royal Pavilion and Museums for four virtual tours, other pictures, and information.

HIP/Art Resource, NY

What They Made

Figure 11.3 Strawberry Hill House, Twickenham, England, built 1747–1776. This Gothic Revival castle was designed by the author Horace Walpole (1717–1797) and several of his friends. It is an early example of the soon to emerge popular Revival styles that would characterize European architecture for the next hundred years. He created it and its interiors as a retreat from his busy London life and to house his enormous collections of eclectic objects, pictures, and furniture. This miniature castle combines and interprets several Gothic elements: such as the crenellations along the roofs and on the circular Norman keep, the spires, the window arches, and an imitation of a typical French Gothic tower. He compared what he was doing to what his neighbor Lord Burlington had done creating a small neo-Palladian villa at Chiswick House as seen in Chapter 10. See http://www.strawberryhillhouse.org.uk

akg/Bildarchiv Monheim

Figure 11.4 This is the Gallery at Strawberry Hill House in the Gothic Revival style. Although it incorporates many scaled-down Gothic details, Horace Walpole wanted it and the entire house to be a "theatrical experience" to express his ideas of Gothic "gloomth." The rooms are basically a museum for his collections and for the first time a personal statement and expression of his taste. Gothic touches are in the wainscoting, groin vaulting, and the fan vaulted ceiling that is based on one at Westminster Abbey. Also notice the ornate mirrors in the niches and the unusual large one in the shape of a Gothic arch at the end of the room with walls covered in red damask. The intricate fretwork in front of the mirrors also reflects Mughal influence as seen in Chapter 19. The fireplace is flanked by two niches with red velvet benches that use an early example of tufting that would come into its own in Victorian times. There are also two sets of three matching Rococo Louis XV chairs.

akg/Bildarchiv Monheim

* During this Romantic period buildings began to be historically "themed" according to a number of revival styles: Gothic Revival, Romanesque Revival, and Greek Revival were extremely popular in both Europe and America. These Revival styles, and others like them, in architecture and furnishings looked to these past periods, but were reimagined in a sentimental and idealized fashion. These will be explored further in the next two chapters.

* At the same time buildings were conceived of as places for useful activity not theoretical, ideal spaces. They were expected to be useful, but could also be highly decorated.

* Interiors exhibited an increased emphasis on middle class domesticity. Homey and comfortable houses featured sitting rooms and parlors.

* Garden style became softer and more natural with the introduction of the English style of "natural" garden design. In these gardens the rigid formality of the Baroque garden was broken by a natural-looking landscape of trees, meadows, and meandering streams. Larger gardens often featured romantic vistas and ruins and even included exotic birds and animals. Gardens gained in popularity as the middle class grew and could afford them.

* The world's first railroads were developed in Britain in the 1820s and along with the perfection of cast iron building construction began a building revolution that would continue throughout the century.

* With the advent of trains travel in Europe and also the United States became far easier and more affordable, and made remote and exotic locations more accessible thereby widening the scope of the Grand Tour.

How They Decorated

Figure 11.5 This is a large bed of Chinese inspiration, designed by Thomas Chippendale in 1754, Badminton House, UK. This is an early example of a Western form, the four poster tester bed using chinoiserie motifs, such as the Chinese temple roof shape with turned up corners with dragons and rounded tile edges. The wooden parts are typically gold and red lacquer and the backboard uses a variation of an Oriental swastika pattern. The yellow satin bedding is full and opulent and the curtains would have been closed at night.

Gianni Dagli Orti/The Art Archive at Art Resource, NY

* Revived interest in Gothic emotionalism and mystery in art and architecture was now joined with sentimentalism in early Romanticism, and resulted, for the first time, in a huge variety of commercial, factory-produced decorative objects for the house and garden.

* Middle class women in towns and cities were increasingly responsible for domestic life as men were working in factories and offices. Women surrounded themselves and their families with romantic and sentimental furnishings and decorative images—often inexpensive color prints, and other objects.

* The Regency Period in England is generally considered from 1810 until Queen Victoria's ascension to the throne in 1837. During this time George IV acted as regent for his incapacitated father and the Regency style continued while he and his brother were kings. George IV was an avid collector and patron of the arts, architecture, and theater. Because of his affection for spectacle he developed the English monarchs' use of ceremonial rituals and pageants. See his Royal Pavilion at Brighton, Figures 11.1 and 11.2.

* The Paris Opera had tremendous artistic clout as a theatrical style setter in both Europe and America. It aided the new Historicism by decreeing for the first time that scenery, props, and costumes had to be historically researched to suit the period of the performance and to be specifically designed for each scene in order to be truthful to the story.

* Gas lighting appeared in theaters around 1820 and allowed for more realistic stage pictures. This technology enabled designers to be more dramatic and expressive in their images, settings, and scenery.

Building and Décor Keywords

Historicism – The conscious use of historical motifs in the arts and décor. Often used in a sentimental way during the Romantic period. This period marked the beginning of many revival styles based on past historical eras reimagined by contemporary Europeans and Americans. See Figures 11.1, 11.2, 11.3, and 11.4.

Gothic Revival – An architectural and interior design and décor style popular in the late 1700s and 1800s in England and America, influenced by medieval and Gothic forms and ornamentation. It became the unofficial style for church design and much of the architectural and interior design of the 19th and early 20th centuries. See Figures 11.3, 11.4, and 12.3.

Regency – The period in England named for the Prince Regent, the future King George IV, under whose patronage there was much building in London in the Neoclassical Regency style, including the remodeling of Buckingham Palace and Windsor Castle; and also the construction of the Royal Pavilion at Brighton—noted for its Mughal-inspired exterior. See Figures 11.1 and 11.2.

Exoticism – The adoption of style motifs and characteristics from the Far East, Egypt, Africa, Turkey, and the Indian subcontinent and their application to Western forms in décor and costume. See Figures 11.1, 11.2, 11.4, and 11.5.

The Romantic Clothing and Costume World

Figure 11.6 William Powell Frith, English genre and portrait painter (1819–1909). *Portrait of Annie Gambart* in a Romantic-style gown. This period reintroduced structure into women's garments and laid the foundation for Victorian nostalgia in clothing design. The structured horizontal and low neckline characterized much of women's fashion. Firth's paintings would be useful for designers for costumes, props, landscapes, and architecture of this and the Victorian era. Many of his paintings can be seen on the Internet.

Private Collection/Christopher Wood Gallery, London, UK/Bridgeman Images

How They Dressed

Figure 11.7 *Left:* A colored engraving of exuberant French women's fashion, c. 1830 from *Petit Courier des Dames*. The low, wide profile was characteristic of this style, which used the low, straight neckline, wide shoulders, and leg-o-mutton sleeves, and hemlines that stayed at the ankles. This is a prime example of leg-o-mutton sleeves at their height in the 1830s. This look frequently included shawls, often many imported from Persia and India and large highly decorated bonnets.

Gianni Dagli Orti/The Art Archive at Art Resource, NY

Figure 11.8 *Below:* A cartoon *Morning, Noon, and Night* by William Heath from an English woman's fashion magazine, c. 1820s. It shows the same fashionable lady at three times during the day. Notice how her decorative brightly colored dress changes and becomes more slender and formal for evening and her nightcap becomes a giant bonnet with trailing ribbon, and is then replaced for eveningwear with an equally vertical hairstyle.

Private Collection/The Stapleton Collection/Bridgeman Images

Figure 11.9 This is an 1840s engraving from a Paris fashion (*Modes de Paris*) illustration titled, *Petit courier des dames*. The three men are wearing fashionable evening clothes that accentuate the tall vertical look with slim waists, long pants, and tight sleeves. The two to the right are wearing overcoats, the first with a flared frock coat, sometimes referred to as a "Prince Albert coat," and the other in a longer looser one, but both with wide lapels. The gentleman to the left is wearing formal evening attire, "white tie and tails." Their tall top hats also add height to their outfits. Their carefully trimmed facial hair and hairstyles are representative.

Archives Charmet/Bridgeman Images

* In the 1820s the Romantic female clothing styles abandoned the simplicity of the Empire and Neoclassical style and brought back structured and tailored garments and the return of whimsy and gaiety. Exaggeration of these design elements increased through the period. See Figures 11.6, 11.7, and 11.8.

* Women's costumes featured wide skirts with low waistlines and hemlines that rose above the ankle. The dresses had off the shoulder necklines and large wide, puffed sleeves, which were long for day and short for eveningwear. There was a return to flamboyance and complexity in the skirts and bodices, which were often decorated with flounces and embroidery. See Figures 11.6, 11.7, and 11.8.

* Women's hairstyles consisted of highly involved arrangements of ringlets, hairpieces, and upswept hairstyles with curls. They were usually embellished and intertwined with feathers, fabric, ribbon, and/or flowers. See Figures 11.7 and 11.8.

* Men's Regency clothing for the upper classes and nobility was characterized by increasingly romantic extravagance and frivolity and gave its name to the dandified, pleasure-oriented Prince Regent and his associates. What primarily distinguished it was the expert tailoring and the quality of expensive fabrics. See Figure 10.18, "Beau" Brummell.

* Because of the practical demands of business activity, most men were working for large companies instead of in small shops or for themselves and this period saw a more sober and conservative style of business dress evolving.

* The style and fit of the clothes continued in the more restrained fashions of the Neoclassical period, with long, fitted trousers with jackets and coats that had a seamed tight waist and now had a flaring peplum. Instead of high boots they wore flat shoes and also abandoned the tricorn and bicorn hats in favor of caps and top hats. Their color palette was now limited to dark greys, browns, and black. See Figure 11.9.

* There was a clean break from the past and men abandoned all feminine affectation in favor of the more somber, practical business attire. Color and frivolous detail were seen only on women's dresses and some young males.

* Beau Brummel had set a precedent and by the mid-1800s and the Romantic period, for the first time men could use hairstyles as personal expressions. Particularly with literary and artistic people there were different and freer rules. See Figure 12.17.

Clothing and Costume Keywords

swallowtail – A men's double-breasted cut-away tailcoat with knee-length tails that was made popular by Beau Brummell. Usually it was in dark colors with little decoration or trim. It was worn with trousers, a shirt, short vest, and neckwear. This basic outfit has stayed substantially the same with minor modifications until the present for very formal "white tie" occasions. See Figures 10.18, 10.19, and 11.9.

shawl – A women's loose garment worn over the shoulders, arms, and sometimes head, which could be of various lengths and widths, oblong, or more commonly a folded triangle. It could be of bright colors and patterns and of a contrasting fabric from the dress. The fabric varied by locale, climate, and season. See Figure 11.7.

petticoat – Women's skirt-like undergarments used to give fullness to fashionable dresses.

crinoline (CRIN-olin) – At first a stiff horsehair petticoat that was padded, but later a wood and wire frame connected with fabric strips to enlarge and support a skirt. Unlike the prior pannier and farthingale, the later caged crinoline was extremely popular as it was not so heavy and was worn by all classes. See Figures 11.6, 11.7, and 11.8.

leg-o-mutton (gigot) sleeves – These were sleeves that started as tie-ons in the 16th century and were reintroduced starting in the 1820s. These were now sleeves on dresses that were stuffed with fabric and puffed out at the shoulder and tapered to a narrow cuff. They resembled the popular cut of meat after which they were named. The height of their popularity was in the 1830s and again in the 1890s. See Figures 7.17, 11.7, 14.6, 14.9, and 14.10.

réticule – This was a small ladies' handbag often with a drawstring and decorated with embroidery.

umbrellas – These were becoming popular in England and somewhat earlier in France, and used for both protection from sun and rain and carried by men and women. See Figures 12.13 and 13.27.

CHAPTER TWELVE

Early Victorian: 1837–1870

Figure 12.1 Félix-François-Barthélémy Genaille, *Vue de Salon de la Comtesse de Salverte*, 1854. This painting shows a comfortable French upper class parlor. Although this room is more elegant, it would be a model for the growing English and Continental middle class homes that reflected their taste for comfort and increased prosperity and gave them the ability to afford many and larger furnishings. The new style of tufted chairs and sofa, rug-covered tables and mantelpiece, the plethora of mementos, and pictures speak to the increased wealth and well-being. Notice the very high ceiling and window and the draperies on the walls, which as well as adding a touch of refinement would help to keep the room warm, and the ornate wall to wall carpet would help as well. Lighting was still by candle and the large mirrors would help to distribute it. The figure of the woman and her wide, full dress and cap are very typical of the time. See Figure 12.15.

Christie's Images/Bridgeman Images

A Little Background

The continuation of Romanticism into the Victorian era and its influence on England and America as well as the optimism that surrounded the newly crowned Queen Victoria of England resulted in an assortment of architectural revival styles. Huge increases in material comfort brought on by the Industrial Revolution and colonialism of European powers characterized this upwardly mobile society. Variety and abundance in architecture, décor, and costume became widely available to the upper and middle classes in Europe and America.

This was an era that saw enormous changes in most aspects of life—including industrial, political, scientific, and cultural advances in many parts of the world.

In the United States the California gold rush in 1848 opened the way for the rapid westward expansion. After the Civil War in 1865, institutions like universities, libraries, and museums were well established in the US and there was little distinction between the US and Europe in their cultural affinities, styles, and fashions.

Who They Were

* In 1837 Victoria began her reign as a constitutional monarch. During her 64 years as Queen the role of the monarch evolved and although she had relatively little political power she did maintain and exerted considerable influence. After her marriage to Prince Albert in 1840 he played a dominant role in her life for 20 years until his death. During her reign she increasingly became a popular icon of middle class values—of family, comfort, security, and sentimental romanticism.

* The period saw the rapid spread of British and European colonialism that eventually resulted in imperialism. The aim of colonialism was to extract goods and raw materials from colonized nations; imperialism went further and controlled the client nation's government and its economy.

* The Shakers started in the 1750s in England and immigrated to New England in 1774. They were a religious communal society and eventually established 19 self-sufficient communities in the US. They were the most successful of the Utopian societies started in the first half of the 19th century in the US. They believed in the equality of men and women, but were celibate and depended on conversions and the adoption of orphans; and by the beginning of the 21st century they had only a few members. Their design sense was very distinctive and has been influential on modern design. Many of their communities are now museums and there are many websites about them. The Shaker Museum and library is at Mt. Lebanon, NY. See Figures 12.10 and 12.18.

* Garibaldi and his 1,000 "Red Shirts" volunteers were instrumental in unifying the many Italian city-states and in 1861 it became The Kingdom of Italy under King Victor Emmanuel.

* Germany also became unified in 1871 as the German Empire with Wilhelm of Prussia as Emperor and Bismarck as Prime Minister, which lasted until 1918.

* The westward US expansion, industrialization, and the spread of slavery were accelerated and promoted by new railroads, which also led to the growth and development of cities and suburbs.

* The American Civil War ended US slavery in 1865. This would be the last war on US soil and resulted in the death of 600,000 people on both sides.

* This period saw continued dramatic scientific progress and many major contributions, such as: Darwin's theories on evolution, Mendel's ideas on genetics, and Pasteur's experiments with vaccinations and pasteurization of milk. This saw the beginning of modern medicine and germ theory.

* In the US and many European countries there continued to be growing prosperity and the rise of the middle class into professions, such as teachers, lawyers, scientists, doctors, and other professional and business workers. This also included people in the arts and cultural fields.

* The Victorian era was a time of enormous social division; frequently Charles Dickens (1812–1870) was associated with it through his novels and social criticism, as he poignantly depicted the life of this time, especially the poor and downtrodden. He was the most famous and popular writer of his time and also introduced the serial form of publishing, which has had a lasting influence in writing and also in episodic film and TV shows.

* For the majority of the populations the beginning of industrial mass production of goods resulted in the social and financial misery of poor men, women, and children. They worked 12-hour workdays and 6½ day workweeks in factories and also did "piece work" at home.

* The full flowering of Romanticism with its emphasis on love and emotionalism in art and culture and its taste for sentimentality and exoticism in everyday life continued at this time.

* Historicism and Exoticism continued to influence all the arts including the decorative arts. Exoticism complemented Historicism and took it farther by including settings and locales in places like Egypt, China, and Turkey.

* This era developed a fascination with death and repressed sexuality especially in artistic expression.

* This period saw the creation and celebration of the public image of the artist as a romantic, solitary, tortured genius.

* The invention of photography in the 1830s revolutionized art and communication. There was less of a need to paint realistically and especially in France and England in the 1860s, painters and designers reacted to this Historicism and Romanticism by developing the essentials of Impressionism.

* More and more women were writing for books and magazines. Women were also a growing and significant audience and consequently more was being aimed and written for them; several prominent and influential magazine examples were Godey's *Lady's Book*, *Vanity Fair*, and *Harper's Bazaar*.

* Harriet Beecher Stowe wrote *Uncle Tom's Cabin* in 1852. This was an iconic abolitionist, anti-slavery book that had tremendous and immediate impact both in the United States and abroad. It was not only the largest-selling novel of the 19th century, but after the Bible the largest-selling book.

* Romanticism would predominate in literature in the US and Europe. In the US Transcendentalism would also introduce many writers, including the Alcotts, Thoreau, and Emerson.

* Novelists: Dickens, Thackeray, Cooper, Melville, Poe, Irving, Hawthorne, Hugo, Dumas, Stendhal, and George Elliot, George Sand, and the Brontë sisters.

* Poets: Walt Whitman, Emily Dickinson, Elizabeth and Robert Browning, and Tennyson.

* Composers: Chopin, Mendelssohn, Paganini, Schumann, Smetaena, and Johann Strauss I.

* Artists: French Impressionists—Monet, Renoir, Degas, Pissarro, Morisot, and Cassatt. Also French—Courbet, Manet, and Daumier.

* In the US, the Hudson River School (1825–1875) started by Thomas Cole would now have a second generation of painters like Bierstadt and Frederick Church. In Germany, there were many Romantic painters, which led to the Dusseldorf School of Art.

* The films: *Her Majesty, Mrs. Brown* (1997), *The Young Victoria* (2009, Academy and BAFTA awards costume design Sandy Powell)*, *Great Expectations* (1946 film,* though there are many other TV, film and stage adaptations), *Tess of the D'Urbervilles*, *Jane Eyre* (1943, 2011)*, *Middlemarch* (TV 1994)*, *Dracula* (1992* Eiko Ishioka Costumes, F.F. Coppola, Director), *The Piano* (1993)*, *Gone with the Wind* (1940)*, and *The Portrait of A Lady* (1996)* would be useful resources.

The Early Victorian Material World

Figure 12.2 This Greek Revival style house in Saratoga Springs, New York, built in 1832, is an excellent example of the American version of this style, and usually here it was made out of wood rather than the English, German, and Italian that were made from stuccoed stone and brick. Generally this style in the US started about 1825 and continued on until the turn of the century. The Greek Revival style in the US symbolically emphasized the simple strengths of democracy for Americans.

Susan E. Pease/age fotostock/SuperStock

What They Made

Figure 12.3 The Church of The Cross, Bluffton, SC, built 1857, is an Episcopalian Church in the Carpenter Gothic style, which is a uniquely American naïve interpretation of European Gothic forms. It keeps the pointed Gothic arches and high steep roofs and also frequently uses diamond pattern windows. In the arches over the windows are fanned or Saw palmettos—a typical South Carolina plant. The Sabal palmettos, pictured in front, are the state tree. Two particularly good examples of this domestic architecture are Rose Mansion, also in Bluffton, SC (see their website) and Oak Hill Cottage in Mansfield, Ohio. There are many examples of churches, especially in Florida but also houses—see "Carpenter Gothic" for many pictures.

Author photo

Figure 12.4 Italianate style house. Front Elevation for Villa No. 1, from *Architectural Designs for Model Country Residences....* by John Riddell, 1861, colored lithograph. This was a practical book of architectural elevations and ground plans for different styles of houses, a number of which were built in the Philadelphia area. The digitized book is available on the Internet—"John Riddell, architect" will take you to the website. Notice the porch, which is a new architectural idea that spans and extends beyond the façade with its stripped decoration and cast iron arched openwork, the nearly flat roofs, and overhanging eaves with prominent brackets that are all found on Italianate style houses. The rectangular tower with its little balcony, which in this case is central and steps away from the building, has a small pedimented roof that echoes the larger one below and is also a marker for the Italianate style. In this case the building is completely symmetrical but often this is not true and the towers and chimneys can be in other positions. Also the double and triple Romanesque arch windows are another stylistic feature, but also don't always occur.

Christie's Images/Bridgeman Images

Figure 12.5 This is a wooden New England version of the Italianate style house that became popular in the 1860s. Like the previous one (Figure 12.4) it shows a porch and an additional enclosed wraparound one, a central square tower, deep overhanging roof eaves with prominent brackets. There are small attic windows that are sometimes referred to as "lay me down on my tummy windows." Also markers are the nearly flat roofs and the popular shallow topped arches.

Author photo

Figure 12.6 This is another example of an Italianate style house now using an asymmetrical composition, but retains many of the features already described. Notice the tower is still over the main entrance but to the side and has the typical single and double Romanesque arch windows. The roof has a steeper pitch and the rectangular windows make it likely that this was a colonial house that was remodeled in Victorian times.

Author photo

Figure 12.7 The Crystal Palace, London, England. This enormous building was designed and construction was supervised by Joseph Paxton for the Great Exhibition of 1851 in Hyde Park. After the exhibition in 1852–1854, it was reconstructed in Sydenham, an upscale London suburb, as a popular destination for concerts, exhibitions, sports, and a beautiful garden and public park, as well as a showpiece of architecture. This was one of the first and most dramatic uses of cast iron and glass as building materials, which was made possible by the recent invention of cast plate glass in 1848. This type of construction would continue to be used for commercial buildings, greenhouses, and conservatories throughout this period and would anticipate more complex building applications that would be used later in the 19th century and 20th century. There are many references to it and images on the Internet.

akg-images/Archie Miles

* The development of cast iron manufacturing caused a revolution in building construction. Building parts were cast in iron in factories, shipped, and then assembled on-site, which saved tremendous time, labor, and therefore money. This was the antecedent to more contemporary building methods of prefabricated and modular designs. See Figures 12.4 and 12.7.

* At this time architecture and décor developed many historical revival styles, often used eclectic elements and occurred simultaneously; and borrowed from several different periods.

* The Gothic Revival continued throughout this period and profoundly influenced church architecture and art in Europe and America. With few exceptions, especially in remote areas, most church construction was done in this historical style.

* Carpenter Gothic was its simpler and more rustic cousin that was adopted in rural areas and used wood construction for church and residential buildings. See Figure 12.3.

* A new building design style that arose later in the period was the Italianate style based on rustic Italian farm architecture. It dominated much town and country domestic and commercial architecture in both England and America until the end of the century. See Figures 12.4, 12.5, and 12.6.

How They Decorated

Figure 12.8 Furniture was also affected by the fashion for revival styles. This 1841 French sofa and chair are in the extremely popular Neo Rococo style and tufted furniture makes its appearance at this time. The size of the couch is much larger and bulkier than true Rococo furniture and the legs underneath are filed in, whereas in a Rococo chair they would be open like the side chair. It is primarily the shapes and carving of the backs that mark the Rococo style. The side chair is more similar to the Rococo in its shape but now has an exaggerated and elongated back. In both examples the colors of the upholstery and wood are now darker instead of pastel colors and gilt.

Private Collection/The Stapleton Collection/Bridgeman Images

* Mass production in factories of furniture, decorative, and utilitarian objects, as well as clothing greatly increased the number and speed of identical products that were previously done by hand and thus encouraged and consequently led to the rapid turnover and variation of décor styles. See Figures 12.8 and 12.9.

* John Henry Belter (1804–1863) created iconic intricate furniture and almost single-handedly made the transition from hand crafted to machine made. He was instrumental in developing machines to speed the factory production of high quality furniture. There are a number of antique dealers and websites that have examples of his furniture under his name. See Figure 12.9.

* The proliferation and expansion of railroads during the boom years from 1830s to 1860s in the US and Europe enabled the wide distribution not only of these objects but also building materials and labor. Railroads also led to leisure travel that exposed people to a wide range of architecture, decorative objects, and art, which also contributed to style changes.

* Domestic interiors were characterized by a continuation of Romantic design with the addition of exotic elements from Africa, India, and the Far East. This was partially due to the spread of colonialism and increased contact with and exposure to the colonial nations.

Figure 12.9 This is a mid-19th-century Neo Rococo style armchair with a large heavily carved molded back. Again the size of this example is much larger and more complex than a true Rococo chair and the upholstery and wood are darker. This chairs looks very much like the furniture of John Henry Belter, who was mentioned on p. 184.

akg-images/De Agostini Picture Library

Figure 12.10 This is a typical bedroom at Shaker Village of Pleasant Hill, Kentucky, often known as Shakertown. The restraint and minimalism of Shaker designs were an important influence on modern design. Notice the two railings that go around the rooms usually with pegs and used to hang their furnishings and clothes. For the most part their communities were self-sufficient and they made and grew most everything themselves. At their height in the mid-19th century, they also sold many of their products including furniture and smaller artifacts, but also farm implements, seeds, and plants. There is a video on the Internet about this community, *Shaker Village of Pleasant Hill*, and also many of the others have websites.

Library of Congress

Figure 12.11 Log cabins were some of the American colonies' first buildings and noteworthy are the ones Washington used at Valley Forge and Abe Lincoln's childhood home. This is a well-appointed one as there are a number of tools and many cooking implements of different metals, pottery, but also wood. Even though the East Coast by now was quite sophisticated most people lived in very simple dwellings like this, sod and dug out and simple frame houses with few rooms and with few possessions. The fireplace served as the primary heating, cooking, and lighting source similar to the Romanesque uses, but now at least there was a chimney and also the center of activities in the house. On the left in the fireplace is an arm that allowed pots to be raised or lowered on a chain, and also there are cast iron Dutch ovens used to cook over the coals, as there is no other kind of oven. Notice the huge size of the logs, floorboards, and ceiling beams and rafters.

TimAbramowitz/iStock

* Queen Victoria had a very opulent, elaborate, and complex structured household. By her example and influence she promoted the proliferation of many decorative and utilitarian objects. As an illustration, she multiplied the formality of dining that used a vast array of very involved and specific tableware and then encouraged china, glass, and silverware factories to create them and in multiple patterns. This would be true for textile, clothing, and furniture manufacturing as well.

* Victoria and Prince Albert brought the candle-lite and decorated Christmas tree to Windsor Castle in the 1840s and wealthy people emulated it across Europe. By 1850 an illustration of Prince Albert and the Royal family surrounding the tree appeared in the US and shortly thereafter it began the Christmas tradition.

* This was also a highpoint in the use and hierarchy of servants and tradesmen, especially in aristocratic and upper class residences. Many people have now been made aware of this from the TV shows *Upstairs Downstairs* and *Downton Abbey*.

* The first use of gas lighting in theaters was in Philadelphia in 1816, but by the 1840s it was used in most theaters in the US and in Europe. The position of lights was similar to the earlier oil lamps as they were used in chandeliers, footlights, vertical strip lights or "ladders" in between the wings, but now they added horizontal strip lights, also between the wings.

* In 1832, the first practical box sets were used in theaters, which used three walls for a room.

* Mary Ellen Best (1809–1891) was a prolific English painter. It is believed that she did about 1,500 paintings of English and German mostly interiors of various rooms and domestic life and often reflected a comfortable Victorian life, eclectic furnishings, and many objects. Her renderings are similar to traditional "box theater sets," looking straight on and using three walls. http://www.art.com/gallery/id--a33992/Mary-Ellen-Best and other websites have information about her and other women artists.

Building and Décor Keywords

Greek Revival – An American architectural and interior design style of the 1830s–1860s that utilized the simple lines of Doric or Ionic orders, pediment, and columns of Greek architecture. Americans saw it as a reference to the purity of ancient Greek democracy, which they saw themselves emulating. See Figure 12.2.

Carpenter Gothic – This was a naive American mid-19th-century style loosely based on simplified European Gothic forms without much regard to accuracy. It retained the pointed Gothic arch, high pointed roofs, and the diamond pattern windows. This style was always executed in wood because of its wide availability, ease of construction, and also the invention of the fret saw, which made curved forms easier to cut. Generally it was used for relatively small rural houses and churches and did not require many or sophisticated builders, but relied on local carpenters. See Figure 12.3.

Rococo Revival – An embellished Victorian furniture and interior décor style of the 1850s to 1870s, which featured elaborately carved parlor furniture, triple crested sofas, and balloon backed chairs. It was in imitation of the Louis XV style, but used heavier construction darker woods and fabrics. See Figures 12.8 and 12.9.

Cast Iron style – The 19th-century architectural construction technique used in England and America. In this process a factory cast the structural and decorative features of a building from iron and then they were assembled on-site in modules. This method was a precursor to modern construction methods. The resulting open and often lacy look of buildings built in this technique was very dramatic and was extremely popular. It was used both structurally and decoratively from large buildings to garden furniture. Prominent examples were the conservatory (greenhouses) at Kew Gardens and the Crystal Palace in London. See Figures 12.4 and 12.7.

Shaker style – This was the architecture, interior design, and especially furniture design style developed by the self-contained communal, religious Shakers in the US. They emphasized elegant simplicity and inventive utility of design and among other things, they originated the one-piece clothes-peg, i.e. pin, the oval nesting boxes, the circular saw, flat broom, apple peeler, and perfected the cast iron stove. PBS has an interesting website, *Shakers for Educators PBS*, with many links to related sites and Ken Burns' 1985 film *Shakers: Hands to Work, Hearts to God*. See Figures 12.10 and 12.18.

Italianate – This was a new 19th-century American and English architectural style based on traditional Italian farm architecture that featured a low pitched metal or tile roof, overhanging, bracketed roof eaves, round-topped windows, and a square tower. The buildings were often finished in brick or stucco. This style was also adopted for commercial and factory buildings. Both the domestic and industrial versions were designed in this simple but strong style. See Figures 12.4, 12.5, and 12.6.

balloon back – The type of Rococo Revival couch or chair in which the back was shaped as one or more ovals. See Figures 12.1, 12.8, 12.9, and 13.18.

tufting – This was heavily padded upholstery pierced by a regular, geometric pattern of buttons that was very characteristic of Victorian furniture. See Figures 12.1, 12.8, 12.9, and 11.4, 13.18.

arabesque – A type of flat ornament derived from Arabic forms, which used intricate, overall patterns that formed sweeping, curved paisley compositions. It became popular in fabric designs and in garden layouts.

Victorian garden style – Known as the Victorian bedding or carpet beds, this was a popular style that used colorful seasonal and frequently exotic plants in arabesque and other patterns similar to those found on Oriental rugs and Elizabethan designs. They changed seasonally and the plants were grown in the new greenhouses. This was very similar to the styles we now find in the US in commercial and residential complexes.

The Early Victorian Clothing and Costume World

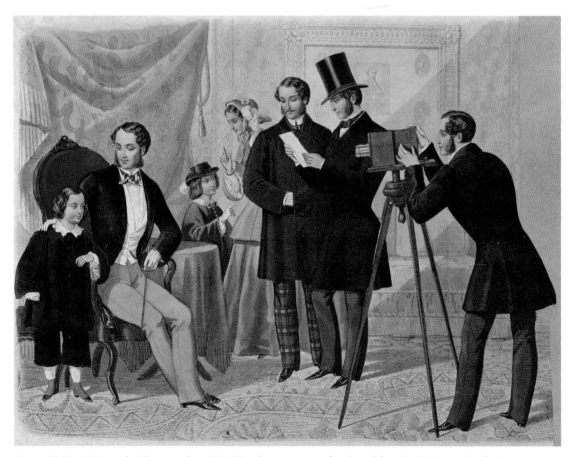

Figure 12.12 *A Visit to the Photographer*, 1857. This shows a range of male and female clothing styles for the upper middle class of various ages. The man seated in the chair is wearing formal attire as noted by his cut-away with tails and white waistcoat and the young boy to his left is wearing an outfit created especially for children, which for the first time is not just a miniaturization of adult clothing. All of the other men are wearing daytime wear, the two on the right have the more fitted frock coats and the man in the center, a looser overcoat. Notice the variety of hairstyles and also facial hair. The lady is wearing the new wide crinoline-style dress. This would be a very early use of the camera and pictures like this would be taken in a photographer's studio often with a painted scenic backdrop and props, like this chair that has a close resemblance to the one in Figure 12.9. This would be standard procedure for formal photographs into the 20th century and other examples will be shown. In the image of the Shakers (Figure 12.18), although outside, the camera and tripod would have been very similar as the hand held camera was not invented until the 1920s.

How They Dressed

Figure 12.13 *Summer Fashions for 1841*. Finely dressed men, women, and children parade in front of Windsor Castle, England. They are displaying the latest summer fashions. Ladies' profiles are more restrained than in the Romantic period and now have higher necklines, drooping shoulders, pinched waists, and the sleeves are tight at the wrists. The young child is wearing a shorter dress and pantelettes. The men are similar to the previous chapter and to stay fashionable and emulate Prince Albert they wear the tight waist with flared frock coat and for the most part slender white summer pants to retain the vertical look. But notice the variety of neckwear and that they are all wearing the same style of shorter top hat. Queen Victoria and Prince Albert are shown in a carriage disappearing up Castle Hill.

HIP/Art Resource, NY

* The sewing machine was introduced in the 1850s and its improvements in technology facilitated garment making in the home and factories. The introduction of machine-made clothes greatly enhanced the speed with which they were made, the availability of a wider range of styles and also the number of garments people could have.

* Printed paper clothing patterns were now available and published in a number of magazines for ladies to sew at home.

* The use of sewing machines also encouraged the use of pleats, frills, braiding, and other ornamentation on women's dresses. See Figure 12.15.

* The invention of artificial dyes by William Henry Perkin in 1856 and machine printing of fabrics broadened color and design possibilities and made clothing, decorative fabrics, and wallpapers available on a commercial scale.

* Victoria and Albert's wedding in 1840, a romantic love match of Royals, popularized and formalized decorative staged weddings as a woman's transition into adulthood and the bride as an object of worship. This wedding marked the introduction of the fashion of the white wedding dress that

Figure 12.14 Although this photo is from later in the period it shows three teenage young men in 1897, but two of them are wearing a style of jacket called a sack coat that started in the 1850s. It would continue in popularity through the Victorian era and eventually become the standard for daywear. It was worn buttoned up high on the chest and generally worn with a high stiff collar in this case with rounded not folded down tips and with cravats and neckties. The hairstyles with short center-parted slick-backed hair and their short leather boots would have been more typical of the 1890s. The young man on the left is wearing a military school uniform with ornamental braiding called frogging. Also notice the short stand-up mandarin collar, which is still in use today by US combat soldiers.

Louisa Rawle

Figure 12.15 This is a photograph of Queen Victoria, c. 1860. Until Albert's death in 1861 and since her coronation in 1837 she was fashion conscious, not overly ostentatious, but had a quiet elegance. As we have seen the fashions for men and women usually patterned on the King and Queen and so she set the standard. Her dress has the tiered crinoline shape and flounced dress layers. After the 1850s dresses would get wider and needed something to support them and that is when the cage crinoline was introduced as can be seen in this photograph. This is a day outfit and so dresses would have high necklines and be worn with bonnets or other hats and gloves. Also notice she is wearing a fitted jacket with flared sleeves. The 2009 film *The Young Victoria* had outstanding costumes by Sandy Powell that won her an Academy Award.

Private Collection/Bridgeman Images

symbolized the purity and virginity of the bride. It also established the wedding ceremony as a social necessity and a cultural rite of passage for women.

* For the aristocracy and wealthy women this period and the next were characterized by a highly elaborate hierarchy of clothing and manners that continued to grow more complex.

* By the beginning of this period fashion was becoming less flamboyant and hemlines dropped down and by the 1840s women were wearing a heavy padded crinoline that was stiffened with horsehair and many petticoats to make the dress wider. Instead of long coats they were wearing short jackets and shawls.

* During the 1850s and into the 1860s stylish women's garments became increasingly wider and again more elaborate in their styles. They featured long, wide, bell-shaped ruffled or flounced skirts

64.156

CRINOLINE in its NAKED MONSTROSITY shows that great difficulties have to be overcome in order to disguise the human form.

Figure 12.16 *Crinoline, its Difficulties and Dangers*, 1850s. This is one of 20 cartoons of the problems of wearing crinolines by *Quiz* magazine. The cage crinoline like this was introduced in 1856. This picture also shows the camisole and the flimsie, two additional cotton undergarments.

Museum of London/The Art Archive at Art Resource, NY

Figure 12.17 Frederick Charles Worth (1826–1895) was a pioneering English fashion and costume designer based in Paris, and founder of the House of Worth in 1858. He is credited as the father of haute couture and was one of the first to use live models to show his designs. Worth dominated French fashion in the last half of the 19th century, and French fashions led the fashion world; his family continued the business until 1952. His elegant and often theatrical gowns used luxurious materials and also frequently incorporated historical elements. There are many examples of them in costume collections in the US and Europe as he designed for many wealthy and famous patrons, as well as opera and theater stars such as Jenny Lind, Sarah Bernhardt, and Lillie Langtry. He also designed costumes for the theater and stylish and popular masquerade balls. This photograph of him shows an example of the flamboyant "artist's attire," which was a newly created style for all kinds of artists and critics. They often wore a beret and large cape and similar clothes can be seen on Wagner, Whistler, Sargent, and others.

The Art Archive at Art Resource, NY

Figure 12.18 Group of Mount Lebanon Shakers posed with Elder Evans, New Lebanon, New York, c. 1890. Their austere and uniform clothing reflects their beliefs and simple, rural lifestyle. These would be their "Sunday going to meeting" clothes for the photographer and not their more utilitarian work clothes. Although this photo is from a slightly later date the clothes would have been basically the same in this earlier period. The women have long plain skirts, long sleeves, simple capes, and all have cloth caps to show piety. The men are wearing modest dark suits with white shirts and no ties and also notice their hair and beards. They would have grown and made most of their fabrics and clothes. Also notice the range in ages; this small group would have been from only one of the residential houses, as Mt. Lebanon was the largest of all of their communities and had hundreds of buildings over 6,000 acres. The average man and woman in the US and most of Europe would have worn variations of these simpler clothes through this and the next period.

Culver Pictures/The Art Archive at Art Resource, NY

with a waistline that returned to its natural place and tight, fitted bodices. For daywear, necklines were high and more modest, with a low sloping shoulder line, and long sleeves. They were worn with bonnets and other hats and gloves. At night sleeves were usually short and puffy, worn with long evening gloves, and commonly they also wore a shawl. See Figure 12.15.

* The cage crinoline, introduced in 1856, had large steel and tape hoops to support all these skirts and despite the caricatures and cartoons was more comfortable as it was much lighter and more flexible and therefore more popular with women. See Figure 12.16.

* The 1860s was when the crinoline style reached its widest. See Figure 12.16. After 1862 the profile would have a flatter slimmer front and would push out in the back with the new addition of the crinolette, a different shaped undergarment. See Figure 12.15.

* All of this was worn over foundation garments, which continued to use the boned corset, chemise, and layers of petticoats. In addition women also wore pantalettes that were made of linen or cotton and decorated with broderie anglaise or lace. They were ankle length and meant to show under the skirt; younger girls wore shorter skirts and theirs went to mid-calf. Pantalettes have often been confused with bloomers, but they were different. See Figures 12.13 and 12.16.

* In the 1840s women's hair was parted in the middle with puffs or curls around the ears. Later it was worn long and low on the back of the neck or in braids curled around the head.

* The hair, with the highly structured bodice and the puffed or flared sleeves, then the long full skirt completed the desired A-line silhouette.

* Purses, réticules, hats, parasols, shawls, and a variety of different styles of gloves became necessary accessories for the well-dressed lady.

* Ladies' hats varied considerably for outdoors during this time, but close-fitting cotton or linen caps and bonnets also with broderie anglaise were worn indoors throughout. See Figure 12.15.

* Introduced in 1850 by Amelia Jenks Bloomer, as a style that was not so restrictive and therefore healthier, were loose pants gathered at the ankles and worn under a short skirt; borrowed from Turkish pantaloons, they were known as the "Turkish dress" and later the moniker-bloomers. They were a craze that was taken up by the suffragettes and became a symbol of feminist reform. After the Civil War they fell out of fashion, but would reappear at the end of the century in an altered way.

* Hats and gloves were required for both sexes.

* Men's garments continued to be sober and businesslike with small variations in jacket length and the fullness of trousers, which increasingly used a tubular shape and were used for both day and night. The genteel and aristocratic man wore well-tailored clothes made of fine fabrics. See Figures 12.12, 12.13, and 12.14.

* The desired look for men was tall and slim with a large chest and corseted waist to mirror Prince Albert. The typical outfit included the flared frock coat, decorative vest, slim trousers, top hat, and heeled leather shoes. See Figures 11.9, 12.12, and 12.13.

* Men's styles featured longer hair and mostly they were clean-shaven but sideburns were popular and by 1865 also goatees.

* Writers and artists adopted flamboyant "artist's attire" featuring capes, scarves, and berets in contrast to the sober dress of businessmen. See Figures 12.17.

Clothing and Costume Keywords

flounce – The decorated horizontal bands of fabric forming layers or tiers on a skirt that made a wide profile. See Figure 12.15.

Garibaldi shirt – This was a red shirt supposedly introduced by Empress Eugénie in France in honor of the Italian patriot, which then became popular with women in the US and Europe in the 1860s. It was the precursor to the blouse.

camisole – This was essentially the same as a chemise and was worn next to the skin to help keep more expensive garments clean and usually made of cotton, linen, or muslin, but like its use today, could be decorated with trim. See Figure 12.16.

flimsie – This was similar to our slip and was usually a cotton garment with a drawstring at the waist and worn as an additional undergarment under petticoats and could also have ruffles or lace at the hem. See Figure 12.16.

broderie anglaise – This was a type of white work embroidery that combined it with cutwork to look similar to lace, usually on cotton or linen. It was extremely popular from the 1840s to 1880s and was used on ladies', young boys', and girls' dresses. It was prevalent as trim and on underwear and bonnets. See Figures 14.9 and 14.11.

cage crinoline – This was the wide-hooped structure introduced in 1856 that tied around the waist and was worn under petticoats to make skirts larger and bell-shaped. See Figures 12.15 and 12.16.

crinolette – In 1862 after the demise of the caged crinoline, the crinolette created a shape that now had a flatter stomach and pushed out behind. It also tied around the waist.

bustle – This was a whale bone, padded fabric, or steel half-cage worn under the petticoat that created a "pouf" on the back of the dress, which resulted in a train of fabric. It was often worn with leg-o-mutton and pagoda sleeves (funnel-shaped) in the 1870s and early 1880s during the day. See Chapter 13.

snood – a woven bag-like net worn over the hair, which was gathered at the base of the neck.

zipper – The female garment closure using two rows of interlocking teeth joined by a sliding catch was invented in 1851, and originally called "the hookless fastener."

waistcoat (WES-cut) – The basic men's vest made with fine fabric on the front and lining fabric on the back. At this time it had a pronounced waist. See Figures 12.12, 12.13, and 11.9.

Prince Albert coat – This was a long double-breasted frock coat with satin, silk, or velvet lapels favored by Prince Albert that flared at the waist. See Figure 11.9.

sack suit – This was a style of men's suit that was introduced in the 1850s and would develop into the matching three-piece suit with thigh-length jacket, vest, and straight trousers. Eventually it would become the standard business suit. It started out quite baggy and got more slender as it evolved. It was single breasted and usually worn buttoned and frequently with a bowler hat. In England this was called a "**lounge suit**." An excellent website with pictures and information is Sack suits/Mass Historia—Walter Nelson. See Figures 12.12 and 12.14.

bowler hat – A rigid felt hat with rounded crown created for everyday wear in 1849 by London hat makers Thomas and William Bowler. It was famously worn by Charlie Chaplin as "The Tramp" in his early silent films.

string tie – A type of bowtie neckwear made out of ribbon, which had long tails.

stovepipe hat – This was a tall, cylindrical hat with a narrow brim that we now associate with Abraham Lincoln. See Figures 11.9 and 12.12.

frogging – This was a distinctive type of decorative braiding that could be used to close a jacket or be ornamental. It was popular from the 17th to 19th century, especially on military uniforms. See Figure 12.14.

mandarin collar – This originally developed in Imperial China and was adopted in the West primarily on military uniforms. It was also worn in India by Nehru and known then as the Nehru collar and came full circle back to China and was worn on the Mao suit. It is part of the Eastern Orthodox cassock. In films it is often worn by the "bad guys"—see James Bond films, *Austin Powers* and *Star Wars*. See Figure 12.14.

suspenders, galluses – These were a pair of straps that went over the shoulders and buttoned to the top of men's pants. They were commonly worn through the middle of the 20th century when they were supplanted by belt loops and belts.

CHAPTER THIRTEEN

Late Victorian: 1870–1901

Figure 13.1 The Palais Garnier, Paris, as it was often called to distinguish it from the old Paris Opera, founded by Lully at the Palais-Royal in 1673 and later moved to the Salle Le Peletier. This was the new theater home of the Paris Opera built in 1861–1875 and named after its architect Charles Garnier. It is in the Beaux-Arts style showing the enlarged Neo-Renaissance features that characterized this new Parisian style. These architectural elements feature the horizontal orientation and symmetrical unified façade. Notice the abundance of decorative elements, such as the many statues, windows, arches, and "the giant orders." This theater inspired the design of opera houses throughout Europe and the Americas. For the Opera Garnier, Wikipedia has a photograph of the façade referencing all the statues.

ilolab/Shutterstock.com

A Little Background

The latter half of Victoria's reign coincided with the full development of American and European secular culture. The complete spectrum of cosmopolitan, social and cultural, and recreational institutions that we take for granted were developed: theaters, opera houses, museums, concert halls, spas, casinos, libraries, schools, clubs, sporting associations, hotels, restaurants, galleries, and civic and church organizations. Revival architectural styles continued to be popular and were accompanied by an increase of scale and complexity of motifs in public buildings, but this was not necessarily so in most residential architecture, which still stayed complex and eclectic, but with the exception of the palatial homes, stayed in smaller scale.

New contact with the insular Japanese culture prompted another wave of interest in Asian art and culture. America was expanding westward, which prompted a domestic building boom that spread Victorian revival styles across the continent. Opera houses and theaters began to employ new production technologies based on the use of electricity in auditorium and stage lighting. Clothing and costume reflected the growing level of wealth and sophistication of both European and American cultures through an increasingly rapid series of style and fashion changes driven by the availability of a wide variety of fabric and accessory choices, the sewing machine, and manufactured clothing.

Who They Were

* The solidification of European imperialism and British control of India and their other colonies made Britain the dominant player in international affairs. "The sun never sets on the British Empire" was coined to highlight England's domination over one quarter of the Earth.

* The deaths in the 1860s of Prince Albert, Victoria's mother, and many of Britain's colonial adventurers, Lincoln's assassination, and the carnage of the American Civil War led to a social culture of mourning, which had extremely specific rules and codes of dress and behavior.

* After Albert's death, Victoria remained in deepest mourning for many years and only wore black. Prompted by Disraeli, her esteemed Prime Minister, she was convinced to re-emerge and she resumed significant influence. Her reign was noted for much royal pomp and circumstance, enormous public celebrations and spectacles: 1851, The Great Exhibition; 1861, Prince Albert's funeral; 1863, Prince Edward and Princess Alexandra's wedding; in 1877 she became Empress of India; 1887, The Golden Jubilee; 1897, The Diamond Jubilee, and her funeral in 1901.

* The continued use of Historicism to reinterpret the past in a moralistic way resulted in the popularity of historical revival movements in the arts and architecture.

* This period was the height of the Industrial Revolution with vast improvements in technology, transportation, and communication.

* The inequity between owners and producers with their labor force continued to grow even more pronounced. Trade unions were legalized in England in 1871 and during this period they came into being in the US and most European countries.

* There continued scientific and medical progress that was represented by the discovery in medicine of radiation and the prominence of the psychoanalytical theories of Freud.

* In the late 19th century the invention of the internal combustion engine and the beginning of petroleum production led to many inventions and the development of the automobile. These advanced technological innovations happened very rapidly from the 1880s to 1908 when Henry Ford introduced the popular Model T car in the US. This spurred the development of mass transit and great advances in social contact and personal mobility.

* Baron Haussmann was the designer who rebuilt Paris in the monumental French Second Empire style (French Renaissance Revival), which influenced urban design and planning in Europe and America for decades. This movement popularized city planning and beautification movements in many major cities in Europe and America and resulted in the reorganization and renovation of many of these city centers.

* While the original Paris Opera was known for its groundbreaking Historicism in its use of historically accurate scenery and production elements, the later Garnier Paris Opera was among the first theaters to employ innovative new production technologies such as the use of the carbon arc light in projectors and follow spot lighting.

* The Garnier Paris Opera was the setting for *The Phantom of the Opera*, the 1910 serialized novel, which later had numerous other adaptations for film, television, operas, cartoons, and children's books. Its most famous adaptations are the 1925 movie with Lon Chaney and the 1986 stage musical by Andrew Lloyd Webber.

* The invention of radio, sound recording, and film technology began an era of rapid communications and entertainment expansions.

* Freud's theories of psychoanalysis sparked new dramatic and literary works based on hidden fears and the emotions of the unconscious in characters. He also suggested an additional life phase called adolescence between childhood and adulthood that helped to encourage popularization of children's fantasy literature and illustration.

* The rising popularity and influence of commercial illustrators, such as Pyle, N.C. Wyeth, Gibson, Jessie Wilcox Smith, Rackham, and Doré energized the market for children's books and magazines.

* Fairy tales of Perrault, the Brothers Grimm, and Hans C. Andersen, as well as the Islamic classic *The Arabian Nights* all played a large role in Victorian children's upbringing. This was also the time of the classic English writers J.M. Barrie—Peter Pan stories and play, Lewis Carroll—*Alice in Wonderland*, Edward Lear—nonsense verse, Kipling—*The Jungle Book* and *Just So Stories*, and slightly later in the 1920s A.A. Milne's Pooh stories and poems. Many of these have had many other adaptations including film, theater, and TV.

* This continued the "Great Age" of the 19th-century novel where Realism and Naturalism would prevail. Novels: Balzac, Zola, Flaubert, Proust, Longfellow, Stevenson, H. James, Twain, Hardy, Stoker's *Dracula*, and H.G Wells. The 19th century in Russia was known as the "Golden Age"; it started with Pushkin, then followed Tolstoy, Gogol, Turgenev, and Dostoyevsky. There are many film adaptations of these novels; the 2012 adaptation of Tolstoy's *Anna Karenina* is an interesting one.

* Playwrights: Wilde, Ibsen, Strindberg, Chekhov, Rostand—*Cyrano de Bergerac* and *Les Romanesques,* which was adapted to the musical *The Fantasticks*, Sardou, Musset, and Feydeau. There are also many TV and film adaptations of these.

* Composers: Borodin, Brahms, Debussy, Rimsky-Korsakov, Johann Strauss II, known as "the Waltz King," and Tchaikovsky.

* Opera composers: Verdi, Wagner, Meyerbeer, Berlioz, Puccini, Gounod, and Offenbach. Traditional productions using Victorian costumes and sets by any of these would be useful. Many opera houses have recorded video productions and many are on YouTube.

* Artists: Winslow Homer, Mackintosh, Whistler, Sargent, Beardsley, Rodin, Cézanne, Van Gogh, Matisse, Gauguin, Toulouse-Lautrec, Mucha, Gaudi, and Horta.

* There are many movies and TV mini-series about the Victorian era; some suggestions would be: Oscar Wilde's *The Ideal Husband*, *The Importance of Being Ernest*, and *The Picture of Dorian Gray*, with several adaptations. Edith Wharton's *The Age of Innocence* (1993)* and *The House of Mirth* (1981)*, *Sherlock Homes* (2009)*, *Dr. Jekyll and Mr. Hyde* (1941), several adaptations of Henry James' novel *The Heiress* to *Washington Square*, the play and movies. Any other adaptations of the above writers and particularly Dickens for sets and costumes would be useful.

The Late Victorian Material World

Figure 13.2 Neuschwanstein Castle, Bavaria, Germany. This Neo-Romanesque fantasy castle was built for King Ludwig II as a personal retreat and although large it was not meant for court life. The late 19th century in Germany was a time of romantic rebuilding of castle ruins and this castle was conceived by Ludwig and a theatrical designer, Christian Jank. Ludwig was passionate about the mythological operas of Richard Wagner and many of the rooms were inspired by them. As it was also a pastiche of Gothic and Norman features it is now considered a significant example of Historicism. It has been the site of several movies and the inspiration for Disney's castle at Disneyland.

Robert Harding Picture Library/Superstock

What They Made

Figure 13.3 The golden Grand Foyer of Opéra Garnier, Paris. The opulent architectural details and the beautiful crystal chandeliers recall the splendor of Versailles and the Baroque and the ceiling is also using images in the compartmentalized Baroque style. The chairs right and left give a sense of the enormous scale.

Circumnavigation/Big Stock Photo

Figure 13.4 The grand double staircase of the Opéra Garnier in Paris. The staircase was designed as a stage on which wealthy theatergoers could see and be seen.

gary718/Big Stock Photo

Figure 13.5 Museum of Science and Industry at the Chicago World Fair of 1893. The Beaux-Arts movement delighted in these enlarged Classical monuments. It is an over-scale and complex version of a Greek temple, but built on a Roman scale. The fair was one of the first major public displays of incandescent electric lighting and at night the buildings and grounds were also lit by a profusion of different kinds of lights.

Ernitz/Dreamstime.com

Figure 13.6 This is one of the Vanderbilts' seasonal estates and is in Hyde Park, New York. Designed by the pre-eminent 19th-century New York City architectural firm McKim, Mead, and White and built 1896–1899. This was one of America's premier examples of the country residence built by wealthy industrialists during the Gilded Age. It uses the Beaux-Arts style on the exterior and "the American Renaissance style" in the interiors. This round portico is on the garden or back side façade, using the Composite order. The front façade is based on the Petit Trianon at Versailles.

sphraner/Big Stock Photo

Figure 13.7 Bow Bridge is an iconic element in Fredrick Law Olmstead's Central Park in New York City and depicted in countless films and photographs. The bridge was designed by Calvert Vaux and built between 1859 and 1862 making it the second oldest cast iron bridge in the United States. Central Park was the first large-scale public park in America and its popularity gave rise to the City Beautiful Movement across the US. See New York City Central Park website for more photos and information.

Chris Tiné

Figure 13.8 The façade of the house, Casa Batlló, Barcelona, Spain, designed by the brilliant Catalan architect, Antonio Gaudi and built between 1904 and 1906. His work was characterized by its asymmetry, his use of organic shapes, and his unusual and often flamboyant use of colors. This façade is covered with pieces of glass and mosaics of colorful tiles. The roof is also covered with iridescent ceramic scales. This is an excellent example of the Art Nouveau style as applied to architecture. There are many websites that have pictures and information—Google "Casa Batlló."

Mark52/Shutterstock.com

Figure 13.9 This is a stick-style house that is another revival style in the US and England in the late 19th century and gets its name from the use of "stickwork"—small pieces of wood used for decoration on the exteriors of houses. Some of its characteristics featured here are the bracketed eaves, the ornate oval openings with their trellis designs (sticks) on the upper and lower porches, the railings, and the contrasting colored trim are also representative of this style.

Author photo

Figure 13.10 The Carson Mansion, Eureka, California, in a 1930s photograph. William Carson was a Western lumber baron who built his house as an oversized Queen Anne redwood palace in 1884–1885. The exterior is an eclectic mix of styles, making it uniquely American, but Queen Anne predominates because of the overhanging roof eaves, the little porches, and the multiple shapes of turrets, towers, and cupolas with steep roofs. The interior has many original Arts and Crafts details. The house has been well preserved and since 1950 is a private club "The Ingomar Club"—their website has many pictures and a history.

NGS Image Collection/The Art Archive at Art Resource, NY

Figure 13.11 A New England version of a Queen Anne house that uses ribbon windows, scalloped shingled siding, with both of the small porches recessed, and although the corner porch is unusual, it is indicative of Queen Anne as is the curved wall on the other side. On the second story left is a bow semi-circular window and the shape continues under the porch roof to the porch floor. Notice that most of the windows have square panes, using 16 over one large one.

Author photo

Figure 13.12 The Belfast Grand Opera House in Northern Ireland, 1895, designed by Frank Matcham, the most prolific theater architect of this period. This is an example of the "eclectic style" that was typically used for the all-purpose "Opera Houses," found in England and America in medium and large cities in the Late Victorian era. This attests to the popularity of opera and its more informal cousins, operetta, vaudeville, burlesque, and melodramas, and in England and Ireland music hall and pantomime performance spaces, all of which would have similar buildings and were called "opera houses." www.virtualvisittours.com/the-grand-opera-house/Belfast

incamerastock/Alamy

Figure 13.13 The Buxton Opera House, Derbyshire, England, 1903. This is an interior of a similar medium-size theater by Frank Matcham. The configuration of the circular seating with high balconies was adapted from the Paris Opera on a much smaller scale and was popular in the last half of the century. See http://en.wikipedia.org/wiki/Frank_Matcham. He also designed two famous London theaters: the London Palladium (1910) and the London Coliseum (1904). See their websites.

John Warburton Lee/SuperStock

Figure 13.14 Ames Memorial Library, North Easton, Massachusetts. Henry Hobson Richardson, architect. Richardson popularized a revival style nicknamed Richardson Romanesque that was his version of Neo-Romanesque. It was used on both intimate buildings and monumental commercial ones. This shows an example of rustication stone technique and his use of the Romanesque arches. His work was influential on many architects of the late 19th century and early 20th century, including McKim, Mead, and White, whose work is seen in this chapter, and Louis Sullivan and Frank Lloyd Wright in the next.

Wikimedia Commons

Figure 13.15 This is a Second Empire-style house in Lancaster, Ohio. Its most distinguishing feature is the mansard roof with decorative shingles and an ornate cast iron railing, called "cresting," with three practical and ornamental lightning rods. Dormer windows are also common and in this case the two smaller ones are known as eyebrow dormers and the large one shows Dutch influence. Paired columns on the portico and the tall windows with cast iron window trim are also typical elements. Paris was rebuilt during the Second French Empire in the 1870s and this style was enormously popular there and quickly spread to the US for municipal, commercial, and residential buildings through the 1880s.

Mshake/iStock

* Civic and governmental architecture became monumental often on a Baroque scale. Building design was often Classical, Romanesque, or Gothic inspired and often supported multiple uses, such as railway stations which also had restaurants and bookshops in the same building complex. These were the first massive multi-use secular buildings since Roman times. See Figure 13.5.

* The Neo-Renaissance and Neoclassical Revival style continued to dominate palatial mansions and sometimes also civic building projects like the exterior of New York's Grand Central Station.

* Extensive use of the French Renaissance Revival style for commercial, governmental, and domestic buildings was extremely popular in the United States and Europe. See Figure 13.1 and Philadelphia City Hall.

* At the same time, the Beaux-Arts movement in Europe and the City Beautiful Movement in America emphasized Neo-Renaissance designs on a giant, formal scale and applied them to planned and refurbished cities. Older cities in America and Europe were rebuilt and incorporated new mechanical, electrical, sanitation, and transportation systems.

* The City Beautiful Movement in the US and comparable movements in Europe arose partly as a reaction to the terrible urban conditions that existed mostly due to population increases and immigration. On a large scale they introduced gardens, parks, landscaped cemeteries, and grand boulevards into cities. In the US this also saw huge monuments and statues erected, particularly to Civil War memorials epitomized by the sculptor Augustus Saint-Gaudens. See Figure 13.7.

* The Art Nouveau style developed among young artists in France, Belgium, Spain, and Austria as a break with Historicism and Victorian pomposity in the 1890s. It emphasized the abandonment of the formality and Classicism of the prevalent Victorian designs and replaced it with free-form and organic shapes. It spread quickly at the end of the century and died out almost as fast about 1910, but has had lasting influence. See Figures 13.8, 13.20, 13.21, 13.22, 13.23, 13.24, and 13.25.

How They Decorated

* Interiors continued to elaborate the period revival styles of the mid-century but they were enlarged in scale and their decoration was mixed with seemingly unrelated styles in the same building.

* The development of indoor plumbing, bathrooms, electricity and lighting, central heating, and the elevator revolutionized residential and industrial design and buildings.

* The greater use by the middle class of resident servants, and especially nannies, increased the need for living space and the size and complexity of houses.

* Homes continued the development of specialized rooms that answered the needs for comfort, diversion, and utility. Separate domestic areas were set aside for men (study, smoking room, library, and billiard rooms), and for women (drawing room, ballroom, music room, gallery, conservatory, and sewing rooms), and for children (nursery, bedroom, playroom, school rooms). Servants' quarters (kitchen, pantry, linen, silver, and china storage, and servant living quarters), garages, repair shops, and other outbuildings were also added.

* The importation of the veranda from India created a desire for outdoor porches and living spaces as an addition to the Victorian home. See Figures 12.2, 12.4, 12.5, and 12.6, Figures 13.9, 13.10, and 13.11, and Figures 15.3 and 15.9.

* Industrial mass production of furniture and decorative arts satisfied a huge middle class market for household articles and domestic decoration. See Figures 13.18 and 13.25.

Figure 13.16 One of the Neo-Rococo bedrooms in Marble House, the grand Vanderbilt summerhouse in Newport, RI. The house and its interiors were modeled on the Petit Trianon at Versailles. The flat ceiling and the deep moldings of the boiserie technique mark this as an example of the Rococo Revival style. Built from 1888 to 1892 it was one of the first transforming houses to make Newport the style-setting summer resort for the very wealthy. They called them "cottages" in reference to the simpler wooden houses that were in Newport—although not simple, see The Hunter House in Chapter 10. Palatial mansions in this style like this room often used authentic period furniture to enhance the illusion of a period room. As an example, in the other Vanderbilt Hyde Park residence Sanford White was in charge of buying all of the antiques. See Preservation Society of Newport Mansion's website.

Newport Preservation Society

Figure 13.17 The Oak Room in Wightwick Manor, Wolverhampton, UK. This Queen Anne-style house was built in 1887 and alludes to its Tudor ancestors. This is a comfortable middle class Victorian parlor and it is an excellent example of an interior using the Arts and Crafts style. For example the angled wooden recessed niche above the fireplace, the de Morgan tiles, and smaller cottage-style windows with square panes and stained glass. The interiors have many original details, objects, and furniture like the square upholstered chair and William Morris fabrics and wallpapers. See websites of the Wightwick Manor and Gardens, William Morris, and William de Morgan.

National Trust Photographic Library/Andreas von Einsiedel/Bridgeman Images

Figure 13.18 This triple-backed crested sofa was extremely popular in Europe and the US and every middle class family owned one. They were based on Rococo shapes but expanded to three seats and continued to use the popular tufted upholstery. Compare this to Figure 12.8 and see that it has gotten longer but the proportions have gotten more delicate especially in the arms and legs and therefore more like the original Rococo style. The great proliferation of this furniture was made possible by its mechanization in factories. See the bullet point in Chapter 12 about John Henry Belter (p. 184).

Author photo

Figure 13.19 This painting by John Hammond titled *The Commemorative Book of the Royal Visit in 1884* shows Princess Alexandra and her daughters at William Armstrong's home, Craigside. William Armstrong was a prominent inventor, engineer, and developed and manufactured modern armaments during the Crimean and US Civil War. He was an early advocate of hydroelectricity and solar power and was also one of the wealthiest men in Europe. This is a richly furnished room with classically themed decoration and is an example of an affluent Victorian interior that was made popular at this time. This is a good example of a French Empire table decorated with marquetry, as is the box. The pair of jardinières are sitting on a Chinese-style table and the pots are likely Chinese. The columns support a massive marble fireplace surround. Sir William's dress is subdued and standard upper class attire and notice his high collar with the wings turned down. Alexandra is dressed in a tastefully restrained bustle dress with three-quarter-length sleeves and with her hair up and with curls. Her daughters are also in stylish, modest dresses, but because they are younger they wear their long hair pulled back and down their backs.

National Trust Photo Library/Art Resource, NY

Figure 13.20 The shapes of these Tiffany & Co. lusterware glass vases are very representative of the Art Nouveau movement, particularly the tall, slender one. Louis Comfort Tiffany popularized the custom handmade style of this and the Arts and Crafts style in furnishings and décor. His vases and particularly his stained glass lamps are extremely representative of this period. Maybe less known are his windows for both residential and church architecture that can be seen at the New York Met Museum. Many are not aware that he employed three hundred people in his studio and many of them were women. Clara Driscoll was one of his lead designers and did several of *his* iconic images including the wisteria lamp. The New York Historical Society did an exhibition in 2007 and also has many of his objects. Their website is extremely informative and also has many links and videos to other sites: http://www.nyhistory.org/explore/louis-comfort-tiffany

Bridgeman Images

Figure 13.21 This is the dining room in Victor Horta's Art Nouveau house in Brussels, built 1898–1901, at the height of this style. Horta was among the first to design the whole house interior and exterior and also much of the décor and furnishings. Art Nouveau was a movement by young designers that rejected Victorian formality and Classical forms and imagery, and showed its connection to Rococo in that it also favored organic and curvilinear forms. We can also see this with the Arts and Crafts such as Wightwick Manor, Figure 13.17, and William Morris, and also in the US, Frank Lloyd Wright with his American Prairie style. The house and studio are now a museum and have many of the original contents—see website: hortanima.be.

Erich Lessing/Art Resource, NY

Figure 13.22 This is the stairway skylight in Musée Horta, Brussels, 1898. The lighting behind the panels uses incandescent lights to mimic the sunlight outside, which was a popular technique of Art Nouveau designers. Also notice the stained glass used like bracketing to attach the curvilinear forms to the ceiling. These metal structures are also typical Art Nouveau forms.

akg-images/Hilbich

Figure 13.23 *The Heart of the Rose*, 1902. This design is by Margaret MacDonald Mackintosh. This complex and semi-abstract image features two women with a rose between them concealing the figure of a child and is very representative of her painting, textiles, and embroideries. She was the wife of Charles Rennie Mackintosh and they often worked together. The Hunterian Art Gallery, Glasgow, has an online catalogue of much of her work.

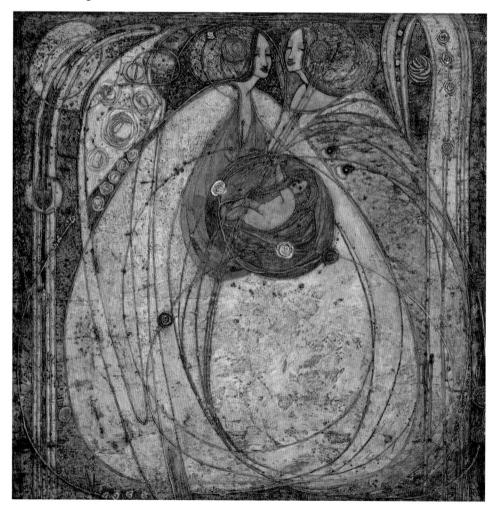

Figure 13.24 This is a high-backed chair designed by Charles Rennie Mackintosh in 1897 and this seminal design was often copied. Like Horta he was an architect, interior designer and created many of the furnishings. His two most famous projects are the Glasgow School of Art (1897–1909) and the interiors and furniture for the Willow Tearooms, Glasgow (1904). Also like Frank Lloyd Wright, he was very specific and demanding in his interior and exterior designs and the methods of their construction. Many of the architectural drawings and designs were done by his wife, Margaret MacDonald. He and Margaret were also textile designers and he worked for the famous company Liberty of London—see their website for their cotton fabrics. There are a number of reference books about him and several good websites.

The Fine Art Society, London, UK/Bridgeman Images

Figure 13.25 This Thonet chair is the universal bentwood chair in its original form. Thonet was a German-Austrian cabinetmaker, who in the 1830s pioneered the novel idea of steam bending and laminating simple pieces of beech wood. With the addition of two more bracing elements on the back it became "chair No. 14"—"the coffee shop chair"—and in 1867 he won a gold medal at the Paris World's Fair and so his fame and fortune were assured. His other innovation was that the chair, now eight pieces, screws, and a woven cane seat shipped unassembled in boxes—similar to Ikea—could be assembled at a store or by yourself. The chair and its variations are still popular today and have influenced many modern designers such as Ray and Charles Eames, Joseph Hoffmann, Adolf Loos, and many others.

De Agostini Picture Library/A. Dagli Orti/Bridgeman Images

* With the rise of materialism, personal objects became more important in defining social status. Wealthy and middle class homes were often seen as a shrine to the owner and his family. The prominent display of personal mementos and bric-a-brac underlined its function as a personal museum.

* The intensified feelings of romantic emotionalism in art and then photography also affected clothing and home furnishings by catering to the exotic and sentimental.

* Gilbert and Sullivan wrote 14 comic operettas from 1887 to 1896 and the Savoy Theatre, London was built for them in 1881. These operettas are still popular and they directly influenced musical theater.

* In 1881 incandescent lights were first introduced in the Savoy Theatre and by the 1890s were in most theaters in the US and abroad. Also because of electricity the elevator stage was invented and first used at the Budapest Opera in 1884, and then the revolving stage in Munich in 1896. See Figures 13.3, 13.4, 13.13, 13.16, 13.21, 13.22, and 13.32.

Building and Décor Keywords

French Second Empire (French Renaissance Revival) – The architectural style used by Haussmann and based on the style of Jules Hardouin Mansart from the Baroque period in the rebuilding of Paris. It emphasized centralized city planning and combined new residential apartment buildings with commercial buildings that featured over scale Renaissance façades with Gothic details and decoration. This style popularized the Mansard Roof, named for his great uncle, François, an earlier 17th-century architect. (Spelled Mansard in America, Mansart in England and Europe.) See Figure 13.15.

Beaux-Arts style (Beautiful Arts) – A Neo-Renaissance style of architecture in the US, Latin America, and Europe at the turn of the 20th century, combining Renaissance symmetry and Baroque axial planning and decoration on a massive scale. It was most often exemplified by large public buildings, parks, and private estates. In the US it was featured in many buildings at the Chicago World's Fair of 1893 that popularized this style and contributed to the City Beautiful Movement. See Figures 13.1, 13.3, 13.4, 13.5, 13.6, and 13.7.

Giant Order – An architectural system started in the Renaissance in which a large order is superimposed over one or more smaller orders that are behind it. The Giant order could be the entire height of a building and was only used on large and significant buildings. Palladio and Michelangelo used this in a number of their important municipal buildings and churches and it has been used by architects ever since. See Figure 13.1.

axial planning – The layout of a building or a group of buildings, usually seen in the Beaux-Arts style, along a single axis implying a processional pathway. It was derived from Baroque architectural palace design and applied to Late Victorian civic and commercial structures. The Chicago Exposition used this, but it is not shown in this image.

City Beautiful Movement – The American response to the European adoption of the city planning principals of Haussmann in Paris. Many cities remade their downtown areas to include wide boulevards, parks, bridges, and fountains in response to the Parisian innovations. See Figure 13.7.

Arts and Crafts – This style that included architecture, garden design, and all the decorative arts flourished from the 1880s to 1910s. It was started in England by William Morris (1834–1896) and quickly spread to the continent and North America, where it was often called "**Craftsman style**." The movement was a reaction to the gaudy, factory, mass-produced furniture and featured simpler forms and stressed excellent, often handmade, craftsmanship. It was heavily influenced by romantic interpretations of medieval decorations. The US examples are the Prairie style of architecture of Frank Lloyd Wright and Mission style furniture of Gustav Stickley. See Figure 13.17.

Stick style – A variation of the Queen Anne style in England and America in which exterior decorative features such as railings, brackets, windows, and half-timbered effects were executed with multiple small wooden members, either turned or sawn. See Figure 13.9.

Queen Anne (Cottage) style – A late 19th-century American and English suburban and rural architectural style based on revived and reinterpreted English Tudor features like shingled siding in geometric patterns, large overhanging oriel windows, projections, turrets, hidden second-story porches, decorative half-timbering, and asymmetrical compositions, often with one or more round towers. It was not related to the 18th-century furniture style of the same name. See Figures 13.10, 13.11, and 13.17.

Richardson Romanesque – The style of the public and civic buildings designed by the American architect Henry Hobson Richardson in a Neo-Romanesque style, which featured heavily rusticated stone construction. It was especially popular for church and institutional applications. See Figure 13.14 and Figure 13.2. Neuschwanstein Castle is not Richardson but is Neo-Romanesque.

Eclectic – This term referred to a style that delighted in combining architectural elements and furniture and accessories of various periods. See Figures 13.10 and 13.12. See R.M. Hunt and R.N. Shaw.

Shingle style – The late 19th-century and early 20th-century style of American domestic and cottage architecture that featured shingled walls as well as roofs based on vernacular New England farm and fishing cottages. This style was initially popular in New England and Long Island, but later further inland, but its simplicity was not about fishermen's huts as it was usually summer "cottages" for the wealthy, a good example is the former President Bush's 1903 home in Kennebunkport, Maine. For other examples see the websites: http://architecture.about.com/od/housestyles/ss/shingle and http://en.wikipedia.org/wiki/Shingle_style_architecture

Colonial Revival – Reproductions of classic 18th-century American styles of domestic architecture, furnishings, and décor were popularized during the American Centennial celebration in 1876.

Art Nouveau – The decorative architectural and interior décor style developed in France between 1890 and 1910 characterized by the use of free, sinuous movements of organic and plant shapes in fantastic and imaginative compositions. It was an outgrowth of the Arts and Crafts movement in England and America, and the Vienna Secessionist movement in Europe. See Figures 13.8, 13.20, 13.21, 13.22, 13.23, 13.24, and 13.25.

Mansard roof – There were a number of variations of this, but generally it was a four-sided gambrel-style roof characterized by two slopes with the lower slope at a steeper, more vertical angle than the upper slope that was nearly flat. Dormer windows often punctured it. It often used slate instead of wooden shingles. It was representative of the French Second Empire style of 1855–1880. See Figure 13.15.

gambrel roof – This was a double-sloped roof with the lower slope at a steeper angle than the upper slope; often found on farm and barn buildings.

hipped roof – A pitched roof style where the tops of the end gables were chamfered or cut away at an approximately 45 degree angle. See Figure 5.12, Stokesay Castle.

dormer – This was a window with a roof of its own that projected from the shingled slope of any roof style. See Figure 13.15.

veranda (va-RAN-dah) – The covered porch, often with a railing, added to homes in this period. It derived from British colonial buildings in India, South East Asia, and Australia.

porte-cochère (PORT co-SHARE) – An archway in a building or a freestanding covered structure open at the sides that was large enough to accommodate and protect a vehicle and its passengers traveling to or from the street to a large house.

rusticated (rust-eh-KAY- ted) – This was the decorative architectural technique that left stone building surfaces and façades in a rough, unfinished state. See Figure 7.5 and Figure 13.14.

bric-a-brac (knick-knack) – Low-cost and often highly sentimental decorative chinaware, decorative objects, and paintings meant to be displayed on a table or in a cabinet.

The Late Victorian Clothing and Costume World

How They Dressed

*   During the Victorian period masquerade and themed parties and balls continued to be popular as they had been in the earlier royal courts. Frederick Charles Worth (Figure 12.17) among others was a noteworthy designer for them, and the young lady as Rapunzel (Figure 13.31) is an example of a costume.

*   Elaborate rituals and social customs of dressing and formal visiting developed partly as a way of expressing wealth and status and partly as a way of socially excluding newcomers.

Figure 13.26 This is an elegant Philadelphia lady in the late 1880s' bustle-style evening gown with voluminous ruffles and train. The short sleeves and low round neckline are also characteristic, as is her hairdo. This photo was taken in a professional photographer's studio in front of a painted 19th-century Rococo set.

Louisa Rawle

Figure 13.27 This is a collection of day dresses and hats in the bustle style from a Paris fashion plate of 1888 from *Journal des Demoiselles*. Americans copied French styles faithfully and would have been influenced by illustrations such as this and been eager to have their seamstresses and milliners copy the latest designs. The bustle styles were also worn by younger women and girls, but with shorter skirts. Notice the variety of colors, decorated hats, gloves, and the low-heeled, high shoes that would have laced up with a buttonhook. Hair for older women was always worn up with this style and for younger women it was long and down the back.

INTERFOTO/Alamy

Figure 13.28 Pierre Auguste Renoir (1841–1919): *Luncheon of the Boating Party*, 1880–1881. One of the reasons this painting is so useful is that it shows a great assortment of Renoir's actual friends in a real restaurant that are outfitted in many different kinds of clothes and with props on the table. Particularly the men are shown from their underwear to the very formal wealthy gentleman with a top hat talking to the young man with a student cap and the middle class businessman with brown suit and bowler hat and man in the light summer jacket, which would evolve into the "boating suit." The women are also shown with a wide variety of clothes such as the relaxed blue and white dress to the young woman lower left with a more formal, fashionable outfit with a bustle to the woman by the railing in boating costume, and also showing an array of hats and bonnets. Renoir would also be a good source for costumes—see the website: P.A. Renoir The Complete Works.

Bridgeman Images

Figure 13.29 The beach at Staten Island, New York, 1898, showing a man and woman in bathing suits. Notice that she is almost fully covered with stockings and skirt. The two men are wearing tank tops and tight pants of different lengths. At this time most of these "bathing costumes" were made of wool and now people were actually going into the water, whereas before they sat or walked on the beach.

Museum of the City of New York/The Granger Collection, NYC

Figure 13.30 Mrs. George J. Gould in a wasp-waist gown. In the 1890s women disfigured themselves with these extremely tight and long to the thigh corsets to achieve this look and to stay abreast of fashion. The desired ample bust line could also be augmented with padding. Unlike the women in day dresses this would be an evening dress with its low neckline and small shoulder sleeves and was usually worn with long gloves. Also notice the extremely long ropes of pearls, the small tiara, and jeweled bodice.

Library of Congress

Figure 13.31 This is a young lady dressed up as Rapunzel in a photographer's studio with its theatrical 19th-century scene painting and the small flax spinning wheel. She is wearing a Victorian adaptation of a "princess dress" with puffy sleeves and a fichu. It is interesting to compare it to contemporary Rapunzel costumes such as the 2010 Disney film *Tangled* and *Shrek—The Third*; Barbie as Rapunzel, and the stage and film versions of *Into the Woods*.

Louisa Rawle

* Women's complicated costume continued with modifications such as the bustle and wasp-waist styles that resembled Rococo shapes with upswept, wig-like hairstyles, but returned to simplicity at the end of the century. See Figures 13.19, 13.26, 13.27, and 13.28; and wasp waist, Figure 13.30.

* In the late 1860s the crinoline style was declining and the bustle was introduced in the 1870s. At the beginning of the style the skirt was narrower at the top and fell more gently and was wide and fuller at the hemline in a "waterfall look" that often had a train. In the 1880s, as seen in Figures 13.26 and 13.27, the bustle had a more shelf-like appearance and the dress had a pronounced "pouf" behind, often with frills and a train, which became very exaggerated. The bustle went out of fashion after 1888.

* The 1890s introduced the new style of the wasp waist where the skirt had a tiny waist that accentuated the hips and pushed the bosom higher. To accommodate this look corsets became longer and were more rigidly boned and covered the stomach. For daywear the sleeves were wrist length and fitted and also had leg-o-mutton sleeves, and for evening, like the image of Mrs. Gould, necklines were low and with small sleeves or straps. See Figure 13.30, wasp waist.

* Women's hair was worn long and predominantly upswept high on the head with tight curls. Hats became a fashion necessity and developed a wide variety of styles that at the beginning of the period were high and narrow and ended low and wide, which transitioned into the Edwardian period. Small hats with artificial flowers and birds and feathers were also popular. Both for modesty and fashion, women wore facial veils. See Figures 13.27, 13.28, 13.32, and 14.10.

Figure 13.32 *The Gardens of Paris or The Beauties of the Night*, 1905, by Jean Béraud (1849–1935). This painting shows the transition into the freer Edwardian fashions. The men's clothes are still pretty much the same—white tie, waistcoat, and tails—but see that some of them are wearing the traditional top hats, but others have the more casual straw boater. This is a wealthy time prior to the First World War so the ladies have lots of extra fabric and softer dresses with a dropped waist, shawls, and capes, and their hats are flattened and wider. There is a lovely playful, romantic feel to this painting that is also captured by the theatrical use of electric lighting. Béraud was a popular French painter in his time and painted many Parisian people, interiors, and exterior scenes in all times of the year and is an excellent source for designers. There are many of his images on the Internet.

Giraudon/Bridgeman Images

* Men's formal and business costume continued dark and conservative, but after the death of Prince Albert, who was slim and also corseted, profiles became fuller. Coats, waistcoats, trousers, hats, gloves, and a cane were the rule with few variations. All extravagance was abandoned in favor of conservative dress geared to urban living. See Figures 13.19 and 13.32.

* In the 1870s the silhouette of the sack coat was getting narrower and was buttoned high on the chest, but in the 1880s it was often worn open or partly open to show the waistcoat and pocket watch. Knotted neckties and bowties were worn with both styles.

* As the century progressed, the sack coats got more tailored and the hems could be straight or recurved. Formal starch shirt collars were turned up, exposing the necktie, with the tips folded down in front. Contrasting colored vests continued to be worn with coats. See Figures 12.14, 13.19, and 14.1.

* By the 1890s the three-piece suit with creased pant legs was standard men's attire and would be from then until now. See Figures 13.19, 14.1, and 15.26.

* Toward the end of the century, the introduction of the tuxedo from the US as formalwear with no tails for middle class men signaled the importance of this rapidly growing segment of society. It was comparable to the European smoking jacket.

* Men wore their hair collar length and developed many decorative facial hairstyles, such as mutton chop whiskers and various beard and mustache styles. Facial hair increased during this period, but

by the end it was acceptable for them to be clean shaven. This was augmented by a variety of top hat styles. See Figures 13.28, 13.29, and 13.32.

* The beginning of sports attire appeared with boating and seaside wear and uniforms for the newly popular team sports like cricket, rugby, baseball, and football, which also often carried team logos. Women started adopting tailored men's attire particularly for sporting clothes, but this did not include trousers. See Figure 13.29.

* Croquet, tennis, and bicycling were wildly popular and they also developed specialty clothing.

* In the 1890s bloomers reappeared for women's sports activities; also known as knickerbockers or "rationals," they were now skirt-less, baggy, knee-length trousers fastened below the knee.

* Middle class men and women copied the fashionable clothes often in simpler ways and with less expensive fabrics and trims. They were made at home or by dressmakers or tailors. The poor relied on donations and also second hand shops and altered them over and over until the destitute wore rags.

Clothing and Costume Keywords

wasp waist – The women's fashion that became popular in the 1890s, which featured an unnaturally small waistline that was achieved by the use of very tight corsets. Some larger women had their ribs surgically removed to achieve this look. See Figure 13.30.

bustle – This was a whale bone, padded fabric, or steel half-cage worn under the petticoat that created a "pouf" on the back of the dress, which resulted in a train of fabric. It was worn with leg-o-mutton and pagoda sleeves (funnel shaped) during the day and at night with short sleeves. See Figures 13.19, 13.26, 13.27, and 13.28.

réticule – A small, decorated fabric purse worn on a cord hanging from the wrist that was often beaded or embroidered.

top hat – A tall, cylindrical men's hat that now had a wider curved brim. It was made of beaver skin or later silk and sometimes was collapsible. See Figures 13.28 and 13.32.

mutton chop whiskers – A men's shaving style of the 1880s and 1890s, which allowed the sideburns to become elongated and very full around the cheeks in a shape similar to a big lamb chop.

handlebar mustache – This was the men's mustache that had two upward s-shaped halves similar to bicycle handles.

gaiters – These were a protective covering for men's shoes and/or boots and lower trouser leg to shield them from dirt, snow, and rain. They were also part of clerical, equestrian, and military dress.

CHAPTER FOURTEEN

Edwardian: 1901–1919

Figure 14.1 This striking portrait of Count Robert de Montesquiou (1855–1921) was painted by Giovanni Boldini (1842–1937) in 1897. The slim lines and affected, relaxed pose point towards the easy informality of this period. Daytime and sports clothing for both men and women became more informal and eveningwear stayed more structured. Boldini, originally Italian, became a successful portrait and genre painter first in London and then in Paris with his fashionable portraits like this one. His paintings would be good costume sources—see "Giovanni Boldini The Complete Works" on the Internet.

Giraudon/Bridgeman Images

A Little Background

The death of Victoria and the ascension of her son Edward VII to the throne freed Victorian society from the stiffness and formality of the former years and introduced a period of relaxed optimism and energy in both Europe and America. Architecture, décor, and especially clothing became more comfortable and informal; often it adopted country, leisure, and sporting themes. The massive Beaux-Arts formal architecture continued for civic buildings, but domestic architecture trended toward the rural Queen Anne, Shingle, and Cottage styles. The European Art Nouveau architectural, craft, and graphic style had a brief popularity in America at the turn of the century.

Who They Were

* This was the era of the second industrial revolution when there were many advances in science and technology and the growth of many industries.

* There was a continued expansion and sophisticated improvements of municipal technological systems, such as electricity, telegraph, telephone, steam, rapid transit, road, and highway building.

* The 1956 musical play *My Fair Lady* perfectly encapsulated English Edwardian life. It was based on George Bernard Shaw's play *Pygmalion* of which there have been many adaptations for TV, film, and stage. Shaw, like Dickens, was known for his social criticism and was a moral conscience of this time. The 1956 New York production won Tony awards for Oliver Smith's sets and Cecil Beaton's costumes and it was followed in 1964 with the stunning film version with art direction and costumes by Cecil Beaton—a superior resource for this period.

* The Eiffel tower was built for the Universal Exhibition of 1889 in Paris by Gustave Eiffel (1832–1923) as a radio transmitter but quickly became a popular attraction, which it has remained; it became a symbol of Paris, technology, and the French spirit.

* In France this was the period after the Franco-Prussian War and the start of WWI from 1871–1914 known as the "La Belle Époque" and was noted as a stable, joyous time of "joie-de-vivre."

* This was roughly comparable to the Edwardian time in England and the Gilded Age in the US and shared many characteristics. One important one was the rise of a new wealthy class often referred to as "the nouveau riches," who intermarried with old aristocratic European families and created a lavish lifestyle with palatial houses as seen in the previous chapter, both in the US and Europe. The TV mini-series *Downton Abbey* is a good resource as were John Galsworthy's novels, *The Forsyte Saga* with adaptations to movies and the TV mini-series 2002*.

* In Germany it was the period of Kaiser Wilhelm II and in Russia Czar Nicholas II and his wife Alexandra, where many of the old traditions continued with a large division between the aristocracy and the rest of the population that would end with WWI. See films: *Nicholas and Alexandra* (1971) and *Dr. Zhivago* (1965 and TV 2002).

* The rising prominence of US naval and military might after the Spanish American war signaled the United States' entrance onto the world stage.

* The conquering of Native American cultures and the addition of the western states to the Union completed the Western colonization of the American continent. This period was often seen as an American "Golden Age of Innocence."

* This was the time when Americans began to collect and appreciate Native American art and artifacts and the start of "American West" painting, including landscapes, paintings of cowboys and Native Americans. Frederic Remington was a good example and a rich resource for the designer: Wikipedia has an excellent website with many images.

* The influence of Chinese and Japanese art and culture grew as a result of continued trade with them. These cultures and their art influenced designers and artists in the West and produced another wave of "Oriental" designs.

* In the middle class in reaction to Victorian rigidity there was also a growing desire for simpler, more natural styles of furnishings and clothing that sparked an interest in emulating rural simplicity. See Carl Larsson, www.clg.se/engallery.aspx

* Professional sports teams and sporting activity for the general public developed at this time, which in turn spurred the growth and popularity of leisure and specialized sports clothing and equipment. See Figures 14.12 and 14.13.

* Paris was renowned for its vibrant life and was famous for its intellectuals and artists, as well as the more frivolous and ostentatious nightlife. This was especially true in the artists' quarter of Montmartre where the famous Moulin Rouge cabaret with its red windmill attracted people of all classes to mix together. This was where the can-can dance started and led to the introduction of cabarets throughout Europe. There have been many movies, music videos, and documentaries about it from a silent movie in 1898 to the 2001 Baz Luhrmann film.

* The Folies Bergère was another distinctive nightspot that featured exotic dances with frequent nudity, but also outlandish extravagant costumes and sets. In the 1880s they invented a new theater form the musical review. Florenz Ziegfield, Jr. brought this to Broadway and created The Ziegfield Folies from 1907 to 1931 that starred the "Ziegfield Girls" and started many important theater careers. There have been numerous movies about both Folies—Paris and New York City.

* George M. Cohan (1878–1942) was America's first show business star and known as "The Man Who Owned Broadway," as he did everything from song and dance to writing and composing to directing and producing. He was also known "as the father of the American Musical" and his statue is in Times Square, NYC. James Cagney won an Oscar for portraying him in the 1942 film, *Yankee Doodle Dandy*.

* Isadora Duncan and Loïe Fuller were instrumental in starting modern dance. Fuller also designed her own silk costumes and made important discoveries in the use of colored stage lighting.

* Film had its early beginning steps in the 1890s and by the 1910s there were full-length movies and newsreels, which were silent until the late 1920s. *Wings* (1927) was a groundbreaking silent WWI aviation film that introduced the superstar "It Girl," Clara Bow, who personified the 1920s Hollywood silent movie star. A lovely film about silent movies was *The Artist* (2011).

* By 1929 most films had sound. There are now many contemporary movies set in this time and Merchant and Ivory films were well known for their carefully researched and lavish productions and costume designs that would be excellent resources.

* Any movie or TV adaptations of these writers would be useful if set in this period. Also further suggestions: the TV mini-series of PBS, *Manor House* and *Upstairs Downstairs*. The films: *Meet Me in St. Louis* (1944) with Judy Garland, *The Miracle Worker* (1962), about Helen Keller, *Titanic* (1997), *Enchanted April* (1991), and *Michael Collins* (1996), the Irish Revolutionary. In addition there are many WWI movies, but these are a few good ones: *Gallipoli* (1981), *All Quiet on the Western Front*

(1930), *Le Grand Illusion* (1937), *Paths of Glory* (1957), *King of Hearts* (1966), *Atonement* (2007), and *War Horse* (2011).

* Anton Chekhov with Ibsen and Strindberg were considered the beginning of modern playwriting. Chekhov's four seminal plays were directed by Constantin Stanislavski at the experimental Moscow Art Theatre. He was a chronicler of Russia rural life, which at that time was dealing with the turmoil of change, which still resonates with us today. His sensitive portraits of women in crisis were especially powerful. The plays were considered comedies because of their ironic use of misunderstandings and the subtle subtexts. From a designer's point of view they can be interpreted from simple abstract sets to more traditional realism rather than many of his contemporaries such as Ibsen, who depended on more concrete details. There are a number of films of his plays and short stories and an exceptional little-known one is *An Unfinished Piece for the Player Piano*, 1977. Aaron Posner's irreverent adaptations have been hugely successful and called "meta-theatrical."

* Playwrights: Chekhov, Strindberg, Shaw, Maugham, and Gilbert and Sullivan. Burlesque, music hall, and Edwardian musical comedy were also popular and led to the later US vaudeville and American musical comedy.

* Composers: Elgar, Rachmaninoff, Dvořák, Janáček, Bartók, Joplin, and Sousa.

* Artists: Rossetti, Burne-Jones, Whistler, Sargent, Alma-Tadema, William Morris, Augustus and Gwen Johns, Boldini, Henri Rousseau, Bellows, Chase, Glackens, Steichen, and Sloan. In England Walter Sickert painted many interiors and theater-related subjects and was part of a group of painters known as "The Camden Town Group," many of whom could be useful, http://www.tate.org.uk/about/projects/camden-town-group, also "The York Art Gallery."

* Illustrators: This and the late Victorian era were "The Golden Age of Book Illustration"—Randolph Caldecott, Beatrix Potter, Maxfield Parrish, Walter Crane, Kate Greenaway, and many others made an important impact with their pictures and have had lasting influence.

* Writers: Important novelists and poets continued the 19th-century traditions, but some who typified this period and were significant and/or who were innovative were: Edith Wharton, Willa Cather, T.S. Elliot, Edna St. Vincent Millay, James Joyce, Virginia Woolf, and the Bloomsbury Group, E.M. Forster—*Howard's End* and *A Passage to India*, both adapted to plays, TV, and film.

The Edwardian Material World

What They Made

* The Arts and Crafts movement in the US, Cottage style in England, and Jungenstil in Europe reacted against Victorian mass-produced furniture and decorative arts and emphasized the virtue of simple handmade crafts using natural materials, and expressed youthful, middle class values.

* English architects and designers William Morris and Charles Eastlake were the most well-known practitioners of the Arts and Crafts style; they believed a house and its contents should be beautiful, useful, and handcrafted, emphasizing honesty and sincerity.

* The Cottage style of architecture in England was based on scaled-down Tudor Revival styles and celebrated the virtues of rural yeomen simplicity.

Figure 14.2 This is a grand, elaborate Edwardian home built for Sir Ernest Debenham, the department store magnate, in 1905–1907, London. It is in the Arts and Crafts style and uses the return of relatively flat Neo-Classical, Renaissance ornamentation on its façade and the interior also uses many Arts and Crafts details, including de Morgan tiles. Notice both the basement and attic windows, as these would be servants' quarters for kitchen and utility rooms and the attic for sleeping. It has been used in many TV shows and films. Debenhams is now an international store and architecturally runs the gamut from past styles to the Postmodern one in Bury St. Edmunds, UK.

Angelo Hornak/Alamy

* Civic and governmental architectural styles in Europe and America continued to be based on revivals of Gothic, Tudor, and Renaissance forms and were hardly influenced by the new youth-oriented Arts and Crafts and Art Nouveau movements.

* Edward Lutyens not only designed many English country houses but starting in 1912 designed and planned the new British colonial seat of government and capital in the city of Delhi, India—now known as "New Delhi" and sometimes "Lutyen's Delhi."

Figure 14.3 This is an English manor house with a period greenhouse. Gardens and conservatories such as this became showplaces and emblems of wealth and more relaxed living. They were often connected to the house like this one, and treated as an additional room and were often the site of informal entertainments like afternoon tea.

Figure 14.4 Fulbrook House in Surrey, UK, was designed by the major English architect Edward Lutyens (1869–1944) and was built in 1896. This is an early photograph. In this early period Lutyens was known for designing country houses in Surrey using local idioms combined with historic styles and modern conveniences such as plumbing and electricity. The left side of the house is in the Neo-Gothic style, characterized by the small windows and the size, detailing, and positioning of the large chimneys. The right side with the shingled tower and the large sash windows with square panes reflect English Renaissance and Gothic architecture. He used this flared-shape roof over the doorway on a number of houses. The steeply pitched roofs are a marker for both periods. Lutyens and garden designer Gertrude Jekyll became partners and designed and created hundreds of iconic gardens in the UK, Europe, and the US that still have lasting influence. They established a new style away from Victorian formality that combined architectural elements such as stairways, walls, and balustrades, and furniture with luscious and colorful perennial borders and shrubberies.

Figure 14.5 Edward Linley Sambourne's (1844–1910) Edwardian townhouse at 18 Stafford Terrace, London. Row townhouses like these often featured mansard roofs, bay windows, and classical moldings. This modern photograph has a contemporary window greenhouse that would not be of this period, but it is showing two houses with balconies and balustrades. Each house had two entrances; the owners entered through the door with the staircase, and the servants and trades people went in through the door to the lower right of it, and the iron railings and gates closed them off. Sambourne was the major cartoonist for the satirical magazine *Punch* after 1901; his black and white drawings have a strong, distinctive style that was based on accurate details. He also did book and advertising illustrations. The house and furnishings are now "Leighton House Museum" and there are also many of his images on the Internet.

Bridgeman Images

How They Decorated

Figure 14.6 *A Friendly Call* by William Merritt Chase (1849–1916), 1895. Seemingly a small drama is occurring between these two genteel ladies, who are enjoying an afternoon social call in a large informal drawing room, with the large rag rug, small cushions scattered on the floor, and the soft satin pillows that would not have been seen in a more formal Victorian parlor. Notice in his composition the interesting use of rectangles and the juxtaposition between the large mirror with Rococo frame and the simple straight lines of the other art and the long banquette, also with its casual covering, and the one-point perspective with its focal point right above the two ladies' heads. Wicker and bamboo chairs were recently introduced, probably from British India. Electric lighting was also a new introduction in grander homes and a lamp with fringe is reflected in the mirror. Both ladies are wearing the new softer style of Edwardian summer dresses in lighter colors with high necks and soft leg-o-mutton sleeves. The visiting lady is wearing a decorated hat and veil and has a lacy parasol (also an Indian detail), and her friend a yellow fan.

Bridgeman Images

* William Merritt Chase was an American Impressionist painter known for his portraits, particularly of fashionable ladies, but also of landscapes and genre paintings, both in the US and abroad. He would also be a good period source. See http://www.william-merritt-chase.org

* Pre-Raphaelite painters returned to the pre-Renaissance styles influenced by the Romanesque and Gothic spiritual style of painting. Their flat, direct compositions of medieval subjects influenced a generation of artists, illustrators, and designers.

* There are a number of Edwardian period painters that were doing detailed pictures of interiors, landscapes, genres, and portraits. This website gives a broad spectrum and then you can find more images from these names and it also has other useful links to books, theater, TV, and film. See http://edwardianculture.com/2013/05/02/one-hundred-edwardian-paintings

* Two other Scandinavian artists who are also useful are Carl Vilhelm Holsøe (1863–1935) and Carl Larsson (1853–1919).

* Carl Holsøe was a Danish painter, who primarily painted interiors that were similar to upper middle class English ones, and showed many pieces and arrangements of furniture. Interiors at this time were moving away from the high Victorian to a simpler yet cosmopolitan style. There is a tranquil

quality that is reminiscent of the 17th-century Dutch genre paintings and particularly Vermeer. His atmospheric use of lighting was stunning and he also captured its effects off of surfaces and reflections and their shadows. See the Carl Vilhelm Holsøe Athenaeum website and also a video on YouTube for many images.

* Carl Larsson was a Swedish painter, working mostly in watercolor, of domestic life using his house "Little Hytthnäs" in Sunborn and his wife and his many children as models. Together with his wife, Karin, they created a vibrant home filled with furniture, painted décor, textiles, and other furnishings. She designed and made many of these objects, which are representative of the Swedish Arts and Crafts style. The house is open to the public in summer months. There are many books with his images and many are also on the Internet. This is another excellent resource for designers.

* The introduction of Japanese motifs popularized by their woodblock prints greatly influenced artists in Europe and US and once again the emphasis was on foreign and exotic subjects.

* Graphic design and illustration were also influenced by them and in things like theater, advertising, commercial posters, and menus used flat, two-dimensional compositions as seen in the work of Toulouse-Lautrec and Alphonse Mucha among many others. Both of these artists have many images on the Internet and "1910 Vogue Covers" would all be good costumes references.

* The brief flowering of Art Nouveau and the Vienna Secessionist movements in Europe also emphasized the handmade and natural, and combined them with highly unusual organically derived structural forms. Primarily the graphic, decorative objects, and jewelry of Art Nouveau affected American design as seen in the work of Louis Comfort Tiffany; there was little interest in building and clothing in that style.

* The ascendency of the automobile as a necessary conveyance for the wealthy; and the continued development of all forms of communication technology increased the tempo of life. See Figure 14.8.

* The proliferation and popularization of children's books and the commercial illustrations that accompanied them generated a huge demand for writers and illustrators.

Building and Décor Keywords

Arts and Crafts style – The decoration and furniture style popular in America and Europe in the late 19th and early 20th century that embodied a reaction against mass-produced Victorian furniture and decorative arts. Their adherents wanted to replace them with unaffected, genuine design, skilled craftsmanship, and natural materials. They also wished to emphasize the authority of the individual craftsman. It was known as the Aesthetic Movement in America, also the Cottage style in England, and the Vienna Secessionist Movement in Austria and Germany. See Carl Larsson books and Internet.

William Morris style – This style took its name from the English designer who was one of the leaders of the Arts and Crafts movement. He is known for his decorative pattern designs used in interiors, primarily fabrics and wallpapers and established the firm Morris and Co. He also started the Kelmscott Press, which was a limited edition handmade book press that used illuminations like medieval manuscripts. His aesthetic urged for improved design, good craftsmanship, and a better quality of life for the middle class that influenced many interior, furniture designers, and architects. There are many images on the Internet and also useful are the William Morris Society and V&A museum—William Morris.

The Edwardian Clothing and Costume World

How They Dressed

* Both men's and women's fashion became lighter and more simplified during the Edwardian period. Fabric choices were wider for both sexes and leisure and sportswear broadened the clothing palette.

* In 1912 men's and women's ready-to-wear fashion was introduced in shops. See Figures 14.11, 14.12, and 14.13.

Figure 14.7 *Walzer* (The Waltz). This is a German lithographed postcard, c. 1900. The ladies are dressed in the stylish pastel colors with the more simplified, relaxed evening gowns of this period, which has the complexity at the bottom and the skirt forming a trumpet shape. They retain the low necklines and short puffy sleeves, now frequently with lace ruffles at the elbow and long white gloves. Not so noticeable here but the desired, characteristic look was to have an "s" shape as mostly seen by the lady on the right in the white dress. The fashionable style was to have long swept-up hair pinned on top and worn very full, but it could also be a large bun at the nape of the neck. As noted before men's formal fashions will not vary significantly into the 20th century, but as seen here they did wear short white gloves for dancing as a way of keeping ladies' gowns clean. Generally men wore their hair shorter, beards were mostly eliminated, but well-groomed mustaches in different styles were characteristic.

akg-images

Figure 14.8 Millicent Sutherland-Leveson-Gower, Duchess of Sutherland (1867–1955), was an English society hostess, an advocate for social reform, wrote plays, novels, and memoires and was president of the Ladies Automobile Club in France, where she lived much of her life. This is an early example of an open automobile and is most likely a Peugeot – notice its large brass horn and carriage-like seat. The Duchess is wearing a long coat with wide lapels and turned-back flared sleeves, a fancy version of a "duster." Drivers and rugged horseback riders wore an overcoat at this time to protect their clothes from dust while driving in open cars or riding in the American West. She also has a large flat hat tied with a large bow to keep it from blowing off as is her daughter's more decorated softer bonnet. Notice the child's shorter dress with the petticoat showing beneath the hem, black stockings, and high-buttoned shoes.

Private Collection/Bridgeman Images

Figure 14.9 This shows a mother and two girls in summer fashions looking like they are either going to or coming from a garden party. The woman has a high-waisted long but slimmer skirt; notice popular details such as the lightweight fabrics, the criss-cross decoration on her bodice and an extremely large soft garden party hat decorated with plumed feathers. Her jacket and small purse are also good details. The little one is wearing a full cotton dress with collar and puffy sleeves, but notice that they are not tight at the wrists as is common on adult clothes, and also that you can see her petticoat with its typical broderie anglaise. Because of its dark color it is difficult to see many details in the older child, but it does show the higher waist and diagonal details that are style markers of the end of the period. Their short white socks and shoes are also good costume references. Also note the use of the trelliage in the background.

Kim Schott/iStock

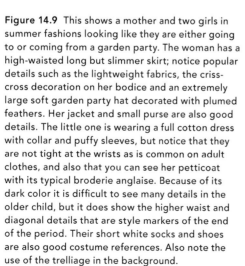

Figure 14.10 *Left:* Two stylish ladies posed in their winter coats, c. 1912, in a photographer's studio. The lady on the left is quite dignified and she is wearing a short jacket with a long fur stole over a long wool skirt with conservative trim. The other woman is more fashionable with her well-tailored coat with high collar and gigot sleeves. Her hat is more flamboyant with the bird perched cockily on it and her hemline is shorter and you can see her lace-up shoes.

marlenka/iStock

Figure 14.11 *Below:* This is a photograph, c. 1916, of a large recent immigrant family, who came to find "the American dream." With hard work, they quickly prospered and this shows them in subdued middle class Edwardian clothes. The women are wearing a number of different styles of loose dresses with long tight sleeves and also a variety of collars and necklines. The men are also in traditional business attire like modern suits with little variation other than their collars, which are starched, curved, or winged. The two children are boys and the baby is in a cotton broderie anglaise dress. The other boy is wearing an updated version of "The Little Lord Fauntleroy" velvet suit but with a large tie instead of the large lace collar, but still the long white stockings and high-buttoned shoes. Also notice the wide range of all of their hairstyles.

Author photo

Figure 14.12 This is the cover of a *Household Ledger* magazine, from June 1903, which was an American ladies' magazine that offered household hints such as cooking, gardening, baby and medical care to fashion, news, and stories with many illustrations and ads for current products. This one shows a picture of a current style of tennis costume that featured the separate shirtwaist blouse that became standard for sports, work, and casual wear. Also now the game would no longer be indoors for royalty as we saw in Chapter 7, Renaissance, Figure 7.18, but upper and perhaps even some middle class people would have access to it through newly organized tennis, cricket, and golf clubs from the 1880s and 1890s onward on both sides of the Atlantic.

Heritage Image Parnership LTD/Alamy

Figure 14.13 This is an English "Advertisement for Hinds Cream," c. 1900. Sports and leisure activity became popular and were heavily marketed. The man is wearing the traditional Scottish and English golfing costume with pants that were called "plus fours" and had been popular from the 1860s on. They were like knickerbockers, but were four inches longer and allowed for more movement and were popular for sports. They were often worn with knee socks, a squash cap, neckties, a shirt, and a sweater or the tweed Norfolk jacket. The woman's golfing clothes show a new style of fashion that prefigures the 1920s. It has a narrow ankle-length skirt, a long-fitted buttoned jacket that resembles a man's, but subtly it is still featuring the narrow waist and pigeon breast, and a soft fitting hat like a large cloche.

Heritage Image Parnership LTD/Alamy

Figure 14.14 This is the work of illustrator Charles Dana Gibson, who popularized the confident, independent "Gibson Girl" image, which became the epitome of "The New Woman" from the 1890s through the 1920s. He frequently used his wife, Irene, and her four beautiful sisters as his models. The woman on the left is dressed for business because of her white shirtwaist and separate long ample skirt, which was the symbol of the emancipated woman. In the center is the classic Gibson Girl look and on the right is a more aristocratic lady in a gracious outfit with a typical Edwardian hairdo. Gibson was a prominent and successful magazine and book illustrator from the 1890s until WWII. The Library of Congress had an exhibition called "The Gibson Girl's America" and now has many images on their website.

ClassicStock.com/SuperStock

* The rigidity of the late Victorian manners and dress was eliminated, but the floor-length skirts, hats, and veils of that style were retained. Edwardian ladies' garments now aimed for a more relaxed, comfortable style with ease of movement that had a more casual, flowing line, especially in eveningwear. See Figures 14.6, 14.7, 14.8, 14.9, 14.10, 14.12, and 14.14.

* In the beginning of the decade a new corset was introduced and called a "health corset." It made a continuous line of the bosoms and went straight across the top of the chest and pushed it up and out and was often referred to as the pigeon breast. It also pushed the backside out, which created the desired "s" shape that was the fashionable look. It usually had a separate cotton, sometimes ruffled, covering. See Figures 14.6, 14.7, 14.9, 14.12, 14.13, and 14.14.

* At the end of this period the waist rose to almost Empire height for both day and night. Diagonals were also used on the bodice to emphasize the bosom and make a dramatic statement. See Figure 14.9.

* The shirtwaist was a fashion innovation that accompanied women's entrance into business, factories, and sales. It consisted of a separate dark ankle-length skirt of a serviceable fabric worn with a white cotton or linen long-sleeved, collard blouse. A men's necktie and miniature boater were often worn with the set. See Figure 14.14.

* Ladies' hats became flat and wide with overhanging brims and were made of softer, more flexible materials. Veils were still popular in more formal and religious settings. See Figure 14.9.

* Men's casual clothing included the Norfolk Jacket and straw boater for outdoor sports activities as well as lighter-colored versions of the single-breasted suit and vest for relaxed daytime wear. Shoes were often worn with spats.

* Specialty clothing developed for work, art, recreation, sports, travel, and household use. There were also different fabric materials and slight style modifications for seasonal use. See Figures 14.7, 14.8, 14.9, 14.10, 14.12, 14.13, 14.14, and 13.28, and 13.29.

* Charles Lewis Tiffany established "Tiffany & Co." in the 1830s and designed for and served the wealthy and royalty in Europe and the US with exquisite jewelry, silver, and other fine things. In 1886 he introduced the diamond engagement ring, as we know it today. He was an innovator in corporate identity and launched the "Tiffany blue book" in 1845 as the first catalogue of its kind and the "Tiffany blue box" that are still used.

* Louis Comfort Tiffany took over his father's prestigious company, as its first art director in 1902, and designed jewelry using Art Nouveau lines of organic and natural shapes with an innovative mixture of semi-precious and precious stones. His designs were often inspired by many past historical and cultural styles. He also expanded the business to create the many innovations in glass. See his vases, Figure 13.20.

Clothing and Costume Keywords

Edwardian – The costume style popular during the reign of Edward VII in England featured a simpler, slimmer line and lighter fabrics for both men and women. There was less elaboration and softer, looser fabrics for women. Ladies' hats were still required but became flatter and softer. The introduction of sporting and recreational attire broadened fashion choices for both sexes. Children were now dressed in fashionable daytime and sports clothes.

fedora (fe-DOR-ah) – A soft, felt hat with a crease down the crown and two pinches at the front. Originally it was a woman's hat with the name derived from the title of the 1882 French play *Fedora!* in which the hat was prominently featured. See Figures 15.26 and 15.31.

homburg – Smaller and firmer than the fedora, it was a more rigid felt hat with a crease running down the center of the crown but with a rigid upturned brim. It was appropriate for business and semi-formal settings and was popularized by Edward VII.

straw boater – The men's flat, woven straw hat with a grosgrain ribbon that was worn for boating and leisure outdoor activities and by clerks in the business arena. It was used primarily in the summertime. Women also wore a smaller version. See Figures 13.28, 13.32, and 15.9.

Inverness (INN-ver-ness) – The men's full-length cape with a half cape attached at the neck. Originally a Scottish rural hunting garment of rough tweed but eventually it was adapted to cosmopolitan settings and fabrics. It was named for the area of Scotland where it originated.

deerstalker – This was a small tweed cap with matching small brims at front and back and with earflaps tied at the top. It was often worn with and in a matching fabric as the Inverness. The fictional literary character Sherlock Holmes was originally pictured wearing this outfit.

knickerbockers or nickers – These were loose or baggy men's and young boys' trousers that gathered at the knee. In the UK they are girls' underpants. In the 1920s they were briefly fashionable with young women.

plus fours – Men's and boys' knee-length pants derived from nickers gathered at the knee, and that extended four inches below them and therefore the name. They were worn with a belt and long socks for sporting occasions and often paired with the Norfolk Jacket and became the pants for golf outfits. They were introduced to the US by the future English King, Edward VIII, on a trip in 1924. The outfit, complete with argyle socks, was brought back in the late 20th century by the American pro golfer Payne Stewart. See Figure 14.13.

Norfolk jacket – The first men's sport jacket for informal occasions. It was a tight and short, single-breasted buttoned jacket with a narrow lapel, sewn in belt, and pleats front and back. It was usually made of tweed.

spats – These were short gaiters covering the top of the shoe and the ankle.

Gibson Girl – The image of the free, confident young woman created by the illustrator Charles Dana Gibson that became emblematic of the Edwardian style. It also referred to the upswept, loose women's hairstyle made popular by those illustrations. See Figures 14.7, 14.12, and 14.14.

shirtwaist – This was a white cotton or linen long-sleeved, collared blouse and the ensemble with a long skirt and tie was introduced for women in the workforce. See Figures 14.12 and 14.14.

middy blouse – In reference to midshipmen sailors, this was a loose blouse that featured a sailor's collar and decorations and was often worn with a pleated skirt and as casual wear, and also worn by young boys and girls.

boating dress – This was a lightweight, loose ladies' one-piece casual dress in blue with white trim at the collar worn for boating, picnicking, artistic, and outdoor activities. See Figure 13.28.

bloomers – They were now a fixture of athletic dress that would continue for many years, even in girls' schools in the US and Europe into the 1980s, but they got shorter and were gathered above the knees. They also became a regular staple of women's underpants popular from 1910 through the 1930s, but in different lighter-weight fabrics and gathered either at or above the knee.

duster – A long linen or canvas overcoat worn by both sexes while driving automobiles to protect clothing underneath from road dust. Men accompanied it with goggles and a canvas hat and ladies wore a veil and wide-brimmed hat for protection. See Figure 14.8.

CHAPTER FIFTEEN

Modern: 1919–1980

Figure 15.1 This is the Bauhaus building in Dessau, Germany, that was designed by Walter Gropius in 1925–1929. This design school was a leader in introducing the "Bauhaus style" or Modernism that would lead to the "International style." The surface of the building is stripped of decoration and it uses pure materials in its rectilinear, horizontal asymmetrical composition. Also notice the new modern typeface and off-center placement on the building's signage.

imagebroker.net/Superstock

A Little Background

The shock of the First World War carnage by mechanized warfare (20 million killed), the influenza epidemic of 1918 (another 20 million killed), and rapid industrialization spurred a new modern attack on traditional Classical design as a symbol of outdated and corrupt Victorian thinking. In a reaction to industrialization the rise of political movements like Socialism and Communism in Europe promised an ideal future but fell short of providing it.

A short period of speculative prosperity in the 1920s ended with the US stock market crash and was followed by a worldwide depression in the 1930s. The Second World War followed this in the 1940s, which ended up being a more widespread conflict than the First World War. This was followed shortly by the Cold War nuclear standoff between the US and Russia in the 1950s through the 1980s. After the collapse of the Soviet Union in 1989 the US was left as the sole remaining world superpower.

Modern architecture, costume, and design flourished in the years before, during, and just after the Second World War. Western European and American Modernism dominated world design after the war. Despite the tensions of the Cold War American and European prosperity continued; increasingly broadcast media and public entertainment defined the public character of national cultures.

Who They Were

* The hugely destructive First World War period, when millions of people suffered severe emotional and austere material conditions, was followed by an exuberant one. In the US this period was known as the "Roaring '20s," a world of high living, short-lived stock market profits, and styles.

* The age of Modernism also witnessed the rise of the American Musical Comedy and Jazz as art forms.

* The 1920s were known as "The Jazz Age" as the music became popular and Jazz bands proliferated. F. Scott Fitzgerald's 1925 novel *The Great Gatsby* has been called the supreme portrait of this era and has been made into numerous films from 1926 to 2013, TV, theater, opera, ballet, computer games, and radio adaptations.

* Prohibition of alcohol in the US initiated the crime wave of the 1920s and 1930s as gangsters tried to circumvent the law and sold and distributed illegal alcohol. Bars and nightclubs went "underground" and were called speakeasies, where they served "Bathtub Gin." Many gin-based cocktails were invented to mask the terrible taste and are still with us.

* There were a great many movies about gangsters between the war years, and several others were *The Godfather* films, 1972, 1974, and 1990, which top many lists, *Bonnie and Clyde* (1967), *Chicago* (2002), *The Untouchables* (1987), and the inimitable *Some Like it Hot* (1959).

* During the 1920s and 1930s more and more cars and trucks were used and people began a migration from rural America to cities to find work in factories. There was also a movement from the cities to the suburbs, which spawned a new distinctively American culture that became epitomized and romanticized in the 1950s and 1960s.

* Charles Lindbergh made the first transatlantic flight from New York to Paris in May 1927 and became an instant international celebrity and did much to promote aviation. See http://www.charleslindbergh.com

* In the 1930s and especially after the Second World War the airplane became a standard feature and way of travel that would play a major role in 20th-century life.

* The world financial depression of the 1930s ended the lavish living of the 1920s and led to government programs to bolster the economy and support for the arts in both Europe and the US.

* The Allied victory in the Second World War confirmed US dominance in world affairs and set the stage for US world political, corporate, and cultural expansion. It also began the Cold War in which tensions between Russia and the US, who were former Second World War allies, ran high but never ignited.

* Corporations grew larger and became important international players by wielding tremendous economic and influential taste-making power. Corporations adopted the International style of architecture that became the icon of corporate power. See the Seagram building in Figure 15.6.

* The US led the development of a consumer-based society whose aim was to provide material goods and prosperity for everyone.

* There was an increasing division between "popular" and "high" art and this period witnessed the birth and growth of advertising and the entertainment industry worldwide.

* The proliferation and democratization of art forms and techniques continued from the 19th century and became even more pervasive.

* Playwrights: Brecht, Grass, Pirandello, Ionesco, Genet, Cocteau, Coward, O'Neill, Williams, Inge, Anita Loos, Wilder, Miller, Osborne, Pinter, Beckett, Albee, Kushner, and Simon.

* Bertolt Brecht and Kurt Weill in Germany in the 1920s rejected traditional Victorian dramatic theatrical forms and invented a personal, confrontational, and didactic theater style. Their work continued to have a strong influence on European and American theater throughout the century.

* Musical and Jazz composers: Kern, Rogers, Gershwin, Weill, Lerner, Kander, Charles Strauss, Bernstein, Lloyd-Webber, Sondheim, and Schwartz. Ellington, Armstrong, Basie, Joplin, Waller, Parker, Brubeck, and Gillespie.

* *The Jazz Singer* featured the superstar Al Jolson in 1927 in the first full-length movie to have a "vitaphone system" that had synchronized dialogue and it was the advent of "the talkies."

* The 1920s also saw the era of the Big Bands that developed into Swing music in the 1930s and 1940s, mostly centered in New York City, Chicago, and Kansas City and had many notable composers, lyricists, bandleaders, instrumentalists, and vocalists. There are also many films, videos, and biopics like *The Glenn Miller Story* (1954), *Hollywood Hotel* (1937), *The Benny Goodman Story* (1956), *The Gene Krupa Story* (1959), and *The Fabulous Dorseys* (1947).

* Composers: Prokofiev, Stravinsky, Shostakovich, Mahler, R. Strauss, Hindemith, Barber, Menotti, Ives, Copeland, Bernstein, Britten, Cage, Glass, and Adams.

* Writers: A non-alphabetical and random sampling of prominent writers of this period is: Faulkner, Updike, Cheever, Welty, Capote, Dorothy Parker, Wolfe, Hemingway, Margaret Mitchell—*Gone With the Wind* (1939)*, Roth, Agee, Fitzgerald, Dos Passos, de Beauvoir, Sartre, Gertrude Stein, Pasternak, Gorky, Nabokov, Solzhenitsyn, Doctorow, Eco, Dr. Seuss, Haley, Havel, Huxley, Kafka, Steven King, D.H. Lawrence, Mailer, McCarthy, McCullers, F. O'Connor, Marquez, and Sontag.

* Poets: Stevens, Frost, Eliot, Pound, Jeffers, Kerouac, MacLeish, Plath, Dylan Thomas, Auden, Kalib Gibran, Sandburg, Yevtushenko, Brodsky, Mishima, and Billy Collins.

* Artists: This is also a random selection of visual artists of this period: Arp, Bacon, Basquiat, Chagall, de Chirico, Close, Dali, Escher, Frankenthaler, Giacometti, Haring, Hopper, Indiana, Johns, Judd, Kandinsky, Klee, Klimt, de Kooning, Krasner, Lichtenstein, Magritte, Motherwell, Munch, Nevelson, Nagouchi, O'Keefe, Claes Oldenburg and Coosje van Bruggen, Picasso, Pollack, Rauschenberg, Ray, Rivera, Rothko, Schiele, Serra, Shahn, Stella, Warhol, Andrew and Jamie Wyeth.

* A major force in entertainment was the emergence, dominance, and fall of the American film studio system. Begun in the 1910s and 1920s films were seen as a product for public consumption and were produced in "factory studios" on an industrial scale with actors, writers, directors, and designers as long-term employees, who produced multiple films on contract. A lovely film about silent movies was *The Artist* (2011).

* American movie palaces were at their apex in the 1920s with over 20,000 theaters in every conceivable and outrageous architectural style, with Egyptian especially popular. Two of the largest and most opulent that still exist are Grauman's Chinese Theatre in L.A. and Radio City Music Hall in New York City.

* This was the Golden Age of American Animation. The first short Walt Disney films began in 1923 and added sound cartoons in 1928. *Snow White and The Seven Dwarfs* was their first full-length animated film in 1937. Although he was the most prominent, others were Max Fleischer with *Betty Boop* and *Popeye*, and Hanna-Barbera's TV cartoons including *Tom and Jerry*, *The Flintstones*, and *The Jetsons* among many others.

* This was followed after the Second World War and throughout the last half of the century by the European "New Wave" film movement, and there and in the US the rise of the Independent films.

* This movement changed the dynamic of film making from the old model of industrial production to one in which films were carefully crafted individual works of art by directors, writers, and designers. They no longer needed the huge old studio movie lots as camera and film technologies allowed location shooting, and casts and crew were hired for individual projects. The studios still functioned as producers, fundraisers, controlled distribution, and provided publicity.

* *Show Boat,* based on the book by Edna Ferber, was a 1927 seminal American musical with music by Jerome Kern and lyrics by Oscar Hammerstein II and sets by Joseph Urban. It was the first to combine a story with music and lyrics with dance and sets and costumes; and in this instance it dealt with several serious issues.

* Ferber would collaborate with George S. Kaufman on three great comedies—*The Royal Family* about the Barrymores, *Dinner at Eight* (see Figure 15.17), and *Stage Door*, also adapted into an all-star movie.

* Oscar Hammerstein would later collaborate with Richard Rogers and created some of the best-known American musicals including *Oklahoma!*, *Carousel*, *South Pacific*, *The King and I*, and *The Sound of Music*.

* *Enchanted Evenings: The Broadway Musical, from "Show Boat" to Sondheim and Lloyd Webber*, by Geoffrey Holden Block, 2009, is an excellent resource.

* The introduction of TV, particularly in the US, would have a profound effect on American life. It would also give rise to variety shows, soap operas, and "sit-coms." There were a number of iconic shows that epitomized their times such as *Leave it to Beaver*, *The Brady Bunch*, *The Honeymooners*, *I Love Lucy*, *All in the Family, Dallas,* and *Cheers,* which all provide examples for designers to reference sets and costumes. *The Goldbergs* was unique in that it was on radio from 1929 to 1946 and TV from 1949 to 1956.

* The rise and dominance of photography, film, and electronic media reduced the influence of the traditional arts and theater, and began the fragmentation of media that characterized the last third of the 20th century.

The Modern Material World

Figure 15.2 Villa Savoye in Poissy, by Charles-Édouard Jeanneret known as Le Corbusier, built 1928–1931. This is an iconic house and was one of his most famous buildings and served as a model for architects all over the world and hence its pervasive influence on the "International style." The house also addresses Le Corbusier's "5 Points." First notice that the pilotis (the round column-like structures) are supports that go from the ground all the way up through the building. They also allowed the space underneath to be used as a garage, as he thought cars were important, as a garden, or for other leisure activities. Visually this open space also allows the house to float. Second, because the pilotis are the structural supports there were no internal load-bearing walls, creating an open, flexible plan. Third, the façades also have no structural purpose or decoration. Fourth, the flat roof could also function as a garden or terrace. At the time this was considered a negative as it would lead to leaking and now in the 21st century is considered an important eco-friendly feature with the use of "green roofs." Fifth were the long horizontal "ribbon windows." It was also one of the first houses that used concrete as an aesthetic material.

Universal Images Group/SuperStock

What They Made

* The Modern style of architecture and design began when Walter Gropius founded the Bauhaus Design School in Germany in 1919 to teach the principles of Modernist design. This type of design developed into what was known as the International style in architecture. See Figures 15.1, 15.2, 15.5, and 15.6.

Figure 15.3 This is Frank Lloyd Wright's Robie House in Chicago, built 1908–1910, and is a prime example of his "Prairie School" of architecture. This is the first real American style that was not derived from past European historical styles. The horizontal design reminded him of the mid-West American prairies and he achieved this not only in its form, but also by the horizontal banding of the bricks and mortar, which was a unique technique; the house is also an early example of brick and steel construction. The cantilevered windows and roofs also emphasized the horizontal and were another new feature in domestic architecture. Wright also designed the interiors and much of the décor and furnishings in this and many of his other houses. The open plan of his interiors permitted for a flexible arrangement of furniture that influenced the Bauhaus style and future modern architecture. His use of 30/60-degree angles in windowpanes, tapestries, gates, and other elements is another of his markers.

View Pictures Limited/SuperStock

Figure 15.4 This is Le Corbusier's Chapel Notre-Dame-du-Haut, in Ronchamp, France, built in 1954. It is an example of his later more organic style and is primarily built of reinforced concrete and local stone. Like the Romans he used recycled stone from previous chapels from this sacred site that was used even before the Romans. The two main interior lighting features are the deep, randomly placed small windows and the hidden clerestory windows between the top of the walls and the cantilevered roof, which cast a mysterious light. His organic approach is not only with the curvilinear walls and soaring roofline, but also in his sensitive awareness of the environment in which he took advantage of and incorporated the sloping ground.

Mihai-Bogdan Lazar/Shutterstock.com

Figure 15.5 This is the Farnsworth House in Plano, Texas, designed by Ludwig Mies van der Rohe in 1951. Mies van der Rohe was strongly influenced by Le Corbusier's pure, horizontal lines and completely open plan as seen in Figure 15.2. Only the wealthy could afford a house like this as its large picture windows afforded an unencumbered view and interaction with nature and no need for privacy. Again he is using pilotis as the structural element but in this case he has raised it off the ground only a few feet to help with ventilation in this hot environment and like Le Corbusier's it adds a floating appearance. It has also stripped down the domestic experience to its essentials with few rooms and an open plan.

akg-images/VIEW Pictures/Grant

Figure 15.6 This is the Seagram building at 375 Park Avenue in New York City and is an iconic example of the "International style" steel and glass skyscraper. The exterior was designed by Mies van der Rohe and many of the interiors are by Phillip Johnson, another important 20th-century architect as well. The sparse, sleek unadorned industrial façade characterizes this building and in 1958 it was a radical idea. He wanted the structural beams exposed but due to New York City fire laws they weren't allowed so he added the bronze-colored vertical skins over them to suggest the exterior beams. The building is isolated in a park and set back from the street that is also part of the modern style and influenced many other buildings and zoning laws. He is also known for saying "God is in the details" as he was extremely exacting even to the design and use of the window shades. This is the building website and is an excellent resource particularly for the interiors showing architectural details, furnishings, and much contemporary art. See http://www.375parkavenue.com

Chris Tiné

Figure 15.7 This is an urban apartment building and shows the strong vertical thrust of an Art Deco building. It uses a steel frame with a curtain wall that in this case is hidden by the applied concrete masonry. The upright "fins" on the building and water tower have an aeronautically inspired look, another feature of Art Deco style, which used industrial and geometrical designs. This is also captured in the ordered striping under the windows, which have a machine-made quality.

Chris Tiné

Figure 15.8 This is another Art Deco building in the resort town of Miami, Florida, that features the exuberant bright child-like colors often characteristic of this style. Its design has a strong focus on geometry with its use of squares, rectangles, circles, and cylinders and the absence of classical details, replaced by this streamlined look.

Kamira/Shutterstock.com

Figure 15.9 This is a typical New England Victorian clapboard house and shows a 1920s conversion into a mom and pop grocery store. The most significant remodeling was the façade of the lower level extending out to the street and the complete revamping of the interior, which will be shown later in Figure 15.12. Also notice the porch on the third floor has been shortened to a balcony and the stairs leading to the second floor porch and entrance door were added as prior to the store, access would have been from inside. Coco-Cola advertising is prominently displayed on both levels. In this case the owner and his large extended, multi-generational family lived above the store and he is proudly shown standing in front in the typical white cotton outfit for grocers and butchers of the day and with his straw boater.

Author photo

Figure 15.10 Balloon construction framing was invented in the 1830s in the US as a way of expediting the cost and time to build a wooden house and simplified and streamlined the way that they were built. It was characterized by small, dimensional framing members, called studs, placed at regular intervals that formed load-bearing walls and created an exterior membrane (balloon). In most cases this technique has now been amended with a similar one called platform framing, which treats each level as a separate unit and in the 21st century they sometimes come prefabricated in modular sections to the building site.

gmnicholas/iStock

* The Bauhaus aesthetics rejected Classicism as corrupt and replaced it with the radical idea of finding a design aesthetic in machines instead of nature or myth. Modernism looked for beauty in industrial materials and shapes, and focused on the functionality of an object or work of art. The members of the Bauhaus promoted Modernism first in crafts and then in interiors and lastly in architecture. Gropius and others attempted to unify arts and crafts through the doctrines of Modernism. See Figures 15.13, 15.14, and 15.15.

* Modern art and architecture became characterized by a single-minded concern with purity and abstraction. It sometimes became doctrinaire and resulted in slogans like "Form Follows Function" and "Less is More" to describe its relevancy.

* Two architects were the seminal forces of the Modern movement in Europe and America; Le Corbusier was freer and more expressive in his designs, and Mies van der Rohe was more severe and puritanical. They represented the soft and hard sides of Modernism. Both of them used and embraced the high-rise form of Modernist building construction. See Figures 15.2, 15.4, 15.5, and 15.6.

* Art Nouveau influence persisted into the early 20th century and evolved into Art Deco as a result of the 1925 Exhibition of Society of Decorative Arts in Paris. See Figures 15.7 and 15.8.

* Art Deco promoted Modernism in the US and adopted many European styles as well as ancient Egyptian motifs and adapted them to our culture. It included all of the decorative arts as well as architecture. It featured colorful, geometric, and abstracted forms and used large sculptures and

Figure 15.11 A housing explosion followed the Second World War that demanded millions of homes in the late 1940s and 1950s. It was the beginning of planned suburban communities and inexpensive tract housing like Levittown in Long Island. They were all being done in traditional styles like this one and not using modern idioms. Similar types of developments would continue into the 21st century, but now in many different styles and price ranges with gated and planned communities and also residential townhouses, condominiums, and graduated care facilities. Standing in front of the "American dream" home is the "American dream" family in their typical summer dress-up clothes.

ClassicStock/Alamy

murals. It often combined metals such as stainless steel, aluminum, and bronze in relief patterns in both interiors and exteriors and private and public buildings. It was partly influenced by film design, and used Classical and Rococo revival forms treated in a streamlined way, and often had a playful manner. See Figures 15.7, 15.8, 15.17 and see reference in Figure 18.8.

*   The American architect Frank Lloyd Wright introduced Japanese, Native American, and pre-Columbian design motifs to American Modernism. He wanted his buildings to be in harmony with their environment and called his aesthetic "organic architecture," which wedded buildings to the earth and landscape. He featured low profiles and strong, clean, horizontal lines and the use of natural materials—first in the American prairies, later at his house, Taliesin West, in Scottsdale, Arizona, and his most iconic 1935 building "Fallingwater" in Pennsylvania. See Figure 15.3, http://www.franklloydwright.org/about/taliesinwesttours.html, and http://www.fallingwater.org

How They Decorated

Figure 15.12 This is the interior of the same 1920s mom and pop grocery store shown in Figure 15.9. The large object on the left is a scale, and notice the wooden shelves and planked ceiling and flooring and the long counter. The front of it would be drawers to hold loose products like spices, flour, and vegetables; the few packaged and canned goods were on the shelves behind as most items were not pre-packaged, pre-made, or frozen. The proprietor is wearing a typical white cotton butcher's outfit. The young boy is wearing woolen stockings, hat, and sweater and is still young enough to be wearing shorts and not long pants. The man behind him is wearing a typical workingman's outfit with long pants and a buttoned cardigan sweater and straw boater. The other younger man is in dressier clothes with a white dress shirt and tie and with a jacket tucked into his belted pants, which would have been a "hipper" look.

Author photo

Figure 15.13 This is a brass, silver, and ebony tea infuser and strainer designed by Marianne Brandt, c. 1924, and made in the Bauhaus School as a prototype for mass production that could use expensive or cheaper materials depending on the market. In all cases Bauhaus wanted the objects to combine beautiful art simplified and undecorated with functionality. Brandt made this while a student and she was the only woman in their metals workshop. Its asymmetrical form is a good example of the attraction of modern design.

The Fine Art Society, London, UK/Bridgeman Images

Figure 15.14 Marianne Brandt (1911–1983) and Hin Bredendieck (1904–1995) worked at the Bauhaus metals workshop in the 1920s and designed a number of lighting products together. This was their 1928 prototype for a flexible bedside lamp that is still popular today and used mostly as a desk lamp. Brandt designed a number of the Bauhaus's most lucrative and significant objects that were mass produced by Kandem (Korting & Mathiesen), Leipzig, Germany, and that influenced many other Modernist designs. See the "Marianne Brandt: Life in Design—Dieselpunks" website http://www.dieselpunks.org/profiles/blogs/marianne-brandt-life-in-design

CNAC/MNAM/Dist. RMN-Grand Palais/Art Resource, NY

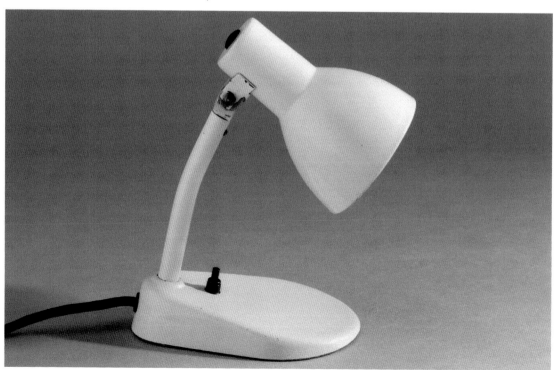

Figure 15.15 This revolutionary and seminal Modernist chair was designed by Marcel Breuer (1902–1981) and named "B3 Wassily Chair" in 1925 after a former Bauhaus colleague and is made out of tubular steel with leather straps. Originally manufactured by Thonet, who also made Breuer's other iconic, cantilevered chair that used tubular steel with cane seating. They are still manufactured and often copied today. Breuer left Germany at the start of the Second World War and eventually started his own architectural firm in New York City; he is noted for his use of cantilevers and concrete construction and the design for the 1964 Whitney Museum of Art, New York City. http://breuer.syr.edu

DeA Picture Library/Art Resource, NY

Figure 15.16 Jean Dunand (1877–1942) was a Swiss artist who lived and worked in Paris and was noted primarily for his lacquer work on wood or metal and was regarded as a great Art Deco designer. This is a lacquered metal vase, c. 1925, in which he uses free-form and geometric images on a simple, elegant round vase that is typical of his handmade luxury work. He also used several styles in his furniture designs, but also like his use of lacquer there is specifically a Japanese influence.

The Metropolitan Museum of Art. Image source: Art Resource, NY

Figure 15.17 This is Jean Harlow in *Dinner at Eight*, the 1934 "comedy of manners" film with an all-star cast. This is an example of an Art Deco interior; costume and film production design was extremely influential in connecting Modernism to popular art. Sleek, streamlined sets and elegant costumes projected wealth and class in the depression years and offered an inexpensive escape into a glamorous sophisticated world. The movie, directed by George Cukor, produced by David O. Selznick, was adapted by Frances Marion and Herman Mankiewicz from the play by George S. Kaufman and Edna Ferber for MGM Studios. All of these people played an influential role in the 1930s and 1940s in movies and theater and are worth looking up.

MGM/The Kobal Collection

Figure 15.18 *A Streetcar Named Desire*, 1947–1949, by Tennessee Williams, directed by Elia Kazan, with set and lighting designs by Jo Mielziner. The Stanislavski "method style" of acting asked actors to recall and use their own emotions to portray a more natural style of acting, which was introduced into the US in the 1930s and it affected stage and lighting design and started a new style—"Poetic Realism." Jo Mielziner's work in this play was a milestone in production design as it gave the gritty realism of the play a poetic basis. This style would dominate productions for the next 50 years. Ultra realistic plays like this about the trials of the lower classes struck a sympathetic chord during the war years and later in the 1950s and 1960s in England with "the kitchen sink dramas." This play has had many different adaptations and revivals on stages around the world, opera, ballet, and TV, and several film versions—Kazan's 1951, and Woody Allen's 2013 *Blue Jasmine*.

Photofest

Figure 15.19 This is the Festival Theater in Stratford, Ontario, Canada. Sir Tyrone Guthrie and Tanya Moiseiwitsch in 1962 created a new theater form by grafting a Greek theater onto a Shakespearean stage. Their new configuration had the circular raked seating wrapping around 210 degrees like a Greek theater bringing the audience in close proximity to the action and the actors on stage and creating a thrust stage. At the rear of the stage was a two-story stage house similar to the Elizabethan theaters. The arena stage was a later development with the audience surrounding it on all sides and with the elimination of the stage house.

Peter Smith/Stratford Festival/ Stratford Festival Theater in 1962. Lois Quail, lquail@stratfordfestival.ca

Figure 15.20 This WOW! girl is similar to the Pop Art styles in the 1960s and reflects the silkscreen portraits made by Andy Warhol such as *10 Marilyn's*, 1967, and *Mao*, 1972. Using straightforward colorful, two-dimensional art and graphic style Pop Art was a fresh new art style brought to popularity by Warhol, Roy Lichtenstein, Peter Max, and the sculptures of Claes Oldenburg and his wife Coosje van Bruggen, among many other artists. They all elevated everyday objects and mass-produced images to an art form as a reaction to Abstract Expressionism. It often was making social commentaries using irony, parody, and humor.

Goldmund/iStock

* Automobile, industrial, and home furnishing design became large industries that followed Modernist principles. Commercially derived design dominated the industrial and home products of this century.

* This period saw the development of a huge market for consumer goods, which also included entertainment like movies and video games.

* Some iconic US 1950s objects/props were large TV sets with rabbit ears, portable record players, small 45 rpm vinyl records, juke boxes, black dial phones, princess phones, and outdoor pay phones.

Figure 15.21 This is a 1970s living room with long, low white sofa and burr elm modular wall unit, which resembles an abstract Mondrian painting with its strong use of horizontal and vertical lines. The elimination of moldings and the use of white and off-white walls prompted designers to use interiors as backgrounds for their compositions of furniture and décor. The zebra head on the wall and the rest of him as a rug on the floor is a bit of an ironic Postmodern touch.

SGM/age fotostock/SuperStock

Figure 15.22 This sleek red, black, and white bathroom has clean lines and bold shapes that mark this as a modern 20th-century room. The minimalism of the design is another modern feature. The freestanding soaking tub is an adaptation of the 19th-century footed bathtub.

archidea photo/iStock

* Although they had existed before, this period saw a huge rise and popularity of spas, restaurants, and casinos, all designed in these modern styles.

* Modernism favored the materials of industry for architecture and décor: steel, aluminum, chrome, glass, enamel, and also plastic for furniture and decorative objects. Natural materials played a secondary role to machine-made and non-organic finishes. See Figures 15.13, 15.14, 15.15, 15.16, 15.17, 15.21, and 15.22.

Building and Décor Keywords

Art Deco (Arte Moderne) – The highly popular commercial and fine art, architecture, and costume style of the 1920s and 1930s, which emphasized streamlined interpretations of Classical forms rendered in shiny metallic, white, and silver finishes. It was also made popular in films and graphic art. Bryn Mawr College has a good website with examples in Philadelphia and explanations about the style. See Figures 15.7, 15.8, and 15.17. http://www.brynmawr.edu/cities/archx/05-600/proj/p2/npk/historydeco.htm

Bauhaus – The German design school, which began in the 1920s, that espoused principles of Modernism, functionalism, and utility in architecture and industrial design. It was also the name applied to these design principles. See Figures 15.1, 15.13, 15.14, and 15.15.

International style – The commercial style of architecture of the mid-20th century in America and Europe developed from Bauhaus and Modernist principles of functionality and pragmatism. It was characterized by buildings built with high-rise modular steel frames, glass curtain walls, flat roofs, and integrated mechanical systems. These buildings came to be characterized by blank, monumental exteriors devoid of any Classical detail. The buildings were sometimes defined as "machines for living." The style was adopted by the rapidly growing corporate business world. See Figures 15.1, 15.2, 15.5, and 15.6.

Prairie style – The style of American domestic architecture popularized by Frank Lloyd Wright that emphasized the integration of the horizontal line, texture, and setting of a house within its natural site. Wright's intention was to reject all European influences and he looked to Native American and pre-Columbian cultures for decorative inspiration. See Figure 15.3.

Brutalist – An architectural style of civic and urban buildings prominent in the 1970s and 1980s, characterized by the use of massive, blank or textured concrete walls with tiny windows. These buildings had a frankly defensive aspect and were often built in blighted urban neighborhoods. See http://www.dezeen.com/2014/09/10/dezeen-guide-to-brutalist-architecture-owen-hopkins and http://en.wikipedia.org/wiki/Brutalist_architecture

balloon framing – This was the type of wooden house framing that developed in the US during the 19th century and was characterized by multiple studs placed at regular intervals that formed load-bearing walls that created an exterior membrane (balloon). It replaced the old method of construction that had four massive posts that bore the weight of the building on the colonial style frame houses and barns. This new construction was dependent on the invention of power saws in lumber mills in the 19th century that were worked by wind, water, and steam or by animals and people. See Figure 15.10.

curtain wall – In Modern architecture this was a non-structural wall usually of metal and glass that was hung from the horizontal structural framing members of a building and carried the windows and wall paneling. See Figures 15.6 and 15.7.

modular design – A design system in which a single, measured unit (the module) was either multiplied or divided to derive all crucial measurements. See Figures 15.1, 15.7, and 15.8.

Brechtian – The style of theatrical production developed by Bertolt Brecht in the 1920s that rejected conventional theatrical sentimentality and artifice in favor of an aggressive and confrontational realism.

New Wave – The French and Italian style of film making of the late 1940s and 1950s characterized by ultra-realism, independent productions, low budgets, and frequently stories of the downtrodden.

Abstract Expressionism – The painting movement centered in post-Second World War New York City that sought to do away with all pictorial representation and to treat the canvas as a surface for the direct expression of raw emotion. Jackson Pollock with his drip style of painting was a prime example. See http://www.jackson-pollock.org

Pop Art – Pop Art started in the mid-1950s in England, but really came into its own in the US in the 1960s and 1970s and was art that was based on media, advertising, and product design, and popular culture. It used simple, colorful, two-dimensional art and graphics and like Lichtenstein often incorporated comic book styles and printers, Ben-Day dots and sought to bring a cool, unemotional appreciation to the aesthetics of everyday objects and subject matter. It looked at the production of art as a business—famously, Andy Warhol called his studio "The Factory." There are numerous examples to be found online.

The Modern Clothing and Costume World

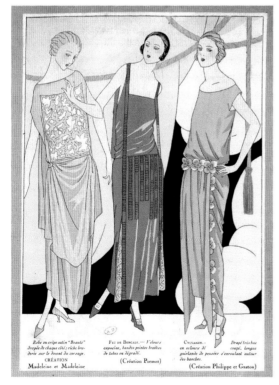

Figure 15.23 Fashion designs for evening dresses: "Beauté" by the House of Madeleine & Madeleine, "Feu de Bengale" by the House of Premet, and "Cyclamen" by the House of Philippe et Gaston, 1922. French fashion in the 1920s slimmed down all profiles and removed all outward structure to achieve a clean, modern look.

Archives Charmet/Bridgeman Images

How They Dressed

Figure 15.24 This is the iconic look of the Roaring '20s and this simple graphic illustration of a young woman doing the Charleston dance in her typical flapper dress, with rope of beads, black stockings and high-heeled shoes, hairstyle, and cloche hat says what the epitome of 1920s flapper fashion was all about. The dance and this look expressed the energy and exuberance of this period and defined what was worn by young, usually unmarried women.

lambada/iStock

Figure 15.25 This is a formal 1920s wedding photo. The tip-off is the raised hemlines on the short dresses with dropped waists, long pearls, strapped shoes, and hats. The bride's decorated hat and long train are nice 1920s touches as are the two flower baskets with the matching flower girls, with their decorated knee socks. The men are in traditional formal white tie and tails. Queen Victoria's 1840 wedding set this custom in motion and it was continued in the US and in Europe, first by the wealthy and aristocratic, and by the 1920s was a common practice at middle class weddings.

Author photo

Figure 15.26 Jean Harlow with fellow Hollywood star William Powell about 1936. A pronounced waist was beginning to appear for women in the 1930s and hemlines varied from ankle to mid-calf. The over-the-shoulder look of her sumptuous fur coat was often copied and a popular trend. Notice her carefully styled and permed hair that is also seen in her other picture (Figure 15.17); this was now a common style in the US and Europe. Powell's long, double-breasted overcoat with wide lapels is very typical as is his plaid suit with creased pants and cuffs, shirt and tie with wide fedora hat.

Pictorial Press Ltd/Alamy

Figure 15.27 This outfit would be typical of a stylish urban European or American 1940s woman. Her suit, still the most popular style, has a short, narrow-waisted jacket and emphatically padded shoulders. She has an ample flared skirt that during the war years due to shortages of fabric would become narrower. This model carries an envelope clutch purse and wears a simple brimmed hat, scarf, and gloves. Simplified versions with less expert tailoring would have been worn by office workers and middle class women.

Everett Collection/SuperStock

Figure 15.28 "Women of Style" exhibition at the Fashion Museum, Bath, UK. These are all fashions by haute couture designers and worn by Dame Margot Fonteyn de Arias (1919–1991), the English prima ballerina. The dresses are by Hardy Amies (1909–2003), British fashion and costume designer (*2001: A Space Odyssey*, 1968) and Christian Dior (1905–1957), the French fashion designer. On the left is a black brocaded silk evening gown by Bianca Mosca, which Fonteyn wore at a reception in New York after her opening performance of *Sleeping Beauty* in 1949, showing the important fashion detail of an asymmetrical bodice and hemline. Mosca was a prominent French and British couture and costume designer and also helped establish this museum. The puffball ensemble on the right is also by Christian Dior and was worn at her wedding to Roberto de Arias in 1955. This image is useful as it shows the variety of skirt styles, widths, and hemlines that were used during this time.

Bridgeman Images

Figure 15.29 *The Wild One* (1953) was a classic movie, which started the "outlaw biker" film genre. It starred Marlon Brando as the leader of a rebellious motorcycle gang and projected him as the image of a disaffected, estranged young man with a Triumph motorcycle. He wore sideburns, blue jeans, black leather boots, leather cap, and leather jacket, which caused a sensation and he became a hero to a generation and Rock and Rollers like Elvis Presley and The Beatles. James Dean also wore blue jeans in his iconic film *Rebel Without a Cause* (1955) about a disturbed youth that catapulted him to fame and he also became an idol and symbol for young people.

Columbia Pictures/Album/SuperStock

Figure 15.30 This shows two 1950s bobbysoxers. The term was started in the 1940s when fans of swing music took off their shoes and danced in their bobby socks in school gyms, events known as sock hops. This would continue into the 1950s and young women affected a casual style with a sweater over a light-colored blouse, pleated, knee-length skirt, and white athletic socks—bobby sox—with either sneakers, saddle shoes, or penny loafers. Notice the young man's white sweater with banding called a tennis sweater and usually it had a V-neck. Both of their hairstyles were very typical—a short pageboy with a headband for the girl and a short flat top, buzz or crew cut for boys.

ClassicStock.com/SuperStock

* In women's fashion, after the First World War Edwardian romanticism and sentimentalism gave way to the stripped-down silhouettes, with flat chest, short hemlines, glittering fabric surfaces, and bobbed hair of the Roaring '20s. Thinness became a fashion virtue and the desired and predominant look. The straight line of the dress with slightly flared skirt and low waist were characteristic of the dresses of the time. See Figures 15.23 and 15.24.

* Although the image of the girl doing the Charleston (Figure 15.24) was the epitome of the age, in reality hemlines went up and down continuously. In the beginning of the 1920s hems were long then they went up and by the end covered the knees to the top of the calf. The important characteristic was the long slim vertical line.

* The 1920s fashion styles and their innovations introduced new undergarments like bras, girdles, garter belts, and different styles of panties, silk sacks, and lingerie, that were replacing more structured corsets. These and the explosion of different kinds of clothes and many types of fabrics have stayed with us.

* In the 1920s French fashion designer Coco Chanel was quoted as saying "A woman needs just three things: a black dress, a black sweater, and on her arm, a man she loves" and "Fashion changes, but style endures." She was famous for many designs, but especially her iconic "Chanel Suit," the little black dress, and the perfume, Chanel No. 5. Her legacy and style have endured. There have been a number of films about her and a 1969 American musical *Coco* by Alan Jay Lerner and André Previn. A wonderful video about her and Paris can be found at http://inside. chanel.com/en/paris-by-chanel/video

* Hats and coats for women were also necessary items and came in a number of variations, but generally the coats also expressed the slim verticality and often had fur trim, which could be removable and mixed or replaced with other pieces. In the 1930s these fur collars became very large and exaggerated and repeated on the cuffs and were made of beaver, skunk, or fox. See Figure 15.26.

* Through the 1930s women's fashion became more structured and fitted. High fashion was carefully tailored and produced by the couture houses in Paris and New York. Film design and celebrity clothing influenced fashion design. Hemlines dropped again to mid-calf and even lower for formal evening ball gowns. See Figures 15.17 and 15.26.

* Luxurious satin and silk lingerie, negligees, peignoirs, and bed jackets were extremely fashionable and also often emulated movie stars' costumes.

* In contrast, these were two films about the depression era and poor people that have good references: *Grapes of Wrath* (1940) and *They Shoot Horses Don't They?* (1969).

* There are many wonderful 1930s and 1940s movies and musicals that use set and costumes for the designer to reference. There are too many to mention, but they can be looked up on the Internet by decades, i.e. "1930s musical films," etc. to find resources.

* The invention of nylon and other synthetic fabrics in the 1930s allowed for lower cost and a greater variety of fabric choices. Nylon stockings were now in nude or pastel shades and replaced the much more expensive silk stockings; they were simply called "nylons" and the word "Silk-Stocking" meant wealthy or aristocratic. The lighter tones also put more emphasis on the shoes, which came in a wider variety of styles and colors.

* The Second World War years of the 1940s and the introduction of the "New Look" for women raised hemlines to calf length, flared skirts into an A-line, and brought in padded,

Figure 15.31 This is Gregory Peck in *The Man in the Gray Flannel Suit*, the 1956 film adaptation of the 1955 Sloan Wilson novel that dealt with problems of corporate and suburban life in post-war America. This was the required business uniform for young executives.

20th Century Fox/The Kobal Collection

Figure 15.32 This is designer Ken Scott at Frank Usher's showroom in 1966. Ken Scott was known for his colorful fabrics using wild combinations of flowers. At first they were on his cotton dresses like these, but later as his popularity increased during the 1960s they appeared on all kinds of clothing, textiles, home furnishings, bags, and suitcases. He became a cult figure in the 1970s. Heavy make-up went with the modern look of the 1960s. There are a number of websites that have colorful images of his products.

Daily Mail/Rex/Alamy

Figure 15.33 Twiggy became an overnight sensation when a fashion journalist launched pictures of her in a newspaper and called her "the face of '66." She became the first international supermodel at the age of 16 and among other clothes, popularized the miniskirt. Her small teenage figure started a craze that began using sweet, A-line, mini dresses and neckties. She always wore the latest Mod fashions as seen above with the two dresses and the bellbottoms. Several important designers started using androgynous details in their styles that became popular and that filtered down as minimalistic, "unisex" designs and hemlines went higher and higher through the 1960s. Twiggy would later have a successful acting and singing career. There are many websites about her and "Twiggy—The official Web Site" is a good reference.

Figure 15.34 The Afro hairstyle (sometimes called "fro" or "natural") became popular with young African-Americans of both sexes in the 1960s and 1970s. This was partially a result of the American Civil Rights Movement, and "black is beautiful" became a buzzword. The hairstyle became a political symbol of "black pride" and was worn by members of the Black Panther Party. It was also famously worn by Angela Davis, Jimi Hendrix, The Jackson 5, and The Supremes as well as a number of athletes, significantly Arthur Ashe.

RollingEarth/iStock

square shoulders, tight blouses, halter tops, low wide hats, and hair worn shoulder length. See Figure 15.27.

* The exclusive Paris Couture Houses and their imitators dominated early modern fashion until the Second World War. Increasingly after the war fashion became democratized and more personal.

* After the Second World War Americans began to replace the French as arbiters of taste and the fashion center moved from Paris to New York.

* "The New Look" continued into the early 1950s. Women's hair was now worn in a wide assortment of styles from short to shoulder length to up and often in a French twist. Heavy eye make-up and lipstick were common on younger unmarried women. Fashion varied a great deal in this decade and waists were a major component, as some liked the fitted Dior look, often with a belt, and others the looser "sack dresses." The decade was sometimes referred to "as the wandering waist." The period is also noteworthy as women were freer to choose their look, partly based on their size, and many more styles of clothes were available in different price ranges. The 1950s skirts were typically wide and circular in plan. Women wore flats, like ballet shoes, and high heels, and loafers were introduced for men and women as casual wear.

Figure 15.35 *Hair: The American Tribal Love-Rock Musical* (1968–1972 Broadway), which used the famous song "The Age of Aquarius." The musical romanticized the discontented youth of the counterculture years of the late 1960s and the anti-war peace movement. It was the first rock and roll musical and used a small band with loud, raucous singing and dancing and also a young racially mixed cast. It is about a soldier headed to Vietnam meeting up with a group of New York City hippies, who introduce him to illegal psychedelic drugs and the sexual revolution, which was explicitly shown in its controversial nude scene. The ending had a new twist and invited the audience on stage and to join in singing and dancing—a "be-in." There were New York and London revivals in 2009 and 2010. There was also a film adaptation with many changes to the plot and songs directed by Milos Foreman and choreographed by Twyla Tharp (1979). See "Hair the musical official web site."

Photofest

* 1950s girl's dresses, skirts, and the famous flared poodle skirt were worn with stiffened petticoats and crinolines and also popular were plaid kilts. Matching sweater sets with small scarfs tied at the neck and blouses with peter pan collars were also typical as were cat-eye glasses. Older women used a more conservative version of these with lower hemlines and many different necklines and sleeves.

* Men's clothing began to change with the simplification of the suit, the abandonment of the cravat in favor of the tie, and the ubiquity of the fedora hat. The men's single-breasted suit with a button-down collar shirt, and wing tip shoes became the fashion uniform of the corporate culture; the briefcase and trench coat completed the image. See Figures 15.26 and 15.31.

* Men's fedora hats were a necessity for business dress until the 1970s when all hats for businessmen were abandoned. After this men wore many different kinds of hats often for specific activities like sports and job applications and seasonal and geographic locations.

* Men's casual fashion became looser and less formal through the 1960s. Blue jeans, chino pants with open shirts that showed the top of a white undershirt were popular for men and boys.

* There was an increased emphasis placed on youth culture and young people's access to independent income. This sparked the growth of the independent designer movement of the 1960s both in the US and Europe and freed clothing design from the established couture houses. More and more in this decade and into the 21st century fashion and accessories would be driven by and marketed to the young.

* *The Outsiders* (1983) was an iconic young adult novel/film of social class conflict in 1960s Tulsa, Oklahoma, and was a useful costume resource as it showed both sides of the tracks, and the 2005 re-release had additional footage. *West Side Story* (1961) adapted from the stage musical would be another one for New York City.

* The 1960s saw radical changes in men's and women's fashion. It started out quite conservative, but by the mid-1960s London burst into view not only with Twiggy and the Beatles but Carnaby Street, the fashion and music district in London, that epitomized the "Mod" and "Swinging London." The clothing fashions were characterized by a colorful, childlike look and an expensive "thrift shop" aesthetic that emphasized individual style. It produced the miniskirt and bell-bottom trousers and used "Op Art" images and patterns of wavy lines, stripes, and dots with bold colors on fabrics. See Twiggy, Figure 15.33 and her website, and "Mod."

* In the late 1960s and 1970s women were wearing pants for work and evening and the pants suit was introduced as acceptable business wear. Legs of pants would get wider and were often worn with jackets and long blouses or tunics. The introduction in the 1970s of hot pants, famously worn by Brigitte Bardot, the French starlet, and jump suits in many different fabrics from tough utilitarian ones to luxurious velvets and satins were new looks.

* The homemade and the thrift shop aesthetic of the Hippie Look of the 1970s popularized blue jeans as everyday wear and this time for women as well as men.

* The 1970s for men's and women's clothes were less exuberant and the biggest introduction was the use of polyester as the new fabric. Clothing for both would get tighter and as the decade ended the main colors were black, white and neutral greys. The couture industries, which had been floundering since the Mod fashion designers, introduced "Ready to Wear" clothing, which again increased the personal choices.

Clothing and Costume Keywords

flapper – The popular name given to the liberated young women of the 1920s and to the tight-fitting and revealing clothes they wore. See Figure 15.24.

cloche (CLOSH) – This was the simple, spherical, close-fitting women's hat of the Roaring '20s. See Figure 15.24.

finger curls – The hairstyle of the 1920s that featured short, wave-shaped curls worn tight around the face.

vaudeville – The extremely popular early 20th-century variety shows performed in neighborhood theaters all over the US three or four times a day before radio and television.

"The New Look" – The fashion style introduced by Christian Dior in 1947 that featured longer A-line skirts, tight jackets, and upswept, tightly coiffed hair. See Figure 15.27.

penny loafers – Girls and boys wore these slip-on leather shoes with a low-heeled sole and decorative false tongue with a slit on the front, which they filled with a penny. Loafers also had tassels and were worn by women and men.

halter top – A woman's blouse or dress top made of a single piece of fabric attached at the waist, crossed in front at the stomach and chest and drawn up and behind the neck revealing the arms and back. Popular in film costumes and for both leisure and formal wear in the 1940s and 1950s. For casual wear it was often worn with shorts.

snood – A loose weave fabric or net bag worn at the back of a woman's hairdo to contain long or loose falls of hair or a bun. It was popular in the 1940s and earlier at the time of the American Civil War.

zoot soot – A comical men's suit and hat worn by young hipsters in the 1940s. It usually consisted of outsized trousers with suspenders; a matching oversized jacket, multicolored shoes, a giant watch chain, and a flattened and exaggerated contrasting-colored fedora hat. It was made popular by vaudeville and TV star Milton Berle.

pencil skirt – This was a knee-length straight skirt popular in the 1950s and 1960s, usually with a back vent or pleat especially for office wear. The straight skirt was introduced in the 1940s by Dior and Amies, often as part of a suit. See Figure 15.28 for the longer 1940s style. See Figure 15.23, in pink, and also its predecessor in Figure 14.13.

blue jeans, blue denim – These pants were invented by Levi Strauss and Jacob Davis in 1873 in San Francisco for cowboys and gold miners, and then worn by field hands and factory workers. Jeans were made popular by James Dean and Marlon Brando in the movies and were worn by young, middle class and rebellious teenagers during the 1950s and 1960s, but often were outlawed in movie theaters, restaurants, and schools until the 1970s when they became the standard casual pants still worn today. See Figure 15.29.

corporate attire – Men's business attire of the mid-20th to early 21st century consisted of a conservative single-breasted suit, white shirt, tie, laced shoes, and until the 1970s, a fedora hat. See Figure 15.31, grey flannel suit.

trench coat – This was originally a military coat worn in the First World War trenches and continued into the 1950s when it was adapted for business use and became part of that uniform. The image was popularized by Humphrey Bogart in the film *Casablanca* and later by Peter Sellers as Inspector Clouseau.

Hippie – The free-spirited youth of the 1970s counterculture, who strove for a purer, more natural lifestyle that looked for personal and sexual freedom ("love-ins"). They reacted against the uniformity of American commercial culture by "dropping out" of society; and some experimented with recreational and hallucinogenic drugs, some lived in simple agrarian communes that emphasized ecological farming practices and oneness with nature, some embraced Eastern religions, and some lived in urban centers like San Francisco, New York City, and Amsterdam. See Figure 15.35.

leisure suit – This casual two- or three-piece suit for men became popular after John Travolta wore it in the 1977 movie *Saturday Night Fever*; because of this it was sometimes called the **disco suit**. The suit was often in bright colors or white and made of polyester or a blend. It was frequently worn with a floral or patterned shirt with large wide, open collars over the jacket lapels.

CHAPTER SIXTEEN

Postmodern: 1980–Present

Figure 16.1 This is the Guggenheim Museum, in Bilbao, Spain, designed by Canadian-American architect Frank Gehry in 1997, showing the riverside view. Gehry's swooping shapes could not have been built without computer technology and this and other of his buildings are among the most admired in contemporary architecture. The computer, CAD, and 3D modeling programs have revolutionized Postmodern design. This technology has influenced how architecture, engineering, and the construction industry have expressed these design elements. This digital technology has further expanded the scope of the artist's vision in the entertainment world of theater, film, themed entertainment, and digital and electronic media.

Matthi/Dreamstime.com

A Little Background

Postmodern style is another relatively small, elite movement exerting a large impact on the arts, media, and personal expression. It arose as a result of the multiplication of art forms and communication channels available as well as being a reflection of the multiple and fragmentary nature of modern life and the dominance of popular culture. Postmodernism seeks to reconcile the spontaneous impulses of modern life and entertainment with the more focused purpose of past styles. It often does this through irony and meaningful juxtaposition of disparate design elements (deconstruction), with a remixing of classical themes in a contemporary context. Sometimes it is done with a purposeful emphasis on transient artistic events in social settings and in nature. Architecture, décor, and costume all embrace environmental consciousness in their sourcing and use of materials.

Who We Are

* The collapse of the Soviet Union in 1989 left the US as the world's only superpower.

* Postmodernism celebrates Celebrity and Mass Communications as art forms and encourages their influence on fashions and art. It was popularized by Andy Warhol in the 1970s with his dictum that "everyone will have 15 minutes of fame." Postmodernism rejects Modernism as hostile to the human spirit and values: "Less is boring."

* Technological innovations produce multiple artistic and entertainment choices: radio, TV, recorded sound, audio and videotape, CD and DVD technology, the Internet, personal computers, and handheld personal entertainment systems all coexist and the list expands every year.

* Postmodern design is striving for a marriage between art and technology similar to what the Bauhaus was doing, but they were primarily interested in functionality and purity of form without decoration. Postmodernism on the other hand acknowledges the role of decoration and delights in it and frequently uses whimsical superfluous flourishes and bright colors.

* The rise of environmental consciousness in art, architecture, interiors, and clothing becomes a powerful motivator of new social and artistic experimentation.

* Artists: Again this is a random selection of artists and it is in no way complete, but does cover a range of styles and mediums: Eric Fischl, Vanessa Beecroft, Chris Burden, Cindy Sherman, John Baldessari, Chihuly, Nam June Paik, Nancy Rubin, Andy Goldsworthy, Fred Wilson, Christopher Wool, the team of Christo and Jean Claude, and ballet, set and costume designer David Salle.

* Rock concerts, music videos, and spectacular events like the opening ceremonies of the Olympics and the Super Bowl halftime have also had significant influence on design and the use of technology and especially now the use of lighting technology and design. The 2013 play *The Curious Incident of the Dog in the Night-Time* shows these influences with pioneering sound and projection designs.

* Cirque du Soleil started as a few street performers and moved to Montreal in 1984 under Guy Laliberté. With thousands of employees they perform around the world to thousands of spectators and have melded traditional circus arts with the most advanced technologies and superior inventive uses of all aspects of design. In 2014 they announced partnering with Grupo Vidanta and that they planned to open a huge theme park in Nuevo Vallarta, Mexico, in 2018. See https://www.cirquedusoleil.com/en/press/kits/corporate/cirque-du-soleil/history.aspx

* Theater set designers: David Rockwell, Ming Cho Lee, John Lee Beatty, Tony Walton, Michael Yeargan, George Tsypin, Doug Schmidt, Derek McLane, and Julie Taymor are good examples that have set high standards and are frequently emulated.

* Opera has moved to the cutting edge and a number of traditional ones have new interpretations in different or even fantasy periods and are now accessible. As examples, several new interesting productions are Stravisnky's *Oedipus Rex* (1992) in a mesmerizing production by Taymor/Osawa in Japan; Met Opera's version of Bellini's *Sonnambula* (2009), in which director Mary Zimmerman and

set designer Daniel Ostling set it in a rehearsal room with the cast in contemporary clothes. Also the Salzburger Festspiele and the Dutch National Opera's production of Verdi's tragic *La Traviata* uses Willy Decker's symbolic large semi-circular set and giant clock and the omnipresent figure of death who never speaks, but interacts with the singers. The musical *Rent,* based on Puccini's *La Bohème,* started as a tiny 1994 workshop, moved to Broadway and became a lavish 2005 film. A young contemporary German composer, Detlev Glanert, has written a number of operas, one of which is an adaption of Albert Camus' 1939 play, about the Roman Emperor, *Caligula* (2006).

* Postmodern film like architecture and décor blends assorted styles with different perspectives or genres. It also frequently manipulates reality with juxtapositions of time, and uses non-linear narrative story lines and plot developments. The films of Charlie Kaufman like *Being John Malkovich* (1999), many of the Coen Brothers' films, like *Raising Arizona* (1982), and the Monty Python films are good examples. There are many others, but these would also be good examples: *LA Story* (1991), *Who Framed Roger Rabbit* (1988, the first animated live action film), *Naked Lunch* (1991), *Magnolia* (1999), *Total Recall* (1990), and *Birdman* (2014).

The Postmodern Material World

Figure 16.2 This is the exterior of the Pompidou Center in Paris. It was designed by Renzo Piano and Richard Rogers in 1977. This revolutionary museum structure placed the previously hidden service pipes on the outside of the building in a colorful and playful way that has served as an influential interior and exterior model for other Postmodern architects, as well as artists and fashion designers.

Jorge Felix Costa/Shutterstock.com

What We Make

The Powerhouse Museum in Sydney, Australia, is home to a wide variety of examples of Postmodern art and technology. Museum curator Anne-Marie Van de Ven describes her view of the nature of Postmodernism, saying "Post-modernism emerged as a cultural reaction to what had become the excessive conformity, conservatism and utopianism of the Modern movement, in tandem responding to changes in societal attitudes being negotiated through the Post-Colonial movement. Postmodernism also emerged in tandem with the Punk movement leading and planting the seed for Craft Punk where freedom of expression and truth to materials remain core values. Why Postmodernism? Sometimes entrenched traditional or conservative views just have to be turned upside down, turned on their head, to ensure culture and society remain relevant, democratic and dynamic." (http://www.dhub.org/postmodernism-themovement-we-love-to-hate; this is a useful website with many additional links)

* Postmodernism celebrates all artistic and personal expression that is created by, delivered by, or filtered through electronic media.

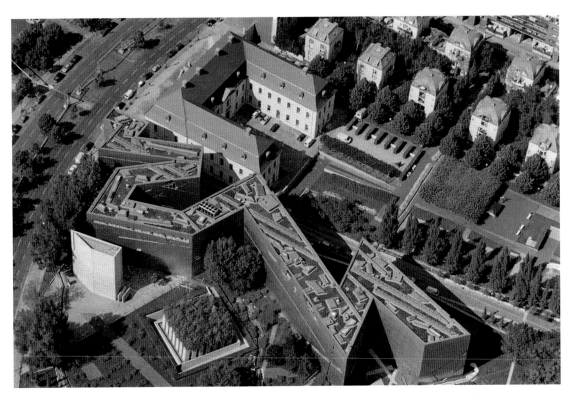

Figure 16.3 The Jewish Museum, Berlin, Germany, designed by Daniel Libeskind and built 1993–1999. The expressive dark metal building twists through a Jewish neighborhood that was destroyed by the Nazis. The zigzag shape touches significant places in the neighborhood and the lines on the roof trace the pattern of the streets that it has replaced. The Jewish Museum is seen here next to the older baroque "Kollegienhaus" building, which formerly housed the Berlin Museum. See the Jewish Museum, Berlin, website for information and pictures; also informative are Libeskind's comments in "Between the Lines."

akg-images/Reimer Wulf

Figure 16.4 and 16.5 The Venetian Resort Hotel Casino in Las Vegas was built from 1997 to 1999 at a cost of $1.5 billion. The opening ceremony included the Italian actress Sophia Loren and owner Sheldon G. Adelson, dedicating the resort and the first motorized gondola with singing gondoliers, trumpeters, and white doves. Both the exterior and interior of the complex have a number of scaled-down Venetian landmarks including the Rialto Bridge, St. Mark's Piazza with its Campanile, and canals. Inside the canals with their gondolas are lined with shops under a painted sky that uses lighting effects for day and night for a complete theatrical experience. Themed entertainment designers and fabricators created all of this. There were similar painted skies in the Würzburg Residenz, Figures 9.2 and 9.4.

Chris Tiné

* Computers and the development of the Internet are revolutionizing art, architecture, and engineering by making possible complex calculations and by speeding the delivery and sharing of information. See Figures 16.1, 16.2, 16.3, 16.4, and 16.5.

* Computer-aided design and manufacturing streamline and diversify the decorative arts, design, and the production of clothing and furnishings, enabling individual designers to design, source, manufacture, and market their own creations without corporate involvement.

* Non-traditional media are being explored as a means of artistic expression, and world cultures provide fertile ground for new artistic creations. The Internet and cell phones are used by Postmodern artists to instantly access and share visual, audio, and intellectual information from around the world.

* Postmodernism in architecture, costume, and décor is reintroducing historical consciousness, playfulness, irony, and theatricality to the cultural arts.

* The Scottish Parliament Building complex in Edinburgh, Scotland, was designed by Spanish architect Enric Miralles. Its exteriors and interiors are an excellent example of Postmodern architecture, using an eclectic mix of styles and decorations. Built from 1999 to 2004 it has been very controversial in its application of Postmodern style to traditional government buildings. These two websites are useful: http://www.scottish.parliament.uk/visitandlearn/15914.aspx and http://www.archdaily.com/111869/ad-classics-the-scottish-parliament-enric-miralles

*   A new Postmodern Frank Gehry project is the business school at the University of Technology, Sydney (UTS), Australia. The building is named the Dr. Chau Chak Wing as he contributed the money for its construction. These websites give interesting information and images about the project:

http://www.dhub.org/chau-chak-wing-a-gehry-icon-in-the-making/

http://utsmasterplan.com.au/index.php/component/content/article?id=15

http://www.theguardian.com/artanddesign/2014/nov/12/frank-gehrys-uts-building-a-first-look-inside

How We Decorate

Figure 16.6 This Postmodern interior is in the Judge Business School at Cambridge University, Cambridge, UK. It is a renovation of the Addenbrooke's Hospital founded in 1766 into a modern facility. The windows have been reconfigured into asymmetrical patterns, the addition of the large tall columns, the use of child-like bright colors in the interiors, and the modern cantilevered stairs contrast it with the original 18th-century building.

Chris Tiné

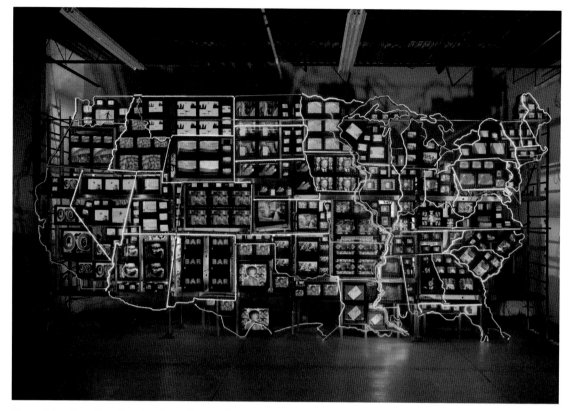

Figure 16.7 Nam June Paik (1932–2006) was a Korean-American who is considered the founder of "video art." *Electronic Superhighway,* 1995, this massive installation uses closed circuit televisions and shows scenes from *The Wizard of Oz, Oklahoma!,* and other classic video images. The size of the installation and the use of video technology are his commentary on the pervasive influence of film and television on American culture. Paik is credited for coining the phrase "Electronic Superhighway." He also did the first international satellite "installation" mixing video, taped TV with a live event in the 1984 *Good Morning, Mr. Orwell,* linking people, including John Cage (music), Salvador Dalí, and George Plimpton between New York City, Paris, and South Korea.

Smithsonian American Art Museum, Washington, DC/Art Resource, NY

* The emergence of High-Tech style in the 1980s merged Modernist clean, sleek forms with the love of fantasy structures derived from Sci-Fi and film.

* The 1980s also saw the popularization of grid patterns in furnishings and fabrics.

* Michael Graves, as well as his numerous architectural projects, has designed hundreds of products for Alessi, Steuben, Dansk, J.C. Penny, and now for many years for Target, with a beautiful, sophisticated, and utilitarian product line for the mass market. His home accessories and furniture use Postmodern aesthetics and colors; and like his Alessi tea kettle which is reminiscent of Marianne Brandt's, both are emblematic of their time. See http://michaelgraves.com

* Philippe Starck is a French designer, and since the 1980s is known for his industrial, architectural, interior, and far-ranging and prolific household and furniture designs, which often translate historical periods and motifs into contemporary designs, and frequently with an ironic or lighthearted touch. See http://www.starck.com/en/#

* The Steampunk style of the early 2000s is a sub-genre of fantasy and science fiction and often merges period features with Postmodernism. It is now global and encompasses all the arts and media, costumes, props, décor, restaurants, fairs, and other events. See Figures 16.11 and 16.16.

Figure 16.8 Christo and Jeanne-Claude: *Running Fence*, Sonoma and Marin Counties, California, conceived in 1972 and completed in 1976. It was 24.5 miles long and 18 feet high using a heavy nylon fabric on steel poles. This famous French duo have created their environmental sculptures all over the world and are often ephemeral, lasting only for short periods of time. This installation was removed after two weeks and everything was donated to the ranchers whose property it was on and they left no trace behind. It was designed to be viewed by driving 40 miles of roads with open parts for wildlife, cattle, people, and cars to go through. They pay for all their projects through sales of their artwork, models, and drawings. A more recent site-specific work was the February 12–27, 2005, *The Gates* in New York's Central Park. See their website for pictures and drawings—christojeanneclaude.net/projects

CNAC/MNAM/Dist. RMN-Grand Palais/Art Resource, NY

Figure 16.9 This sofa and cushions are made entirely of molded plastic, with tubular chrome legs, which are reminiscent of Breuer's chairs. Its playful shape characterizes it as a Postmodern design. The cartoon colors complete the carefree image.

da-kuk/iStock

Figure 16.10 More rigid in its shape than the sofa in 16.9, this room is carefully hiding and disguising its function by weaving it into the wall pattern. This bathroom shows the quirky nature of Postmodern design, using geometric shapes.

Auris/iStock

Figure 16.11 This is a collection of Steampunk props and shows the imaginative use of an unusual assortment of parts that characteristically utilize anachronistic features; such as steam engines, gears, or jet wings reimagined or combined with digital or modern elements or controls.

Andrew Kraemer

* A mash-up of design styles characterizes early 21st-century design. Historical periods with Modernism mingle and coexist and create Postmodern style.

* Postmodern art is often created in an environmentally conscious manner showing the influence of environmental considerations in the work. See Figure 16.8.

* Andy Goldsworthy (1956–) is a Scottish artist who is famous for making "Land Art," ephemeral art projects that make an ironic statement about the impermanence of art. There are several books about these. More recently he has been working in stone, building cairns and walls (See Strom King Art Center). These websites have excellent bibliographies, images of his unique sculptures, and his photographs:

http://www.goldsworthy.cc.gla.ac.uk

http://en.wikipedia.org/wiki/Andy_Goldsworthy

Building and Décor Keywords

Postmodern – The style of art and architecture of the late 20th century and early 21st century that rejects the abstraction and formalism of the Modern style and reintroduces traditional and classical influences, often in an ironic and playful manner.

Deconstruction – Originally the process of confronting a work of art by treating it as a text to be reinterpreted and revised in contemporary language while devaluing or ignoring the original intent of the artist. In architecture and design, the literal exposing or "pulling apart" of the structure of a building or composition and reordering its parts in a confrontational way. See Figures 16.1 and 16.2.

High-Tech – An interior design style of the late 20th and early 21st century continuing Modernist principles and emphasizing exposed mechanized parts and clean, machine-made finishes. See Figures 16.6 and 16.10.

Steampunk – The style of entertainment, décor, and costumes of the early 21st century combining late 19th-century industrial machinery with modern digital technology. Often it gives an otherworldly look to fanciful and often oversized objects reminiscent of the levity of the Pop Art of graphic artist Robert Indiana ("Love" and "Eat"), the quirky machines of Rube Goldberg, and whimsical sculptures of Claes Oldenburg and his wife Coosje van Bruggen. See Figures 16.11 and 16.16.

Rube Goldberg (1883–1970) – Cartoonist and inventor of complex imaginative machines often using diverse parts. His name is now an adjective to imply "an overly complex solution to a simple problem" and often involving complex circuitous physical machinery resulting in a comical effect.

A. MacGyver – Angus MacGyver was a fictional TV special agent on a show from 1985–1992, who was always fixing or repairing broken objects with simple household things and always had his Swiss Army knife and duct tape. His name has also become an adjective for the act of creating a sophisticated solution out of commonplace and transient materials.

The Postmodern Clothing and Costume World

Figure 16.12 This 1988 Christian Lacroix (b. 1951) wedding dress shows a departure from traditional styles using tulle fabric, flowers, and butterflies sewn into the skirt, and in the hair to create a humorous effect. He is a French fashion and costume designer, who has had a haute couture Paris firm since 1987 and is known for his theatrical, flamboyant, often fantasy creations like this. He often uses a mix-up of historical styles and details from clothing from all over the world. He has had a full line of accessories, including perfume as well as an interior design department. See http://www.christian-lacroix.com/en

Camera Press Ltd/Althea Simms/Alamy

How We Dress

Figure 16.13 Marilyn Monroe in *Gentleman Prefer Blondes*, 1953. This is an iconic film image of Marilyn Monroe in a pink satin strapless gown with diamond jewelry.

AF archive/Alamy

Figure 16.14 This is Madonna from the *Material Girl* video. In this music video Madonna reimagines the classic Marilyn Monroe image and shows a common element of Postmodernism in which one stylistic feature is referenced and commented on by another artist.

Photofest

* This period sees the continued dominance of individual designers and small design houses focused on the youth market and a fast-moving fashion scene. Now designers are operating worldwide through Internet communication and computer-aided design and manufacture.

* Casual clothes produced by both small manufacturers and large corporations often in low-wage countries dominate the market, and increasingly have a global style heavily influenced by relaxed and informal US fashions.

* Eiko Ishioka (1939–2012) was an extremely influential Japanese graphic and costume designer, and prominent art director. Her extensive body of work in multiple media from theater to movies to the Olympics to Cirque du Soleil, included both contemporary designs and the imaginative use of elements derived from historical styles. She was also known for her sumptuous and innovative use of materials and fabrics. There are many websites that reference her and many pictures of her work.

Figure 16.15 The fashion illustrated here shows a woman wearing a corset which is hand painted to become a decorative fashion element. This is characteristic of the work of many designers who expose the interior of clothing, and decorate it to use it as a fashion element. This is reminiscent of the architectural innovation of the Pompidou Center where interior features are used as a decorative exterior treatment. This is a new idea for this era but references past styles used in Gothic and other cathedrals that wore their structural elements like flying and diagonal buttresses on the outside. See Figures 3.6, 6.5, and 16.2.

Mlenny/iStock

* Tattooing, body piercing, and highly personal hair and make-up styles define youth culture. See Figures 16.15, 16.17, 15.34, and 15.35.

* Conservative business dress retains the suit and tie of past decades for men and women with little acknowledgment of Postmodern variety.

* Women were also entering the higher ranks of corporate business, professional, and political realms and dressed in expensive, tailored "power clothes" with skirted suits, pants, wide shoulders, and spiked heels by designers such as Armani, Lauren, Klein, and Mugler.

Figure 16.16 Steampunk clothing generally includes goggles, gadgets, and props. Originally about the Victorian British Empire or the American "Wild West," it has become enormously popular around the world and integrates these with many styles from American and Celtic to Samurai. High fashion designers have seized on it and now it is part of their couture and mainstream lines.

Andrew Kraemer

*   Luxurious gowns for "Red Carpet" events continue to generate attention for designers and the celebrities of fashion, film, reality TV, and the music industry. These are often highly theatrical occasions and the designs use innovative interpretations and materials. These designs get modified and become the dresses for weddings, proms, and festive celebrations.

*   Design and fashion for clothes and costumes are never static and always move into the future. The best and most enduring designers capture these moments and often cycle back and around, reinventing and incorporating past historical styles.

Figure 16.17 Devices often used by young people to individualize themselves include body art, tattooing, piercing, body modification and the dramatic use of color in hair, make-up, and clothing.

Blend Images/Alamy

Clothing and Costume Keywords

Postmodern – Beginning with Hippie clothing of the 1960s a whole repertoire of casual and personal clothing developed for men and women often based on sports, worker's, and non-Western garments; and accentuating the development of a personal style mixing commercial products, garments, and accessories from unconventional sources.

tattooing – Ink dye applied under the skin to create permanent decorative patterns and text on the body. It was borrowed from South Sea Island cultures particularly after the Second World War with returning sailors and later in the 1980s from African cultures and used both decoratively and to make a personal or political statement. See Figure 16.17.

body piercing – Inserting wood, metal, or gems as decorations through the skin of the body, usually around the face and ears. Also borrowed from African and Asian cultures. See Figure 16.17.

mohawk – A youth hairstyle in which the head is closely cropped or shaved except for a ridge of longer hair down the center of the skull. Named for the Native American Indian tribe who originated the hairstyle.

Punk – This was an alternative style for both sexes characterized by its rejection of traditional styles and often including shocking or challenging elements such as mohawks, body piercing, tattooing, face painting, and the use of torn or distressed clothing, military equipment, and even corsets and underwear used as clothing. It has also been embraced by high fashion and the Met Ball is a stylish celebration for the fashion industry. See Met Ball 2013, whose theme was "Punk: Chaos to Couture." See Figures 16.15, 16.16, and 16.17.

CHAPTER SEVENTEEN

Pre-Columbian Cultures: Maya: 291 BCE–c. 1200, Aztec: 1325–1521 CE, Inca: 13th Century–1527

Figure 17.1 This shows the city of Teotihuacan, Mexico, and the great Pyramid of the Moon and "the Avenue of the Dead."

Chris Tiné

A Little Background

The Native American nations of Mesoamerica (central) and South America developed a built culture of temples, cities, roadways, and royal residences as early as the 3rd century BCE that continued until the European conquest of the 1500s CE. Expert planning of complex cities, roads, and temple compounds was complemented by sophisticated siting of sacred structures and by accomplished carved symbolic decoration. All three major civilizations achieved a high level of architectural and decorative sophistication without iron tools, the wheel, or the radial arch. Exceptions were the Maya, who had a written language, and the Inca, who were the only ones that used llamas as draft animals.

These two films are not specifically about these cultures but would be of interest and others will be cited in the different sections: *1492: Conquest of Paradise* (1992), Columbus discovered the New World, and *Aguirre, the Wrath of God* (1972), directed by Werner Herzog about conquistadors in the Peruvian Amazon rainforest that was shot on location.

These two American museums have significant collections of pre-Columbian art and information:

http://www.doaks.org/museum/pre-columbian

http://en.wikipedia.org/wiki/University_of_Pennsylvania_Museum_of_Archaeology_and_Anthropology#Mesoamerica

Who They Were

The Maya

* The Maya civilization was the oldest in the New World. The first recorded date on an extant Maya calendar was November 4, 291 BCE. Their culture began earlier than that with the prehistoric Olmec of whom little is known.

* The Maya were located on the Yucatan peninsula and to the west and south of current-day Mexico, Belize, Guatemala, El Salvador, and much of Honduras.

* They were mostly a peaceful farming and trading people who built great roads of stone blocks that connected their jungle cities that were centered on sacred pyramidal temples.

* Their civilization reached a high point in the arts, architecture, agriculture, and the sciences, including mathematics and astronomy; and these were particularly developed in the cities of Tikal and Chichén Itzá, from 600 to 900 CE. See Figures 17.2 and 17.3.

* They had rich traditions of painting, carving, and illustration that decorated their temples and sacred sites.

* They were the only pre-European culture in the New World with a written language of glyphs and hieroglyphics (sacred writing), most of which has now been deciphered. See the documentary film *Breaking the Maya Code* (2008).

* The Maya measured time more accurately than their contemporaries in Europe and developed a 365-day calendar and also used the zero as a number.

* In 1546 the Spanish finally conquered them, but their civilization had been in decline for several centuries. However, Maya people and their traditions and customs still are found primarily in the Mexican provinces of Yucatan, Tabasco, and Chiapas.

* There were several films: *Kings of the Sun* (1963), *Apocalypto* (2006), and two documentaries: *Breaking the Maya Code* (2008) and *Dawn of the Maya* (2004).

The Aztecs

* The Aztecs were a warrior people located in central Mexico who appeared before 1300 CE. They referred to themselves as the Mexica, where we got the word Mexico. They saw themselves as the descendants of the Toltecs and had great reverence for them, their myths, and civilization. The Toltecs thrived earlier in this same area, and it is unclear to historians today what precisely was myth or historical fact as it was an unrecorded culture.

* The city of Teotihuacan and its civilization was even earlier than the Toltecs; scholars believe it was settled in c. 100 BCE and the city built from the 1st century CE until the 7th century CE. The name means "the place where the gods were created." About 30 miles northeast from present-day Mexico City, it was the largest city in pre-Columbian America and was a model for large-scale urban planning and architecture for most civilizations in the Mesoamerican region. It comprised temples, palaces, markets, and large multi-story apartment complexes that were laid out along a longitudinal axis on a two-kilometer "Avenue of the Dead." See Figures 17.1, 17.5, and 7.11.

* The Toltec civilization was positioned between these other two, c. 800–1000 CE, and they founded their capital city of Tollan or Hispanicized-Tula northwest of present-day Mexico City. It was an important archeological site with its main pyramid dedicated to Quetzalcóatl and their rulers, who they believed were his descendants. Quetzalcóatl was the feathered serpent god who was worshiped all over Mesoamerica. On top of the pyramid are four basalt statues of Toltec warriors, which were actually pillars that held up a roof. See Figure 17.6.

* Tollan was also the first place that the chacmools were used and they would become common throughout Mesoamerica. See Figure 17.16 for an example of an Aztec one.

* The Aztecs founded their capital city of Tenochtitlan in 1325, which was mostly destroyed by Cortés in 1521. The city grew to an estimated 200,000 people and included complex civic and religious architecture. It was one of the largest cities in the world at the time.

* The Aztecs were highly militarized and practiced a bloody, war-like religion based on human sacrifice. They had simple but effective weapons for both close and far combat. The most important was the *maquahuitl* that has been compared to a European sword, and also bows and arrows, lances, and spears. There are many pictures and references on the Internet: http://www.mexicolore.co.uk/aztecs/artefacts/maquahuitl

* They were expert and extensive traders and were skilled craftsmen in metallurgy, which in addition to weapons and utilitarian objects included jewelry and ceramics.

* By 1440 under their king, Moctezuma, the Aztecs controlled most of central Mexico, with an estimated population of 5 million.

* Aztec legend said that when Moctezuma II, the last king of the Aztecs, received news of the landing of Cortés and his men in 1519, he thought that Quetzalcóatl had returned and welcomed them.

* Cortez and his Spanish troops defeated the Aztecs in 1521.

* The National Anthropology Museum in Mexico City has many good and useful images:
http://www.visitmexico.com/en/anthropology-museum-in-mexico-city
http://en.wikipedia.org/wiki/National_Anthropology_Museum#mediaviewer/File:Musee_National_Anthropologie-

* A film about the Aztecs is *The Other Conquest* (2007).

The Incas

* The Inca were a conquering civilization that rose to prominence in about 1300. In 1438 Emperor Pachacuti began his expansion, which lasted until 1525 under his sons and heirs with their enormous armies. Eventually the empire spanned 2,600 miles of the Pacific South American Andean coast, from present-day Colombia to southern Chile, an area that was larger than China or the Roman Empire. It comprised high mountains, rain forests, coastal plains, and deserts. See http://historyworld.net/timesearch/default.asp?conid=timeline&getyear=1000&keywords=%20%20%20Incas

* The Inca conquered and strictly controlled roughly 100 different tribal nations and scholars estimate that the Inca Empire at its height had 6 million people, but these statistics vary widely. For the most part the people had peaceful trading, fishing, and farming communities.

* Emperor Pachacuti made Cusco (Spanish-Cuzco) in present day Peru his capital city in c. 1440 as the religious and administrative center, with population estimates of 150,000 at its peak. By eyewitness accounts at the time of Pizarro's conquest in 1524, it was a spectacular city covered in gold and studded with jewels.

* The government was a benevolent despotism in which everyone worked for and was supported by the state.

* The Inca built a system of 15,000 miles of roads for commerce, communication that was principally for administrative purposes, and for military movements. These roads were equipped with lodgings and way stations for the armies and travelers.

* The Inca mastered massive dry stonewall building construction of precisely cut and fitted boulders that were used for royal, religious, military, and residential buildings. Few of them remain intact today, as the Spanish purposely destroyed them and used the rocks for other structures. There are, however, a number of historical sites of ruins, mostly near the ancient capital city of Cusco and along the Inca Trail. See Figures 17.7 and 17.25.

* The Inca built the large complex of Machu-Picchu about 1450 in a remote area in the Andes Mountains. Although its exact purpose is still being debated, it featured royal residences and dependencies in this large-scale stone construction and was spread over a vast area on steep slopes and valleys with connecting terraces. For unknown reasons, it was abandoned about the time of the Spanish conquest, but scholars doubt that the conquistadors were ever there as nothing was defaced or destroyed as in other places. See Figure 17.7.

* They had a highly developed system of agriculture constructed into the mountains and valleys that used terraces and stairways to maximize land use for crops and water systems for drainage and reservoirs, which also used huge blocks of stones. They grew potatoes, corn, quinoa, amaranth, peanuts, squash, avocados, papayas, and many other native plants and also mastered freeze drying and storage techniques. See Figure 17.7.

* They also raised guinea pigs, ducks, and dogs. They domesticated llamas and alpacas and used them for food, and the fibers and leather for textiles. Most importantly, they also used llamas as draft animals.

* The mountains were rich with veins of silver, minerals, and other gemstones, and the rivers with gold.

* The Inca believed that gold was "the sweat of the sun" and the sun was their primary god, so they believed they were to treasure and protect it. They fashioned many artifacts out of it such as jewelry, vessels, and figurines, and also for decoration of their temples and palaces. All gold belonged to their Emperors and in the end it was one of the causes of their defeat.

* The Inca and some of their conquered people, especially on the Peruvian coast, were particularly skilled at ceramics, which came in many sizes, shapes, and with a wide variety of decorations. They also made statues and figurines in clay as well as gold. See http://www.veniceclayartists. com/peruvian-pottery

* They had no system of writing but were skilled in farming, textiles, inlay, metalwork, and surgery. There were several contemporary accounts about them and recent archeological work has brought some light to their civilization, but we know very little of the workings of their culture.

* Contact with the Spanish Francisco Pizarro and his conquistadors in 1524 began their downfall. The Spanish were primarily interested in taking their gold, silver, and precious gems and plundered many of their buildings and towns and destroyed or stole their artifacts.

* *The Royal Hunt of the Sun** was a 1964 play by Peter Shaffer; lighting design in the 1965 Broadway production by Martin Aronstein used exposed lights for the first time and incorporated them as part of the set design; there was also a 1969 movie and 1977 opera by Iain Hamilton. *Wara Wara*, a 1930 film, was restored in 2010.

The Pre-Columbian Material World

What They Made

The Maya

Figure 17.2 This is The Kukulkan Pyramid known as El Castillo in the Maya settlement at Chichén Itzá, Mexico. It is known as a supreme example of the blending of Toltec and Maya architecture showing graceful proportions and excellent construction and decoration. The temple is 75 feet tall and thought to have been built partially for astronomical purposes as during the Spring and Autumn equinox the sun makes a path down the stairway (shown on the right) that looks like a serpent wiggling down the stairs to meet its feathered stone head at the base. Kukulkan was a Maya ruler, who took this name, which translates as feathered serpent. A good link is http://archaeology.about.com/od/archaeo logic7/ig/Chichen-Itza/Chac-Masks-at-Chichen-Itza.htm#step-heading

gumbao/Shutterstock.com

Figure 17.3 This is known as the Group of a Thousand Columns, in the north or new section of Chichén Itzá. The columns once supported a painted frieze and a roof and it is believed that these were meeting halls. Remains of the frieze are decorated with Chac masks, which refer to the rain god and an earlier priestly class, who ruled the city.

Figure 17.4 This is a Maya corbel arch in Uxmal in the Yucatan. This narrow-shaped arch is very typical and a distinctive feature of Maya architecture and was found throughout the Empire. This also shows two important elements of the earlier Puuc style architecture with a plain lower section and an elaborate carved upper one. Uxmal was connected to the city of Kabah with a huge 5-meter-wide raised path way, called a *sacbé*, which had enormous arches like this at entrances to both cities. This arch was also used in other cultures such as Egyptian, Greek, Islamic, and Indian architecture.

* Their permanent architecture consisted of pyramid temples, rectangular palace structures, ball courts, and sometimes residences. Often their sacred precincts were located on high ground in the jungle or on the coasts as is Tulum.

* Some of their greatest architecture was at Chichén Itzá, which had a variety of architectural styles and decorations. Although there was an earlier settlement, it reached its peak in the 9th and 10th centuries with the second settlement when the Toltecs migrated south and blended the two architectural styles. This was seen primarily in the north section with the El Castillo Temple Pyramid, the great ball court, the skull wall, El Caracol, a round building that is believed to be an observatory, and the Group of 1,000 Columns among others. There were also a number of chacmools here in a variety of forms. See Figures 17.2 and 17.3 and the Aztec chacmool in 17.16.

The Aztecs

* There is a model of the center of the ancient Aztec city Tenochtitlan that was founded in 1325 and much of it was built over by present-day Mexico City. The model shows the central sacred complex that featured massive stepped temple pyramids, several smaller stepped temples, a circular temple, an elite school, and a sacred ball court that played a large role in the Aztec religion. In other sections of the city were secular and manufacturing buildings and fields for agriculture. See http://commons.wikimedia.org/wiki/File:TenochtitlanModel.JPG

Figure 17.5 This is another view of the Teotihuacan complex showing the Pyramid of the Sun in the distance. It is an example of *talud-tablero* architecture and also several simple undecorated, geometric pyramids as contrasted to the sculpted and painted surfaces at the Quetzalcóatl Pyramid.

Vadim Petrakov/Shutterstock.com

Figure 17.6 These are the four basalt statues of Toltec warriors on top of the Quetzalcóatl Pyramid in the city of Tula (Tollan), showing their butterfly breastplates, feathered headdresses, and arm bands; not shown are the sun shields on their backs and their spears. These and the other structures shown here were actually pillars that held up a roof.

Niciak/iStock

* Royal palaces and religious buildings were constructed of carved stone blocks, which in many cases were highly decorated with symbolic sculpted carvings and paintings. They generally used oak or pine for support beams and doorjambs. See Figures 17.11, 17.12, 17.13, 17.14, 17.15, and 17.16.

* Simpler and private buildings were of wood posts in the ground that supported thatched roofs and stone sides. In the ancient city of Teotihuacan archeologists have also found the ruins of large apartment complexes.

The Incas

* The most remarkable of Inca sites is the 15th-century building complex at Machu Picchu, which is over 2,000 meters high in the Andes. It incorporated approximately 200 royal, religious, residential, and agricultural buildings built in the classical Inca style with polished hand carved stone walls. Like other sites it had many steep terraces and complex water systems. In addition, an altar oriented to the sun's movements in four directions across miles of terrain completed this highly sophisticated compound.

Figure 17.7 This photograph is of the Royal Sanctuary at the Inca site at Machu Picchu showing its spectacular and sophisticated positioning that integrated the buildings with the environment. These ruins are now considered one of the seven wonders of the world. See http://ngm.nationalgeographic.com/2011/04/inca-empire/pringle-text

Vladislav T. Jirousek/Shutterstock.com

* This precise stone construction needed no mortar and the architecture featured clean rectilinear lines and usually trapezoidal inward-leaning walls with windows and doors and thatched roofs. There were several different styles and variations, mostly based on geography, that were used for all their buildings. See Figures 17.7 and 17.25.

* The capital city of Cusco, meaning "the navel of the world," was an ancient town by the 13th century and under the rule of Pachacuti in the 1440s became the central royal, religious, and administrative city of the Inca Empire. It demonstrated precise urban planning, with intricate baths, irrigation channels, and their buildings used expert stone wall construction that continues to withstand numerous earthquakes.

* The holiest site in the city was Coricancha or the Sun Temple, dedicated to the sun god, Inti. It was covered with sheets of gold and had many gold statues and precious jewels. The Spaniards destroyed it, took the gold and gems and used its stones to build a cathedral on top of it. See http://www.delange.org/Qoricancha/Qoricancha.htm

* Their carvings and cut stones were also used for smaller artifacts, food preparation, and storage as well as walls, bridges, tunnels, and even their weapons.

How They Decorated

* Exterior architectural decoration on temples and palaces was either relief carved stone or stucco or applied stucco forms, and they were colorfully painted inside and out.

* None of these pre-Columbian cultures used movable furniture; they sat or knelt on the ground for food preparation, eating, ceremonies, and sleeping. The primary exception was the throne for the king. See Figure 17.25.

* They all used wood, bone, shells, ceramics, stone, and metals for their utensils and food preparation, all of which they widely traded.

* Alabaster, obsidian, turquoise, and jade were also highly prized and valued and used for jewelry, many decorative and ornamental purposes. Obsidian, a very sharp natural glass, was used by the Aztecs for these things as well as for tools and weapons, most importantly the *maquahuitl*.

* Metals like gold and silver were used for ceremonial vessels, jewelry, figurines, and for decorative purposes on clothes, temples, and palaces. These metals were one of the primary reasons the Spanish wanted and conquered these lands. They plundered the sites and temples, stole the gold and silver objects, and took much of it back to Spain.

The Maya

Figure 17.8 This is the Palace of The Chac Masks at Kabah, Mexico, which is in the Western Yucatan and features the older Puuc style architecture. It is dedicated to Chac, the rain and lightning deity, who was also the god of agriculture, most important in a farming and arid region. The façade is covered with hundreds of stone masks, which show his big round eyes and dangling, hooked nose (the grey foot-like structure) that repeat over and over.

arturogi/iStock

Figure 17.9 This is a detail of one of the Chac masks. Puuc architecture is noted for its highly ornate carvings, often with layered, cut and carved stones set into concrete.

mofles/iStock

The Aztecs

Figure 17.10 This is part of the "Avenue of the Dead" in Teotihuacan and shows an excellent example of *talud-tablero* architecture, which is a distinct style of architecture prominent in Aztec and Maya civilizations. It started very early in this pre-Aztec city and is a notable and very influential architectural feature. It varied in its forms from different pyramidal temple complexes as it spread across Mesoamerica. Also notice the stonework, texture, and colors.

Anton_Ivanov/Shutterstock.com

Figure 17.11 Also at Teotihuacan, this is a wall with carved and painted images and also shows the way doorways were constructed using a wooden lintel (missing at the top) mortised into stone verticals.

Chris Tiné

Figure 17.12 Left—This is another detail showing the same carved and painted floral images and the facing of the platform showing more painted details and colors.

Chris Tiné

Figure 17.13 Right—Notice the same repeat pattern of the white and red circles and this time a jaguar on a striped background.

Chris Tiné

Figure 17.14 Palace of the jaguars at Teotihuacan, showing an interior stone wall with an additional lower one with a painted image of a crouching jaguar wearing a headdress and blowing into a feathered conch shell. The painting was done on a thin coat of plaster in a typically flat style using mostly red but also some green, blue, and yellow paints. The technique is reminiscent of Egyptian, Classical, and European frescos. Scholars do not know what the repeating images at the top mean.

Chris Tiné

Figure 17.15 This is a carved stone image of Quetzal-cóatl, the sacred Aztec feathered serpent god. Traditionally he was the god of the morning and evening star and the symbol of death and resurrection. His worship involved human sacrifice. The pointed rays behind his head are really his "feathers."

Jesus Eloy Ramos Lara/Dreamstime.com

Figure 17.16 This image is of an Aztec chacmool, c. 1500. They are usually found in or outside Aztec and Maya temples and are quite common. It is thought that they were to receive religious offerings as they are frequently seen holding a bowl or basket. Notice his attire all of which would have been worn by real men; the feathered headdress, his large round gold earrings, the collar made of jewels and/or ceramic beads, the wrist and ankle bands, which were also of gold and set with large rounded turquoise stones.

Michel Zabe/AZA/INAH/Bridgeman Images

Figure 17.17 This is the Aztec calendar also known as the sunstone or Cuautixicalli, which is the most famous piece of Aztec sculpture. Shortly after the Spanish invasion it was buried under the central square—Zócalo in Tenochtitlan (Mexico City)—and was discovered in 1790. There are many theories about it, but the exact purpose is unknown. In the center is the sun with his outstretched tongue, which represented the sacrificial blade, as he demanded blood in order to stay strong, which is why they sacrificed animals and people to him. He holds a human heart in both his hands. It is thought that the wheel within a wheel represents their perception of time and space as the inner one has 365 days and the four seasons and the outer sacred one is about the individual gods who ruled each of the days.

pchoui/iStock

The Incas

Figure 17.18 These are contemporary boats and houses on the Uros Islands in Lake Titicaca, Peru, which is a huge sacred lake high in the Andes, which they believed is where the world began. These structures have stayed relatively unchanged since very ancient times. Unlike Inca stone architecture this conquered Uros tribe built floating islands out of totora reeds and also used them for their houses and boats. These boats, called balsa, could be small fishing boats or large enough to hold 20 people and have a very distinctive style and type of construction, also notice the curved stern and prow with animal heads. The boats are similar to others found in several and widely dispersed parts of the world and also very similar to ancient Egyptian papyrus boats.

Yana_N/iStock

Building and Décor Keywords

Maya pyramid – Originally a series of small temples placed on a stepped platform. They were rebuilt numerous times, entombing the previous temple inside. These temples were finally enlarged to form massive four-sided pyramid complexes. The pyramid at Cholula is the largest in the New World and was influenced by the temple at Teotihuacan, it was started in the 3rd century BCE and was worked on until the 9th century CE. See Figure 17.2.

Maya corbelled (COR-belld) **arch** – This was a narrow structure of cut stones that formed a triangular arched opening and was used both inside and outside of Maya religious and secular buildings. Its distinctive feature was that each row of ascending stones was placed a little closer to the center of the arch. It was also adapted as the corbel vault and formed the interior of a roof structure. See Figure 17.4.

chacmools (TCHK-mool) – Chacmools were found throughout Mesoamerica and came in a variety of forms and used different kinds of rock and ceramics. But what they all had in common was a reclining male figure with bent knees, elbows on the ground, and the arms on the chest, generally holding a disk, bowl, or basket. The head was at 90 degrees from the body and the face was toward the viewer. They were usually found outside Maya and Aztec temples. The ones from Chichén Itzá (Maya) and Tollan (Aztec) were surprisingly similar to each other. See Figure 17.16.

roof comb – The carved decorative crest that sometimes surmounted Maya pyramid temples.

Aztec pyramids – The large four-sided pyramids that typically supported one or two temples dedicated to their gods and reached by two parallel flights of steep stairs. These temples were the sites of ritual animal and human sacrifice. Smaller, more rectangular pyramid temples had two long sides and two short ones, as seen in the model of Tenochtitlan. See Figures 17.1 and 17.5.

talud-tablero (TAL-ud-tab-LER-oh) – In all its different manifestations it consisted of a flat horizontal structure, the *tablero*, and a sloping side called the *talud*. As well as in Aztec temples it is found in many Maya sites throughout its range such as Tikal, Palenque, Copan, and Tulum. See Figures 17.1, 17.5, and 17.10.

coatepantli (COAT-e-PANT-lee) – The carved outer or freestanding walls in Aztec temple complexes that often featured images of the sacred feathered serpent, Quetzalcóatl.

Quetzalcóatl (Keh-tzal-coh-atl) – Worshiped by most Mesoamerican cultures, he was the most sacred of gods and his image varied from region to region. See Figure 17.15.

atlantean figures – These were large statues of warriors made of various local stones, found throughout Mesoamerica and used as pillars to hold up roofs. These were comparable to the Greek Caryatids. See Figure 1.4 and the Toltec warriors in Figure 17.6.

The Pre-Columbian Clothing and Costume World

How They Dressed

The Maya

Figure 17.19 This is an 1831 watercolor by Johann Friedrich Waldeck of a traditional 19th-century Maya woman in a huipil over a skirt. She is also wearing a traditional headpiece that was made of a large piece of folded cloth. This costume has hardly changed from classic times to traditional villages today.

Newberry Library/SuperStock

Figures 17.20 and 17.21 These two contemporary native Maya men are dressed up to look like Maya warriors from the Yucatan in the Classic period, c. 10th century. Notice the animal sculls attached to their headwear, and their large collars; the one for the man on the right extends down his arms and has bird wings attached to it. They are wearing body paint, loincloths, and sandals. The man on the left has an ax-like weapon made out of wood with a wrapped obsidian head.

mofles/iStock

* They used bark cloth, hemp fiber, and cotton as clothing materials, dyed with plant, insect, and animal dyes in green, purple, black, blue, and red, and usually woven on back strap looms.

* Several natural colors of cotton were indigenous to Mexico and were used for thousands of years before CE and used for utilitarian purposes like rope and fishnets as well as clothing, which they traded widely throughout the region.

* Depending on their wealth and rank this determined the amount, complexity, and quality of the ornamentation and decoration of both men's and women's clothes.

* Symbolic images were used for weaving and embroidery and the use of colors varied as a distinguishing feature from village to village.

* Men's and women's hair was intertwined with cloth in headdresses, decorated less for women and more for men with feathers, gems, and animal hides. Both men and women also wrapped them in a turban-like fashion.

* Men and women wore sandals that usually had one or two thongs and were decorated or plain (see Figure 17.21), and are like our contemporary flip-flops and similar ones in Japan.

* Women wore a skirt and a poncho-like tunic called a huipil, belted or knotted. None of the clothes were fitted and the neck opening was woven in. They also wore a long version of the tunic. Again decoration varied by rank and region. See Figure 17.19.

* Men wore a breechcloth wrapped around the waist and between the legs. They were decorated with feathers for upper classes and left plain for the poor.

* Men also wore the pati, a long square cloth tied around the shoulders and also worn as a sleeping cloak.

The Aztecs

Figure 17.22 This is a detail from a page from a manuscript, the *Tudela Codex*, that is one of a number of pictorial Aztec manuscripts with many paintings in this typical Aztec style. This appears be a god or royal person because of his crown of feathers and tassels and also the two special feathers that were reserved for them. This one was accompanied with annotations in Castilian Spanish written in 1553. There are also some good costume and prop references depicted in this manuscript and there is information and a facsimile copy on the Internet: Google the Tudela Codex.

Album/Art Resource, NY

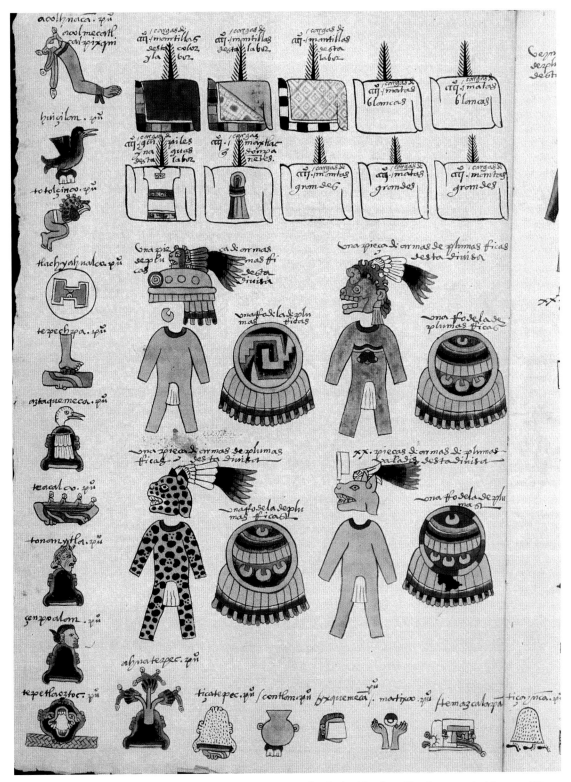

Figure 17.23 This is another page from a different manuscript, the *Codex Mendoza*; Mendoza was the Viceroy of New Spain. It was written in the early 1540s for the Spanish King to list the tribute paid by the conquered Aztecs and also a history and a description of daily life. This one, and other pages like it, shows the tribute from 16 towns of Acuolhuacan: various decorated and plain mantles, women's tunics, and warriors' costumes and shields—notice their similarity to the eagle costume in Figure 17.24. These and other codexes would be excellent resources for the designer for Aztec history, culture, clothing, and props.

Bodleian Libraries, University of Oxford/The Art Archive at Art Resource

Figure 17.24 This is a terracotta figurine of a c. 1480 Aztec eagle warrior with a knife, showing a type of military costume or order. Notice the beak-like helmet and the claws at his knees. We would also know about these from the codexes mentioned earlier and from descriptions of the conquistadors and probably more importantly, the work of Franciscan missionaries—particularly Bernardino de Sahagún, who wrote extensively about them and had them illustrated by local artists. There are several websites about him and his codex.

Gianni Dagli Orti/The Art Archive at Art Resource, NY

* Their clothing was loose fitting and did not fully cover the body. It was usually of woven cactus fiber or imported cotton from other areas of Mexico. They used bright colors, as dyes were freely traded throughout Mesoamerica.

* Men also wore a triangular cloak, the tilma, which they sometimes used as an apron, usually over a simple wrapped loincloth.

* Noble and religious clothing was simple but more highly decorated than daily clothing. Ceremonial dress could include necklaces, earrings, bracelets, furs, and feathers.

* Military clothing varied according to which warrior group a soldier belonged to such as depicted in the illustrations. Heroes were allowed to wear headdresses and more decoration and carried the *maquahuitl*, a sword-like weapon fitted with hard, razor-sharp obsidian glass. See Figures 17.22, 17.23, and 17.24.

* Women's clothing was also simple and like men at the time of the Spanish arrival they were also frequently naked to the waist and often wore only a skirt and sometimes a sleeveless blouse-like short tunic. Like men, decoration and fabric were determined by wealth and rank. See Figure 17.23.

* Sympathetic Spanish missionaries and others recorded much information about clothing and daily life as seen in the *Codex Tudela* and *Codex Mendoza* examples, which were recorded shortly before and after the Aztec Empire fell. See Figures 17.22 and 17.23.

The Incas

Figure 17.25 *Left:* This National Geographic illustration shows an annual Inca festival dance being performed in Cusco's Holy Square. Notice the huge polished stone blocks used for the walls and the three different thatched roofs. In the center was the Emperor on his throne with his princes, other courtiers, and guards holding long decorated staffs. It also shows the wide variations of both the men and women's basic clothing and headwear; also significant are the men's huge gold earrings that pulled their ears to their shoulders, also seen on the stone chacmool in Figure 17.16.

H.M. HERGET/National Geographic Creative

Figure 17.26 *Below:* These two Inca ponchos with woven geometric designs would have been worn by people of a high status. One is decorated with a kind of cat—most likely a sacred Puma—and *cantuta* flowers, which were popular decorative motifs and were also considered sacred during Inca times; now their common name is "flower of the Inca." Notice the simple construction and the colors. These garments are from the south coast of Peru, c. 1380–1520.

Werner Forman/Art Resource, NY

Figure 17.27 This is an image of a beautiful gold and jeweled Inca necklace and shows the sophisticated and intricate degree of workmanship that they were capable of.

alessen/iStock

* The clothing of the Inca was simple, decorative, and strictly controlled by the state.

* Each person was given two sets of clothes, one formal, the other informal, and both were replaced by the state when worn out.

* The Inca imposed their clothing styles on the tribes they defeated.

* Warmer coastal regions wore lighter cotton and higher, cooler regions wore warmer alpaca, vicuña, or llama wool. They were accomplished weavers, knitters, and lace makers and also skilled at embroidery. They used brightly colored dyes and either wove or embroidered their fabrics in imaginative geometric or figurative designs and patterns.

* The fabrics of all these people were woven on basic, low-tech backstrap looms, which were of a simple construction made of sticks, ropes, and yarn or threads. The loom was then attached to a person with a "backstrap" that was worn around the hips or waist. The looms were extremely versatile as they could be used anywhere and produced different styles and sizes of cloth also with woven patterns or decorations. See Figures 17.19, 17.25, and 17.26.

* Inca women wore a one-piece ankle-length dress with a wide ornamented sash at the waist. Similar to the basic Greek dress it wound around the body to form a tube and was pinned at the shoulders. They wore a cloak that was closed at the center with a large, decorative, metal straight pin, called a stopo that could also be used as a knife; and they also wore a headdress. See Figure 17.25.

* Men wore a breechcloth, a sleeveless tunic, which was sewn at the edges, a large cloak tied at the center, and carried a small bag and, in the colder regions, also a knitted or fur cap or hat.

* Inca men began piercing their ears at a young age as a rite of manhood adding increasingly large gold earrings until their earlobes were very stretched. See Figure 17.25.

* Both Inca men and women wore sandals, usually made out of llama hide or woven grasses.

* They all wore much heavy, gold jewelry and frequently body and face paint. See Figure 17.27.

Clothing and Costume Keywords

breechcloth – This is basically the same as a loincloth and is a simple primitive garment worn by men to cover the genitals and has been worn by many cultures around the world. It was a basic part of Aztec and Incan clothing.

maquahuitl (MAK-u-AHOO-itll) – The powerful Aztec sword and symbol of high military rank. There are several good websites.

tilma (TIL-ma) – An Aztec triangular cloak sometimes worn as a tunic.

pati (PA-tee) – A Maya men's garment that was a long square cloth tied around the shoulders and also worn for sleeping.

huipil (WIP-il) – A Maya poncho-like tunic worn by women that often had embroidery, with each village having its own style. It was also a wedding costume intricately woven with feathers, a technique once common in Mesoamerica. See Figure 17.19.

huipil de tapar or bidaniro – The large piece of fabric folded over as a head covering worn by traditional Maya women. See Figure 17.19.

vicuña – A wild camelid similar to the alpaca. Only royalty wore its very fine and warm wool, which was worth as much as gold.

CHAPTER EIGHTEEN

Egypt: 2920–57 BCE

Figure 18.1 These are small gold statues of King Tutankhamun, commonly King Tut, who ruled from 1332 to 1323 BCE in the New Kingdom. It shows him with both crowns of Upper Egypt (South—roughly Aswan to Memphis) on the left with a *uraeus*, and Lower Egypt (North—roughly Memphis to Mediterranean Sea) on the right. He is wearing a pleated kilt and sandals with heavy eye make-up and carrying a large shepherd's crook or *heqa* scepter and flail, both symbols of his power and authority. He is in the typical male pose with one foot slightly in front of the other.

François Guenet/Art Resource, NY

A Little Background

Egyptian culture existed relatively undisturbed for five thousand years in the Nile River valley from Aswan in the south to the mountains of northeastern Africa and the Mediterranean Sea delta. The ancient Egyptian civilization was almost always united under one of a series of kings called a pharaoh who achieved status through battle and lineage. It was believed that he was descended from the gods and when he died he would become a god. They believed in many gods and goddesses who had specific roles and it was critical to recognize and pray to them to keep life in balance and harmony. At different times in their history and in different cities one or more gods would become dominant.

The 1922 discovery of King Tut's tomb and the incredible vast array of its contents prompted international exhibits and popular interest in all things Egyptian, which would have a direct influence on Art Deco architecture, motifs, and clothes. This ancient civilization would have a profound impact and lasting influence on the Western world, particularly in architecture, industry, medicine, arts, and crafts. They were the first to have a written language and to record their own history. Through their hieroglyphics, paintings, sculpture, and models, they depicted their way of life, myths, stories, and accomplishments and so gave us a visual record.

Who They Were

*   Egyptian history was divided into a series of dynasties each of which comprised the reigns of several pharaohs who were either related or allied. Ancient Egyptian history was roughly divided into four phases: the Old Kingdom (2920–2134 BCE), the Middle Kingdom (2040–1640 BCE), the New Kingdom (1550–332 BCE), and the Greco-Roman Period (332 BCE–395 CE).

*   Their society was largely agrarian and the major agricultural zones were limited geographically to the flood plain of the Nile and the northern delta. The cycles of flooding and drought of the Nile River determined most aspects of Egyptian life and its culture, which included food and textile production, seasonal religious observances and performances, and building construction.

*   The river flooded from July to November and therefore as they could not farm this was when most building construction took place. The common people worked for the pharaoh as he provided food, clothes, and shelter, but perhaps more importantly, guaranteed a burial place on the precinct to assure them of an afterlife.

*   Their society was strictly hierarchical with the gods and goddesses, then the pharaoh, his court, the governors of the provinces, the commanders of the army, the priests and priestesses, then scribes, and then the craftsmen and farmers.

*   A basic understanding of their religious and philosophical beliefs is essential to all aspects of Egyptian life as its art and architecture as well as its history and politics were dictated and governed by them. They believed that life on earth was short and that after death there was another eternal new life in another world provided certain conditions were strictly met and enforced.

*   In conjunction with this they believed that everyone had a soul ("Ba") and a spiritual duplicate ("Ka") which was also their "vital life force." "Ka" remained on earth in the burial tomb and "Ba" was

free to travel out during the day but returned to the tomb at night. Eternal life was dependent on them recognizing each other and the body, so corpses were preserved or mummified. A human-headed bird or simply a hieroglyph bird often represented "Ba." During life "Ka" and the person were separate but when a person died "they went to their Ka." The "Ka" symbol was often a figure with two upraised arms. See Figure 18.10, to the upper left of Horus' head.

* The more important the person the larger the tomb, so consequently the pharaohs were buried in the large stone pyramids but everyone was mummified and buried.

* The pyramids were the iconic image of ancient Egypt and were symbolic of their beliefs. Many scholars believe that the peak and the four sides represented the four points of the compass and the rays of the sun. So the sun god, Ra, who was the king of gods in the old Kingdom, shone directly down on the pharaoh and linked them together.

* The majority of the pyramids and tombs were on the west bank as that is where the sun set as it traveled to the other world and would return the next day in the east. Later when Osiris became king of the gods he ruled the underworld and the afterlife and controlled the west bank. Later there would also be tombs and temples on the east bank.

* Like so much else Egyptian art was in the service of religion and to perpetuate and assure the ideas of eternal life and their gods, the pharaohs, and the people. It was not to realistically imitate life but to idealize people and things often with symbolic meanings and images. Especially the gods and pharaohs were idealized and depicted as slim with muscular upper bodies and erect posture. There were strict rules about when and how things could be depicted and this varied little over this entire period.

* The six colors, green, red, blue, yellow, white, and black, were used symbolically and each had a specific meaning that gave an image greater power. Green was symbolic of new life, vegetation, and fertility and the god Osiris was pictured with green skin. Red was the color of power and it symbolized life and victory, as well as anger and fire, and was associated with the goddess Isis and her blood. Blue was the color of heaven and water and symbolized creation and rebirth and the god Amun. Yellow was the color of Ra, the sun god, and gold, and all of the pharaohs, and symbolized the eternal and indestructible. White was the color of purity and was used by priests and priestesses and symbolized the sacred. The color black was for death and was represented by Anubis and Osiris, the gods of the underworld and night and the afterlife.

* There have been a number of films such as: *Exodus: Gods and Kings* (2014), *Gods of Egypt* (2016), *The Ten Commandments* (1956), *Nefertite, regina del Nilo* (1961), *Land of the Pharaohs* (1955), *Faraon* (1966), *Agora* (2009), and the 2002 BBC documentary, *Building the Great Pyramid*, and the 6 part 2005 BBC series *Egypt: Rediscovering a Lost World,* as well as a number of TV mini-series and history shows. There are many versions and adaptations of the story of Antony and Cleopatra but the iconic one is Elizabeth Taylor and Richard Burton's 1963 film *Cleopatra*.

* Four classic operas are Rossini's 1827 *Moïse et Pharaon*, Verdi's 1871 *Aida*, Massinet's 1914 *Cléopâtre*, and Barber's 1966 and 1975 *Antony and Cleopatra*.

* Several helpful websites are:

  http://www.perankhgroup.com/Life%20in%20ancient_egypt.htm

  http://www.aldokkan.com/religion/ba.htm

The Egyptian Material World

Figure 18.2 This is the famous Great Sphinx at Giza and also includes the Pyramids of Menkaure and Khafre in the background. It is thought to have been built during the reign of the Pharaoh Khafre (c. 2558–2532 BCE) and to be a likeness of him. It has the head of a pharaoh with the typical nemes headdress and the body of a lion. It is often supposed that it was to guard the pyramids. It is not uncommon in Egyptian iconography, particularly with their gods, to combine human and animal and bird elements. It is the largest monolithic statue in the world and made of limestone.

plus99/iStock

What They Made

Figure 18.3 These are the three Giza Pyramids built a lifetime apart and at slightly different angles from 2550 to 2460 BCE during the Old Kingdom. There are more than 80 pyramids along the banks of the Nile built from 2700 to 1640 BCE. This image shows the straight-sided and the three smaller stepped pyramids and there was also a third bent or rounded form. They were made of limestone and the center one shows the smooth highly polished facing of Tura limestone.

sculpies/iStock

Figure 18.4 This is the Mortuary Temple of Mentuhotep II (2061–2010 BCE) on the west bank across from Thebes, Middle Kingdom, 2040–1650 BCE. The buildings were composed of two colonnaded levels, the top one set back from the bottom one and surrounded by a flat roofed hall. Colonnades articulated the front elevations and bore early Doric features. Each colonnade consisted of a row of rectangular piers outside, each with a Doric column directly behind it. Although it looks very stark, at the time it would have been heavily decorated and painted in bright colors. Usually there were also many statues of the Pharaoh and his wives, children, also sphinxes, and the gods associated with him, as well as relief carvings, and wall paintings commemorating his life and accomplishments. We know from records that they were also lushly planted such as at the nearby complex of the Mortuary Temple of Hatshepsut where she imported hundreds of trees, shrubs, and plants. In the foreground can be seen a peristyle and the round depressions were most likely where trees would have been. In this case the burial chamber was deep in the rock cliffs and far from the flooding river.

De Agostini Picture Library/G. Sioen/Bridgeman Images

Figure 18.5 This is an entry gate at one of the temples at the Temple of Karnak complex built from 1550 to 332 BCE during the New Kingdom. The area at Karnak was called "Ipet-isut"—"The Most Select of Places"—and this massive temple complex was dedicated to the Theban triad—Amun, Mut, and Khonsu—and marked the ascent of the deity Amun. This view shows the huge cut stones and the typical post and lintel construction. Remnants of the original relief carvings are visible on the walls and inside the posts. The statue of a pharaoh on the left is wearing the double crown of Upper and Lower Egypt, the *pschent*, with the *nemes* underneath and also the rectangular false beard. It was common to have two symmetrical statues at an entryway and also often two obelisks. Both statues are in the typical male pose with one foot in front of the other. Inside the courtyard you can just see the bases of another row of statues. It uses a strong processional axis through a series of aligned courtyards and gateways and pylons to the great hall of columns or hypostyle hall, which culminated in a sacred sanctuary. These pylons are similar to the later pylon gateway at the Temple of Edfu, 251–257 BCE, seen in Figure 18.8.

waupee/Big Stock Photo

Figure 18.6 These are the huge lotus bud–shaped columns in the ruins of Luxor Temple. This temple was also built for the worship of the gods Amun-Re, his wife, Mut, and son, Khonsu, known as the Theban Triad. It was built during the Middle Kingdom and the early New Kingdom, c. 1550 BCE. Unlike most temples it was oriented on a north–south axis, to align it with the northern Karnak Temple complex and the avenue of Sphinxes connects the two. The buildings that still exist were built by Amenhotep III and Ramesses II. Clearly visible in this picture are the parts of an Egyptian column starting with the top architrave, then the rectangular abacus, the capital, then the shaft, and finally the base. Often capitals were plants such as lotus and papyrus. Stone shafts were carved to resemble tree trunks or bundled reeds or plant stems. The shafts were often decorated with colorful depictions in painted and/or carved relief, and hieroglyphics and remain some of the most interesting architectural elements in Egyptian structures. See http://www. touregypt.net/featurestories/columns.htm#ixzz3P5wBYU78

uchar/iStock

Figure 18.7 This modern rendering of an interior Egyptian palace is based on historical reconstructions, wall paintings, and models found in tombs and shows their use of the central court plan that we will see later in Greece and Rome. It also shows the colossal scale and lavish and colorful decorations, which they used inside and out. In Egypt piers were called polygonal square columns and were painted and also often used carved relief and these have painted images of papyrus and lotus. They were also using papyrus for these capitals, but at least 30 different plants have been identified. Columns were placed close together so that they could carry the weight of the large heavy roofs on houses and temples.

HIP/Art Resource, NY

Figure 18.8 This is the cult Temple of Horus at Edfu and built during the Ptolemaic period from 251 to 57 BCE. This is a good and well-preserved example of the Egyptian pylon gateway showing the two large tapering towers decorated with huge relief images of the god Horus dressed as a pharaoh with the double crown, the *pschent*, a queen or his mother, Isis. He was the god of war, sky, and falcons and is usually pictured with a head of a falcon and body of a pharaoh and was considered one of the major gods. Both architecture and the iconography were very symmetrical and over the gate is a round sun disk that has double raised cobras. The rectangular slits on the façade were to hold huge tall flagpoles. Notice the difference between the small mud-baked bricks, which were made in molds and the cut stones. At the base of the gateway are two exquisitely carved statues of falcons that show their direct Egyptian influence on Art Deco and are worth looking up.

LUke1138/iStock

Figure 18.9 These are the entrance doors in tomb no.2 at the Necropolis of the Mustapha Pasha complex in Alexandria. It is from the Ptolemaic (Greco-Roman) period in the 2nd century BCE and incorporates their elements, such as the Ionic columns, the entablature with triglyphs, and the frescoed doorframes with horses and chariots. Sphinxes were common in temples and tombs throughout ancient Egypt and were known as "the terrifying one" or "the Father of Dread."

akg-images/De Agostini Picture Library

Old Kingdom: 2920–2134 BCE

* The Giza Pyramids were tombs for three successive kings that were built from 2550 to 2460 BCE, during the 4th dynasty, and were emblematic of Old Kingdom Egypt. A pyramid had two functions: to thwart grave robbers and to protect the body for immortal life. See Figures 18.2 and 18.3.

* These were some of the first true pyramids and each of the three was of slightly different size and slope. They were built for the kings: Khufu had the largest pyramid; Khafre, his son, the medium pyramid; and Menkaure, the grandson, the smallest pyramid.

* Each pyramid was part of a funerary complex that had a fairly standard prescribed plan. The pharaoh would be brought by royal barge to his complex to the first valley temple, which was a large hall with storage units. He would be embalmed here or in workshops nearby and put in a mummy case.

* This temple was connected to a long narrow covered causeway that led to a mortuary temple where sacred ritual ceremonies called "the opening of the mouth" were performed by Sem priests to prepare him for the afterlife. This ceremony was not just for the mummy but also for all the statues that represented him or her and were known as "Ka" statues.

* When these were completed he was taken to his final burial chamber deep in the ground under the pyramid. This room was lined with granite and decorated with paintings. It often contained statues of the pharaoh. He had been placed in one or more wooden coffins and then finally in a decorated stone sepulchral and the room sealed off. Outside of this were the "Ka" statues and anterooms where all the things he needed in his eternal life were stored. These were the myriad of objects that have come down to us in the modern world and comprise so many different aspects of Egyptian life and culture that allow us to know so much.

* Rectangular tombs for the king's family and courtiers, called mastabas, were built around the pharaoh's pyramid. Even smaller tombs were for the laborers and their families.

* Temples on the western bank of the Nile followed an east–west axis and on the eastern bank a west–east axis.

* The queens had smaller pyramids of their own. Later they would also have special mortuary and cult tombs, especially in the Valley of the Queens.

* The capital of the Old Kingdom was at Memphis, meaning the "city of white walls," and was believed to have been founded by the legendary first pharaoh, Menes. It was the capital of the Lower Kingdom and it remained an important city of commerce and trade due to its strategic site at the head of the Nile delta.

* Through the period the architecture was similar to that at Giza and focused on the construction of royal tombs. Workshops for the construction and other artifacts, necropolises, housing, and sites for food preparation surrounded these.

* About this time, c. 2680–2258 BCE, the characteristic Egyptian style of painting and relief carvings was solidified and known as "the law of frontality," and with minor variations would stay relatively the same through their long history. It showed the human figure with the head in profile and the eyes looking straight ahead, the shoulders in front view and the lower body and feet also in profile. Paint was applied in unblended simple symbolic colors.

Middle Kingdom: 2040–1640 BCE

* Mentuhotep II (ruled c. 2051–2030 BCE) was the founder of the Middle Kingdom and during his reign reunited Upper and Lower Egypt and started the use of the Double Crown to symbolize this.

This was called the *pschent* or *sekhemty*, and combined the red Lower and white Upper crowns. See Figure 18.1 for the separate crowns and Figures 18.5 and 18.8 for the double ones.

* Thebes became its capital and was a cosmopolitan city and center of artistic production. Briefly it was moved to a different northern city, Lisht or el-Lisht, where there was a pyramid complex of Senusret I, but returned to Thebes in the New Kingdom.

* The mortuary complex of Mentuhotep II, 2061–2010 BCE, was the greatest accomplishment of this period. It was a combined temple and tomb in a single structure that was built into the side of a steep mountain. The building was composed of two colonnaded levels, the top one set back from the bottom one and surrounded by a flat roofed hall. Colonnades articulated the front elevations and bore early Doric features. It was a spectacular combination of architecture sited in a dramatic landscape. See Figure 18.4.

* This temple and others of his officials used decorations in their tombs in a distinctive Theban style of low painted reliefs with hieroglyphics of ritual and ceremonial scenes.

* This was the period c. 1981–1975 BCE when many of the small models of daily activities were made that were discovered in 1920 in the tomb of an official, Meketre. They would make excellent research material. These examples are at the Met Museum, New York City, and Egyptian Museum in Cairo.

* On the east bank of the Nile there were 39 tombs of provincial rulers at Beni Hasan built high into the limestone cliffs. Some of them were decorated in a distinctive colorful style of wall paintings that were characteristic of the art of the early Middle Kingdom. These paintings would make excellent resources as they show many aspects of scenes from daily life including the military, agriculture, as well as animals and birds. There are a number of relevant websites, but this one has some good pictures: https://egyptsites.wordpress.com/2009/02/14/beni-hasan also click on "images."

New Kingdom: 1550–332 BCE

* This period was the height of Egyptian civilization and its imperial expansion to the north and east.

* It was the period of the best known 18th Dynasty (1543–1292 BCE) when most of the famous pharaohs and queens reigned.

* During this period the capital moved again back south to Thebes (now Luxor) and was again a thriving major religious and political center. Across the river on the west bank was the Valley of the Kings and Queens with many mortuary and cult temples and the burial place of the kings and queens of the New Kingdom with their tombs in the limestone cliffs.

* The New Kingdom temples on the west and east sides of the Nile consisted of pylons, main gates, peristyles, and hypostyle halls, side rooms, and sanctuaries. Peristyle halls were courts enclosed by columns. Hypostyle halls had roofs or ceilings enclosed by rows of columns. The public was only allowed to enter the peristyle and hypostyle halls for prayers, especially on feast days.

* The New Kingdom was dominated by the Temple of Karnak, which dated from c. 2055 BCE to c. 100 CE. The major difference between Karnak and other temple sites was that it was constructed over an extremely long time and by 30 pharaohs, starting in the Middle Kingdom and continuing through the Greco-Roman period. Because of this there was enormous diversity of architectural and decorative styles, the complexity of the site, and its sheer size. One of them, the Hypostyle Hall was the largest religious building ever constructed at roughly 60,000 square feet and featured 134 columns. See Figures 18.5 and 18.6. There are several good websites including: http://discoveringegypt.com/karnak-temple

* During the brief period of Akhenaten and Queen Nefertiti some different things happened both in religion and politics; but also in art and architecture it was known as the Amarna period (1372–1350 BCE). There was a tendency toward more naturalism and a more delicate style. This had its highpoint in the objects and paintings from the tomb of Tutankhamun. In some sculpture and painting there was often a caricature-like feeling as can be seen in some paintings, relief, and sculptures. See Figures 18.1, 18.11, 18.12, and 18.13; and this website has pictures in this style: http://www.metmuseum.org/toah/hd/phar/hd_phar.htm

* Ramesses II reigned from 1279 to 1213 BCE; he was often considered the greatest pharaoh and was responsible for much construction and imperial expansion. He ended the Amarna period and reinstated its traditional religion and its architectural construction methods, with modifications. His building and rebuilding of existing temples covered all of the Egyptian and conquered territory. He also built his Ramesseum mortuary temple and the Abu Simbel rock temples in Nubia as monuments to himself and his queen Nefertari. He initiated a new technique of deep relief carving to assure that his image and hieroglyphs would survive and also erected enormous statues of himself in many older temples as a means of propaganda to promote his legacy and impress the people with his power.

* This was probably the time of Moses and the Exodus when he led the Israelites out of slavery. Ramesses II was portrayed with him in the movie *The Ten Commandments* (1956) and the animated film *The Prince of Egypt* (1998).

* There were basically two types of residential architecture—urban and country. In the early periods they were made out of mud bricks that were made in molds and later the wealthier homes used cut stone, which was more permanent.

* We know much about their architecture, as there are still many visible ruins with ongoing excavations and also through models and paintings.

* Urban architecture was generally multi-storied and rectangular with small windows usually high up near the ceiling. They often had flat roofs that they used for many purposes including food preparation and sleeping, as they were cooler than the interiors.

* By this period wealthy homes or villas were freestanding and usually the complexes of multi-purpose buildings, gardens, and orchards were surrounded with walls. The buildings were rectangular in shape and often two or more stories high with windows on the second level. Silos for grain storage were beehive shaped. Frequently the main residence had a porch and entrances in the front and back; often the front porch had a roof supported by tall columns based on plant forms. The interior rooms had many different functions and were highly decorated with bold colors. See Figure 18.7.

* They had tables, chairs, beds, and many different styles and sizes of chests and wooden boxes. There were also many different kinds of pottery, faience, metal, and baskets and other woven implements. Again because they were in the burial tombs to support the person in the afterlife many of these artifacts are now in museums around the world.

* Egyptians slept on beds covered with mattresses and used a curved wooden headrest, which was also covered with cloth or straw. These headrests were very similar to those used by Geishas in Japan many centuries later.

* Gardens were associated with the country houses of the wealthy. Usually they were rectangular and symmetrical with a water feature in the center and surrounded by a peristyle or columns. We see this construction and arrangement repeated in Greek, Roman, and also often Islamic, and Indian architecture. See Figure 18.7.

* Fortified cities were enclosed rectangles with high crenellated walls with corners punctuated by defensive towers and strategically placed entrances.

Greco-Roman Period: 332 BCE–395 CE

* Alexander the Great of Greece conquered Egypt in 332 BCE and built the city of Alexandria as the new capital, which reached great prominence for commerce and culture, symbolized by the Lighthouse at Pharos and the Library. Until its destruction some time near the 1st century CE, the Library at Alexandria had "the task of collecting the knowledge of the world." Not only did it house an enormous collection of Egyptian, Greek, and Roman learning, mostly in the form of papyrus scrolls, but it was also a center of scholarship, research, and teaching.

* The reign and military expansion of Alexander the Great (336–323 BCE) was brief but significant as he conquered all of Greece and then the Persian Empire of western Asia and Egypt. Returning back to Greece he died in Babylon at the age of 33. The conquered lands were divided among his generals.

* Egypt was allotted to General Ptolemy, who established the Ptolemaic dynasty. His son and co-regent Ptolemy II revived the tradition of brother–sister marriage practiced by some earlier Egyptian kings by marrying his sister Arsinoe II. This era was noted for its dynastic problems that eventually led to the Roman intervention and conquering of Egypt.

* Its most famous ruler was Queen Cleopatra VII, who was the last active pharaoh and was a descendant of the Ptolemaic dynasty and therefore spoke Greek, which was used on important documents and was one of the reasons the Rosetta Stone was also written in Greek. She claimed to be the reincarnation of the queen goddess Isis. It was during Cleopatra's reign that the Roman Octavian defeated her and her Roman lover, Mark Anthony's armies in 31 BCE. Octavian would change his name and become Caesar Augustus and ruled as a pharaoh.

* Along with Nefertiti, Cleopatra captured the imaginations of the Western world. She was represented in many art forms, including painting, literature, and other media. Several examples were the film *Cleopatra* (1963), Massenet's opera, *Cléopâtre*, Shaw's *Caesar and Cleopatra*, and Shakespeare's *Antony and Cleopatra*, most of which have been adapted.

* Egypt would then become a tightly controlled province in the Roman Empire and it was during this period that Egyptian art and architecture began to take on Late Greek and Roman influences. See Figures 18.9, 18.16, and 18.17.

* The Greeks and Romans were intrigued by the Egyptian civilization and particularly its art and architecture, which they copied and elaborated. This is particularly noteworthy in sculpture.

* The Romans discovered many types of marble in the mountains near the Red Sea and they used them extensively in construction and in sculpture. There was more movement in these sculptures and also rendering of folds and fabric. See Figures 18.16 and 18.17.

Building and Décor Keywords

mastaba (house for eternity) (MAST-aba) – This was a large 30-foot-high type of above ground rectangular tomb with outward-sloping sides and a flat roof. These were the burial places of many important and noble Egyptians, but not pharaohs. The burial chambers were below ground carved out of the rocks and also had statues of the deceased. In the early periods, mastabas were constructed out of mud bricks, which were used for houses and smaller tombs and later like the pyramids and temples used the more permanent stone. There are hundreds of them on the Giza plateau.

semataway – This was a symbol of the unity of the Upper and Lower Kingdoms and often seen on the sides of thrones and in wall paintings. It used the heraldic signs of a lily for the South and papyrus for the North intertwined with a knot.

mortuary temples – These were memorial temples constructed near pharaoh's tombs and planned by them while they were alive. The temples were designed to commemorate the pharaoh or queens and were used by their cult followers after their death. See Figures 18.4 and 18.10.

obelisk – This was a tall pointed, tapered monolithic pillar that often had a square or rectangular base. They were often in pairs at the entrance to temples and usually made of red granite. The pyramid-shape top was often covered in an alloy of gold and silver called "electrum" and all four sides had hieroglyphs. They were particularly influential to the Romans, who had many in Rome. Many were taken from Egypt and were scattered around the Western world and have been adapted to many other cultures.

piers (PEER) – These were large columns often square in plan that supported the roof of a house or temple. In ancient Egypt they were referred to as polygonal columns and could be square or many sided. See Figures 18.4 and 18.7.

post and lintel – This was a basic type of construction where two vertical posts of equal length and width have a horizontal beam or bar placed between and above them and was the basis of most Egyptian architecture. It was characteristic of most built architecture around the world. See Figures 18.4, 18.5, 18.6, 18.7, 18.8, and 18.9.

pylon (PIE-lon) – This was a massive rectangular gateway that used two tapering towers in Egyptian temples. Variations of these were later used in Western churches and towers for modern suspension bridges and highways. See Figure 18.8.

colonnade – This was a row of columns that supported a roof, entablature, or arcade. See Figures 18.4, 18.6, and 18.7.

peristyle – This was a rectangular arrangement of columns that enclosed a courtyard, garden, entryway or other architectural feature. See Figures 18.4, 18.6, and 18.7 and Chapter 1 and 2 for several examples.

hypostyle (HYP-o-STYLE) **hall** – The hall in some Egyptian temples that consisted of a rectangular room filled with rows of massive columns that supported a roof. Refer to Temple of Karnak, Figure 18.5.

hieroglyphs (HI-ro-GLIFS) – The symbolic picture writing used by the ancient Egyptians, where an object represented a sound, syllable, or word. They were finally deciphered in the 1820s, after Napoleon's soldiers found the Rosetta Stone in Egypt. See Figures 18.10 and 18.14.

Rosetta Stone – This stone had a Ptolemaic period, 196 BCE, decree written on it in three languages: Ancient Greek, hieroglyphs, and another Egyptian script, demotic, that allowed scholars to finally decipher ancient hieroglyphs.

cartouche – In hieroglyphics this was either a horizontal or vertical oval often with a line at the bottom that contained a pharaoh's name. It was also a physical amulet often of gold and carved gems to protect him from evil spirits in life and after death. There were tombs and sarcophagi that also used this shape and an example was the one of King Thutmose III. Later in Western civilizations it would have a different meaning and image.

canopic jars – The jars in which human remains were placed when a body was being mummified. The stoppers depicted the heads of the four sons of the god Horus to protect the lungs, stomach, liver, and intestines.

The Book of the Dead – These were funerary spells and sayings written on papyrus scrolls that were placed in tombs to help the person on the journey in the afterlife.

mummy case – This was the case for the embalmed mummy that had a stylized body shape and was highly decorated with colorful painted images and hieroglyphics.

cartonnage – This was a papier-mâché-like substance of linen and papyrus used for mummy masks and cases and was popular during the Greco-Roman period. It was important as wood was scarce and it was also lightweight and easily molded, gilded, and painted.

sarcophagus – This was the final stone or alabaster coffin often rectangular in shape that was built in the burial chamber while the pyramid was being constructed, as they were too large and heavy to move. It was usually decorated with inscriptions, sculptures, or portraits. It contained several smaller ones and the wrapped mummy in its case.

The Egyptian Clothing and Costume World

Figure 18.10 This is a fresco in the Mortuary Temple of Hatshepsut on the west bank and was built c. 1478/72–1458 BCE near the Mortuary Temple of Mentuhotep. See Figure 18.4. It is in "the Birth Colonnade," which has a series of images showing her divine birth. On the left is the god Horus with the typical falcon head wearing a divine kilt, and leg and armbands. It is unclear whether the figure on the right is Hatshepsut or her stepson and successor Thutmose III, as after her death he destroyed many images of her and replaced them with his own. In either case, the figure is dressed in the pharaoh's kilt with starched triangular piece, sash, and bull tail, and with the *nemes* headdress with its raised cobra and false beard. Also notice they are in the typical male stance and both wearing the *usekh* collar. The arms are raised as an offering and respect, with typical small round vessels, but also notice that the pharaoh is pictured larger than Horus, with the implied meaning of more importance. Hatshepsut was a successful and long-reigning female pharaoh from 1503 to 1482 BCE and to solidify her power she dressed as a pharaoh as seen above. Her temple was known as Djeser-Djeseru, "Splendor of Splendors." http://www.ancientegyptonline.co.uk/hatshepsutmorttemple.html

Mariasats/Dreamstime.com

How They Dressed

Figure 18.11 This is the very famous bust of Queen Nefertiti, wife of Akhenaten, who reigned c. 1352–1336 BCE, during the New Kingdom, Amarna period. Her name means "the beautiful one is here." This iconic image is as well-known as the pyramids and sphinx. With her elegant long neck, shapely features, and heavy make-up, and multi-colored *usekh*, it is a beautiful painted sculpture and also has a curious blue cylindrical headpiece unlike any other crown. It was found in 1913 by German arche-ologist Ludwig Borchardt buried in rubble in the excavated workshop of the royal sculptor Thutmose in Amarna, Nefertiti's capital city. This website has many images of her: http://www.gettyimages.com/creative/nefertiti-stock-photos. There are also several websites about Amarna and the excavation work being done there. Google "Amarna."

Vanni Archive/ Art Resource, NY

Figure 18.12 This is a limestone tablet and was a sculptor's or painter's preliminary or test piece depicting a pharaoh and his queen holding a bouquet of flowers. Identification of the royal couple is uncertain and some have suggested that they are Smenkhkare, Tutankhamun's elder brother, and Merytaten, Akhenaten's and Nefertiti's eldest daughter. They also look remarkably like Akhen-aten and Nefertiti in some of the freer drawings of them. In any case it is an image of a pharaoh and a queen wearing typical elegant garments. Notice the heavily pleated clothes and the diaphanous fabric of her gown, which is the royal linen. They are both wearing short-pleated kilts with sashes, large multi-colored *usekh* and blue crowns known as *khepresh* with *uraeuses*. His crown is in the more typical shape and also with round disks and he is also wearing the extended curved pointed toe shoes. He is holding a long staff, a symbol of authority from ancient Egyptian times. Notice that the style of painting is freer in the Amarna style and is also unusual to have a woman painted in red ochre. This website is useful for descriptions and portraits of Egyptian rulers and also has the pic-tures of the drawings referenced above. See http://www.metmuseum.org/toah/hd/phar/hd_phar.htm

Werner Forman Archive/Bridgeman Images

Figure 18.13 This is a modern reconstruction of a statue of King Tutankhamun, who reigned 1332–1323 BCE. It is wood and gilded bronze and it was one of two that stood outside the sealed entrance to his sepulchral chamber; it is an example of a "Ka" statue. Notice the typical *nemes* with the raised cobra, *uraeus*, the stiff triangular pleated apron of his kilt, the complex patterned shawl, the gold arm and wristbands, his bull tail, and a variation of the staff, called a "mks" staff with a collar halfway down. These "Ka" statues were so "Ba" could recognize the correct tomb and also in case the corpse deteriorated or was lost, so they could still unite and have eternal life. Usually there were at least two outside the chamber and one or more inside as well as frequently a portrait on the sarcophagus itself.

HIP/Art Resource, NY

Figure 18.14 This wall painting of lady musicians is from the Tomb of Rekhmire, Dayr al-Bahri, Valley of the Nobles. They are playing a version of the lute and harp. They are shown wearing the traditional white linen sheath dress and in both instances with one wide shoulder strap and both with typical long straight hair. The top of the dress comes to just below her breasts on the figure on the left. In Egyptian painting they frequently show scenes stacked on top of each other with a narrow black band as is visible here, in lieu of perspective showing things in front and behind. Also note that the chair above and the harp have animal feet, and customarily they would go in the same direction like a real animal. Also notice that the women all have their feet side by side unlike male figures.

AISA—Everett/Shutterstock.com

Figure 18.15 This is from the Tomb of Nakht, Dayr al-Bahri, Valley of the Nobles. This painting shows laborers picking grapes. The two men on the right are wearing a typical skirt that wrapped around the body and tucked in at the waist. The man to the left is wearing a simpler loincloth typical of laborers. Also notice the large pottery wine vessels. Both wine and beer making were important industries, and as well as on wall painting they are depicted in miniature models found in the tombs.

AISA—Everett/Shutterstock.com

* Textile production was second only to food production as the main occupation of the lower orders of society.

* Linen was the main clothing fiber. It was made from flax, which was grown along the banks of the Nile. With some exceptions, linen was not dyed but used as a natural off-white. In the New Kingdom c. 1550 BCE colors were introduced.

* Silk came to Egypt from the East during the Ptolemaic period and was a favorite of Cleopatra VII.

* Cotton was introduced and grown after the Roman conquest and became an important fabric and commodity.

* Hieroglyphic and wall painting images show figures and garments that were associated with rank. Generally in the images, less clothing indicated lower rank and more clothing indicated higher rank, but this wasn't always the case.

* As it was very hot most of the time, people often wore as little clothing as possible except for ceremonial occasions. Linen fabric was cool and easily washed, which the Egyptians valued as they thought cleanliness was important.

* Egyptian clothing was relatively simple and stayed fairly consistent from 3000 until c. 1550 BCE and the New Kingdom. See Figures 18.1, 18.10, 18.12, 18.14, and 18.15.

* In the early periods men's clothing was very simple. It was a rectangular piece of linen wrapped around the body and tucked in at the waist. See Figure 18.15.

* Clothing styles for both sexes were of two basic types: wraparound and fitted. See Figures 18.1, 18.10, 18.12, 18.13, 18.14, and 18.15.

* Women wore two types of dresses: wraparound or V-neck. Either way they

Figure 18.16 This marble statue of a young boy is from the Greco-Roman period in the 1st century BCE. The young boy is draped in a chlamys after a sporting event—notice his typical Roman hairdo with brushed forward short hair. The statue is in the Greco-Roman Classical style that we saw in Chapter 1 and 2 and probably would have been painted as we saw in Figures 1.12, 2.18, and 18.17.

Erich Lessing/Art Resource, NY

Figure 18.17 This is a marble funerary bust of Persephone showing her fully wrapped in a himation-like garment and also showing a painted statue. This might have been real linen fabric that they plastered on a carved or molded statue, which was a technique developed at this time. It is from the 1st-century CE Greco-Roman period and again shows the mingling of Egyptian and Classical styles for sculpture. For centuries Western culture thought all Greek and Roman clothing were white because the colors on the statues had bleached white. It wasn't until statues like this and King Tut and Queen Nefertiti appeared that they realized differently. Persephone was the Greek goddess of the underworld and also the goddess of the Spring awakening. These funerary statues, called *ushabti*, were common in tombs and originated in the Old Kingdom (c. 2600 to 2100 BCE). Many were small and produced in multiples and scattered around the chamber. This appears to be quite large and more finely crafted.

could be cut into a sheath pattern and could also be long- or short-sleeved or sleeveless. They were often shown as tight, but in reality could also be looser. See Figure 18.14.

* In the Old and Middle Kingdoms women's dresses were long sheaths held up by shoulder straps and came to below or above the breast. Wealthy women also had long-sleeved gowns that had pleats or folds. See Figure 18.14.

* Along with the kilt, *shendyt*, high officials of the Old Kingdom wore ornaments such as necklaces and pendants, and leg and armbands. See Figures 18.1, 18.10, 18.11, 18.12, and 18.13.

* By the Middle Kingdom women also wore an outer garment that was pleated or straight and was pinned or knotted at the chest or tied. See Figure 18.12.

* Men and women were also wearing shawls and capes that could be tied in the center in decorative ways or with a knotted fringe and were made of linen or wool. See Figure 18.13.

* By the time of the Middle Kingdom wealthy men were wearing kilts, which got longer and more complex over time. These kilts, called *shendyts*, had fronts that folded down into a stiff triangular or a longer rectangular shape or sash, and also, they could have complicated pleats. Men also wore tunics with sleeves and a short cape. All of these were fitted garments. See Figures 18.1, 18.10, and 18.13.

* By the New Kingdom, 1550 BCE, women's clothing was made of two or more pieces, usually in white, but sometimes in pastel shades. Wealthy and noble women wore elaborate long gowns and wigs and much jewelry.

* New styles appeared for both men and women nobles and officials, and they are shown wearing long robes with pleated sleeves that flared at the elbow. Sometimes they were worn with short kilts under these long transparent ones as seen in Figure 18.12.

* By the New Kingdom higher ranks wore longer ankle-length tunics that were held up by a strap around the neck. Other high officials wore a pleated kilt or a kilt with an apron over it and a pleated shirt. A short, wide sleeveless cloak was also worn.

* During the Greco-Roman period both men and women adapted their clothing and added more fabric in more complex ways. They used variations of the himation, chlamys, and chitons and held them together with sashes, belts, and pins. See Figures 18.16 and 18.17.

* Men's and women's status was shown by how elaborate the decoration was and how fine the quality of the fabric. See Figure 18.12 and 18.13.

* The wealthy wore sandals of finely worked papyrus or leather, usually just for special occasions. These were of simple construction with a thong between the big toe and a strap around the top of the foot. They also had a woven pointed shoe with a thong and strap. Mostly everyone went bare footed. See Figures 18.1 and 18.12.

* Royal and elite status for men and women was shown by shaving the head and by the use of a variety of wigs that could be quite complex and highly decorated. They also styled their hair using scented unguents, which they melted on their hair.

* Kings and Queens wore colorful and embroidered linen clothes, which were often decorated with feathers, gems, and beadwork and the elaborate *usekh* collar. They wore woven sandals, leather shoes, sashes, and belts. See Figures 18.1, 18.10, 18.11, and 18.12.

* The Queen wore a Vulture headdress to emphasize her rank and also to show she was the mother of the next pharaoh.

* Pharaohs' clothing changed very little over time. Typically they wore the striped nemes headdress and the double crown, *pschent*, often with a false rectangular beard attached. See Figures 18.1, 18.5, and 18.8 for the separate crowns; and Figures 18.2, 18.5, 18.10, and 18.13 for the *nemes*.

* For official duties and appearances they wore a different type of pleated kilt that was wound counter-clockwise around the body. The royal apron was often worn over the kilt and was covered with accordion pleats, or a different style was rigid and not pleated. See Figures 18.10 and 18.13.

* It was known from the contents of King Tut's tomb that pharaohs had many different kinds of clothes including kilts, robes, undergarments and outer garments, shoes, socks and sandals, and different styles of gloves and much of these were richly and elaborately decorated.

* The royal linen was almost transparent and much softer and whiter than other linen; it can also be seen in the queen's costume. See Figure 18.12.

* Only royalty were permitted to use animal skins. Sem priests wore a whole leopard skin, including head, paws, and tail.

* Priests and priestesses only wore long white linen robes and white papyrus sandals as all other materials were not considered holy. White was symbolically the color of purity and the sacred. Male priests generally shaved their hair.

* Tradesmen and craftsmen wore short kilts and leather for their loincloths.

* Servants were sometimes pictured as mostly naked—men with a simple loincloth and women with scant panties and the *usekh* or other jewelry.

* Children and laborers were naked.

* Soldiers wore a close-fitted short or long outfit with bone or metal fish scale-like elements and also a short-sleeved jacket. Foot soldiers also wore a short skirt often with a rectangular piece or sash that hung down the middle of the front.

* Soldiers also wore a padded leather helmet, which often had raised circular patterns and was called a *khepresh* and was usually blue. Sometimes they wore a sleeveless leather corset supported by straps and they went barefoot. See Figure 18.12. This website has several pictures of them: http://en.wikipedia.org/wiki/Khepresh

* Everyone including children wore many types of jewelry. It was frequently elaborate and made of gold, silver, precious gems, and beads. They excelled at jewelry making and metallurgy and because they were buried with them many examples still survive. There were gold and copper mines in Egypt and they traded for other metals like silver and gemstones. See http://www.allaboutgemstones.com/jewelry_history_egyptian.html

* Cosmetics and perfume were important in this society to men and women, both for symbolic and aesthetic reasons. They placed extreme emphasis on the eye, which they decorated in the iconic almond shape; and made the black outline with kohl and shadowed with ground malachite. They used red ochre for their lips and cheeks and henna to color their hair and nails. They mixed these products with animal fat and stored them in small, sometimes imaginative boxes and jars, which were later also found in burial tombs. See Figure 18.11.

Clothing and Costume Keywords

meses (MEH-sis) – The Egyptian name for the bag-tunic, which was a simple cylinder of rough fabric that was the typical garment of workmen and tradesmen.

kalasiris (KAL-ahs-IRIS) – This was the basic sheath dress worn by women throughout its history. It was usually ankle length and could rise to under or over the breasts with one or two shoulder straps. It was basically a tube, which was usually pictured as very tight, but for practical purposes probably was looser. It could also be decorated. See Figure 18.14.

shendyt (SHEN-dite) – This was the men's kilt, which eventually had many adaptations, including a stiffened triangular panel like an apron that could be worn over a short or long version. See Figures 18.1, 18.10, 18.12, and 18.13.

pschent – This was the double crown that was adopted after the unification of Upper and Lower Egypt. The red lower crown, *deshret*, was like a throne or chair and usually had the *uraeus*; and the white upper *hedjet* was more like a bowling pin with the curled asp coming out of the center. See Figure 18.1 for the separate crowns and Figures 18.5 and 18.8 for the double.

nemes (NEM-ess) **headdress** – This was the Pharaoh's striped linen headdress that was characterized by the large folds on the sides and back that fell to the shoulders and behind the ears. Usually it had the raised cobra, the *uraeus*, in the center above the forehead. It was often pictured in blue and gold stripes and symbolized their power and could also be worn under the double crown. The iconic image is of the death mask of King Tut. See Figures 18.2, 18.5, 18.10, and 18.13.

khepresh – This was also a royal and military headdress and is sometimes called a blue crown. Made of leather or cloth it was blue and often had round disks, and a *uraeus* if worn by a pharaoh. See Figure 18.12.

red ochre – This was a natural mineral that was used medicinally and as the basis of make-up as seen in Figure 18.11. It was also an important pigment for painting: see Figures 18.7, 18.10, 18.12, 18.14, and 18.15, and was usually used for male figures, and generally females were paler.

uraeus – This word was from the Greek "on its tail" and from Egyptian *iaret*, "rearing cobra" and was the stylized, upright form of an Egyptian cobra (asp or serpent) used as a symbol of the pharaohs, and deities, and their divine authority. It was almost always a part of the pharaoh's crown. Technically he was only recognized by wearing the *uraeus*, which symbolized his legitimacy. See Figures 18.1, 18.2, 18.10, 18.12, and 18.13.

usekh – This was the wide collar worn by men and women. It could be made out of gold or other metals and decorative gems or beads. Many examples exist as they were frequently buried in tombs and also pictured in wall paintings and sculptures. See Figures 18.10, 18.11, and 18.12. Notice in Chapter 3 how similar this was to the *maniakis*, and also the collar on the chacmool, Figure 17.16, and the Inca necklace, Figure 17.27.

ankh – This is an iconic Egyptian image. It was a symbol for life and immortal existence. It was often pictured with the gods and pharaohs holding one in each hand or crossed on the chest. See Figure 18.10.

flail – Like the ankh this was a symbolic object often associated with the pharaohs. It was a short rod with three strings of beads attached to it. Gods and pharaohs were often seen holding one or both of them and sometimes with their arms crossed over their chests. It has been ascribed with different meanings but usually as a symbol of power or authority. See Figure 18.1.

***heqa* scepter** (or shepherd's crook) – This was associated with the pharaoh and like the flail was often pictured crossed over his chest as a symbol of authority. In later periods it and the flail were shown with alternating bands of blue and gold. See Figure 18.1.

scarabs – These were gems or other artifacts representing the dung beetle that were considered sacred amulets and provided protection from many evils. One of the beliefs was that the beetle like the sun was reborn and so was a symbol of the rising sun and rebirth. Many scarabs still survive in multiple colors and forms, some with hieroglyphics and out-stretched wings. Their use varied through the different dynasties, but by the New Kingdom heart scarab amulets were placed with mummies.

CHAPTER NINETEEN

India: 320–1858 CE

Figure 19.1 This is an 18th-century silk embroidered textile from Kashmir during the Mughal period. The illustration is of Shiva and his wife Parvati praying to their son, Ganesha, from the *Bhagavad Gita*. One of the best-known Hindu deities he was worshiped by all Hindu sects and also Jains and Buddhists. He was the patron of arts and sciences and throughout the different periods was shown in many variations, but always with an elephant head and big belly. This figure has four arms, and typically holds an axe in the left and a goad in the right and is often eating or holding a sweet in his lower-left hand and a broken tusk in the other. As he is pictured here, he is frequently seen sitting on a lotus and with a parasol, a symbolic sign of royalty. He is also the god of beginnings, and is honored at the start of many rituals and new ventures and thought to bring success. In most parts of the country people would have a statue of him and pray to him. Shiva (in Sanskrit: Śiva, means "The Auspicious One"), also known as Mahadeva, "Great God," was considered the Supreme god. His wife, Parvati, was the mother god and was the gentle, benevolent, and nurturing aspect of the Hindu goddess Shakti.

bpk, Berlin/Art Resource, NY

A Little Background

Early Indian culture was divided into a series of regional dynasties of competing Hindu, Muslim, and Buddhist religions on the Indian subcontinent until the British conquest in the 19th century. Architectural styles were divided between northern and southern regions and influenced in the west by Greek, Roman, and Persian styles, and in the east, by Chinese and South East Asian styles. Much of Indian life and culture were connected to the seasonal monsoon rains and to the network of sacred rivers of northern and central India and their flooding cycles. In a civilization with so many different dynasties there were many different clothing styles and they also varied regionally. Indian culture was relatively consistent artistically but highly fragmented politically.

Who They Were

* The main indigenous religions of India were Hinduism, Buddhism, Jainism, and Sikhism, and they were closely related historically and shared a number of important concepts such as reincarnation, karma, and dharma.

* Hinduism was one of the earliest religions of the Indian subcontinent. Difficult to define as it had many sects and beliefs, but the majority of the population of India was dominated by the religion and its traditions; and it spread from India across South East Asia. Hindus honor a body of ancient Sanskrit texts known as *Vedas*, which were revelations from the gods. With the other religions they believed in "dharma," which had different meanings for each religion, but can simplistically be defined as "cosmic order, values, and laws," and "karma"—the total of a person's present, past, and future lives, and reincarnation.

* Hindu temple sites were found all over India and were built throughout its history and in styles that varied from north to south, but all had several features in common and all were near water. They all had similar plans that had an entrance with stone columns that led to a columned main hall, the *mandapa*, and then to a small, square, and dark unadorned shrine for a deity—the "sanctum sanctorum" with a large tower, *shikhara*, over it. This tower was symbolic of a connection to the gods and to the attainment of enlightenment. One of the most famous Hindu pilgrimage sites was Varanasi on the Ganges River south of Delhi. See http://www.religionfacts.com/hinduism/practices/temple.htm

* Siddhartha Gautama Buddha or simply Buddha or the "awakened one" probably lived between the 6th and 4th century BCE in eastern India. He traveled widely in northern India and preached to the poor as well as nobles. Later his teachings would be written down and these would become the tenets of Buddhism. This was a spiritual tradition that focused on personal development and finding the true nature of life. The path to Enlightenment was through morality and meditation. It spread from India across Asia to China, Korea, and Japan and was widely practiced in several different schools. *Little Buddha* is a 1993 film and a PBS documentary *The Buddha* were films about him.

* Basically they had three forms of buildings: the *stupas* for relics (see Figure 19.4) that developed into pagodas, *chaityas*—prayer or meeting halls that developed into temples, and monasteries—*viharas*. There were many Buddhist temples across all of India that were built throughout the centuries. Their architecture developed along with that of the Hindus and shared many similarities such as the small square shrines, covered pillared walkways, and square columned entrances. Kushinagar is a major site for Buddhist pilgrims and is in the northeast.

* Jainism was founded by Mahavira in northeast India in 599 BCE. He was a prince, the son of King Siddhartha and Queen Trishala, who were members of the *kshatriya* (warrior) caste and followers of the teachings of Parshva. He focused his teachings on a non-violent way of life for people, animals, and the universe as well. They believed that everything had a living soul, including plants, and in reincarnation. They were strict vegetarians.

* Modern and medieval Jains built many temples, especially in western India. The common word for a temple was *derasar*, but this word varied by location. Their iconography of figures was seen in their temples but also in Hindu ones, and they were always naked. The five historic temples of Dilwara, built between the 11th and 13th centuries, were one of the most sacred pilgrimage places for the Jains and were considered their most beautiful temples with stunning marble work.

* Sikhism was founded by Guru Nanak (1469–1539) and was based on his teachings which he borrowed from Hinduism and Islam, and those of the nine other Sikh gurus who came after him. Founded in the 16th century in the Punjab area, northwest Rajasthan, and Pakistan. They believed that there was only one God and that everyone was equal before the Deity, meaning that he renounced the caste system. He also taught that everyone had direct access to the Deity through prayer, meditation, and "keeping God in the heart and mind," so there was no need for rituals and priests.

* The Harmandir Sahib in Amritsar, Punjab, was the holiest shrine in Sikhism and was commonly known as the Golden Temple and has been a major pilgrimage site for Sikhs. Their temples were known as *gurudwaras* and didn't have prescribed architectural features, except that they had a special central raised and canopied platform for their sacred text the *Guru Granth Sahib*. A Granthi, which could be a man or woman, read from the text to the congregation. This person was not considered a priest or priestess, as they did not believe they were necessary. In Sanskrit, *granthika* means "a relater or narrator." Other distinguishing features were the tall flagpoles with the Sikh flag and frequently domes which used the ribbed upside down lotus with a distinctive finial.

* *The Mahabharata*, the apex of Indian classical literature, was written in Sanskrit during the Gupta period, c. 400 CE. Originally a long oral verse epic poem, it was an important cultural, philosophical, and religious source of information about the early development of Hinduism between 400 BCE and 200 CE and also its inter-relationship with Buddhism and Jainism. It was regarded as a text about Hindu law, history, and its early myths. It has been compared in importance to the Bible, the Qur'an, the works of Shakespeare, and Homer. The other great Sanskrit epic poem was the *Ramayana*. See http://www.britannica.com/EBchecked/topic/357806/Mahabharata

* The Gupta dynasties (320–647 CE) produced a culture that was primarily Buddhist and covered most of northern India.

* Science and cultural sophistication flourished and matured under Gupta rule, and it was known as the classical or Golden Age of India.

* Sanskrit became the official language of the Gupta court.

* During the medieval period (650–1526 CE) Hinduism replaced Buddhism as the prominent religion and brought with it the height of the art of temple building and distinct Northern and Southern styles developed.

* Northern and Southern styles evolved during this time not only in architecture but also in art, clothing, textiles, and food.

* The Cholas (c. 850 CE–1250) were a Tamil dynasty that ruled southern India. They had both sea faring and agricultural communities and traded with Western nations, especially in the spice trade. They also had a well-developed religious and intellectual society and left much Hindu art and architecture that endured. The Cholas were noted for metalworking, particularly their accomplished bronze statues that used the lost wax-casting process. The 10th-century cast-bronze statue of Shiva/Nataraja,

the Lord of Dance, was of special significance and influenced many others. See Figure 19.19. See http://www.asiasocietymuseum.org/region_results.asp?RegionID=1&CountryID=1&ChapterID=7

* The Mughal Empire was founded by Babur, a Turko-Mongol, in 1526 by military conquest in the north of India. They brought their Muslim religion and it spread rapidly throughout this region. They established their empire with strong, authoritative government and controlling military power. At the height of their imperial power in the 17th and early 18th centuries, they effectively controlled most of the Indian subcontinent until the British took control in 1757.

* Akbar I (reigned 1556–1605) solidified the empire and brought great economic, political, and cultural prosperity. He established great lavish courts at Delhi, Agra, Fatehpur Sikri, and Lahore as well as traditions of literature, scholarship, and the arts. He also encouraged the merging of Persian culture with the native Indian that became a distinct Indo-Persian culture, and Indo-Islamic architecture.

* Wealthy and royal women were patrons of the arts, architecture, and science. They also played sports and hunted. Like the Romans, elite women had considerable behind-the-scenes power as mothers and caretakers of future rulers.

* Shah Jahan was the fifth Mughal Emperor, who ruled from 1628 to 1658 and marked the high point of the empire and continued the traditions of Akbar with an effective government and powerful military. It was also culturally an important artistic and literary time and was considered the golden age of Mughal architecture, as he built many important and influential buildings. In 1648 he moved the capital from Agra to his new city, Shajahanabad (now old Delhi), and constructed the Red Fort, the enormous fortified royal residence. The magnificence of Shah Jahan's court, with its famous legendary jeweled peacock throne, was written about by his contemporaries, travelers, and ambassadors from other parts of the world. Its size and splendor were compared to the courts of Louis XIV of France (1638–1715). See http://en.wikipedia.org/wiki/Shah_Jahan#mediaviewer/File:Vasily_Vereshchagin_-_Pearl_Mosque,_Delhi.jpg

* The British East India Company started as a purely economic enterprise and from its early beginnings in the 1600s grew until it controlled half of the world's trade in spices, tea, fabrics, such as silk and cotton, indigo dye, and saltpeter that was used in food preparation, but more importantly to the British, a major component of gunpowder.

* By the mid-18th century the Mughal Empire's power had deteriorated and the area reverted to smaller independent warring groups and principalities. Robert Clive, also known as "Clive of India" (Figure 19.26 was an illustration from his album book), was instrumental in gaining British military control in 1757, which led to the British East India Company taking over the governing of India and their political sovereignty and economic dominance continued for 100 years.

* In 1858 as the native and Mughal rulers were defeated India became an English Crown Colony that united most of the continent. Known as the Empire of India or British Raj it was now governed by parliament with a "Viceroy and Governor-General."

* In 1876 Queen Victoria was named Empress of India and it would stay under British rule until their independence in 1947.

* As noted in Chapter 4, Islam, there were a number of Western "Orientalist" painters, some of whom painted in India as well—Edwin Lord Weeks was worth revisiting here as well as the Russian painter Vasily Vereshchagin (1842–1904), particularly his paintings of the Pearl Mosques in Agra and Delhi, and also Jean-Léon Gérôme (Figure 2.21, the gladiators), who had been his teacher. The Indian miniature paintings such as in Figures 19.20, 19.26, and 19.27 and others such as

Figures 19.21 and 19.22 and other album books and art from this time would also be good sources for designers. Several suggestions for images and information can be obtained from:

http://collections.vam.ac.uk/style/mughal/55

http://www.metmuseum.org/toah/hd/mugh/hd_mugh.htm

http://www.metmuseum.org/toah/hd/mugh_2/hd_mugh_2.htm

* This is a somewhat random selection of movies: E.M. Forster's novel was made into a play and then a movie, *A Passage to India* (1984); Rudyard Kipling's novel was made into a movie, *The Man Who Would Be King* (1975); also *Clive of India* (1935) about the British in India, Ray's *The Chess Players* (1977), and *Gandhi* (1982), a biopic, but also about the British leaving India, which won BAFTA and Academy Awards for art direction and costumes.

* *The Apu Trilogy* (1955–1959), directed by Satyajit Ray with music by Ravi Shankar, were set in the 20th century, but were some of the best Bengali/Indian films ever made and worth seeing. There were a number of James Ivory movies: *The Delhi Way* (1964) a documentary, *Shakespeare-Wallah* (1965), and *The Courtesans of Bombay* (1983).

* Telugu cinema was also known as "Tollywood" and was in the Telugu language and later due to their popularity the movies were adapted into other Indian languages. They started in the 1920s as silent films in the southern Indian capital, Hyderabad, and continue now, but no longer just period, historical, and mythological films but with some fantasy and futuristic ones; some of the most famous were: *Patala Bhairavi* (1951), *Malliswari* (1951), *Mayabazar* (1957), *Nartanasala* (1963), *Maa Bhoomi* (1979), *Sagara Sangamam* (1983), and *Magadheera* (English: "Great Warrior") (2009). Sheikh Fattelal and Vishnupant Govind Damle were directors and art directors for many influential films such as *Sant Tukaram* (1936), about a 17th-century saint.

* "Bollywood" films, of which much has been written, were not always musicals, but like Telugu were in their native language of Hindi and their production centered in Mumbai; their golden age was the 1940s to 1960s and a classic was *Mughal-e-Azam* (1960 and 2004 in color). The ancient Indian epic poems (later written in Sanskrit) of *Ramayana* and *Mahabharata* have been adapted to many forms and have had significant influence on all the arts, including film.

The Indian Material World

What They Made

* The early Buddhist temples were cut into rock caves and examples span from the 2nd century through the medieval period to the 16th century. They were frequently near water like the Badami caves in the southwest. There was a famous photograph of the interior of the Chaitya Hall at Karli, taken by Sykes and Dwyer around 1869, which was a temple cut into cliffs with a long columned hall with a vaulted ceiling and a *stupa* at the end. There were many of these caves also for Hindus and Jains: see http://www.buddhist-tourism.com/countries/india/caves

* The Gupta period was a rich artistic period for its temple architecture, painting, and sculpture; unfortunately much of it was destroyed and deteriorated with time. Architecturally the Gupta period was best represented by the Durga Temple at Aihole, 320–647 CE, and the famous Vishnu/Dashavatara Temple at Deogarh, c. 500 CE—see Figure 19.18 for a relief sculpture.

Figure 19.2 This is a huge Hindu temple complex dedicated to Meenakshl In the city of Madurai in the southeastern Indian state of Tamil Nadu, showing the typical Southern Dravidian architectural style. In Tamil this style of temple is called a *koil* or *kovil*, "King's House," and this was built from the 16th to 18th century. This is a large *gopuram*, pyramidal tower entrance gate, decorated with hundreds of colorful statues of deities and depicts their stories and myths, both of which, the tower and the style of decoration, are distinguishing features of the Southern style. The temple complex dedicated to Meenakshi/Parvati and Sundareshvara/Shiva shows their different avatars or incarnations and has two sanctum sanctorums and 14 towers similar to this, pillared halls, and smaller temples. The *gopuram* is topped with this long round horizontal drum-like tube, called a *kalasam* and then stone finials. This is the same temple as in Figure 19.3.

Figure 19.3 This is a different part of the Meenakshi Amman Temple in Madurai. This shows another common element of Hindu temples that have bracketed and pillared covered walkways within the temple complexes. These are on the lower levels and surround the shrines of the deities. The stone pillars are frequently carved with pictures of the gods and goddesses and are another example of Dravidian architecture. Also notice the ceiling with its use of bright colors like the exterior in Figure 9.2. The pillars are also seen in the painting in Figure 19.27.

Saiko3p/iStock

Figure 19.4 This is the earliest Buddhist *stupa* and is known as the great *stupa* at Sanchi, near Bhopal in the north. It is one of a collection of Buddhist monuments at this site and has the earliest stone structures in India. Legend says that it was built by King Ashoka (273–236 BCE), but is dated now as 2nd or 1st century BCE. *Stupas* were not temples but originally mounds that contained relics or sutras from Buddha or his followers or monks. It also shows the ornate gateway, *torana*, with carvings of animals. It was abandoned for centuries and heavily restored in the early 20th century. Both the gateway and the *stupa* form would evolve in China, Korea, and Japan and the *stupa* would become the iconic pagoda.

f9photos/Shutterstock.com

Figure 19.5 This is Sangameshwara Temple, the oldest in the complex of ancient ruins in Pattadakal in Karnataka state in the southwest. It was built by a Chalukya king from 696 to 733 CE. The temple is in the Dravidian style and uses a typical Hindu plan that consisted of a sanctum sanctorum with a distinctive stepped tower over it, and now, because it is in the south, is called a *vimana*, and an outer square hall or court, a *mandapa*, with massive square bracketed pillars. There could be other additional halls, but still using this west–east axis and with a definite horizontal orientation. Notice that the *vimana* has a more pyramidal quality than the more rounded Northern style seen in Figure 19.6. The Chalukyas built many temples here between the 7th and 9th centuries and at this site there are 10 temples including a Jain temple, which looks very similar to this, and other small shrines, mostly to Shiva. They use a combination of architectural styles including this Dravidian, the Nagara (Northern), and their own mixture, the Chalukya style.

Rafal Cichawa/Shutterstock.com

Figure 19.6 This is a temple in a large complex of Hindu and Jain temples in Khajuraho, Madhya Pradesh in the north central part of India and is often known as "the erotic temple." This building is in the Nagara style of architecture (Northern style) that developed in the 5th century CE and the buildings here continued into the 11th century CE and were characterized by more rounded beehive-shaped towers, a *shikhara*, that still sat directly above the sanctum sanctorums of the deity. They were also made up of many layers stacked on top of each other and then topped with a more cushion-like piece, called an *amalaka*, and a finial. Although it might not appear this way the basic plan is the typical Hindu mandala with squares and circles that represented and signified the universe. The temple is covered with many intricately carved statues and this one is sometimes known as the "Kama Sutra temple," but has nothing to do with it and only a small portion of the statues are explicitly sexual. There are many websites and pictures of it. This one has good descriptions and pictures of the complex: http://en.wikipedia.org/wiki/Khajuraho_Group_of_Monuments

waj/Shutterstock.com

Figure 19.7 This iconic Indian image is the Taj Mahal, near Agra, built from 1632 to 1649 by Shah Jahan and is a tomb for his second wife, Mumtaz Mahal, whom he married in 1612 and who died in 1631. She was the mother of 14 of his 16 children. Although it is a magnificent building it is not typical of Indian architecture, but of a Mughal/Muslim style that derived from the Persian. Like the Isfahan mosque, Figure 4.5 the entire exterior surface is covered in calligraphy and intricate floral patterns using marble and precious and semi-precious stones in the mosaics. The extensive gardens are also extremely symmetrical like the architecture and very much in the typical Persian style that featured a long reflecting pool as shown here. Later his tomb was also located here. This website has good descriptions of the building and there are hundreds of images of both interior and exterior available: http://www.tajmahal.gov.in/view_taj.html

saiko3p/Shutterstock.com

Figure 19.8 This is an interior hallway in a building at the Fatehpur Sikri complex also near Agra, built by Akbar, 1571–1585, as his new capital. The intricate screens on the two exterior walls are each cut from an individual piece of stone and serve a triple function: first they are beautiful and decorative, second, they reduce the amount of sunlight acting as shades, and third, they allow for air circulation all of which help to reduce the extreme heat. The two rectangular panels on the facing, interior walls are inlaid marble again using calligraphy as a typical Muslim decorative element. Also notice the subtle and elegant use of the colored marble and the typical Persian arches.

Chris Tiné

Figure 19.9 This is a residential building in the same complex at Fatehpur Sikri and like most of the buildings there is built from red sandstone, known as "Sikri sandstone." It has a small central interior core surrounded by wide shaded balconies with stairs connecting the levels; and also has a flat roof surrounded with a low wall or railing; see also Figures 19.10 and 19.12. This is a nice example as it clearly shows the construction and architecture, and the city and its buildings have a mixture of Persian/Islamic styles with Indian Hindu and Jain influences. The complex is set within a lush garden with greenery and decorative ponds.

Chris Tiné

Figure 19.10 Jaisalmer is a Rajasthani city on the edge of the desert and known as "the Jewel of the Desert," or "the Golden City," as many of the buildings were carved from golden-yellow sandstone. This 19th-century mansion known as Patwon-ki-Haveli was built for a brocade and embroidery trader and is one of the oldest and most stunning *havelis*. It is five stories high and has beautiful *jharokhas* or balconies with their typical curved roofs, *chajjas*, and intricately carved screens and pillars, like in 19.8; and underneath is supported with typical brackets or corbels. This style is character-istic of Rajasthani architecture. Notice that they are very similar to English and French oriel windows like we saw in Shakespeare's birthplace, Figure 6.9.

Chris Tiné

Figure 19.11 This is a throne room in one of the palaces in Mehrangarh Fort, Jodhpur, where construction started in 1459. There are a number of interesting elements to look for that would have influence on and similarities to Western decorative styles. First is the ceiling with its vignettes of portraits similar to the Rococo ceilings in Chapter 9. Also on the ceiling are the use of intricate floral designs, which in French would be called "mille-fleur"—thousand flowers—that were popular there in painting and tapestries in the 15th and 16th centuries and are now believed to have been adopted from Persian art and Oriental rugs; a similar style can be seen in Florentine illumination and stationary styles. The arches again use the distinctive scalloped arch, but notice the carving and gold and white decoration is also similar to the *boiserie* technique seen in Chapter 8 and Chapter 9. Also interesting are the columns that now have a lotus flower at the base rather than the Egyptian ones where it was used as a capital. The parasol was a practical and symbolic covering for royalty, and indicated high rank, and can also be seen in the howdahs and many miniature paintings and Ganesha in Figure 19.1. The colorful and abstract and non-figurative stained glass would definitely have influenced the British, who would use patterns like this for the first time in their Victorian homes. The cut wool Indian-style carpet and Oriental rug are also worth noticing. Part of the 2012 Batman movie *The Dark Knight Rises* was shot here.

Chris Tiné

Figure 19.12 "The Blue City," Jodhpur, 2011. Originally painted blue by the Brahmin or priestly class, people in this Indian city continued painting their houses indigo blue, claiming that it kept the houses cooler and fended off mosquitos. The brown rooftop decoration on the right is also used on many Indian buildings and is similar to Western medieval crenellations. This also shows the typically square residential architecture with the very plain façades and with few windows and typically flat roofs. Similar to ancient Greek and Roman houses they were built like this for privacy and also often had central courtyards.

Chris Tiné

* This period saw the beginning of Hindu carved stone and terracotta deities and also Buddhist figures and Jain *tirthankara* sculptures.

* Jain *tirthankara* were either a male figure standing erect in the pose known as *kayotsarga*, "dismissing the body," or in a contemplative posture seated cross-legged on a throne, *dhyanamudra* with a small lotus flower on his chest. They were often carved out of marble or a variety of highly polished stones or cast in metal and they are always naked.

* Hindu temples developed Northern and Southern styles, but all based on similar axial plans and highly decorated buildings with sculptures, paintings, and wall hangings. See the explanation in "Hinduism" and Figures 19.2, 19.3, 19.5, and 19.6. This website has good pictures and explanations: http://www.templenet.com/temparc.html

* Both styles were highly decorated with carved and often painted mythological figures and deities in stone that were symbolic representations rather than individual realistic portraits. See Figures 19.1, 19.2, 19.6, 19.18, and 19.19 for images and more explanations.

* An important element in both north and south temples were the towers—the *shikhara* and *vimana*—that were directly over the sanctum sanctorums of the deities and visually marked these places and also reached towards heaven. These were a physical and significant symbolic manifestation of man's aspiration to enlightenment and the connection between mortals and gods. See Figures 19.5 and 19.6.

* The Chola dynasties (850–1250 CE) from the south, like other early Hindu, Buddhist, and Jains, built their residences and municipal buildings out of wood and bricks and nothing has survived. But they were also great temple builders and the Vijayalacholeswaram near Pudukkottai was an early example that has survived. See http://www.discoveredindia.com/list-of-world-heritage-sites-in-india/great-living-chola-temples.htm

* The Palitana temples were considered the most sacred of the Jains' pilgrimage sites and the mountain had more than 900 temples, built for hundreds of years starting in the 11th century. There were an additional 3,000 more carved marble temples in the Shatrunjayat hills. Jain pilgrims made a religious journey, a *yatra*, walking and saying prayers over 134 miles.

* In 1569 Akbar I founded the city of Fatehabad, in Persian, meaning "victorious," and later called Fatehpur Sikri, and it served as the capital from 1571 to 1585. It was a walled city with royal palaces and courts, harems, a mosque, private quarters, and other utility buildings. See Figures 19.8 and 19.9.

* In the 17th century, the great Hindu temple at Madura, now Madurai, enlarged the traditional temple grounds and became a walled city with the massive *gopuram* as gateways. It covered a huge area with pillared courtyards and many smaller temples at cardinal compass points; it retained its sanctum sanctorums, but now the towers looked small in comparison. There were 200 columns decorated with stucco images of Hindu gods. See Figures 19.2 and 19.3.

* Under Shah Jahan's rule (1628–1658), Mughal artistic and architectural achievements reached their pinnacle. He had highly refined luxurious tastes in all the arts, architecture, as well his courts, and fine clothes. Among his surviving buildings were the Red Fort and the Jama Masjid mosque in Delhi; and parts of the Lahore Fort—the Naulakha and Sheesh Mahal pavilions, and the Tomb of Jahangir, and Shalimar Gardens, Lahore; as well as his most famous, Taj Mahal and its gardens near Agra.

* In the 16th century Sikh art and architecture began and blossomed in the Punjab area. The Golden Temple previously referenced was a good example. The Victoria and Albert Museum has many artifacts and information about them and the website and its links would be a good place to start.

They also had an exhibition "Arts of the Sikh Kingdom" in 1999. See http://www.sikh-heritage. co.uk/heritage/heritagebritain/sheribritain.htm

* This is a short list of some of the most famous mosques: there were three mosques known as "The Pearl Mosques," the one in Agra, The Moti Masjid, built c. 1647–1653 by Shah Jahan, another one was inside the Lahore Fort, c. 1630–1635, and the third in The Red Fort, c. 1659–1660 by Aurangzeb. For additional mosques see: http://iaslic1955.org/famous_mosques_in_india.html

How They Decorated

* Architectural motifs were frequently reused in furniture and accessories.

* Chairs, tables, consoles, beds, and cabinets used elements like the scalloped Persian arch, intricately carved fretwork, like the stone screens, and delicate and ornate woodcarvings. For architectural fretwork, see Figures 19.8, and 19.10. For the scalloped arch, see Figures 19.11, 19.13, 19.14, 19.15, and 19.16. For an intricate wooden carving see Figure 19.17.

* Pietra dura and marble inlay were used on table and chest tops. During the reign of Shah Jahan, it was one of the most prominent crafts and used calligraphy and floral images. See Figures 19.7 and 19.20. In India it was called *parchin kari*. See http://www.tajmahal.net/augEng/textMM/inlayengN. htm

* Reminiscent of the square stone pillars, furniture also incorporated square posts.

* Indoor swings were an interesting piece of furniture and were either mounted from the ceiling or heavily carved freestanding ones similar to Western porch or garden swings that descended from these.

* Mughal emperors introduced Persian carpet techniques and craftsmen to their courts and the industry flourished. Eventually these Persian designs would merge with more typically Indian designs and they would produce a unique style and the industry would spread all over the subcontinent. These carpets were widely exported and appreciated in Europe from the 16th century forward. See Figures 19.11, 19.26, and 19.27.

Figures 19.13, 19.14, and 19.15. These are three different elephant howdahs in the museum in Mehrangarh Fort, Jodhpur. They are made of silver, mirrors, rich textiles, and had parasols or shades from the hot sun. They were used to carry the Maharajah and royal family members and usually had two seats with railings—one for the royal person and one for the guard. Mostly howdahs were used for elephants but also for camels and were also used in warfare for important military figures. These rooms also feature the typical scalloped arch that is common in Rajasthan.

Chris Tiné

Figure 19.16 This is a painted interior in a small room in the City Palace, Udaipur, which is now a museum. The enormous palace complex was started in 1559 and building continued for hundreds of years. Notice that the wall decorations are not linear or symmetrical, and again we see the use of the scalloped arch both as a practical opening and a blind arch. The zigzag pattern on the floor using different marbles is a typical Indian/Mughal motif and is similar to ones at the Taj Mahal. The technique is known as "intarsia." The German director Werner Herzog made a documentary film, *Jag Mandir* (1991); its subtitle is *The Eccentric Private Theatre of the Maharaja of Udaipur*. Jag Mandir is one of the palaces at the City Palace and was built on an island in Lake Pichola from 1551 to 1652 and is also called the "Lake Garden Palace."

Chris Tiné

Figure 19.17 This is a classic Indian textile from Rajasthan printed with traditional hand-carved wooden blocks and also shows three teak blocks. There are a number of good videos showing the carving and printing of these decorative fabrics, which have been a traditional craft for hundreds of years and were exported in quantities along with silks, chintz, cottons, fine Kashmiri wools, brocades, and carpets.

Chris Tiné

Figure 19.18 This relief panel from the east side of the Temple of Vishnu, often called Dashavatara, meaning the "ten incarnations," is located at Deogarh, in central India. It is an early Hindu stone temple with many sculptures and is a good example of the Gupta style, c. 500 CE. Similar to art in Egypt the purpose was not to recreate reality but to idealize it and to use symbolic images to convey a story or message. These two figures are seated on a raised seat in the position known as *lalitasana*, with one leg bent and resting on the seat and the other leg down. Specific hand gestures known as *mudras* were used to express meaning and also mood; similar to sign language and would be understood by the different indigenous religions. Deities were also identified by objects that they wore or carried and also often by animals, birds, or plants associated with them. See Ganesha, Figure 19.1.

Borromeo/Art Resource, NY

Figure 19.19 This is a bronze Shiva Umasahitamurti and Parvati statue in the Dravidian style, 12th–14th century CE, from southern India, during the Chola dynasty. The idealized female figure has a narrow waist and high, rounded breasts. Indian sculptures don't make a distinction between deities and people and usually both are equally sensual. As in the statue above they are seated on a raised seat in the position known as *lalitasana*, and using symbolic hand gestures. They also both have their hair piled high on their heads and the distinctive large earrings. He has his distinguishing third eye that symbolizes his all-seeing nature. He is holding a small trident known as a *tekpi* and a sacred bull. The following website is a business that sells Indian sculptures and has many images of statues identified by the deity and their materials: http://www.lotussculpture.com/ABUS.html

RMN-Grand Palais/Art Resource, NY

* India, particularly Kashmir, was noted for its hand knotted carpets of silk and wool blends and these were considered the most luxurious.

* A different style was the Indian cut wool carpet that used refined medallions and borders usually in subtle variations and monochromatic colors. See Figure 19.11.

* Stone and marble intarsia were common elements in residential and religious buildings both on floors and walls, see Figures 19.7, 19.8, 19.16, 19.20, and 19.27. Favored in the Mughal Empire and other Muslim countries, they were introduced by the Moors into Spain and were elaborated with realistic figures in Siena cathedral in the 1300s. They became especially popular in Europe during the Baroque period.

* Textiles were an important industry in India from its earliest times both for clothing, decorative applications like wall hangings in homes and religious buildings, and for coverings like pillows and cushions. These could be simple cotton to silk brocades and woven, dyed, printed, or embroidered. For cushions and pillows, see Figures 19.11, 19.25, 19.26, and 19.27. For a decorative piece see Figure 19.1, and a cotton-printed cloth, Figure 19.17.

* Statues were common in all indigenous religious buildings, with the exception of Muslim mosques. The statues and figurines of deities, people, plants, and animals and frequently a combination of these could be monumental or quite small and both carved relief and three-dimensional. They were also in private homes as mentioned in Figure 19.1, and it was common for people to have statues of Ganesha but also other gods and goddesses. See http://www.lotussculpture.com/ABUS.html

* Statues could be carved of wood, stone, marble, ivory, bone, precious, and semi-precious stones. They could also be cast of many metals such as brass, gold, or bronze; as noted the Chola dynasty excelled at metallurgy and was famous for its cast bronze statues. See Figure 19.19.

* Brass, bronze, and iron were also used for common household objects, as were wood, glass, and many types of ceramics, and woven fibers for baskets.

* The early Mughal emperors placed great importance on books, illustrated manuscripts, and paintings and set up workshops, *karkhanas*, where they employed Persians, Muslims, and Hindus to all work together. With this cross-pollination they eventually developed a unique Indian style that derived from the Persian, and encompassed all subject matter from warfare to court life, to illustrations of the epic poems, myths and deities, and flora and fauna. They used a decorative and unusual stylized perspective, colorful opaque paints, and often combined them with gilding and calligraphy. In the 16th and 17th centuries the faces were usually in profile and later more naturalistic. See Figures 19.1, 19.20, and 19.26.

* The Victoria and Albert Museum in London has an enormous collection of Indian art and artifacts. Starting in the fall of 2015 they "will present a series of exhibitions, displays, events and digital initiatives that will explore the rich and varied culture of South Asia, both past and present. The India Festival will mark the 25th anniversary of the opening of the Museum's Nehru Gallery, which displays some of the most important objects from the V&A's South Asian art collection produced between the 16th and 19th centuries." One aspect of this will be the fabrics, textiles, and weavings. See http://www.vam.ac.uk/content/exhibitions/the-fabric-of-india/about-the-exhibition

Building and Décor Keywords

mandala – These were an important symbol in Buddhism and Hinduism and represented the Universe. They came in several different forms with different meanings, but basically used a square with an inner circle. The square symbolized the earth and the circle, which was continuous, symbolized heaven. In architecture, it was a joining or meeting of heaven and earth. In Buddhism it was also the shape of *stupas*.

stupa – Literally in Sanskrit, a heap. Originally a *stupa* was a mounded building that contained a relic of Buddha and later ashes or other relics or sutras of Buddhist monks. See Figure 19.4.

chaityas – These were early Buddhist temples with a *stupa*. The word and space evolved and the meeting and prayer hall became the temple.

torana – This was a type of gateway in Buddhist, Hindu, and Jain architecture and was very similar to Japanese *torii* and Chinese *paifang*. See Figure 19.4.

gopuram (gopura singular) – These were monumental tower gates that were usually heavily ornate, and pyramidal in shape and provided entrances to the walled Hindu temples in the later periods especially in southern India. They were not the same as *shikhara*s. See Figure 19.2.

shikhara or vimana – These were the tall stepped towers on Hindu temples that were over the sanctum sanctorum of the deity. They were in several styles through the different architectural periods, but a distinct peaked or rounded ornate tower and sometimes they also had similar smaller towers. They were called *shikhara* in the north, and *vimana* in the south. These were different than the *gopuram* that were entrance gateways mentioned earlier and that were primarily in the south. See Figures 19.5 and 19.6. See http://www.britannica.com/EBchecked/topic/419263/North-Indian-temple-architecture

mandapa – These were the pillared halls that attached to the sanctum sanctorums and towers and as they developed over the periods there could be several for eating, dancing, and other functions. See Figures 19.5 and 19.6.

chhatris – These were elevated, dome-shaped structures typical on Indian palaces, forts, and mosques and frequently the top of minarets. They could be a simple dome mounted on a platform with four open pillars or on much more complex large buildings or incorporated into or on top of them. They were very noticeable at the Fatehpur Sikri complex near Agra and both Red Forts, and the Taj Mahal. See Figure 19.7. Also see Brighton Pavilion, Figure 11.1.

jharokhas – These were carved stone windows or balconies that projected from buildings and were supported with brackets or corbels underneath and with a distinctive curved eave that jutted out on top, called *chajjas*. They were a prominent feature of Rajasthani architecture both as decoration and as a balcony on houses, palaces, and temples from the medieval through the 19th century. They could also be carved out of wood. See Figure 19.10.

bagh – This was a large garden. See Figure 19.7.

fretwork – These were usually intricately carved patterns using abstract geometric shapes or as seen in much of India, particularly typical of the Mughal empire, floral designs. In India they were carved in stone, marble, and wood and were called *jalis*. See Figures 19.7, 19.8, and 19.10. Also see Brighton Pavilion, Figure 11.1.

pietra dura – (from the Italian, stone hard). This was a type of inlay using marble, precious and semi-precious stones used in furniture and as wall decoration. It was fashionable at Shah Jahan's courts, see Figures 19.8 and 19.20 for wall decoration.

stone or marble intarsia – To make a distinction the term is more often used for architecture for floor, wall, and ceiling inlay technique than for furniture, but this can be confusing. Similar inlaid work can also be done in metal, glass, and wood. See Figures 19.7, 19.8, 19.16, 19.20, and 19.27.

The Indian Clothing and Costume World

How They Dressed

* Geography and climate played an important role in traditional clothing and textiles, as well as ethnicity and religion throughout India's history. The following are generalities, but give suggestions as to differentiations.

Figure 19.20 This opulent miniature painting is of Shah Jahan receiving his three eldest sons and Asaf Khan, his prime minister, during his accession ceremonies. The illustration is from the *Padshahnama*, 1636, which literally is *Chronicle of the Emperor* and is a written and illustrated history of his reign. In an interesting and stylized use of perspective, it shows him in his throne room at the top in a seated position and he appears like this in a number of pictures from the manuscript with his distinctive turban and halo. Behind him on the wall are marble pietra dura images of his favorite flowers. This is on a raised dais with a painted wall below and above it is a marble canopy. Below him are two guards in striped *jamas* standing on golden "platforms." The next image is his "durbar"—"holding court" around the low gilded table or step stool also on a gilded dais and then other courtiers outside the gold fenced area. The clothes are typical of the splendid garments of his luxurious court and show the belted and sashed *jamas* and elaborately decorated *patka* tied around the waist. These can be seen on the royal children and Asaf Khan, and the guards in the upper part of the painting. Also notice the brilliant colors and many patterns in the textiles and the variety of turbans. The facial hair on the Shah is a typical style but obviously there was great variety. The following website has a number of other pictures from the book and also shows Shah Jahan on his throne: http://en.wikipedia.org/wiki/Shah_Jahan See Figure 19.11 for an actual throne room and a similar low table.

Figure 19.21 "Buttu," this is one of a collection of 19th-century British East India Company paintings showing Indian occupations and castes. This shows an upper-caste man from the north wearing the *angaraka*, which is a long robe similar to a *jama*, but has a higher waist and an oval opening over a shirt and pyjamas and a long patterned shawl, an *angavastram*. He is wearing a large distinctive turban and typical curled-up shoes and carrying a smaller towel.

Bridgeman Images

Figure 19.22 This man is probably from the south and it is from the same collection of paintings. He is wearing the more modest *dhoti*, soft trousers or *veshti*, which are still worn in the south, primarily in white. This is a long rectangular piece of unstitched cloth, wrapped around and knotted or tucked in at the waist and pulled up through the legs, resembling long loose pants. The outer garment is a *kurta*, which generally was a long loose tunic or shirt that had long sleeves and was open at the neck with different varieties of closures. He is also wearing a different style of turban, similar in shape to 16th-century court turbans, and an *angavastram* scarf and curled shoes.

Bridgeman Images

Figure 19.23 This is a group of contemporary women wearing the traditional *salwar/kameez* outfits. This traditional costume started in the Punjab region and they are still the most popular classic garments worn by women in India and Pakistan. The *salwar* is a baggy pajama-type of trouser with a drawstring waist, whose legs are wide at the top and narrow at the ankles. Another variation in *salwar* is the *churidar* style where the legs end in small folds around the ankles. The women on the left are wearing a looser form, which are sometimes called Punjabi *salwar* suits. The *kameez* is a long shirt or tunic, which often reaches to the knees, but can vary as seen here. As a symbol of modesty women also wear a *dupatta* across their shoulders. All three pieces can be in matching or contrasting colors and fabrics, but like most Indian clothing are brightly colored and in a variety of fabrics and decorations that attest to wealth and status.

Dennis Albert Richardson/Shutterstock.com

Figure 19.24 This is also a contemporary image of a woman wearing a traditional sari and clearly shows how it is worn, which is wrapped around the waist right to left and tucked and pleated into the petticoat and then one end over or pinned at the left shoulder. They are worn over a drawstring petticoat that goes by several names depending on the language and region—in the north, *lehenga*—and also over a form-fitting short-sleeved blouse with a low neck that leaves the midriff exposed, also with different names, but commonly, *choli*. Like *salwar/kameez* outfits the fabrics can be very simple or extremely expensive and decorations can also vary enormously, again showing wealth and status and they also reflect the occasion. It is often thought to represent female dress in South Asian countries.

szefei/Shutterstock.com

Figure 19.25 These are a contemporary bride's feet and hands with henna stain decoration called *mehndi*, in preparation for her wedding. Muslim and Hindu women have used this and the intricate designs for centuries. A reddish paste is made from the dried leaves of the henna bush and applied by a henna artist, a *mu'allima*, with small brushes or now in prepared cones, and after it has dried the paste is removed leaving the stains. Brides can have complex designs with symbols to ward off evil spirits, attract good fortune, or increase fertility. Sometimes other members of the wedding party, including the groom in certain regions, get similar but smaller decorations. We know that henna was used in ancient Egypt and it is believed that the plants were brought from there to India probably in c. 8th century. Notice the similarity to the cushions on the floor in Figure 14.6 that probably came from British India.

Photosindia.com/SuperStock

Figure 19.26 This is a miniature painting of Mughal *Ladies Feasting and Drinking Wine* from the 18th-century *Small Clive Album*. This album now at the Victoria and Albert Museum contains 62 paintings, drawings, and floral pattern studies. It was thought that Robert Clive was given it in 1765–1767. Because of the Muslim and Hindu custom of purdah, woman lived in separate quarters and often did not wear upper garments, but draped themselves with shawls or wore the *choli*. The women are wearing a variety of clothes and several are wearing the long loose pyjamas. The ladies to the left are wearing long skirts and the one in orange has a diaphanous one, called "Dacca muslin," over slender pants like *salwar*. Notice their jewelry and that they are all wearing some sort of head covering and long straight hair. India was famous for silk brocades; notice the large red pillows, the peacock fan, and the fabric canopy to protect them from the sun.

V&A Images, London/Art Resource, NY

Figure 19.27 This is an early 19th-century miniature painting of a nobleman and his guests watching a traditional "Nautch dance," which were traditional classical Indian dances performed originally in the north in Mughal palaces and later for less wealthy patrons and the British Rajs and officials, but always for men. The men are wearing the over garments that we saw in Figures 19.20 and 19.21, and 19.22—namely the *jama*, the *kurta*, and *angaraka*—over different styles of pyjamas, and again, a variety of turbans. The men to the left are accompanying the three dancers also in "Nautch" traditional costumes with stiff over skirts and in this case a long flowing under skirt, and long shawls—*dupattas*. The two men behind have flaming torches and there are candle sconces on the walls. Notice the interesting use of perspective on the floor, and on the Oriental rug where the beautiful design is evident. The square stone pillars are similar to the ones in the temple in Figure 19.3.

Robert and Lisa Sainsbury Collection/Bridgeman Images

Figure 19.28 This is a different kind of dance, known as "Kalbelia" or "Kabeliya," performed in Rajasthan by nomadic gypsy tribes of that name. These folk dances have been performed by men and women using colorful costumes and loud music from ancient times. They involve a great deal of spectacular, sensual, fast movements, and rapid twirling often with stacks of pots on their heads. The men were the traditional cobra snake charmers and the dances were symbolic of the serpent's movements. Their songs and dances were part of their cultural and oral traditions that were handed down from one generation to the next.

Chris Tiné

Figure 19.29 Kathakali is another form of dance-drama that developed in the southwestern coastal region of Kerala during the 17th century. The stories and music have evolved from myths and legends of the gods, and epic poems, and temple rituals. The performers are all males wearing exuberant, exaggerated costumes and highly elaborate make-up, some of which is glued on as seen in these two men. The actors never speak but use elegant, stylized gestures to act out characters, like the *mudras* referenced in Figure 19.18, to accompany the singers and mostly percussion instrumentalists. The stories are very long and today are rarely performed in entirety. There are many images and further detailed information available: Google "Kathakali," web and images.

Sheri Somers

* In the south, the weather was hot and humid so they preferred lighter-weight and looser clothing and less of it. They also had better and richer soil so it was conducive to growing cotton, and also because they could work outdoors, they developed larger looms so could make bigger lengths of material.

* In the north the weather was cooler, and they used fur and wool from sheep and goats as well as cotton and silk. Because the handlooms were inside they were usually smaller and consequently so were the fabrics, which were often embroidered.

* In the west, there were mixed climates and they had a wide range of styles using embroidery and woven fabrics and also developed good quality printed and brightly dyed materials.

* In the east they grew mulberry trees for silk worms and so it became the center of silk production. Because it was on the Silk Road they exported it across Asia to China. Jute was also an important product and used for rough cloth, matting, and also for rope, fishing nets, and other industrial uses, and was primarily grown in the Bengal area.

* Cotton was grown in the Indus Valley for thousands of years BCE and Indian cotton was found in ancient Egyptian tombs, so it was known to have been traded with them.

* Spinning, weaving, dyeing, and embroidery were important and known from ancient times. Embroidery and weaving patterns varied greatly from locale to locale.

* From early times the trading of fabrics was common here as well as with Egypt, Greece, and Rome and throughout the Middle East and Asia. Later this would also include trade with the European nations and often the spice traders carried these materials as well.

* The Mughal rulers and their courts (1526 to 1757) brought new types of tailored clothes to India from Persia, and textile production was greatly expanded and quickly adapted to the warmer climate.

* For both men and women royal attire was characterized by colorful luxurious fabrics of silks, satins, and brocades, exquisite tailoring, and intricate embroidery often with gold or silver threads and jewels. These fabrics and decorations were prohibited for common people.

* The most typical male garment of the courts was the *jama* that was worn over pyjamas and tied with a sash, the *patka*. Men also wore a ceremonial dagger or *kafar* as a mark of rank, decorated slippers, and various styles of turbans. See Figures 19.20 and 19.27.

* Royal garments for the king were worn only once, no matter how costly. After that they were often taken apart and used in other garments or for lesser court members.

* For centuries a very fine sheer muslin, known as Dacca muslin (now Dhaka, Bangladesh), was produced for the Mughal courts and they made a distinctive garment with fitted long sleeves on the upper part with a wide skirt worn over trousers for both men and women that was often pictured in paintings. See Figures 19.26 and 19.27.

* Also a variation, the *jamdani* was a diaphanous muslin fabric woven in a variety of patterns, but often floral as *jam* was Persian for flowers. Often they were grey and white with gold and might be what the ladies on the right were wearing in Figure 19.26.

* Men always wore turbans in many different styles to signify rank, highly decorated in royal and noble versions with costly fabrics, embroidery, feathers, and gems. The Mughal emperors had a distinct curled feathered ornament called a *sarpech* that had gems and pearls attached to it that later influenced Europeans aigrettes (plumes) headdresses.

* Mughal women's clothing was similar to men's, but women also wore many types of jewelry in gold and semi-precious and precious stones: toe and finger rings, ankle bracelets, many wrist bangles, studs and rings for the nose, and ornaments for hair, and an amulet around the neck called a *ta'wiz* worn by both Muslim men and women as good luck charms.

* In the early periods the *dhoti* was the basic garment for non-royal men and women and usually made of cotton. Basically it was a loincloth for men and sometimes wrapped and draped for women.

* *Lungi* was another type of indigenous Indian clothing. Similar to a *dhoti*, but it was sewn into a tube and also worn by men and women. It was tied in various ways at the waist, but generally with a double knot. They are still popular in the south as they are cooler than pants, and in some parts are still worn by men and women, generally by laborers. For special occasions, festivals, and weddings they can be decorated.

Clothing and Costume Keywords

Because there are so many Indian languages there are many words for similar pieces of clothing and because of translations the spellings can vary. Also as the chapter is over a long period and a huge geographic area, different words were used at different times and places. This website has contemporary images, words, and descriptions of basic clothes, but many others exist and individual words can be referenced: http://www.iloveindia.com/indian-clothing/turban.html

jama – During the 16th and 17th centuries this was an upper garment of a men's formal dress that was worn in the courts of northern and central India. It consisted of a tailored upper garment that crossed at the chest and attached under the arms and at the waist to a knee-length or longer flared skirt that also had tight-fitting long sleeves. For royalty and high officials it was always made from the finest silk and for others, from cotton. See Figures 19.20 and 19.27.

pyjama – These were the loose, lightweight pants with a drawstring waist worn under the *jama* that for royalty and their courts were also of the finest cloth. They were cut in different ways and worn by men and women. Note that in olden times this was the spelling, but during British rule they were introduced to Europe and the spelling changed to pajamas and then were worn with many different upper garments and in different fabrics due to the locale. See Figures 19.21, 19.26, and 19.27.

patka – This was a richly embroidered long sash that tied at the waist and was knotted in the center of the *jama*. See Figures 19.20 and 19.27.

kafar – The ceremonial knife worn on the belt by Indian and Mughal aristocrats.

sherwani – This was another style of over garment from the Persian and Mughal court dress that was adopted in India. It was a long straight coat buttoned to the neck and usually with a small stand-up collar—later called a "Nehru collar" as it was his favorite coat. It was knee-length or longer and worn over a *churidar*, or *khara* pajama or *salwar* pants. Today it is worn for special occasions, weddings, and by movie and rock stars.

angaraka – This was a long robe similar to a *jama*, but had a higher waist and an oval opening over a shirt and was worn over pyjamas, *dhoti*, or *lungi*. See Figures 19.21 and 19.27.

kurta – This was a long loose-fitting shirt or tunic that was introduced in the Mughal period and with variations is still worn today. It had different ways of closing at the neck and could be rounded or narrow. It was similar to the Muslim *thaub* seen in Chapter 4, Figure 4.15. See Figure 19.22.

angavastram – This was a long scarf worn over the shoulders and could be made of fine cloth and decorated or very plain and also worn by laborers. See Figures 19.21 and 19.22.

dhoti – A traditional loose trouser-like garment made of a length of fabric wrapped around the waist and between the legs, and was also known as *veshti* in the south. It had many variations of draping and folding patterns and was worn by the rich as well as poor. In the south where it was hot, it was often worn as a loose skirt and also frequently folded in half to the knees by laborers and others, as it was cooler and less restrictive. In the north it was often worn under the *kurta* with an *angavastram* on the shoulders. See Figure 19.22.

lungi – These were similar to *dhoti*, but they were a stitched skirt that formed a tube. It was worn long or to the knees and also knotted or tied in different ways. If it was white in the south, it was called a *mundu*.

gamchha – This was traditional Indian towel made of a thin coarse cotton fabric and used for drying after washing. But it was also an important item of men's clothing for laborers and farmers, and they were often seen carrying it on their shoulders.

sari, saree, or shari – This was the most iconic South Asian female garment and was worn from ancient times. It was made from a long rectangular piece of fabric draped in various ways around the waist and over one shoulder. It was worn over a short-sleeved blouse and a petticoat. It could be made of luxurious fabrics and decorations or plain and simple. It was widely used in India, Pakistan, Bangladesh, Nepal, and Sri Lanka, and is still popular there and their entire diaspora. See Figure 19.24.

lehenga, pavadai (Tamil) – This was the drawstring petticoat worn under the sari and went by many different names in different regions and the many languages.

choli or in the south, ravika – This was the short-sleeved tight-fitting often low-neck blouse usually of half-length to the midriff worn under the sari and usually made specifically for the wearer. It was often in a contrasting color or pattern for visual interest or effect. See Figures 19.24 and 19.26.

salwar/kameez, shalwar/kameez – Variations of these tunics, pants, and scarves have made up traditional Indian attire for men and women. See Figures 19.23 and 19.26.

sharara – This was a traditional dress worn by Muslim ladies and occasionally men, introduced during the Mughal Empire, but now is one of the major traditional costumes. The *sharara* consisted of a long flowing skirt, and for women a *choli* and a *dupatta* or *chunni* for covering the head. The distinctive feature of the *sharara* dress was the skirt, which was divided like trailing pajama pants that were fitted until the knee and then flared outwards. This was originally worn by Muslim brides and usually in red, but is now worn by others in many different colors and again can be simple or highly decorated. See a male musician in Figure 19.27.

dupatta – It was known by various names like *odhni*, *chunari*, *chunni*, and even just *unni* and was a long rectangular, scarf-like cloth, worn in various symbolic ways over the centuries and fashions on the shoulders or head as a sign of modesty. It could be made of many different fabrics from simple cotton to silk, georgette, and chiffon, and plain or heavily decorated. Often it was worn in a different color or fabric, or pattern from the other clothes. Today it figures prominently as the third element in the *salwar/kameez* outfit. See Figures 19.25, 19.26, and 19.27.

Kashmiri shawl, also cashmere – These were famous and coveted shawls throughout India for their soft fine woven goat's wool, often woven or decorated with fine embroidery. "Pashmina" was the indigenous word for cashmere and is *not* a different animal or kind of wool.

paisley – This was English for an Indian design that was introduced and became popular in Europe in the 18th and 19th centuries on woven and printed fabrics and Kashmir shawls, which in Europe and the US were known as "India Shawls." In India the design was known as *boteh* or *buta* and was originally from ancient Iranian and traditional designs of Persian origin. Often the design was attributed to botanical subjects such as a pine cone, cypress, or palm tree, or tear drop or feather or kidney shape, in any case, it was a distinctive recognizable pattern that could be interpreted in many ways, but always with the same distinctive shape. The design and the shawls were copied in Paisley, Scotland, and that is why it got the name.

topi – This was a small round hat with a flat top worn by men and was very similar to the Islamic *taqiyah* seen in Figure 4.15.

pheta – This was a distinctive type of turban with a top ruffle or fan-like tail, which is still popular today and comes in several styles and a variety of symbolic colors.

dastar – This is also a distinctive type of turban and worn by Sikhs around the world and has important religious and symbolic meaning for them. There are several variations from the traditional oval form that crosses in the center and is used to cover their uncut hair.

CHAPTER TWENTY

China: 589–1912

Figure 20.1 This is the Hall of Prayer for Good Harvests that is part of the Temple of Heaven, Beijing, and was built from 1406 to 1420, at the same time as the Forbidden City. It is considered the most sacred of temple complexes and has had considerable influence on Chinese architecture. This unusual circular temple is in the center of a huge formal arrangement of smaller rectangular temples with woods and gardens, using an axial plan that echoed the Confucian notion that heaven is round (the temple), and the earth is square (the park). The building is made of wood that is highly decorated and colorful and sits on a three-level carved white marble base (*taizi*) and uses the conical Chinese roof. It was visited annually by the Emperors of the Ming and Qing dynasties for prayers and sacrifices for good harvests. See http://whc.unesco.org/en/list/881.

jameswest007/iStock

A Little Background

China had 10,000 years of continuous history defined by a series of dynasties with little outside influences. This continuity established the permanence of a single culture. Much of Chinese society, its culture, and political institutions were formed by the philosophy and religion of Confucianism. However, the teachings and philosophies of Daoism and Buddhism became blended with it and these three together united its people and civilization until the Communist era. The native Han people of central China were briefly invaded and occupied by Kublai Khan and the Mongols. More importantly, they were conquered and dominated by the Manchu people from northern and eastern China, who ruled until the end of the Imperial dynasties in 1912.

Who They Were

*   Society, government, and the economy were integrated into a single system—Confucianism—which was part religion, part social code, and part moral order for the country.

*   The native Han people of central China were an agrarian society and culture that had existed with Imperial dynasties for thousands of years. In 1644 they were conquered and overshadowed by the Manchu people from northern China, Manchuria, who like the Mongols used Beijing as their capital city.

*   The Manchu were a people and culture who took pride in their military facility with horses and bows and arrows. They conquered the southern tribes and their Ming rulers and established the modern period of Chinese culture and society now called the Qing dynasty.

*   There are many movies about China made by and about them. This is a short list: *Little Big Soldier* (2010), *The Good Earth* (1937)*, *The Last Emperor* (1987)*, *Raise the Red Lantern* (1991)*, *Curse of the Golden Flower* (2006), *Marco the Magnificent* (1965), *Snow Flower and the Secret Fan* (2011) and several movies about Genghis Khan. *Crouching Tiger, Hidden Dragon* (2000)*, *Ip Man* (2008), *Dragon* (2011)*, *Dragon Blade* (2015), *The Condor Trilogy* (adaptations of the novels for film, TV, and manhua), and *The Grandmaster* (2013) are important examples of wuxia films, which were originally defined as period films showing martial art skills, but due to their popularity have spread to many media forms such as video games and are now a large component of popular culture in modern China.

The Chinese Material World

What They Made

*   Chinese buildings used a standardized system of modular rectangular units called *jian*. This was a modular building system developed very early by the Han people even in their simple huts. The *siheuyuan* or courtyard house evolved more sophisticated materials and elements, but this system and type of Chinese architecture remained virtually unchanged for 3,000 years. It was the basic framework or template for all buildings. It was also closely allied to their Confucian philosophy and its rigid hierarchical structure of society.

*   The core of the house was the courtyard and the "room" units grew around it, both horizontally and vertically, which allowed for great flexibility and repetition. The extent of the modularity in a building increased with its size, importance, and function.

*   This grid and axial system was then applied to larger housing, Imperial, temple, and monastic complexes as well as government and business establishments.

*   The 10th to 13th centuries were the high point of Chinese architecture and brought with them the perfection of timber-frame construction and decoration.

Figure 20.2 This is the Hall of Heavenly Kings at Nanputuo Temple that is on Xiamen Island in southeast China. Notice the typical upturned tiled roofs with dragons at the corners, the use of calligraphy, the potted trees known as *penjing*, and the animal sculptures. This is an ancient Buddhist temple and monastery complex and is famously known as the "Temple of a thousand years" as it has been built many times; it expresses the architecture and culture of this region. It is also situated in a dramatic landscape with green hills behind it and overlooking the sea, considered the most favorable orientation by feng shui.

claudio zaccherini/Shutterstock.com

* The wood building style was relatively similar throughout China with minor variations to accommodate the wide variety of climates. Wood construction was favored because it was plentiful, easy to transport, to work, and to standardize.

* Major buildings were built in wood and elegantly joined without fasteners or adhesives. Joints fit perfectly and the structures were quick and easy to repair, modify, or replace. See Figures 20.1, 20.2, 20.3, 20.4, 20.5, 20.6, 20.7, and 20.12.

* The success of Chinese architecture was dependent on the skill of craftsmen not designers. There was no formal term for the concept "architect" until modern times. The craftsman who built the temples and secular buildings was called the "builder."

* Temples, tombs, and altars made up much of the ceremonial architecture of Chinese cities. Temples were the primary focus of skilled building and decorating and were meant for public display and were a part of the Imperial religious culture. Their primary structural element was of an interlocking network of wooden supports built on top of a foundation platform that had a decorated roof. This provided the distinctive look of all large wood-framed architecture.

* Imperial and large religious buildings used the wooden *duogong* building system that used a series of interlocking structural posts and beams to support the walls and the roofs. See Figures 20.4, 20.5, and 20.6.

Figure 20.3 This is Biyong Hall at the Confucius Temple and the Imperial College founded in 1306 under the Yuan Dynasty, Beijing. This college was the first and later the last Imperial College and this building is where the Emperors gave lectures. The square hall sits on a raised platform (*taizi*) and is surrounded by a round moat and is another example of the symbolism of the square for earth and round for heaven. The double-tiered roof is covered by glazed tiles, with a gold finial at the top. Between the eaves is a sign with the two characters for Bi Yong, the name of the hall. A sign like this is a typical feature and can be seen on many temples and buildings. The four doors lead to bridges that cross the moat and symbolically stand for the spreading of knowledge. After the Confucius temples of Qufu, it is China's largest. Qufu was the hometown of Confucius and the city contains numerous historic palaces, temples, and cemeteries. http://www.travelchinaguide.com/attraction/beijing/guozijian.htm

akg-images/Henri Bancaud

* Buildings rested on a podium, a *taizi* that raised buildings about 3 to 6 feet. At first they were unadorned but later highly decorated balustrades were added. See Figures 20.1 and 20.3.

* A building's main structure was a series of columns on the perimeter that in larger buildings were slightly slanted inward similar to ancient Greek practice.

* Walls were only enclosing elements. They were not load-bearing walls as used in the West, but "curtain walls" similar to our use in modern skyscrapers. In the north due to the cold climate, they were on or near the exteriors, but in the south they were often just used to divide interior spaces.

* Residential houses varied to some extent from region to region, mainly because of geographical differences and climate, but for the most part they retained the basic format of the *jian* with a courtyard surrounded by rooms. This system functioned for urban and rural dwellings.

* Houses were enclosed by inward-facing high walls with only one or two entrances; according to feng shui the most desirable was the southeast as it brought good fortune and the north was least favorable as it brought cold winds.

Figure 20.4 This is in the Imperial Ancestral Temple, Beijing. This view is a detail of the heavily decorated wooden roof beams and ceiling, showing its *duogong* structure and the large red columns that will also be shown in other buildings.

junrong/Shutterstock.com

Figure 20.5 This and the following photos are contemporary scenes in the Forbidden City, Beijing, 1406–1420. The Hall of Preserved Harmony is a good example of traditional architecture using a low, horizontal, symmetrical profile and the roofline with upturned corners. Because these are Imperial buildings they have red walls and columns; again notice the sign that identifies the building.

Chris Tiné

Figure 20.6 Hall of Preserved Harmony, Forbidden City, Beijing, 1406–1420. This shows a close-up of the wooden surfaces that are elaborately painted with bright colors and gold and also accented with bright ceramic roof tiles. This also shows the *duogong* structure from the outside. Notice the embossed round tile caps that are typical of China and Japan.

Chris Tiné

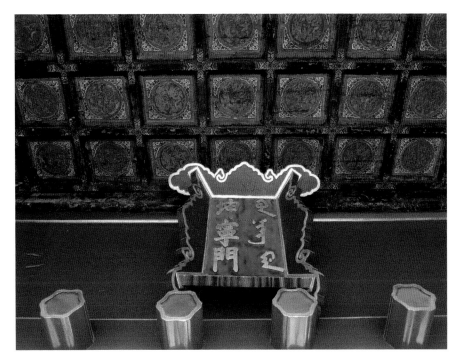

Figure 20.7 Also in the Forbidden City, Beijing, 1406–1420, this shows a detail of an intricately painted ceiling, the ends of the rafters and a different identifying sign.

Chris Tiné

Figure 20.8 This shows more details of roofs in the Forbidden City, Beijing, 1406–1420. Typically the roofs use colorful ceramic tile and are decorated along the roofline and at the corners with animal figures. Imperial buildings usually have dragons and phoenixes, and yellow/gold roof tiles are also reserved for them.

Chris Tiné

* The Emperor-centered Confucian culture was reflected in the typical symmetrical city that was laid out along a central axis, which represented the "correct" spiritual path. Axial planning was also used to imply a direct connection to the Chinese cosmos. See Figure 20.10.

* Cities and towns generally used this axial grid and were enclosed by defensive walls, which had no public gathering places other than the temples. See Figure 20.10.

* Interaction with India in the 3rd century CE brought Buddhist cave sanctuaries, *sutras*, and then the *stupa* form to China. During the Tang dynasty in the 8th century CE the Leshan Buddha was carved into a hill and it is still the largest stone Buddha in the world.

* The Chinese pagoda derived from the *stupa* and usually contained some sort of Buddhist relic. It became popular from the 7th to 10th century. It took on several different configurations and numbers of sides and heights; its unifying element was the upward-curved roofs. There are many references and images available on the Internet. See Figure 20.9.

* The architecture of western China was influenced by the styles of Islam after the 7th century CE.

* Numerology profoundly influenced Imperial and religious architecture and dictated what they used in buildings and how they were constructed.

* Cities, buildings, tombs, and interiors also followed feng shui, literally wind-water, which was the philosophical system of laws that governed their layout and orientation to harmonize with their environment. The most auspicious was south or southeast, and east as it was the direction of the rising sun.

Figure 20.9 This is the Longhua Pagoda built in 977 in the Song dynasty style and is part of the largest Buddhist temple complex in Shanghai. It is seven stories high with the typical upswept grey tiled roofs with small bells at the corners that tinkle in the wind. It is an octagonal hollow brick core that is surrounded by wooden balconies with typical Chinese designs on the railings. Longhua literally means "Luster of the Dragon," as legend says a dragon visited here and it is celebrated with a festival every year. Legend also says it was built to house cremated relics of the Buddha.

Roman Sigaev/Shutterstock.com

* The Forbidden City was started in 1406 and was the primary residence for all the Imperial family and his court and also the political center of government for 500 years. Legend says that there were 9,999 rooms—the ultimate Chinese number before 10,000 that represented heaven. See Figures 20.5, 20.6, 20.7, 20.8, and 20.17.

* The Temple of Heaven in Beijing was the most important and largest temple complex in China and consisted of several temples in a large park, including the one in Figure 20.1. Ancient cosmological laws, feng shui, and the use of numerology in its architecture were important components and were reflected here. Another symbolic element was the dark-blue roof tiles that represented the sky and heaven.

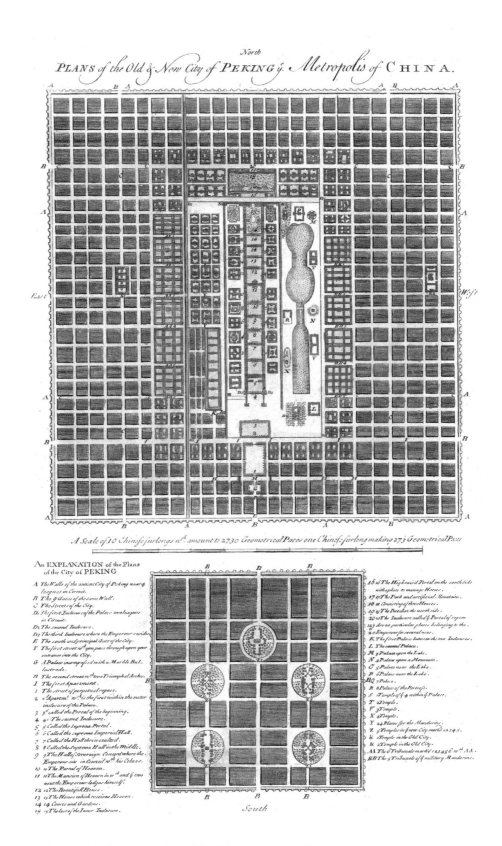

Figure 20.10 These are the formal city plans of the old and new cities of Beijing, by Harris Von John, London, 1790. Shown on the top is the Imperial Forbidden City that is surrounded and protected by a symmetrical grid plan of streets.

akg-images/historic-maps

Figure 20.11 This is a photo of the ancient city of Lijiang with its old castle in the Yunnan Province in northeastern China. Like many traditional Chinese cities it was tightly laid out and contained no public spaces. The castle in the center shows examples of Chinese hipped roofs and the other buildings for shops and common houses use single pitched roofs.

JTB Photo/SuperStock

Figure 20.12 This is a Chinese painting, c. 1800, that shows people approaching a riverside pavilion. The design and construction of the buildings are typical and show several styles of tiled roofs including the hipped, pitched, and upswept. The carved fretwork on the façade provided privacy and air circulation and was used on buildings and furniture; it is also common in Islamic and Indian styles. The footpath on the zigzag wall over the river and the classic arched bridge, whose reflection makes it into a circle, are good examples of landscape architecture. The clothes are typical Manchu attire with pants and tunics for men and women.

Bridgeman Images

Figure 20.13 This is a view of a courtyard of a wealthy Chinese merchant, c. 1800–1805. The interplay of buildings, plants, and water was carefully arranged. Notice the steps leading into the pool and the small pavilion with calligraphy. The merchant is proudly showing his large collection of trained potted plants, an ancient art known as *penjing*. Later the Japanese adapted it and called it bonsai.

British Library Board/Robana/Art Resource, NY

Figure 20.14 This is a colored copper engraving of a "Chinese Village and Peasants" showing a 19th-century Western-er's view of a peasant village and its inhabitants. Notice their clothes and the simple rural structures that did not use the more sophisticated courtyard system; the houses used pitched roofs with small windows.

akg-images

How They Decorated

Figure 20.15 This is a large water cauldron at the Forbidden City, Beijing, 1406–1420, that was forged in bronze and their handles were decorated with the Imperial lion motif. Also notice both the white and iron railings, which are also seen in many palace and temple complexes.

Chris Tiné

* Fired brick and stone and their masonry techniques were later used in the larger religious, secular, and more defensive buildings, such as the Great Wall, as they were more permanent than wood and less likely to burn down. See Figure 20.9 for an early brick pagoda.

* Most important buildings had a hipped roof, secondary structures had a half-hipped roof, and residential structures had gable or gable overhang roofs. See Figures 20.11, 20.12, and 20.14.

* The main and most important beam was the structural top horizontal roof beam, often called the ridgepole, and it was highly painted and decorated, sometimes with relief sculpture. The end decoration of main roof beams had carved images, often of animals, dragons, and fish. See Figures 20.2, 20.5, 20.12, and 20.13.

* Roof tiles were made of clay and came in several colors; blue was often used on temples—signifying the color of the sky. Imperial roof tiles had dragon and phoenix designs and were yellow. See Figures 20.1, 20.2, 20.3, 20.5, 20.6, 20.8, 20.9, 20.11, 20.12, and 20.13.

* All parts of a building were decorated including walls, doors, ceilings, windows, and porticos. Coffered ceilings in buildings were covered in decorative painted detail. More important buildings had figurative detail; less wealthy buildings had simpler, abstract decoration.

* The major colors used in Chinese architecture and décor were red, black, green, white, blue, and gold, and yellow was reserved for Imperial use. See Figure 20.17.

* Colors used on building exteriors could also symbolize the five directions; green for east, red for south, white for west, black for north, and yellow for the center.

Figure 20.16 This is a guardian lion statue from the Ming Dynasty at The Forbidden City, Beijing, 1406–1420. Guardian lion statues are common in China at the entrance to temples and important buildings. In Chinese they are called "Shi," and in the West they are often referred to as "Foo Dogs." The lions are typically depicted in pairs with the male leaning on a sphere, representing supremacy over the earth (yang), and the female leaning her paw on a lion cub, representing nurture (yin).

Chris Tiné

Figure 20.17 This is a Throne Room in the Forbidden City, Beijing, 1406–1420, and is one of many in the complex and has a very theatrical feeling, with the throne on its raised dais looking like a miniature theater as the Emperor presents himself as a god. The room is surrounded by carved screens, which allow light into the hall, and is decorated with bright yellow banners, rich textiles, and traditional Chinese ceramics on very typical Chinese stands. The color yellow on the throne and banners is significant as it is traditionally the most prestigious color and used to denote the Emperor. Again, notice the use of calligraphy.

Chris Tiné

* Every structural element of Imperial, religious, and secular buildings was painted and usually where the colors were used was specified and had a symbolic meaning. Fire = red, yellow = dignity, so these were the colors of the Emperor and the Imperial family and their buildings, furnishings, and clothes. See Figure 20.17.

* Social status, rank, and wealth determined the width, style, color, and decoration of rooms according to Confucian principles.

* The plan of a house also reflected ancestor worship, paternal authority, and filial piety. This hierarchy dictated the order, placement, and size of the rooms and courtyards in an axial symmetrical configuration.

* Chinese gardens evolved over many centuries from vast and magnificent imperial palace and temple garden complexes to smaller gardens for lesser officials, wealthy merchants, poets, and scholars who had gardens to enrich their homes as well. The historical city of Suzhou is famous for its gardens and is a UNESCO World Heritage Site.

* Gardens were an important component of homes and temples and were designed to elevate the beauty of nature to an art form. As in most cultures their function was seen as a natural antidote and a release from the rigid formality of family and court life.

* Axial planning was not applied to gardens as they were conceived as freer spaces and were designed to be an improved imitation of nature. Plantings, water features, rocks, and paths were selected for aesthetic and symbolic significance. They were always asymmetrical. There are many references and images on the Internet, but this link to a US one is also good: http://www.huntington.org/chinesegarden

Figure 20.18 This 18th-century portrait of the Imperial bodyguard, Zhanyinbao, pictures him in his Manchu military garments with the traditional weapons of long sword, bow, and arrows. This is a hanging scroll with the painting and calligraphy mounted on silk. The calligraphy uses Chinese black ink and was considered an equally important art form as the painting; the two are usually integrated. Scrolls were a major feature of décor as were screens, which used paintings, calligraphy, gold, lacquer, carved wood, and lattice.

The Metropolitan Museum of Art. Image source: Art Resource, NY

Building and Décor Keywords

jian – The rectangular Chinese modular unit that consisted of a floor and four vertical posts. These could be added together horizontally and vertically to add another story and to create large and complex buildings.

siheyuan – This was the residential house based around a courtyard that was also the central *jian* module, which was also used for negative spatial compositions.

feng shui – The Chinese spiritual system that harmonized existence with the surrounding environment. All temples were required to meet its standards and it was used to site most other buildings. Its practitioners developed the first magnetic compass.

duogong – The wooden structural support system of ancient Chinese temples in which a series of interlocking structural posts and beams supported the walls and the room. These posts and beams were often intricately carved and painted in bright colors and contained no metal elements. See Figures 20.4, 20.5, and 20.6. See http://en.wikipedia.org/wiki/Dougong

taizi – The masonry base that supported the temple columns. See Figures 20.1 and 20.3.

pagoda – This was a Chinese multi-tiered tower that derived from Indian *stupas* and was usually part of Buddhist temple complexes. They featured the upward-sweeping roofline and always an uneven number of tiers. Usually the roof tiles were grey or black as they believed it encouraged the gods to come to earth. See Figure 20.9.

"china" – It was a term used in the West to refer to ceramics exported from China. It was a type of ceramic that was invented by the Chinese that was a very thin, strong porcelain originally made for the Emperors. Ceramics were a serious and important art form and were practiced in many styles and types throughout China's history.

The Chinese Clothing and Costume World

How They Dressed

* The early establishment of the Confucian hierarchy of social order prescribed clothing worn by the Emperor and the court officials. There were many rules about who could wear what and in what colors and with what decoration and ornamentation; these were strictly enforced during the Manchu dynasty.

* The basic form of Chinese aristocratic garments was established before the first millennium. Silk robes were trimmed with bands showing small closely grouped, colored, patterned borders contrasting with the garment's main fabric. See Figures 20.21 and 20.24.

* Silk was first developed in ancient China thousands of years ago. Originally only Emperors wore it, but eventually other people in the courts and then the wealthy as well. See Figures 20.18, 20.19, 20.20, 20.21, 20.22, 20.23, 20.24, and 20.25.

* The dragon as a decorative motif had complicated and hierarchical rules for its use, but from ancient times symbolized Imperial authority. The number nine had important symbolic connotations, as it was the largest single digit. The Emperor had nine dragons woven into his fabric and later for court garments, but they always covered them with surcoats. This website has good pictures of its many forms: http://en.wikipedia.org/wiki/Chinese_dragon

Figure 20.19 This is a formal portrait of the Qianlong Emperor (1711–1799), the fourth emperor of the Manchu-led Qing dynasty, who ruled from 1735 to 1796. It is painted in a more Western style; notice how realistically he and his clothes are rendered. He is displaying his circular badge of office, luxurious embroidered silk robes, and a typical Imperial round hat. These round badges with dragon motifs were reserved for the Imperial family. Also notice the throne and footstool and the large red pillar, which is similar to the ones seen in the throne room image (Figure 20.17).

Figure 20.20 This Ming dynasty (1368–1644) scroll shows multiple examples of royal 16th-century clothing. The painting is of *The Great Emperors of the Five Mountain Tops in the company of the Great Emperor of Literature and his Assistants*. Mount Tai is one of the five sacred mountains and has been of great significance to Chinese cultural history for thousands of years. For centuries the Emperors climbed the mountain as a symbol of their power and to pray to heaven. Poets, writers, and artists also visited it for inspiration and there are thousands of their poems and paintings. Notice this painting is in a much more typical flat Chinese style, and see the interesting graphic rendering of the clouds.

Figure 20.21 This is a photograph of aristocratic Manchu ladies, c. 1867–1872. This shows the ornate silk fashions and elaborate hairstyles of women from the Manchuria province of northeast China.

Private Collection/Bridgeman Images

Figure 20.22 This is a 20th-century traditional Manchu-style silk robe. It is intricately embroidered in satin stitch with roundels of flowers, butterflies, birds, fish, and bats. Also notice the simple and yet elegant construction.

Christie's Images/Bridgeman Images

Figure 20.23 This is a 19th-century round Imperial badge from a court robe with an intricately embroidered dragon. The dragon was a symbol of power and strength and used for the Emperor and his family, but also as a decorative element on furniture, décor, and architecture. See Figure 20.19 for the Emperor, and Figure 20.2 for a roof decoration.

Werner Forman Archive/Bridgeman Images

* After the Manchu were established they brought several innovations to clothing styles for men and women, also rigidly hierarchical and strictly imposed on the Han population, with the exception of peasants.

* There were two seasons of clothing for the Imperial courts—in summer they used gauze or silk and in winter the robes were padded with silk and lined or trimmed with fur, particularly in Beijing and the north where it was cold.

* There were a wide variety of hats and headwear for men and women, which also denoted rank and wealth and used different materials for winter and summer. See Figures 20.14, 20.18, 20.19, and 20.20.

* Court men wore the *bufu* or surcoat over their robes, decorated with badges of rank for formal wear, or without these decorations at home. See Figures 20.19 and 20.20.

* The basic men's full-length, long-sleeved tunic developed early as two narrow strips of fabric crossed at the chest, and were sewn at the back leaving the front open.

* Aristocrats used less costly versions of royal clothing as wedding attire.

* Skilled artisans produced luxury goods for the wealthy. The impoverished peasantry provided all labor for agriculture and public works.

* Peasant clothing was usually loose-fitting pants and shirts for both sexes made out of rough materials like hemp. See Figure 20.14.

Figure 20.24 This is a 19th-century tempera painting on rice paper. It shows women feeding mulberry leaves to silkworms. They are wearing simple tunics over trousers. Also notice their hairstyles with high shaved foreheads, which is very similar to the Western European Gothic and Renaissance styles. Women did much of the delicate tasks needed for silk production.

HIP/Art Resource, NY

Figure 20.25 This is an 18th-century military parade dress of Emperor Qianlong. It is made of steel and copper, fur, and silk and is decorated with both woven and embroidered elements.

Musée de l'Armée/Dist. RMN-Grand Palais/Art Resource, NY

* After the Mongols invaded in the 13th century they introduced cotton, which was softer and lighter than hemp.

* In ancient China men tied their hair in a knot on top of their head and covered it with a square hat. Monks shaved their hair to show their unworldliness. Prisoners and criminals had their hair cut short as punishment.

* The "pigtail" hairstyle was brought from Manchuria and included a small cap for cold weather.

* Manchu men's rigid soled shoes were derived from horse riding boots. Han men's footwear included lacquered wood sandals and clogs. See Figures 20.18 and 20.19.

* Colored belts and attachments derived from horse riding outfits developed into sophisticated decorative belts and silk and gold ornaments.

* Manchu and Han women wore different styles of clothes and these corresponded to the rank of their husbands.

* The basic Manchu women's dress was similar to the men's with full-length sleeves and consisted of a series of layered decorative long-robed garments. See Figures 20.21 and 20.22.

* Imperial and court Manchu ladies wore a long robe with an asymmetrical closing and two slits on the sides and under it loose pants or a skirt; this could also be worn with the cloud collar or long scarf. See Figure 20.12.

* Han women wore a knee-length jacket also with an asymmetrical closure and embroidered banding over floor-length skirts. They and other Chinese women were not forced like their men to adopt Manchu clothing.

* Women in ancient China coiled their hair and wore decorative combs and elaborate hairpins and headdresses. Young girls were not permitted to pin up their hair until they married. See Figure 20.21.

* Both Manchu and Han women wore many different hairstyles, hats, and headdresses, which also changed seasonally; and they carried fans. See Figures 20.21 and 20.24.

* Foot binding or "Lotus Feet" was a common practice for Han women and a sign of beauty, wealth, and status. Manchu Emperors tried to outlaw this practice, but with little success and eventually their women also adopted it, and it survived into the 20th century.

* Jewelry was worn by both men and women and was a visual way to show rank, wealth, and status. Silver was prized more than gold; but jade was valued more than any other stone or metal, and was also used for other decorative objects. They made exquisite and intricate jewelry pieces for thousands of years including amulets, hair accessories, bracelets, necklaces, pins, rings, and earrings. See http://www.allaboutgemstones.com/jewelry_history_asiatic.html http://kaleidoscope.cultural-china.com/en/10Kaleidoscope6017.html

* In the mid-19th century Chinese-Beijing Opera, known as *jingju* became very popular in the Imperial society. They used highly elaborate and strikingly dramatic adaptations of Imperial and military costumes. See the film *Farewell My Concubine* (1993) for spectacular costumes; other examples of the operas and costumes are also available on DVD and YouTube.

Clothing and Costume Keywords

bufu – The Manchu men's surcoat was worn over their robe and their badges of office were worn on it. See Figures 20.19 and 20.20.

buzi **or mandarin square** – This was the badge worn by court, civil, and military officials on their robes using a variety of animal (military) and bird (civil) images to indicate rank. It underwent a number of stylistic changes and was discontinued in 1912 at the end of the Imperial period. The badges were also worn by their wives. This website has wonderful pictures and descriptions: http://www.pacificasiamuseum.org/rankandstyle/html/pdf/RankandStyle_Section_2.pdf

finial – In addition to the usual meaning of a decorative or architectural feature on top of buildings or furniture, such as Figures 20.1 and 20.3, and many other images throughout the book, in China it was also used on men's civil, Imperial, and military hats as seen in Figures 20.19 and 20.25.

round badges – These round badges were worn by the Imperial family and featured heavily embroidered dragon motifs. See Figure 20.23.

"pigtail" hairstyle or queue – A Manchu hairstyle for men, in which they shaved their hair to the top of the forehead and had a single, long braid worn down the back. This was imposed on all people to show respect for the rulers and non-compliance was an act of treason punishable by death.

qun – The women's skirt-like garment came in several styles, which varied during the Qing dynasty.

chaopao – The Manchu women's court dress consisted of three elements. The first was the *chaopao*, a loose long or knee-length robe of finely embroidered silk cloth. It opened down the center and had long, loose sleeves.

chaoqun – The second layer of costume was a long skirt worn under the *chaopao*.

yunjian **or cloud collar** – The third layer was a decorative collar drawn closely around the neck.

CHAPTER TWENTY-ONE

Japan: 1338–1868

Figure 21.1 A contemporary Shochiku Grand Kabuki production of *Twelfth Night* after William Shakespeare. The scope and language of Shakespeare has become popular in Japan with several different kinds of productions from this stylized kabuki adaptation where all the parts are played by men using their traditional costumes to more classical "Western style" translations and other innovative productions.

Geraint Lewis/Alamy

A Little Background

Chinese culture and technology entered the Japanese islands in the 6th century CE by way of Korea. Until then because of their island location they tended to be very insular. These early Japanese tried to model themselves on the example of a unified Chinese culture but were mostly unsuccessful. This resulted in 900 years of factional strife with a series of local warrior clans pitted against one another, until the relative stability of the Edo period in the 17th through 19th centuries.

Who They Were

* Even during the age of the warring states the Japanese clans shared a common culture and language directly descended from ancient Chinese sources.

* Japanese culture was built on social cohesion, aesthetic development, and isolation from the outside world. It was a family-centered traditional culture that followed its native Shinto religion.

* Buddhism originated in India around 500 BCE and spread with the trade routes across Asia to China in the 1st century CE and then to Korea. In 552 CE it came from Korea to Japan where it comingled with the indigenous Shinto religion. Over the centuries they blended and peacefully coexisted and both played a major role in Japanese culture and society.

* The most important and prominent period in Japanese history was the Edo period (1615–1868). The Tokugawa family of Shōguns, technically military commanders or generals, referred to as the Shōgunate, took over and ran the country from the city of Edo (now Tokyo); theoretically they were under the Emperor, who lived in Kyoto, but he was basically just a figurehead. The Emperor was called the Mikado (also the title of an 1885 comic opera by Gilbert and Sullivan). There was an excellent 1980s US TV mini-series *Shōgun* about the 17th century that was shot in Japan and used many of their actors.

* Zen Buddhism became popular in the Edo period. It emphasized the quiet contemplation of nature and the natural perfection of the world. Its tenets had a direct effect on art, literature, and the social culture that encouraged a minimalist approach to art and material life.

* During this period the nation became politically unified with relative peace and stability and with substantial economic growth. This was a tightly controlled feudal society in which the social order of four classes was frozen and mobility was prohibited.

* In addition to the Emperor and his court, the four classes were the warriors, farmers, artisans, and merchants. It was the artisans and merchants who eventually prospered and contributed to the development of the highly sophisticated artistic, intellectual, and cultural institutions.

* The samurai warriors were the highest-ranking social class in this military government. They were extremely self-disciplined, had rigid rules of conduct, and believed strongly in both Confucian and Zen Buddhist practices. See Figure 21.16.

* The Ninja warriors were from this time and also earlier and they practiced unconventional warfare and martial arts, but during this period they were used as guards and spies. Both of these groups became highly romanticized and were often portrayed in kabuki theater. In our present time there have been many movies, cartoons, video games, and now, in Japan, theme parks about them.

* There are three kinds of traditional theater—noh, kabuki, and bunraku—all of which have several elements in common and incorporate music, dance, and elaborate masks and costumes.

* Noh theater was much like Greek drama and was a very early form of song and dance drama that started in shrines and temples for festivals. By the 14th century it was structured and performed for nobility and it was continually refined through the 19th century and patronized by the nobles, Shōguns, and the wealthy. The stories were based on legends often dealing with the supernatural worlds of gods and spirits, but also history and literature; and also like the Greeks the stories were well known to the audiences, so the performances were appreciated for their subtleties of speech using music and poetry spoken in monotonous tones, slow symbolic movements, stylized masks, and lavish costumes. They are still performed in shrines and temples on an open square stage with a roof with only a back wall with a painting of a pine tree.

* Kabuki was a highly stylized classical Japanese theater, which began about 1600 and used singing and dancing to tell historic stories. Originally it was performed by women in the Yoshiwara district of Edo, the red light area of prostitution; and because of this women were outlawed from performing and it eventually transitioned to all-male adult actors. It used highly extravagant costumes, wigs, and make-up and exaggerated movements. The performances, actors, and their costumes were hugely popular with the general public well into the 19th century; and often they were depicted in the woodblock prints. See Figure 21.1.

* Bunraku was also a form of traditional Japanese puppet theater founded in Osaka in 1684. It uses Ningyōzukai—several puppeteers who work large complex puppets; Tayū—the chanters; and *shamisen* musicians. It had its heyday in the mid-18th century. Bunraku shares many stories with kabuki, but sticks to a strict script whereas kabuki actors can be freer and ad lib lines. *Bunraku* is a US 2010 martial-arts action film and has nothing to do with this art form.

* Manzai was a style of a stand-up comedy that originated in the Heian period (794–1185 CE) for New Year festivities, but became popular all year round and has been a part of Japanese culture since before the 10th century. In it the straight man (*tsukkomi*) smacks the funny man (*boke*) in response to his stupid or misunderstood remarks, using a *harisen*, a theatrical prop meaning "slapping fan" that was a large paper fan. The comedy was similar to the US's Laurel and Hardy's slapstick and Abbott and Costello's routines using puns, double talk, and rapid-fire repartee. *Harisen* and manzai appear regularly today in all types of traditional entertainment media as well as video games, anime, and manga.

* Pleasure gardens were started in the 16th century and were walled-in brothels called *yūkaku* and by the 17th century these women prostitutes/actresses originated kabuki theater in Tokyo. See Figure 21.10.

* By the mid-18th century these women and their male counterparts became more and more differentiated and a highly trained sophisticated type, called geisha, emerged with a unique culture. At first geisha were only men and later principally women who provided entertainment and food to men. See Figures 21.10 and 21.14.

* Wealthy Japanese then created "Floating Worlds," overseen by female geishas now strictly controlled, educated entertainers who were trained in the finer points of music and beauty. This was a private world for men run by women, distinct and exempt from the strict rules of Shōgunate society. See Figures 21.10 and 21.14.

* Geishas were not primarily sex workers and often started their training at an early age. They were taught to sing, dance, play musical instruments—the flute, drums, and *shamisen*—recite poetry, play games, converse at a highly sophisticated level, and serve food. See Figures 21.10 and 21.14.

* In the later phase the Shōguns also had contact with the West. The period of self-imposed national isolation came to a dramatic end in 1853 when four American battleships arrived in Edo Bay. The

US demanded that it be allowed to trade with Japan, with the result that ports were slowly opened to foreigners.

* By this period, the mid-19th century, Japanese culture had a great influence on the art and architecture of the West.

* In 1868 the Meiji Emperor was restored to power and they moved the Imperial capital from Kyoto, and changed the Shōgunate capital name from Edo to Tokyo.

* As well as the films mentioned in other places these would be useful: *Memoirs of a Geisha* (2005), *Woman of the Dunes* (1964), *Rashomon* (1950), and *Ugetsu* (1953). There are also many anime.

The Japanese Material World

Figure 21.2 The Kondo (main hall) of the Sai-in part of Hōryū-ji Temple, Nara Prefecture. This view shows the similarities to earlier Chinese architecture. Japanese buildings were not as decorated as the Chinese and natural colors and textures were favored over the highly ornate and brightly colored painted Chinese ones. See Figures 20.3, 20.4, 20.5, 20.6, 20.7, 20.8, and 20.17. Also notice the podium that the Temple sits on as similar to the Roman ones, see Figure 2.1. The blue tiled roof is very typically Japanese and is used in religious and secular buildings. At the four roof corners can also be seen metal bells and between the second and third roofs are four freestanding vertical dragons, standing on their tails.

CulturalEyes—AusGS2/Alamy

What They Made

* Hōryū-ji was the oldest Buddhist temple complex in Japan and was started in 587 and completed in 607 CE by Prince Shōtoku, who with his father, the Emperor, was also instrumental in introducing Buddhism. A large complex with 21 wooden buildings, it was divided into two parts: Sai-in with

this Temple and an adjacent pagoda and Tō-in where the Prince had his palace and later the site of the seminary and monastery. The complex was significant as it showed the adaptation of Chinese and Korean Buddhist architecture and layout to the Japanese, who would develop a distinct style; and from its founding has been considered the temple that guarded the Empire.

* The four ancient buildings show the Asuka era style (552–710 CE) and are the world's oldest wooden structures: these are the Kondo, the five-story pagoda, the inner south gate, and the "corridor" that wraps around the complex; the features include:

    * "cloud-pattern" brackets (the Y and the circle shapes)

    * a thin block plate beneath the brackets at the tops of the columns

    * entasis—a curved tapering of the top of the columns that were on round stone bases

    * swastika pattern railings, which use various broken cross patterns and were found throughout Asia.

* The building used the Chinese architectural system, which was a modified version of post and lintel construction with intricate bracketing—the cloud-shaped brackets and circles designed to transfer the weight of the heavy tiled roof down to the wooden supporting columns.

* Much of the 7th-century CE art—frescos, statues, and other pieces within the temple complex—as well as the architecture show the strong cultural influences from India, China, and Korea and their interconnection across Asia.

Figure 21.3 This close-up detail of The Kondo (main hall) in the Sai-in part of Hōryū-ji Temple is looking up under the roof and shows its similarity to earlier Chinese roofs and its design and construction. In this image it is easier to see the round cap ends of the roof tiles, which are cast with a raised decoration and also the cloud patterns.

Xiye/Dreamstime.com

Figure 21.4 This is a small ritual storehouse at the Ise Shrine, called *mishine-no mikura*. Notice the thatched pitched roof and its other structures, which are typical of the architecture at this shrine. They used simple stylized building forms based on warehouses or similar utility buildings like this one that pre-date the introduction of Buddhist building techniques. The thatched roof has six decorative round logs located on the ridge, the ridgepole extends beyond the roof, and the bargeboards rise above the roof to form two distinctive forked finals at both ends. Two heavy round freestanding columns support the roof ridge and all of it is made from cypress. All of the buildings at this shrine are rebuilt every 20 years to support the Shinto concept of *wabi-sabi*, the impermanence of all things, simplicity, and rebirth of nature. As they say "they will always be new and will always be original as they are re-built to exacting standards."

Werner Forman Archive/Bridgeman Images

Figure 21.5 This image is in Tenryji Temple in Kyoto and shows traditional architecture that was used in religious and secular buildings, using tatami mats and sliding *shoji* screens, which frame a subtly designed landscape—sometimes known as "borrowed scenery." Great attention was given to siting buildings within their environment, so that when the screens were opened up the whole side of a building included the veranda, which became a part of the interior space. Therefore there could be minimal separation between indoors and out, a symbolic blending of the interior and exterior worlds.

narawon/iStock

Figure 21.6 This shows a simple wooden traditional-style thatched roof farmhouse, called a *minka*, with the upper roof covered in moss; the round upper pieces on the roof ridge were for decoration and generally made of straw, bamboo, or wooden planks. The lower tiled roof extended beyond and would help to provide shade in the summer. The very traditional tied bamboo screen fence would provide privacy. This is in Sagano, a suburb of Kyoto, Kansai region.

paolo negri/Alamy

Figure 21.7 This is a house and garden in autumn in Kyoto. Japanese gardens are characterized by carefully controlled and ordered structures such as basins, lanterns, bridges, and the placement of rocks, and stepping-stones. They feature clipped bushes and trees and control of color and different textures of greenery. They usually have a water feature that might also be a symbolic dry river, pond, or raked gravel.

rawpixel/iStock

Figure 21.8 Kodai-ji Temple, Kyoto, built in 1606. This is the Onigawara-seki teahouse that is one of the four famous teahouses found here. Like this one, teahouses, called *chashitsu*, are usually small rustic wooden buildings, normally situated in private or temple gardens. In the foreground is a typical stone lantern and basin for washing before the tea ceremony and placed next to a dry stone riverbed with a simple granite flat bridge leading to the entrance. The small rectangular door is called a *nijiriguchi*, or "crawling-in entrance," which means you have to bend over to go in, thus showing humility and respect. It also symbolically separates the simple tranquil inside from the turbulent outside world. The windows are covered in translucent paper to allow in light, but also to block out the exterior world and to help focus attention on the tea ceremony inside, which with its specialized implements and ritualized presentation aimed to fuse the spiritual and natural worlds.

Alex Ramsay/Alamy

* During the unstable era of the warring states, the mobility of the early warrior culture located in an island setting combined with the austere Zen Buddhist ideals encouraged a simple way of life, clothing, and customs.

* For religious and Imperial structures the Japanese borrowed the Chinese timber temple, a modified form of post and lintel construction that also featured multiple stacked roofs. The Buddhist Hōryū-ji Temple at Nara Prefecture (670–714 CE) was representative of this style. See Figures 21.2 and 21.3.

* Temple roof shapes were curved up at the corners like Chinese temples and imitated the original bamboo construction with more durable wood.

* Temples were raised on a 3-foot-high podium similar to the Roman podiums. Originally the main structure of the building rested on corner columns, made of unfinished cypress wood that supported a thatched roof. Later they used ceramic roof tiles on wooden beams. The interior space could be subdivided with lighter materials. Both Shinto and Buddhist temples were part of a sacred precinct marked and usually entered by a ceremonial gate and the Torii.

* Many temples, shrines, and palaces have been rebuilt over the centuries, mainly due to fire and earthquakes and often faithfully duplicated the original materials, designs, and finishes. The

Golden Pavilion Kinkaku-ji in Kyoto was originally built as a villa in 1397 and was repurposed to be a Zen temple. It was burned down by a monk in 1950 and recreated in 1955. Google "The Golden Pavilion Kinkaku-ji" for many websites and pictures.

* The example of the Grand Shrine of Ise where the temples date as far back as the 7th century CE and have been reconstructed every 20 years since was unusual and noteworthy. It was the holiest Shinto shrine and known simply as Jingū, which means shrine and was considered the quintessence of ancient Japanese architecture. Ise Jingū is a complex of 123 shrines centered on two main shrines, Naikū, dedicated to the sun goddess Amaterasu-Ōmikami, and Gekū. They were on the island of Honshū, and surrounded by a large national park, also famous for the "wedded rocks"—Meoto Iwa—and Mount Fuji was visible in the distance.

* The Japanese pagoda, usually an element within the temple complex, was their version of the Indian Buddhist *stupa* that was constructed to house a relic of the Buddha or of his disciples or also a symbolic relic like a statue, and other related artifacts like Sutra blocks. Pagodas could be in many different sizes and be simple or highly decorated. Generally they were three to seven stories high, but always an uneven number, and also usually square. Like the temples they had upturned corners on the roofs and often had metal towers or finials on top, which inadvertently acted like lightning rods and so some called them, "demon arresters." Originally in temples, later they were in Shinto shrines, palaces, and private houses. The oldest one is at Hōryū-ji. See Figure 20.9 for a Chinese pagoda and Chapter 19 for an Indian *stupa*.

* *Torii* were the gates into Shinto shrines and also Buddhist temples. They were the symbolic entrance from the secular into the sacred world of temples. They were very similar to *stupa* gates in India. The most famous *torii* is at the Shinto shrine on Miyajima Island known for its "floating" *torii* gate.

* The Japanese also borrowed the Chinese example of symmetrical, axial courtyard layouts but eventually added their own subtle asymmetries that can be seen even in the early layout of Hōryū-ji, where in Sai-in the temple and pagoda are placed next to each other and they do not align sequentially to the other section, Tō-in.

* Many Shinto shrines were directed at agricultural prosperity and conveyed a sense of harmony and balance. The other Grand Ise shrine was the Gekū and was dedicated to the Goddess Toyouke-Ōmikami, the deity of agriculture and industry or "Abundant Food Great Deity." Both of these were in a large forest of cryptomeria trees, which had a special relationship with Shinto shrines. See Figure 21.4.

* During the unstable periods from the 13th to 17th centuries a series of castles were built to resist local warlords and later in the 17th century, Western intruders, who were primarily the Portuguese.

* Castles were similar to European medieval castle compounds. Frequently they were on a hill with a series of fortified walls and gateways that protected a central inside residential zone. See http://www.japan-guide.com/e/e2296.html

* Wealthier housing plans were similar to Chinese models with a main hall oriented south.

* Katsura Imperial Villa (built 1620–1660) was at the beginning of the Edo era typical of wealthy homes that included a shrine and extensive gardens with teahouses and pavilions intended for reflection, relaxation, and artistic pursuits. The flexible and informal plan of the house was determined by the arrangement of the tatami mats, the shoji and folding screens, *byōbu* that could be changed and modified at will, according to the room's use. It is worthwhile to look up this villa.

* Common residential houses, called *minka*, were in a wide range of styles, dependent on geographical locations, urban or rural settings, as well as the social and economic status of the owner. See Figure 21.6.

* In urban settings, houses were usually configured as one-story row houses and often built of impermanent materials. Frequently there were shops facing the street with residential quarters behind. The domestic area had two main sections—a hearth for cooking and heat, the *irori*, and another with a raised floor for dining and sleeping. They had thatched or tiled peaked or upward-curved gable roofs. See Figure 21.9 for an *irori*.

* Floors were made of packed earth and walls were either mud and plaster or lightweight wood and paper screening.

* Windows facing the street were placed above eye level for privacy.

How They Decorated

Figure 21.9 This is a model of an interior of a traditional Japanese house showing part of a room that features the alcove, the *tokonoma*. They are an important element and are found in houses, teahouses, and temples and usually have a hanging scroll, the *kakemono*, which changed with the seasons and a flower arrangement, *ikebana*, which also frequently changed, and sometimes an incense burner or small statue or figurine. Also seen are tatami mats, a *shoji* screen, and a *sudare*, which is the bamboo shade to the left. The square cut out with an iron pot is a traditional Japanese cooking hearth called an *irori*.

Author photo

Figure 21.10 This is a courtyard garden in a brothel in Yoshiwara, the red light district of Edo, c. 1810, showing men and women socializing and playing musical instruments. The garden has some typical Japanese features such as the aesthetically manicured "cloud pruned" trees, the stone lantern, a *tōrō*, to the upper left, and to the right of it is a simple stone Japanese curved bridge, a *hashi*, crossing over the small pond. Also the building in the back has silhouetted figures behind closed *shoji* screens and above them *ramma*, and also paneled railings used mostly on second-story verandas. This image is also useful for costumes, the complex and decorated hairstyles, props such as the typical shapes of ceramics, and the small footed tables. The man in the foreground is wearing a traditional black *montsuki* and kimono with small round badges, called *mons* and he is holding a fan, *sensu*.

Figure 21.11 *Viewing Cherry Blossoms*, by Kitagawa Utamaro, 1790. Polychrome woodblock print with ink and color on paper. He is probably the most famous of the woodblock artists in the *ukiyo-e* genre. He created thousands of images and many of his prints and paintings were of courtesans and kabuki actors, and portraits of beautiful women—known as *bijin-ga*. The openness and flexibility of the Japanese building are apparent in this view showing the shoji screens opened to reveal the interior and elegant men and women leaning over a different type of paneled railing. Notice the traditional oilpaper parasols, *wagasa*, among the trees.

The Metropolitan Museum of Art. Image source: Art Resource, NY

* Interiors were meant to show reverence for the materials they used and to create an atmosphere of simplicity and tranquility to promote reflection. Colors were subdued.

* Living spaces in all Japanese buildings were modular and based on the repeating module of the tatami mats, which were approximately 3' x 6'. The arrangement of the mats determined the room size and its configuration. See Figures 21.5 and 21.9.

* Rooms were also divided by paper or fabric sliding shoji screens into zones of activity that served multiple functions depending on their placement. They also used more opaque screens, *fusama* (see Figures 21.11 and 21.14), and folding screens, *byōbu*, and bamboo blinds called *sudare*. See Figure 21.9.

* Japanese folding screens, called *byōbu*, were especially beautiful and popular in Japan in the 17th century. There are a number of famous ones on the Internet. An outstanding example was by Kanō Sanraku (1559–1635) with a pair of screens of tigers and a storm dragon on a gold-leaf background from the 17th century. He was regarded as one of the best screen painters of his time and did many large panels for temples, castles, and palaces. The Kanō School of painters used genres and nature scenes, and predominated from the 15th to 19th centuries. http://www.smithsonianeducation.org/educators/lesson_plans/japan_images_people/intropage5.html, http://en.wikipedia.org/wiki/Byōbu.

* People of all classes ate, slept, and relaxed on the floor.

* Very little furniture was used in Japanese houses and it was mostly portable with the exception of the stepped or rectangular storage cupboards, known as *tansu*. It consisted of cushions, low tables, and roll-up mattresses, the *shiki* futon, for sleeping. Chairs were not used.

* Decoration in modest homes was kept to a minimum and was usually a niche with a hanging scroll and a flower arrangement that changed with the seasons. See Figure 21.9.

* In more affluent buildings and temples they would have these niches or larger alcoves but also many other hanging scrolls, pictorial folding screens, painted wall murals, and later woodblock prints.

* Like the Chinese cities, Japanese cities were crowded and the houses tightly packed together. They had no public meeting spaces or other amenities. Later, after the rise of kabuki theater, all different classes went and mingled together, which was one of the reasons for their popularity and also why the Shōguns did not like them. The theaters were also surrounded by shops, bars, and teahouses (not for tea ceremony).

* Gardens were found in temples, shrines, palaces, and even modest homes often had a small garden. Their gardens were similar in many ways to those of the Chinese, but gradually they developed their own unique aesthetics and styles, which varied greatly depending on where they were used, i.e. residential, urban, shrine, temple, and geographical locations, but always they were symbolic manifestations and used to mimic nature. See Figure 21.5, 21.7, 21.8, and 21.10.

* A type of Zen garden, the dry, raked gravel garden was designed for inspired meditation and contemplation and consisted only of carefully raked gravel beds and artfully placed moss-covered rock groupings. The most famous was and still is Ryoan-ji in Kyoto.

* Wealthier residential homes, villas, and palaces often had large gardens, which included shrines and one or more teahouses for the performance of the tea ceremony and viewing the gardens. The teahouses and pavilions were carefully placed in scaled and sited gardens. See Figure 21.8.

* At the temple complex at Hōryū-ji there is a treasury that has many ancient Japanese artifacts mostly from the 7th and 8th centuries, including a beautiful wooden statue of the Kudara-Kannon with a round halo with a flame at the top. This halo was frequently seen in Asian including Persian art and in this case it was painted but also could be in relief. There are other Kannon statues and several important miniature shrines, and murals. There are several websites about the temple and these artifacts with pictures, including Wikipedia. The Tokyo National Museum has many of the Hōryū-ji objects, but also has many other useful images of Japanese art, décor, and other objects.

Building and Décor Keywords

Shinto – It was and still is the indigenous and unofficial national religion of Japan. The essence of Shinto was the devotion to spiritual beings called *kami*. Rituals, which let people communicate with *kami*, rather than beliefs, were its core, so it was considered "an aspect of life" rather than a religion. Rituals were practiced at shrines (*jinju*), the sacred places where *kami* lived, of which there are hundreds around the country and also in the home and in gardens. *Kami* was a complex concept and could be many things such as wind, sun, rocks, trees, and mountains. See Figure 21.4.

torii – The entrance to a Shinto shrine and also seen in Buddhist temples that represented the gateway from the earthly to the sacred, spiritual world. They comprised two upright posts and one straight and one upturned lintel. They were made of stone, or more commonly wood, traditionally they were painted vermillion with an upper black lintel. The most spectacular and famous is at Miyajima, which features on many websites and in many pictures.

minka – Literally the word means "houses of the people" and in all of their variations were single-family vernacular dwellings. See Figure 21.6.

***tatami* mat** – An approximately 3 foot by 6 foot woven straw mat with a fabric border used as a floor coverings in all Japanese homes and temples. It also formed the basis of the modular system of dividing interspaces in a Japanese house. See Figures 21.5 and 21.9.

shoji – The delicate paper or fabric that covered lattice-like wood or bamboo sliding screens was an important element in Japanese architecture and was used to divide interior spaces or function as movable outside walls. See Figures 21.5, 21.9, 21.10, and 21.11.

byōbu – These were freestanding folding screens using painting and/or calligraphy. Like many other arts they came from China, but were well established in their own style by the 8th century. These and the Chinese counterparts were particularly popular in Europe in the 17th and 18th centuries. There are numerous images and information and see my bullet point about Japanese folding screens and Kanō Sanraku.

***fusuma* panels** – These derived from *byōbu*, but started to be used about the same time as *shoji* screens in the 17th century and were initially portable opaque wooden screens and later sliding panels that were used as interior room dividers and could be painted or covered with decorative paper or fabrics, usually used for privacy. See Figures 21.11 and 21.14.

sudare – These were bamboo curtains tied with string, wool, or silk, which could be rolled or folded up like Western blinds and used indoors or out to provide privacy or to protect from wind or rain. See Figure 21.9.

ramma – Because the *shoji* screens were short they often added these pieces over them and between the ceilings. Like Western transoms they also allowed light and air into rooms and could be small *shoji* screens or intricately carved of wood. See Figures 21.5, 21.10, and 21.11. Pinterest has some good examples.

***shiki* futon** – It was a roll-up mattress used in combination with a *kake* futon, a comforter traditionally made out of silk, cotton, or down, and with a traditional buckwheat hulled pillow, all items used for sleeping.

tansu – These were stepped or rectangular storage cupboards in Japanese houses. There are many images on the web of both contemporary and antique models.

tokonoma – The niche or alcove in a private house or teahouse that displayed a hanging scroll and a flower arrangement (*ikebana*) and sometimes an incense burner or small statue. See Figure 21.9.

kakemono* or *kakejiku – This was a hanging scroll with a painting or calligraphy mounted with silk edges on a backing; a "roller stick" was attached at the bottom, which provided weight and also so that it could be rolled up for storage. See Figure 21.9.

ukiyo-e – Woodblock prints of the later Edo period frequently illustrated the seductive courtesans and geishas of the urban pleasure districts and floating worlds, and also kabuki actors, sumo wrestlers, and landscapes. They were aimed at the merchant and middle class and not considered high art. By the 19th century these prints were in France and had a huge influence on French painting, particularly on the Impressionists and by the 20th century in the US, where they were also influential in art and architecture, particularly to Frank Lloyd Wright. Their influence can still be seen in the Japanese comic books—manga, graphic novels, anime, and cartoons. See Figures 21.10, 21.11, 21.14, and 21.15.

natsume – These were the tall round stone basins. See Figures 21.7 and 21.8.

tōrō – These were the traditional stone, wood, or metal lanterns, which often resembled miniature pagodas. Originally they were sacred, bronze hanging lanterns used to light pathways in Buddhist temples and later used in Shinto shrines. By the 17th century they were also stone or wood and used as decorations in private and palace gardens and came in several styles and were modified and set on tall or short pedestals on the ground. See Figures 21.8 and 21.10. These are different than the paper lantern in Figure 21.14.

The Japanese Clothing and Costume World

Figure 21.12 *The New Year Game*, illustration in *Kokka* magazine, 1898–1899. The game called *hanetsuki* is similar to badminton and played by girls to celebrate the arrival of the New Year. They are wearing the fully developed kimono and *geta* shoes. The rectangular paddle, a *hagoita*, is used to hit a shuttlecock, *hane*, back and forth. The child in red is pointing to it. Early photographs show almost the same scene with these two evergreen-like trees with other branches on their tops with a rope hanging between them, tassels hanging down, a red decoration in the center, and the trees held up with two straw-like stands. *Hanetsuki* is not as popular as it used to be, but decorative *hagoita* in all sizes are still commonly sold throughout Japan, mostly in December.

Archives Charmet/Bridgeman Images

How They Dressed

Figure 21.13 This is a highly decorated embroidered grey silk kimono lined with orange velvet with cranes, others birds, and scattered flowers. Note its very simple elegant rectangular construction.

Bridgeman Images

Figure 21.14 *Geishas Entertaining*, by Utagawa Kunisada (1786–1865). This is a woodblock triptych by one of the last great, prolific, and popular 19th-century artists. It shows women playing musical instruments—the *shamisen* on the left and right—and in the center a geisha using a *maiougi* (geisha fan) and doing a traditional fan dance. Notice their elaborate geisha costumes, white stylized make-up, and several versions of the extravagant, waxed hairstyles, called *maru mage*, and their *kanzashi*—hairpins. The building also shows the shoji screens open to show the veranda with its typical planked flooring and open wooden railing, and on the right a room divider known as a *fusuma* panel, seemingly covered in a decorative fabric. A curious puzzle is the floor and its color: at this time floors would have been covered with tatami mats, but a similar green floor is used in some of his other prints, so perhaps he is using it as an artistic color choice. There are also examples of lacquered trays and other ceramics. In the distance is a harbor with boats and to the right a high arched bridge with many people. Also notice the typical hanging paper lantern and candle shades and stands. The artist's "chop"/signature are the red, white, and black symbols.

Bridgeman Images

Figure 21.15 *Comparison of Celebrated Beauties and the Loyal League*, Scene 5, c. 1797, color woodblock print by Kitagawa Utamaro (1753–1806). This is one of a series of prints from Utamaro's parody of a famous Japanese story *The Chūshingura*. The woman on the right is wearing a fashionable *kosode*, the forerunner of the kimono, and also the raised wooden thong sandals, *geta*, and carrying a typical paper parasol, a *wagasa*. The woman on the left is wearing a simpler outfit to denote her lower class and is doing the wash in a typical footed wooden wash tub. Also notice the large bonsai pine tree in the "informal upright style" in the large pot.

Bridgeman Images

Figure 21.16 This is a full set of samurai armor from the 16th to 17th centuries and was worn by both foot and mounted soldiers. Even after the period of warfare samurai continued to wear it as a ceremonial display of authority. In the early years it was made of tiny pieces of leather laced together like scales similar to Western chain mail, with additional straw and metal pieces, and all parts of the body were covered. Later they adopted metal breastplates like the cuirass. Samurai armor is also worn by characters in Japanese martial arts movies and samurai films like *Yojimbo*, *The Seven Samurai*, *Shōgun Assassin*, and by Tom Cruise in *The Last Samurai*. The master filmmaker Akira Kurosawa was known for his samurai movies.

HIP/Art Resource, NY

* Fully developed Japanese costume style arose during the Edo period, the era of greatest wealth and sophistication. Both men and women were very style conscious and used their clothes to show their refinement. See Figure 21.15.

* The basic garment for both sexes and all classes was the *kosode*, the forerunner of the kimono. Variations in style, materials, and design communicated wealth and social status.

* The *kosode* consisted of two long panels of cloth that crossed in front and back of the upper garment, always the left side folded over the right. Two wide sleeves joined at the body and were held in place by a sash, the obi, without fastenings. See Figure 21.15.

* Kimonos were worn by men and women and were basically a straight T-shaped ankle-length or floor-length robe with attached collars and long wide sleeves. They were worn over a simple under robe, called *nagajuban*, to help keep the kimono clean. They were wrapped around the waist with an obi sash, which in the later period became greatly enlarged. The shape of a kimono was fixed, its individuality came because of the fabric and decoration; like the *kosode* there was much variety and they could be simple or very luxurious and were changed with the seasons. See Figure 21.13.

* There were different types of kimono for use on different occasions. Women's kimonos for formal wear included the *furisodé* for unmarried women, with long wide baggy sleeves and often flamboyant patterns and colors, and *tomesodé* with normal sleeves for married women; all were worn with the *tabi* socks and sandals.

* Men's kimonos were usually simpler with narrower sleeves and more subdued colors and patterns.

* The formal *montsuki* was a loose black half-coat with three or five mons that were small round family crest badges similar to those of the Chinese. This was worn with the *hakama*, a culotte-like garment that tied at the waist and fell to the ankles, and both were worn over a kimono and a *nagajuban*. The black *montsuki* with *mons* can be seen in Figure 21.10.

* Men's hair during the Edo period was generally worn pulled back and in bun high on the back of the head. Samurai shaved the front of the head, which was why it often appeared blue in the woodblock prints, and also in a similar bun. Generally they were clean shaven. See Figure 21.10.

* The elegance of the garment and its fashion statement came from the selection of color, fabric choice, and pattern, and the subject matter and design of the illustrations on the fabrics. They used embroidery, painting, and elaborate stencils for these illustrations so the clothing took on a storytelling function appropriate for the occasion and the seasons. See Figure 21.13.

* Spectacular and sumptuous versions for Imperial, theatrical, and wealthy individuals were on gold leaf fabrics with intricate appliques and metallic threads.

* Kabuki theater actors became popular and influenced fashion, and the public vied to copy the costumes of the performers. Garment craftsmen competed to provide new fashions for the performers and their patrons. See Figure 21.1.

* Children's clothing was a miniature version of adult clothing.

Clothing and Costume Keywords

kosode – The forerunner of the kimono, it was a robe, which crossed over front and back and tied at the waist. See Figure 21.15.

kimono – Literally "a thing to wear," it was a large often padded robe worn by men and women. Wealthy people frequently wore very elaborate ones made out of silk, silk brocade, and satin weaves that were highly decorated. There were also informal and simpler ones using less costly materials. See Figures 21.10, 21.11, 21.12, 21.13, and 21.14.

haori – This was also a half-coat without insignias for men and women, and due to the occasion varied in length and was usually worn open with sandals and *tabi*.

yukata – It was an unlined informal kimono often made of cotton or linen used at home in summer or at spa resorts, *ryōkan*, and worn by both men and women.

geisha costumes – The formal 19th-century version of the kimono worn by geishas consisted of as many as nine layered rich robes and was kept in place by the wide sash, the obi and its belt, and with an over scale ribbon panel in the rear. They often carried a small bag and a decorated paper fan (*maiougi*). They wore highly stylized ornamental wigs, white make-up, and wooden clogs. See Figures 21.10 and 21.14.

maru mage – This was one of the very complex hairstyles originally worn only by courtesans or geisha and featured a huge bun made of waxed hair, sometimes large waxed side-wings, or two extremely high topknots. Later, common women adopted the look as well and today some brides wear it for their wedding photos. See Figures 21.10 and 21.14.

kanzashi – These were the long decorated hairpins worn by women particularly in the late Edo period. See Figures 21.10, 21.11, 21.14, and 21.15.

tabi – Ankle-high split-toed socks worn by men and women with sandals. See Figure 21.1.

obi – This was the large sash worn around a kimono and it could be tied in a number of different ways to form a simple panel to complex large bows. See Figures 21.10, 21.11, 21.12, 21.13, and 21.14.

obijimé – This was the cord that held the obi in place and could also be tied in different ways that had symbolic meanings.

obiagé – This was what supported the obi.

sensu – According to legend folding fans were introduced in Japan by a monk in the 10th century. They were made of paper on a bamboo frame, usually with a design painted on them. Geisha used them in their fan dances, called *maiougi* (geisha fan), Figure 21.14. Later, in the 16th century Portuguese traders introduced them to the West and they became extremely popular in Europe and the US. Samurai also used several other varieties of war fans, which usually included metal. They are still used today by Shinto priests and in formal ceremonies by the Imperial family.

harisen – Meaning "slapping fan," this was a large variation of a paper fan. A theatrical prop, it was traditionally used as part of a manzai act, a stand-up comedy routine, and a staple of Japanese slapstick culture.

zori – These were woven sandals, which could be simple or ornate, and worn by men and women. They were similar to modern flip-flops. See Figure 21.1.

geta – This was another type of sandal worn by men, women, and geisha. They were made of wood and elevated and sometimes they were worn in rain or snow to keep the feet dry. See Figures 21.12 and 21.15.

netsuke – These were miniature sculpted ornaments, often of ivory or wood, worn by men suspended from their obi. Later they were appreciated as just beautiful art objects. http://www.netsuke.org has links and there are also other sites.

wagasa – These were the traditional oilpaper parasols especially popular in the Golden Age of the Edo era (1688–1704). They came in different colors for different patrons and occasions. They were used in weddings by the matron of honor to cover the bride to avoid evil spirits and were a frequent accessory for geisha and used as props in their tea ceremonies and traditional dances. See Figures 21.11 and 21.15.

shamisen – These were the three-stringed musical instruments similar to Western lutes, played by geishas and other theatrical musicians. See Figure 21.14.

Index

Page numbers in *italics* refer to figures and their captions.

The conclusion of a contemporary production of The Bacchae in the 5th century BCE theater, Syracuse, Italy. Author photo.